Barron's Review Course Series

Let's Review:

Global Studies

Second Edition

Mark Willner
Midwood High School at Brooklyn College
Brooklyn, New York

Mary Martin
Greene Central School
Greene, New York

Jerry Weiner
Louis Brandeis High School
New York, New York

David Moore
Webster Junior High School
Webster, New York

George Hero
Nwood High School at Brooklyn College
Brooklyn, New York

BARRON'S

ACKNOWLEDGMENTS

| p. 107 | Reprinted by permission: Tribune Media Services |

pp. 467, 468   Extract from WORLD CONTRASTS by Brian Nixon. Copyright © 1986, reproduced by kind permission of Unwin Hyman Ltd.

p. 471   Morrish, M., *Development in the Third World*. Copyright © 1983 by Oxford University Press.

p. 477   MacLean, K. and N. Thompson. *World Environmental Problems*. Copyright © 1981 by John Bartholomew & Sons Ltd.

p. 480   Graves, N., J. Lidstone and M. Naish, *People and Environment: A World Perspective*. Copyright © 1987 by Heinemann Educational Books, Ltd.

All inquiries should be addressed to:
Barron's Educational Series, Inc.
250 Wireless Boulevard
Hauppauge, New York 11788

International Standard Book No. 0-8120-1960-1

Library of Congress Catalog Card No. 94-73172

PRINTED IN THE UNITED STATES OF AMERICA

23 22 21 20 19 18 17 16 15 14 13

Preface

• For Which Course Was This Book Designed?

This book was designed to be used as a review text for the New York State course in Regents and RCT Global Studies. The material follows the syllabus in Regents Social Studies: Global Studies, which is used throughout New York State as the basis of a course of study in history on the secondary level. Although the material has been prepared to meet the needs of New York State students, it can be helpful to students in any secondary-level Global Studies course.

• What Are the Special Features of This Book?

The information in this book parallels, for the most part, that of the New York State syllabus in Global Studies. The book has an introductory unit, followed by seven regional units, and an eighth unit, "The World Today." Teachers and students are free to pursue whatever sequence of the seven regional units they wish. However, the sequence in this book follows a specific pattern. That pattern is as follows: I—The Middle East, II—South and Southeast Asia, III—East Asia (China, Japan, and Korea), IV—Africa, V—Latin America, VI—Western Europe, VII—The Commonwealth of Independent States (C.I.S.) and Eastern Europe.

There are several reasons for following the above sequence:

1. The Middle East is a good place to start as it has been, is, and will continue to be very much in the news during the last third of this century. As the site of many well-known ancient civilizations as well as the birthplace of Judeo-Christian culture, it is an area to which Americans can easily relate. Indeed, many of the holidays in the fall semester have their roots in the early history of the Middle East.

2. It is important to make global connections as we move from one unit of study to another. Consequently, knowledge of the Middle East becomes useful as we "travel" into South Asia. Indeed, the flow of history in Asia has been from west to east. This is why, for example, Islam, a religion that began in Saudi Arabia, is the major religion of Pakistan and Bangladesh—two South Asian nations. The best-known structure in India is the Taj Mahal, built by a Muslim ruler and containing writing in Arabic. (Also, we should remember that the largest Islamic nation in the world is Indonesia—a Southeast Asian nation, very far from Islam's birthplace in Saudi Arabia!)

3. Once we are in South Asia, our study of Indian culture helps us learn about Hinduism, Buddhism, and Sanskrit. Aspects of these three cultural patterns spread eastward through a process of cultural diffusion. The Sanskrit language, for example, is linked to some Southeast Asian languages. Buddhism spread to China, Korea, and Japan. This can partially explain why, in

this book, we travel to these last three nations in Unit III, having completed our "trip" throughout Unit II.

4. In Unit IV we go to Africa. Its northern half has absorbed much culture and history from the Middle East. Latin America (Unit V) becomes a logical next "stop" after Africa. Indeed, millions of people today in Latin America and the Caribbean can trace their ancestry to West Africa. There is an additional reason for placing Latin America as the fifth and last of the units on non-Western areas. Of all these areas, it is the one that has had the greatest contact with Western Europe. And it is on to Western Europe that we move in Unit VI, our next unit.

5. Our voyage in Western Europe is very extensive, particularly because knowledge of that area is vital for understanding our own nation's culture, history, and government. Knowledge about Western Europe will also help us to understand its many connections and interactions with the areas covered in the next unit, Unit VII, the Commonwealth of Independent States and Eastern Europe. Indeed, in the 1990s we can see a growing diffusion of Western European economic and political ideas throughout the former Soviet Union and Eastern Europe!

Within each unit, we study a particular area in a certain pattern. This pattern forms a fourfold approach because we look at four features in each area during our travels there: I. *Physical Geography; II. Economic Geography; III. Human and Cultural Geography;* and *IV. History and Political Geography.* This kind of area studies and multi-disciplinary approach will be very helpful to us. It is based upon the kinds of questions we would ask if we were actually about to travel in one of the areas. For example, if you knew you were going to travel to India next week, you would probably ask a travel agent questions such as these: What clothing should I wear? Can I use American money? Do the people speak English? What kind of government is there? Each of these questions would be answered under the features in the fourfold approach.

Another reason for using the fourfold approach is that it gives us an easy way to learn about an area. By studying first about the *physical geography* of an area, we get to know its basic land and natural features. We will then be able to understand certain things about its *economy.* A nation's economy is very closely linked to its physical resources. (Consider Saudi Arabia's dependence on the sale of oil or Japan's lack of oil and nearness to water.) The *human or cultural* features of a nation have important connections with physical and economic features. And finally, the history and politics of an area are best studied once we know something about its geography, economy, and culture. For example, the *history* of the Arab-Israeli dispute in the Middle East can be examined in light of *physical* features (water and deserts), *economic* issues (oil and shipping routes), and *cultural* factors (Jerusalem's status as a holy city).

The fourfold approach therefore is a good way to study any global area. Into this approach, we can clearly fit the themes of the New York State syllabus:

Physical Geography—The Physical-Historical Setting
Economic Geography—Economic Development
Human and Cultural Geography—Dynamics of Change, Contemporary Cultures
History and Political Geography—Historical Setting, Dynamics of Change, Contemporary Nations and Cultures, Region within the Global Context

Both the fourfold approach and the sequence of the seven regional units have been used successfully with secondary school classes. They have helped students to learn and teachers to teach about global areas. The sequence of units has also been recommended by the New York City Association of Teachers of Social Studies/United Federation of Teachers (ATSS/UFT).

This book also explains and has references to the various concepts and issues emphasized in the New York State syllabus. The *fifteen key concepts* are as follows: change, choice, citizenship, culture, diversity, empathy, environment, human rights, identity, interdependence, justice, political systems, power, scarcity, and technology. The *eleven world issues* are as follows: population, war and peace, terrorism, energy—resources and allocations, human rights, hunger and poverty, world trade and finance, environmental concerns, political and economic refugees, economic growth and development, and determination of political and economic systems.

Complementing the text and questions included in each unit are maps, charts, graphs, and political cartoons to help portray necessary information.

Finally, three complete Regents Examinations have been reprinted for testing purposes.

• Who May Use This Book?
Let's Review: Global Studies provides a valuable supplement to a regular textbook in Global Studies as well as those covering individual regions. For teachers in New York State schools, this book will offer an excellent source of review material to prepare students for the New York State Regents and RCT Examinations in Global Studies.

Although the book has been designed to meet the syllabus of the New York State course in Global Studies, any student taking a course in Global Studies will find it to be a helpful source for review and examination preparation.

• Taking the Regents and RCT Examinations
1. Preparation for the Regents Examination begins the first day of class. Good study habits, effective note-taking, completion of all assignments, and a positive attitude throughout the year will make any exam an easier task at the completion of the course.

2. Follow directions closely on the examination itself. Many students are not successful because they do not provide the information asked for or they leave sections of the question out of their answer. The essays have repeatedly used a format like the following: *Select **two** issues and for each **one** give **three** reasons which led to. . .* It is imperative that the student provide the information requested. Graders have their "hands tied" by the directions and cannot provide credit for information that is requested and not given.

3. When answering the Part II essay questions, be aware of the scoring breakdown. It will usually be indicated as follows: (5,5,5) or (10) and (5), etc. Keep in mind, especially if time grows short, that some areas are given greater credit than others and therefore should be answered first.

4. Be aware of key terms in the questions, for example, *show*, *discuss*, *compare*. Underline key words in the directions to the questions.

5. Budget your time. New York State allows three hours for completion of the Regents exam. You have two parts: Part I (48 multiple-choice questions) worth 55 points and Part II (three essays) worth 45 points (15 points each). Wear a watch and plan out your attack while taking practice examinations.

6. Answer all questions. In the Part I questions, use the process of elimination if necessary. In Part II don't get lazy! You can only be given credit for information provided in your answers.

7. Relax and be confident.

The letters RCT stand for Regents Competency Test. The study and test-taking suggestions for the RCT in Global Studies are the same as those described above for the Regents exam. The RCT, however, is made up in a different style. It has a Part I, containing 50 multiple-choice questions. This is worth 50 points. Part II has four essay questions, from which two must be chosen. The essays are worth 20 points, 10 points for each one. For a passing score, a student must get 46 points out of 70. On the Regents, a student must get 65 points out of 100.

• Conclusion
Whether preparing for the Regents or the RCT exam in Global Studies, this book will be very helpful. Good luck to everyone!

Mark Willner

Table of Contents

INTRODUCTION TO GLOBAL STUDIES

The Physical World

Human beings and societies in all regions of the earth share a common *global environment*. This environment is a closed system consisting of a variety of physical features—landforms, bodies of water, vegetation and animal types, and climate regions—which are a result of several natural processes: the rotation and revolution of the earth, geological activity, the water cycle, and biological interactions.

FOUR PARTS OF THE NATURAL ENVIRONMENT

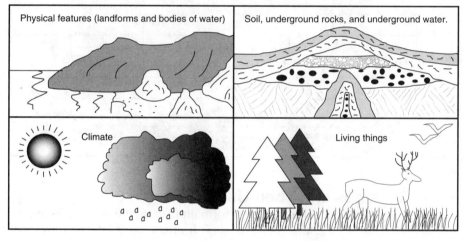

The environment provides humans with a variety of both renewable and nonrenewable resources, which can be used to meet the needs of both individuals and societies. Though these needs are basic to all humans, the different ways in which they are met are determined by the differences in environment that exist from one part of the earth to another.

The land surface of the earth is generally divided into seven large land masses, called *continents*—North America, South America, Europe, Asia, Africa, Australia, and Antarctica. Large bodies of water, called *oceans*—Atlantic, Pacific, Indian, and Arctic—and smaller ones, called seas, cover about 70 percent of the earth's surface. These bodies of water separate some of the continents from one another.

In recent centuries, humans have improved their ability to use more of the earth's limited resources, while technology has created closer contacts among peoples of different cultures. This *global interdependence* has made it increasingly important to understand both the similarities and the differences among cultures. Hopefully, such understanding will aid in solving shared problems and resolving disputes between people of different cultures.

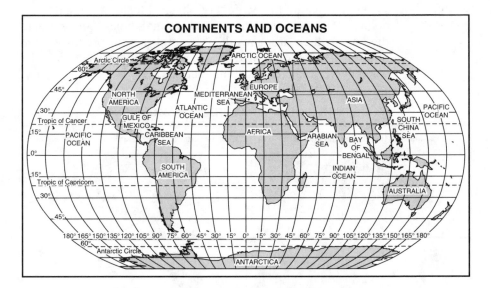

Maps and Their Uses

We can illustrate much information about the world with maps, but we must be aware of their limitations and distortions. Projecting the features of a sphere (the globe) on a flat surface (a map) can distort sizes and distances, especially when we attempt to show the entire world.

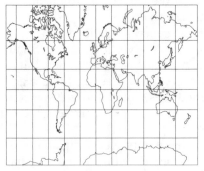

MERCATOR PROJECTION

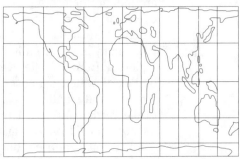

GALL-PETERS PROJECTION

Attempting to illustrate the shapes of land masses correctly can distort the sizes of the land masses. Notice the Mercator projection on the previous page. On the other hand, trying to accurately show size can distort shape, as in the Gall-Peters projection. Thus, maps can convey inaccurate impressions of the importance and influence of certain areas of the world.

Placement or location can also create false impressions of the relationships among regions or the relative importance of an area. For example, in the Mercator projection, with the Atlantic Ocean in the middle, North America and Europe are located top center. This seems to illustrate both their importance and the closeness of their relationship. Compare the Mercator projection with the Japan Airlines map, which centers on the Pacific Ocean, or the MacArthur Corrective Map, which was created by Australians.

Reading maps requires an understanding of their language. The *scale* provides a tool for determining distances. A map's *legend* provides information about the meaning of lines, symbols, colors, and other markings found on the map itself.

GLOBAL
CONCEPTS

Technology

CONCEPTS
GLOBAL

Modern technology has changed how we think about the size of the world. Actual (or absolute) distance has become less important than relative distance—how quickly communication and transportation can move ideas and people from one part of the world to another. Culture regions once separated by thousands of miles or formidable physical barriers now interact with one another.

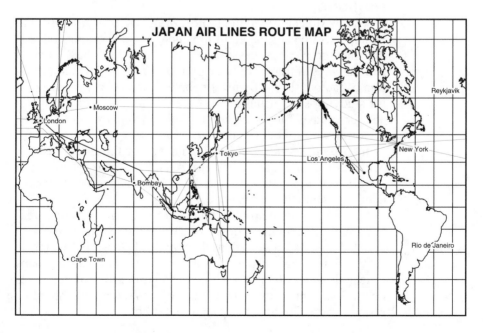

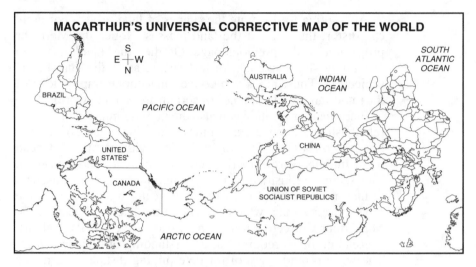

MACARTHUR'S UNIVERSAL CORRECTIVE MAP OF THE WORLD

Maps can present information in many ways. A *topographical map* attempts to show physical features, a *political map* focuses on the way humans divide up their world (the boundaries of nations), and economic maps illustrate the ways in which people use the environment and resources. Comparing specific maps, such as rainfall patterns and population distribution, can be useful in understanding ways of life and the relationships between humans and the world in which they live.

Regions

The world can be divided into *culture areas* or *regions*, that is, large sections of the earth in which physical or cultural features and political processes or economic systems have created similar ways of living for large groups of people. The identification of factors shared by most people in an area provides a tool for studying similarities and differences among regions. It can also be a basis for understanding relationships within a given region as well as contacts between regions.

GLOBAL CONCEPTS
Culture
CONCEPTS GLOBAL

In *Global Studies* we deal with seven of these regions: the Middle East, South and Southeast Asia, East Asia, Africa, Latin America, Western Europe, and the Commonwealth of Independent States and Eastern Europe.

GLOBAL CONCEPTS
Environment
CONCEPTS GLOBAL

Several factors help to define culture regions. Physical features such as mountains, deserts, or water bodies create sparsely peopled regions between densely populated areas, such as fertile river valleys or coastal plains. Water bodies may also unite groups of islands or coastal areas. Climate patterns and resource bases help to determine lifestyles within regions, creating distinctive economic systems and resulting social structures.

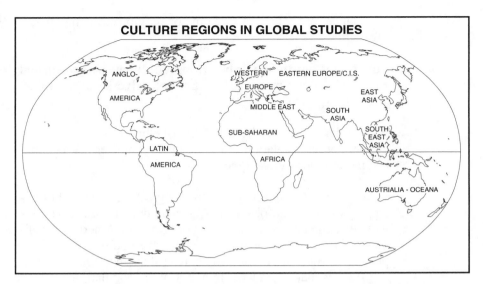

CULTURE REGIONS IN GLOBAL STUDIES

Location + Separation + Climate + Resources = A Distinctive Culture

World Regions as Used in This Course

Each region possesses a set of factors that sets it apart from the others, starting with its distinctive location. Some factors may be shared by several culture regions, but each region has its own special combination of elements:

Western Europe. Judeo-Christian ethic, Greco-Roman tradition, industrialization, temperate climate, Latin and Germanic languages.

Eastern Europe. Slavic languages, Orthodox Christianity, formerly Communist/Socialist economies, totalitarian political systems evolving new forms.

Latin America. Roman Catholicism, Latin-based languages, Spanish/Portuguese colonialism, Native American cultural influence.

Sub-Saharan Africa. Tropical climate, triple religious traditions (animism, Christianity, Islam), negroid physical type, oral tradition, ethnic-group social organization, pattern of shifting agriculture.

Middle East. Connecting waterways, crossroads location, Islam, Arabic language and culture, arid climate, mineral (oil)

abundance, birthplace of three major religious systems, ongoing conflict.

South and Southeast Asia. Monsoon climate, Hinduism and Buddhism, flood-plain agriculture, extensive seaborne trade, colonial experience.

East Asia. Confucian/Taoist/Buddhist ethic, hierarchical social system, sense of isolation and uniqueness, character-based alphabet, mongoloid physical type.

Within individual regions, there are great differences. For example, Western Europe consists of more than a dozen countries with differing languages and traditions. In Latin America, the climate varies from tropical in the Amazon to desert on the Altiplano. Sub-Sarahan Africa has hundreds of distinct ethnic groups.

Muslims make up a large minority of the population in South and Southeast Asia. Israel, Turkey, and Iran are exceptions to the predominantly Arabic culture of the Middle East. In East Asia, Korea provides a bridge between Communist China and capitalist Japan, and the religious and national variety that existed before Communism took hold is reasserting itself in Eastern Europe.

In addition, there are transition or diffusion zones between the major culture regions, where cultures meet, mix, and produce unique combinations. The Caribbean region combines Anglo-European, Latin, and African traditions. The Central Asian nations that were formerly part of the Soviet Union mix European economic practices, Islamic religious traditions, and a variety of political forms.

The Impact of Resources, Demography, and History

The natural features of a region create both possibilities and problems, and culture regions today are a product of centuries of history. The rich river plains of India and China have great potential for agricultural production and dense population but also suffer the ravages of flooding. The mineral wealth of Latin America and the Middle East has created great empires but has also attracted conquerors and exploiters.

An imbalance or scarcity of resources can cause conflict and the movement of large groups of people. Both Western and Eastern Europe have experienced widespread and lengthy wars and extensive migration. Most of Japan's large population lives on the nonmountainous 13 percent of that nation's four islands.

The Meaning of Culture

GLOBAL CONCEPTS

Culture

CONCEPTS GLOBAL

Social scientists use the term "culture" to define the total way of life of a group of people. It includes actions and behaviors, tools and techniques, ideas and beliefs. Culture is preserved by the group, taught to and learned by the young, and provides a pattern of interrelationships for the group, as well as a way for them to use their natural environment.

Elements of Culture

Social scientists look at cultures from a variety of viewpoints, concentrating on specific factors as they try to discover the ways in which cultures are similar to and different from one another.

Cultural Diffusion

GLOBAL CONCEPTS

Change

CONCEPTS GLOBAL

Ideas and techniques have spread from one culture to another throughout human history, but modern technology and global interdependence have increased both the speed and extent of this cultural diffusion. Some see these recent developments as creating a global culture in which similar styles, tastes, and products will be universally acknowledged.

WORLD ISSUES

War
and
Peace

Trade, aid, migration, conquest, slavery, war, and entertainment have all promoted this process, with both positive and negative results. Useful traditions can be destroyed or replaced; social and economic patterns can be disrupted. But new technology can also bring improvements in standards of living, and new ideas can bring variety and enrichment to any culture.

GLOBAL CONCEPTS

Choice

CONCEPTS GLOBAL

Increased contact between cultures can also bring about exploitation and help to create or at least emphasize differences in prosperity and standards of living from one culture region to another. The "developed" regions—Europe (East and West), Anglo-America, Japan, and Australia/Oceana—have been greatly influenced by the Industrial Revolution. The people of these regions have a more abundant supply of material goods and personal services.

GLOBAL CONCEPTS

Technology

CONCEPTS GLOBAL

In the "developing" (once called "less developed") regions, the populace generally has fewer comforts and conveniences, and significant numbers of people may survive at a subsistence level. A major goal for most countries in these areas is economic development—an increase in the capacity to produce goods and services in order to make life safer and healthier.

ELEMENTS OF CULTURE

How a group of people react to some or all of the following:

CONFLICT

Causes and Effects •
Competition: Human vs.
Nature • Human vs. Human
• Philosophical • Physical •
International • Domestic
Resolution • War • Peace •
Compromise • Cooperation
• Control • Change •
Violence • Prejudice

ENVIRONMENT

Geography • Geology •
Landforms • Weather/
Climate • Natural
Resources • Vegetation •
Soil • Bodies of Water •
Minerals • Land Use •
Latitude • Elevation •
Time/Space Patterns •
Ocean Currents •
Tectonic Activity • Wildlife

TECHNOLOGY

Tools • Shelter/Housing •
Resource Extraction •
Machinery • Production
Systems • Energy Use •
Clothing • Science •
Medicine • Electronics •
Simplicity to Complexity •
Training • Skills •
Industrialization

MODES OF EXPRESSION

Language • Communication
• Spoken • Written •
Physical • Electronic •
Music • Art • Literature •
Dress • Entertainment •
Education • Transportation •
Travel • Migration •
Diffusion

CULTURE

SOCIAL ORGANIZATION

Groups: Role/Status •
Rules • Clan • Tribe •
Race • Social Class •
Age • Occupation &
Peer Groups •
Hierarchies • Ethnicity •
Lineage • Family
Structure • Generation •
Household

VALUES/RELIGION

Origins: Human/Divine •
Superstitions • Answers •
Questions • Major Belief
Systems • Mythology •
Theology • God • Founders
• Scriptures • Doctrines •
Animism • Monotheism •
Polytheism • Atheism •
Secular Humanism

POLITICS/LAWS

Rules • Power/Influence •
Government • Bureaucracy
• Monarchy/Oligarchy/
Autocracy/ Democracy/
Dictatorship/Totalitarianism
• Constitutions/Rights •
Parties/Elections • Leader-
ship • Citizenship/National-
ism • Authority • Legitimacy
• Sovereignty

ECONOMIC ORGANIZATION

Agriculture/Industry • Labor
Scarcity: Needs & Wants •
Resource Base • Carrying
Capacity • Goods & Services
• Money/Trade • Poverty/
Prosperity • Capital Supply
& Demand • Distribution •
Capitalism/Socialism/
Communism • Markets

RESULTS IN

The distinctive CULTURE of that group

The existence and operation of these factors in a culture's past makes up its *History*

REVIEW QUESTIONS

Multiple Choice. Select the letter of the answer that correctly completes each
statement.

1. Which phrase best describes the meaning of the term "culture"?
   A. the advancement and progress of a nation
   B. the ability of humans to appreciate art and music
   C. all the ways in which a group of people lives
   D. all the products that a group of humans makes and uses

2. Social scientists who study human culture are called anthropologists.
   Their work would most likely involve
   A. examining the environment in which people live
   B. determining the operating principles of modern machinery
   C. learning the reasons that certain groups of people live as they do
   D. discovering the influence of climate upon types of plants and animals

3. Which aspect of culture is most directly affected by the physical
   geography of an area?
   A. religion
   B. language
   C. food
   D. music

4. In dividing the world's population into culture groups, social scientists
   are most concerned with
   A. weather and climate patterns of different regions
   B. political boundaries separating countries
   C. similarities and differences in styles and patterns of living
   D. present political systems in various nations

5. Below are three proverbs.
   "Mighty oaks from tiny acorns grow." (United States)
   "The journey of 1,000 miles begins with a single step." (China)
   "A little rain each day will fill the river to overflowing." (West Africa)

   Which conclusion is best supported by these proverbs?
   A. Humans in all cultures make excuses for their shortcomings.
   B. All cultures are concerned with transportation and conservation.
   C. Natural resources are a major concern for people in all cultures.
   D. Though cultures may differ humans view many situations in similar
   ways.

6. The popularity of baseball in Japan and karate in the United States are examples of
   A. cultural diffusion
   B. technological development
   C. ethnocentrism
   D. cultural isolation

7. Which of the following statements about maps is *not* correct?
   A. A topographical map would show mountains and water bodies.
   B. Political maps emphasize boundaries between countries.
   C. An economic map might show areas of agricultural production.
   D. Demographic maps generally show types of governments.

8. Culture regions as defined in this course
   A. are for the most part quite small and isolated
   B. usually contain very little cultural variety
   C. have developed as a result of geographic and historical factors
   D. change frequently as political parties and governments change

9. The so-called developing regions of the world are generally located on which continents?
   A. Asia, Africa, and South America
   B. Europe, Africa, and Australia
   C. North America, South America, and Asia
   D. North America, Australia, and Europe

ESSAY

"The world is at our doorstep." In a concise four- to five-paragraph essay, explain the meaning of this statement. Be sure to include the following concepts:

A. Global interdependence
B. Cultural diffusion
C. Communications technology

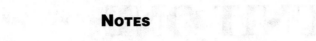

NOTES

UNIT ONE

The Middle East

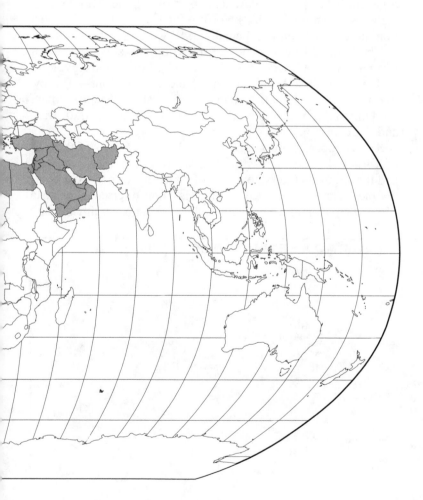

I. PHYSICAL GEOGRAPHY OF THE MIDDLE EAST

Overview

The region known as the Middle East includes parts of three continents—Europe, Africa, and Asia. Because all three continents seem to intersect here, the region has also been called "the crossroads of the world." However, these names, as well as another commonly used name, the Near East, seem appropriate only when one looks at a world map with Western Europe at the center. The African portion of the Middle East includes the area known as North Africa, while the Asian portion includes what might be called SWASIA (Southwest Asia).

The North African portion of the Middle East is made up of five nations—Morocco, Algeria, Tunisia, Libya, and Egypt.

The Southwest Asian portion includes 15 nations—Turkey, Syria, Lebanon, Israel, Jordan, Saudi Arabia, Yemen, Oman, the United Arab Emirates, Bahrain, Qatar, Kuwait, Iraq, Iran, and Afghanistan.

The European portion of the Middle East consists of the part of Turkey that lies across the Dardanelles from the Asian part and that contains the famous city of Istanbul (formerly Constantinople). The Asian part of Turkey is often referred to as Asia Minor. (This reference is a geographical one, not a political one.)

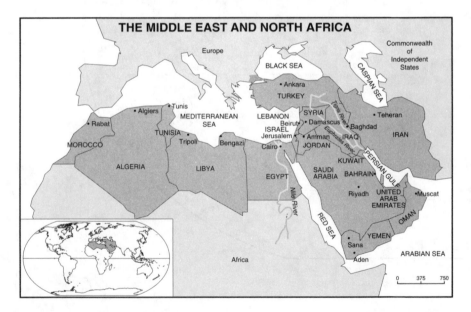

THE MIDDLE EAST AND NORTH AFRICA

4

Topography

Throughout the Middle East, which is about twice the physical size of the United States, the most common landform is desert. The aridity (dryness), lack of vegetation, and barrenness of its desert territories have had profound effects on the history and culture of the Middle East. The nomadic (wandering) lifestyles of such people as the Bedouins, Arabs, and early Israelites put an emphasis on sharing, group values, and conformity over individual values. Close family and clan ties and frugality (thriftiness) were also important. As deserts make up over 80 percent of the land area, population distribution has been uneven. Human settlements were and are still found mainly near the precious water bodies. Armed struggles have occurred throughout history for access to and control over water. The emptiness of the deserts may also have had an impact on the growth of strong religious feelings in the Middle East. A society's religious devotion may become heightened when people live amid harsh natural conditions. Scholars also note that three central religious figures had profound experiences when they were alone in the desert—Moses (Judaism—at Mount Sinai), Jesus (Christianity—in the wilderness), and Muhammad (Islam—in a cave). The major deserts of the Middle East are the Sahara in North Africa, which is the largest desert in the world, the Sinai in Egypt, the Rub-al Khali ("the empty quarter") and the Nafud in Saudi Arabia, the Negev in Israel, and the Dasht-i-Kavir in Iran.

Topographical variety can be seen in the mountain ranges. The Atlas Mountains lie in northwest Africa, separating the Sahara Desert from land near the Mediterranean Sea. Since this land area is arable and has a comfortable Mediterranean climate, there are large cities located here, such as Casablanca, Rabat, Algiers, Tunis, and Tripoli. The Elburz Mountains in Iran and the Taurus Mountains in Turkey are a link between the Himalayas of central Asia to the east and the Alps of Europe to the west.

The Arabian Peninsula, sometimes called Arabia, is shaped like a huge boot. It is mostly desert and contains several nations, the largest of which is Saudi Arabia.

Water Bodies

The scarcity of water in the Middle East is an important fact of life and is crucial to understanding the region's history. Apart from their life-sustaining importance, water bodies have also had vital maritime and strategic influences.

The largest bodies of water in the area are the five surrounding seas—the Caspian, Black, Mediterranean, Red, and Ara-

GLOBAL CONCEPTS

Empathy

CONCEPTS GLOBAL

GLOBAL CONCEPTS

Scarcity

CONCEPTS GLOBAL

GLOBAL
CONCEPTS

Culture

CONCEPTS
GLOBAL

bian. They have always been a source of fish. The "pathway" provided by the Mediterranean and its Suez Canal link to the Red Sea and then to the Gulf of Aden has brought Europe "closer" to the southwestern, southern, and eastern parts of Asia. The Mediterranean has served as a highway of conquest, commerce, and culture. In ancient times, Roman legions traveled across the Mediterranean eastward to the Levant (lands touching the eastern Mediterranean, such as modern-day Syria, Lebanon, and Israel), and Phoenician traders traveled westward from the Levant to North Africa. The Persian Gulf, which leads into the Arabian Sea, was a crucial battleground in the Iran-Iraq War of the 1980s. It was also important in 1991 during Operation Desert Storm (also known as the Persian Gulf War), which involved a U.S.-led coalition against Iraq. The Persian Gulf area contains most of the world's oil reserves, and so it is a strategic route through which oil tankers pass, many bound for Japan, the United States, and Europe. Finally, the Bosporus–Sea of Marmara–Dardanelles Strait route from the Black Sea to the Aegean Sea and Mediterranean Sea is of paramount importance to Russia and the Ukraine. As it was for ships of the former Soviet Union, it is the only way for ships of these nations to reach the warm navigable waters.

WORLD ISSUES

War and

Peace

From ancient times until today, the four major rivers of the Middle East have greatly affected patterns of settlement. They are the Tigris, Euphrates, Nile, and Jordan. Because of the region's arid climate, these water bodies are very valuable. Except for the coasts of Turkey and the Levant, rainfall is practically nonexistent in the Middle East.

1. The Tigris and Euphrates rivers originate in the Taurus Mountains of Turkey and flow southeastward a few miles from each other. They converge (meet) in Iraq and flow as one, the Shatt-al-Arab, past the Strait of Hormuz into the Persian Gulf. The Shatt-al-Arab region, like all delta areas, has rich soil. It is also of strategic value because of the nearby oil deposits and ports. Consequently, it was the scene of much fighting during the 1980s Iran-Iraq War and the 1991 Persian Gulf War.

WORLD ISSUES

World

Trade and

Finance

The area between the Tigris and Euphrates rivers was referred to in ancient times as Mesopotamia. Because it was well irrigated and able to support large numbers of people, it was the site of one of the early river valley civilizations. It was part of an arc-shaped region called the "fertile crescent," which extended from the eastern shores of the Mediterranean Sea to the Persian Gulf. The ancient city of Babylon was in Mesopotamia. Modern-day Baghdad, the capital of Iraq, lies on the Tigris River, just north of the ruins of Babylon.

2. The other major river valley civilization in the Middle East arose in ancient Egypt, along the Nile River, the world's longest river. The Blue Nile, with its source in Central Africa, and the White Nile, with its source in East Africa, converge in the Sudan and flow northward into the Mediterranean Sea. When the Nile overflows its banks, the waters deposit silt and make the nearby land very fertile. The Aswan High Dam was built in 1970 to control the Nile's floodwaters. Since over 95 percent of Egypt is desert, the vast majority of Egyptians live along the narrow strip of land along the Nile River. The ancient cities of Thebes and Alexandria (in the delta) are on the river, as are the present-day Egyptian capital of Cairo and the Sudanese capital of Khartoum.

3. The Jordan River is smaller than the other three rivers, but it is vital to the peoples of Lebanon, Syria, Jordan, and Israel. It flows southward from highland areas in Lebanon, Syria, and Israel and makes irrigation possible along its banks. However, use of its waters has led to political quarrels between the nations through which the Jordan River runs.

The Jordan River has had historical and political significance. It was an important source of water in ancient times. Jericho, one of the earliest urban sites in the world, lies only six miles from the Jordan River. Since 1967, the river has been a disputed political boundary between Israel and the nation of Jordan. The land portion just west of the river, now administered by Israel, is called the West Bank as well as by its biblical names—Judea and Samaria. It was under Jordanian control

GLOBAL
CONCEPTS

Environment

CONCEPTS
GLOBAL

WORLD ISSUES

Economic

Growth and

Development

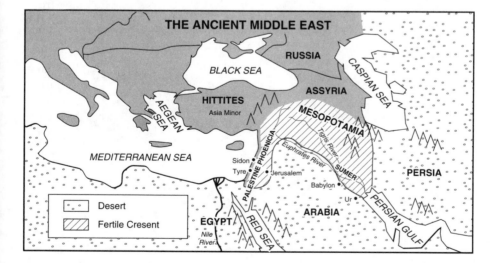

THE ANCIENT MIDDLE EAST

7

until Jordan's attack on Israel during the Six-Day War of June 1967. (See Section IV of this unit for further information.) The river is also important because of its biblical significance. For Jews and Christians, the Jordan River is especially noteworthy for beliefs about events that occurred near it concerning such figures as Moses, Joshua, and Jesus.

The Jordan is also economically significant. Its waters flow into the Sea of Galiee and, farther south, into the Dead Sea. The Sea of Galilee has been a source of fish from ancient days until the present. The Dead Sea is the lowest point on earth and is the end point for the Jordan's waters. Unique natural conditions have made the Dead Sea area a valuable source of chemicals, such as potash and phosphates. Israel has constructed a major chemical complex there and has invited Jordan's participation.

REVIEW QUESTIONS

Multiple Choice. Select the letter of the answer that correctly completes each statement.

1. Which phrase refers to only one continent?
   A. Near East
   B. Middle East
   C. SWASIA
   D. "crossroads of the world"

2. Which pair of water bodies is incorrectly matched?
   A. Tigris River–Persian Gulf
   B. Persian Gulf–Strait of Hormuz
   C. Nile River–Arabian Sea
   D. Jordan River–Dead Sea

3. The "fertile crescent" was known historically for the early growth of
   A. manufacturing
   B. civilizations
   C. architecture
   D. water conservation

4. The Rub-al Khali refers to a
   A. city
   B. desert
   C. seaport
   D. mountain

5. The Middle East has been described as the "crossroads of the world."
   Which fact would best support this statement?
   A. Most of the world's oil reserves are there.
   B. The Suez Canal is an important waterway.
   C. Parts of three continents intersect there.
   D. Water bodies surround the region.

6. The area between the Tigris and Euphrates rivers was once known as
   A. Arabia
   B. Palestine
   C. Asia Minor
   D. Mesopotamia

Fact or Opinion. If the statement is a fact, write F. If the statement is an opinion, write O.

1. Desert people live a nomadic lifestyle.

2. The best place to live in the Middle East would be in the Sinai Desert.

3. Peace would come to the Middle East if Jordan and Israel agreed to build a canal between the Mediterranean Sea and the Dead Sea.

ESSAY

Geography can affect the lives of many people in many ways. For each geographic feature listed below, explain two ways in which it has affected people in the Middle East.

1. desert
2. water bodies

II. ECONOMIC GEOGRAPHY OF THE MIDDLE EAST

Agriculture

It is important to remember that barely 15 percent of the land in the Middle East is arable (good for farming). Moreover, inadequate rainfall, large desert areas, and a scarcity of water are obstacles to agricultural development. In addition to these natural obstacles, the traditional system of landownership, with only a very small number of people controlling the little arable land, has also made it difficult to grow enough food to support the increasing population. The major crops are cereal grains, such as wheat and barley, and olives, grapes, and dates, which have been cultivated since ancient times.

Israel's ability to grow oranges and other citrus fruits while "making the desert bloom" has enabled it to export food. Egypt has built up a substantial cotton industry. The Aswan High Dam along the Nile has added to Egypt's agricultural productivity.

Over 75 percent of the people in Arab countries are farmers (fellahin), who have traditionally leased the land as tenants from wealthy landowners. However, recent land-reform laws in several countries, including Egypt, Syria, and Iraq, have redistributed the land so that more farmers have become landowners. Nevertheless, primitive farming techniques prevent farmers from getting high crop yields from their lands.

In Israel's kibbutz movement, land is held collectively by a large group of people who work the land. There are few private landowners. Advanced farming techniques used in Israel have resulted in food surpluses.

Ever since biblical times, sheep herding has been carried on. Consequently, lamb has been a basic part of the diet of the people of the Middle East.

Industrial Production

The major natural resource in the Middle East is oil. Most of this precious resource is found in nations such as Saudi Arabia, Kuwait, and Iran, which border the Persian Gulf. It is estimated that most of the world's oil reserves are in the Middle East. Since the oil-rich nations produce more than they need, they are able to export millions of barrels a year. From these exports, the oil-rich nations have become very wealthy.

Growth of the Oil Industry. From about 1900 to 1970, oil production in the Middle East was dominated largely by foreigners—British, French, Dutch, and American. The chief reason for this was that foreigners were able to supply most of the factors of production. (The four factors of production are land, labor, capital, and management—those things that are necessary to make a product.) While the Middle Eastern nations had the land on which oil was first discovered in the early 1900s, they did not have enough of the other three factors of production to produce the oil themselves. Foreigners supplied the other three factors: labor (skilled workers), capital (this refers to both money and machinery, such as oil wells and drills, necessary to produce the oil), and management (skilled managers and engineers).

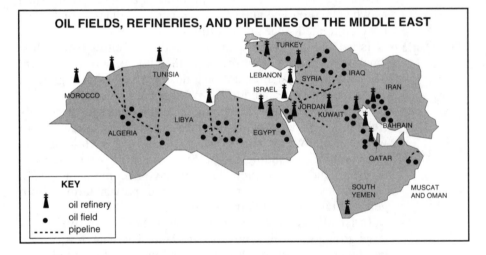

OIL FIELDS, REFINERIES, AND PIPELINES OF THE MIDDLE EAST

KEY
♦ oil refinery
• oil field
------ pipeline

In any economic relationship, both sides agree to give certain things to each other. By providing labor, capital, and management, the foreigners received concessions (permission to use the land) from the oil-rich nations. The foreigners also promised to produce and sell the oil and to give royalties (a percentage of the money earned by selling the oil) to the oil-rich nations. Some foreign companies also agreed to train people from these nations in oil-production techniques.

By the 1970s, these nations wanted higher royalties and more control over the oil industry. Some of them nationalized (took over) the oil fields. Creation of OPEC (Organization of Petroleum Exporting Countries)—an organization of major oil-rich nations in Asia, Africa, and Latin America that is dominated by the Arab nations—was another step in reducing foreign influence in the oil industry. As the 1990s began, the oil-rich nations had achieved complete control over their oil and had become very wealthy.

Impact of Wealth Gained by Oil. The Arab nations became very wealthy from the large amount of money ("petro dollars") paid to them by countries that had to import oil. Because they controlled so much oil, the OPEC nations were able to charge almost any price they wanted. The acquisition of vast amounts of money has had important consequences both internally (inside these nations) and externally (relations with other countries).

1. *Internal impact.* Although some Arab rulers have used the newly acquired money for themselves, the general tendency has been to use this wealth in ways that would benefit their people. As a result, a dramatic increase in the standard of living has occurred in such nations as Saudi Arabia, where new highways, houses, hospitals, and schools have been built. This rapid increase in modernization has, however, clashed with some traditional values regarding marriages, child-rearing practices, and

GLOBAL CONCEPTS

Diversity

CONCEPTS GLOBAL

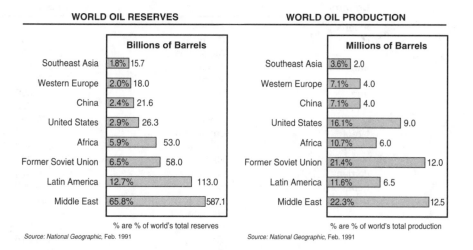

WORLD OIL RESERVES

	Billions of Barrels
Southeast Asia	1.8% 15.7
Western Europe	2.0% 18.0
China	2.4% 21.6
United States	2.9% 26.3
Africa	5.9% 53.0
Former Soviet Union	6.5% 58.0
Latin America	12.7% 113.0
Middle East	65.8% 587.1

% are % of world's total reserves

Source: National Geographic, Feb. 1991

WORLD OIL PRODUCTION

	Millions of Barrels
Southeast Asia	3.6% 2.0
Western Europe	7.1% 4.0
China	7.1% 4.0
United States	16.1% 9.0
Africa	10.7% 6.0
Former Soviet Union	21.4% 12.0
Latin America	11.6% 6.5
Middle East	22.3% 12.5

% are % of world's total production

Source: National Geographic, Feb. 1991

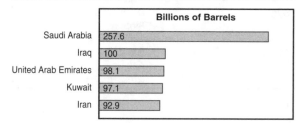

MIDDLE EAST OIL RESERVES

	Billions of Barrels
Saudi Arabia	257.6
Iraq	100
United Arab Emirates	98.1
Kuwait	97.1
Iran	92.9

Source: National Geographic, Feb. 1991

attitudes toward women in the region. The increased emphasis on material comforts and secular (worldly, nonspiritual) concerns associated with increasing wealth has been one reason for the growing influence both of modernization and of Western values on traditional Islamic culture.

GLOBAL
CONCEPTS
Interdependence
CONCEPTS
GLOBAL

2. *External impact.* The oil-rich nations of the Middle East have gained more power and respect in international affairs because of their control of oil and because of their newly acquired wealth. For example, by refusing to export oil or by increasing its export of oil to a given nation, an Arab nation can "pressure" that nation to do things a certain way. (Saudi Arabia's embargo [denial] of oil shipments to the United States in 1973 to 1974 was designed to get the United States to behave in a certain way towards Israel.) Many "petro-dollars" have been used by Arab investors to buy up property and businesses in other nations. (An increasing amount of land in New York City and London has been sold to Arabs.)

WORLD ISSUES

World
Trade and
Finance

MAJOR CITIES IN THE MIDDLE EAST

Country	City	Population
Algeria	Algiers	1,507,241
Egypt	Cairo	6,052,836
	Alexandria	2,917,327
Iran	Teheran	6,042,584
	Isfahan	986,753
Iraq	Baghdad	4,648,609
	Basrah	616,700
	Mosul	570,926
Israel	Jerusalem	493,500
	Tel Aviv	317,800
	Haifa	222,600
Jordan	Amman	936,300
Lebanon	Beirut	1,500,000
Libya	Tripoli	591,062
	Benghazi	446,250
Morocco	Casablanca	2,139,204
	Rabat	518,616
Saudi Arabia	Riyadh	1,308,000
	Jidda	1,500,000
	Mecca	550,000
Syria	Damascus	1,361,000
	Aleppo	1,308,000
Tunisia	Tunis	596,654
Turkey	Istanbul	5,475,982
	Ankara	2,235,035
	Izmir	1,489,772

Current Economic Issues

1. Many Middle Eastern nations need foreign aid to help them meet economic problems. Egypt and Israel are among the five largest recipients of U.S. aid.

WORLD ISSUES

Population

2. Overpopulation and a growth in cities have put a strain on the economy in some areas. Growing numbers of people are demanding that their governments do more to improve living standards. These demands are part of the movement described as a "revolution of rising expectations."

3. Extensive spending on military weapons, especially in Libya, Egypt, Syria, Jordan, Iraq, and Iran, has taken away funds needed for economic and social development. With the exception of Egypt, the military threat posed by these nations to Israel has forced Israel to spend large amounts of money on arms for defense.

GLOBAL
CONCEPTS

Choice

CONCEPTS
GLOBAL

4. Greater regional cooperation could help the nations of the Middle East in finding solutions to common problems. For example, removal of political barriers between Israel and all the Arab nations, as well as those between some of the Arab nations themselves, could lead to increased trade, reduction of arms spending, and improved desalinization projects. (These projects would purify sea water and make it drinkable by removing the salt content.)

GLOBAL
CONCEPTS

Interdependence

CONCEPTS
GLOBAL

5. The frequent changes in world oil prices often lowers the income received from "petro-dollars" and affects the region's economy. Also, the search for alternative sources of energy combined with energy-conservation measures may affect the global demand for oil. Thus, in 1994, when a surplus of world oil supplies led to a drop in oil prices, Saudi Arabia cut its budget by 20 percent. This meant that the government would have to reduce spending on medical care, fuel, and food for its people. These reductions could result in political tension, since the Saudi Arabian population had grown accustomed to large government expenditures for these items.

WORLD ISSUES

Energy:
Resources and
Allocations

6. Political tension linked to an economic issue can also be seen in a decision by Turkey to build a series of 22 dams in Anatolia, its southeastern region. The dams, part of the GAP project and including the massive Ataturk Dam, would aid irrigation and produce great amounts of energy in Turkey. GAP, an abbreviation for Turkish words, is the name for Turkey's massive agricultural and hydroelectric power project. The project would, however, affect the flow of water along the Tigris and Euphrates rivers, whose sources are in Turkey. Both Syria and Iraq are worried about the project's impact on water in their countries and have voiced their concerns to the Turkish government.

WORLD ISSUES

Economic
Growth and
Development

7. Israel's economy has improved during the 1990s, particularly with the growth of high-tech industries. Of significance has been the emigration of Jews from the former Soviet Union, many of whom are highly skilled engineers and scientists. Yet Israel must find ways of housing these immigrants as well as those from Ethiopia (Falasha Jews).

8. Since the end of the Lebanese Civil War in 1990, the capital city of Beirut has slowly regained its status as a major commercial center. Evidence can be seen in the increasing number of banks, businesses, hotels, skyscrapers, and restaurants.

9. Tourism continues to be a prime source of income for those Middle Eastern nations that have sites of religious and historic importance. Among them is Egypt, where the government has been concerned about attacks on foreigners by Islamic militants.

REVIEW QUESTIONS

Multiple Choice. Select the letter of the answer that correctly completes each statement.

1. During the first half of this century, foreign oil companies provided all the factors of production needed in the oil industry except for
   A. labor
   B. capital
   C. land
   D. management

2. What did these foreign companies expect in return for their supplying important factors of production?
   A. petro dollars
   B. territory
   C. pensions
   D. concessions

3. Arable land is land that is good for
   A. growing food
   B. producing oil
   C. manufacturing steel
   D. building highways

4. The Aswan High Dam has increased the agricultural productivity of
   A. Syria
   B. Iran
   C. Egypt
   D. Israel

5. Which action by OPEC nations would most upset foreign oil companies?
   A. desalinization
   B. nationalization
   C. modernization
   D. Westernization

6. The decision by Arab governments on how best to use their petro dollars is an issue that can be described as
   A. human
   B. cultural
   C. physical
   D. economic

7. Most of the oil-producing regions of the Middle East are located around the
   A. Dead Sea
   B. Mediterranean Sea
   C. Persian Gulf
   D. Suez Canal

8. Turkey's dam project is of grave concern to people in those nations whose capital cities are
   A. Cairo and Riyadh
   B. Baghdad and Damascus
   C. Teheran and Kuwait City
   D. Amman and Beirut

ESSAY

Describe one way in which each of the following has affected economic activity or productivity in the Middle East:

1. OPEC
2. kibbutz system
3. Aswan High Dam
4. military spending
5. emigration
6. tourism
7. world oil prices

III. HUMAN AND CULTURAL GEOGRAPHY OF THE MIDDLE EAST

Overview

As a region covering parts of three continents and often described as "the crossroads of the world," the Middle East contains a variety of people. Three major religions developed here— Judaism, Christianity, and Islam. People live in both small villages and large cities. Over 90 percent of the people of the Middle East can be described as Semites or Semitic. These terms describe a family of languages that includes Arabic and Hebrew. The terms are also used to refer to anyone who speaks one of these languages and who belongs to an ethnic group that follows certain customs. An Arab is a person who speaks Arabic and who follows traditions associated with an Arab way of life, that is, traditions connected with existence in a desert environment in the Middle East. Although most Muslims in the Middle East are Arabs, the word "Arab" does not refer to a particular religious group. (A small number of people in Egypt, Israel, and Lebanon consider themselves to be Christian Arabs. Muslims in Turkey and Iran do not consider themselves to be Arabs.)

THE MIDDLE EAST: POPULATION, DENSITY, AND INCOME

Country	Area (thousands of square miles)	Population (millions of people)	Density of Population (people per sq. mi.)	Income Per Person in U.S. Dollars (per capita)
United States	3,615	251.3	68	19,780
Egypt	386	53.1	138	650
Iraq	173	17.7	105	2,420
Israel	8	4.6	584	8,650
Jordan	37	3.1	92	1,500
Kuwait	6	2.1	312	13,680
Lebanon	4	2.9	751	690
Saudi Arabia	870	14.1	16	6,170
Syria	72	12.1	169	1,670

The population of the Middle East continues to grow at a very fast pace. Saudi Arabia, for example, had a population growth rate in the mid-1990s of 3.8 percent (or 38 people per thousand). This is one of the highest rates in the world. (The growth rate of a nation is based upon the difference between both the number of births and migrants entering and the number of deaths and people leaving the nation.) Egypt also has a high population growth rate. As these rates continue to increase, high population density or severe overcrowding in cities occurs. The demands for electricity, food, telephone service, and other daily needs can easily outpace what a government can provide.

Islam: The Main Religion in the Middle East

Islam is the religion practiced by over 90 percent of the people in the Middle East. It was the third major religion to develop in the area, Judaism being the first and Christianity the second. Many Islamic beliefs come from Judaism and Christianity. The most important element common to all three religions is monotheism, or the belief in the existence of one God, which was first stated by the Jews. The followers of Islam call this one God Allah. People who are followers of Islam submit themselves to the will of Allah and are called Muslims. The word "Muslim" is a religious term, while the word "Arab" is a cultural term. The word "Islam" is defined as "submission."

GLOBAL
CONCEPTS

Culture

CONCEPTS
GLOBAL

The Importance of Muhammad. Muhammad lived from 570 to 632 in what is now Saudi Arabia. Muslims believe that he was the fourth and most important prophet chosen by God (Allah) to teach and spread holy ideas and thoughts. Muslims accept most of the teachings of Judaism and Christianity and therefore accept the existence of Abraham, Moses, and Jesus as prophets. However, Muslims view these leaders as simply preparing the way for Muhammad. The life of Muhammad is essential for understanding Islam, as the lives of Abraham and Moses and Jesus are essential for understanding Judaism and Christianity. All four leaders are considered to have had direct communication with God at specific moments when each was alone. Events in the lives of each have profound religious meaning for the faithful; for example, Abraham with Isaac at Mt. Moriah, Moses at Mt. Sinai, the birth and crucifixion of Jesus.

Muhammad, who was born in Makkah (formerly spelled "Mecca"), claimed to have had revelations from God and visions while sleeping in a cave. These revelations, received through the angel Gabriel, were collected and written down in the Quran (formerly spelled "Koran"). The Quran—"the recitations"—became the holy book of Islam. Muhammad began to preach, but he was scorned and driven from Makkah. He fled to Medina in 622. This flight from Makkah to Medina is called the Hijra (formerly spelled "Hegira"), and it is considered a very holy event by Muslims. The year 622 marks the first year in the Muslim calendar. Muhammad gained many followers in Medina, raised an army, and was able to take over

GLOBAL
CONCEPTS

Empathy

CONCEPTS
GLOBAL

Makkah. Makkah was an important city because of its economic activity and because it contained a holy shrine called the Kabbah. The Kabbah is a black stone building, approximately 45 feet high. Muslims believe that it stands on the site where God commanded Abraham and Ishmael, one of his sons, to build a place of worship. Today, the Kabbah lies within the Great Mosque at Makkah. Muslims thus consider Makkah to be their holiest city, with the Kabbah their holiest site.

Muhammad died in Medina, which is Islam's second holiest city. Muslims also believe that one night, Muhammad rode to Jerusalem on a winged mare and stepped on a rock before going to heaven. He then returned to the rock and rode back to Makkah by dawn. (This rock is the one on which Jews believe Abraham was going to sacrifice his other son, Isaac.) In 637 Muslims conquered Jerusalem and soon thereafter built a mosque over this rock. This building is called the Dome of the Rock. Consequently, Jerusalem is considered Islam's third holiest city.

Basic Beliefs of Muslims. The five basic obligations, or "pillars," of Islam, are described in the chart below, with corresponding similarities in Judaism and Christianity.

The Five Obligations	Islam	Judaism	Christianity
Proclamation of faith	"There is no God but Allah, and Muhammad is his prophet."	"Hear oh Israel, the Lord our God, the Lord is one."	"There is but one God, creator of heaven, earth, and all things."
Prayer	Five time a day, facing Makkah.	Three times a day for some Jews, facing Jerusalem.	Some Christians in the Middle East pray seven times a day.
Fasting	During Ramadan, fasting from sunrise to sunset. (Ramadan was the month when the Quran was revealed to Muhammad.)	Fasting on specifically designated days during the year (i.e., Yom Kippur).	Abstinence from certain foods on specifically designated days during the year (e.g., Lent, Advent).
Almsgiving (charity)	"Whoever does not know that his need of the reward for giving is greater than the poor man's need of the gift is donating his charity in vain."	"The poor person does more for the giver than the giver does for the poor man."	"It is more blessed to give than to receive."

The Five Obligations (cont'd.)	Islam	Judaism	Christianity
Pilgrimage (visit to a holy area)	An obligation to make the *haj* (a visit to Makkah) once in a lifetime. One who makes the haj is called a haji.	Jerusalem is holy because it is the site of the first two Jewish temples and contains the Western Wall.	Bethlehem is holy as the birthplace of Jesus; Jerusalem is important as the site of his crucifixion.

Other Items

	Islam	Judaism	Christianity
Holy Books	Quran contains 114 suras or chapters. The Shari'a is a code of law based upon the Quran.	Old Testament (also called the Tanach, containing the Torah and other writings). The Talmud has commentaries on the Tanach.	The Bible (contains the Old Testament and the New Testament.)
Groupings	Sunni Muslims and Shi'ite Muslims. Sunnis are the larger group. Shi'ites live mostly in Iran.	Orthodox, Conservative, and Reform.	Catholic, Protestant, and Eastern Orthodox.

(For information on the spread of Islam, see Section IV of this unit and the units on Africa and on South and Southeast Asia. For a comparison between Islam and Hinduism, see the unit on South and Southeast Asia.)

Important Information About Islam

1. Shi'ite Muslims in Iran, as well as scattered groupings of Muslims in other countries, claim that many traditional Islamic values are being lost in the 20th century. They would like to see a return to traditional, fundamental values and thus have been called Islamic fundamentalists. They are worried about such things as the growth of materialism, introduction of Western values, and changing the role of women. Their protests against some Arab governments as well as their preaching have been a source of concern. An example of an Islamic fundamentalist was the former leader of Iran, Ayatollah Khomeini.

GLOBAL CONCEPTS
Identity
CONCEPTS GLOBAL

2. The crescent and the star, symbols of Islam, are found in the flags and currencies of many Islamic nations.

3. There is no central controlling figure for all Muslims, similar to the position of pope for Catholics.

4. Muslims believe that the Quran was revealed to Muhammad in Arabic, and translations were not allowed. In order to

read the Quran, one had to know Arabic. Therefore, Arabic became a common language for all Muslims, whether they were Arab, such as people in Egypt, or non-Arab, such as people in Pakistan and Indonesia.

Language

GLOBAL
CONCEPTS

Change

CONCEPTS
GLOBAL

As you read previously, Arabic is the most widely spoken language in the Middle East. Along with Hebrew, spoken mainly in Israel, it is a Semitic language. Several other languages are also spoken in the Middle East. Farsi, or Persian, is spoken mainly in Iran. Turkish is spoken in Turkey. The Turkish script is written in Latin letters instead of Arabic, the result of a change made by the Turkish leader Kemal Ataturk in 1928. This was a break with tradition, as was his decision to translate the Quran from Arabic into Turkish. European languages are spoken mostly in areas that were under European influence. Thus, English is used in Egypt, while French is used in Lebanon and Syria.

REVIEW QUESTIONS

Multiple Choice. Select the letter of the answer that correctly completes each statement.

1. Which pair of languages has the most in common?
   A. Arabic and Turkish
   B. Turkish and Hebrew
   C. Hebrew and Arabic
   D. Turkish and Farsi

2. Shi'ites and Sunnis refer to groupings of people who are
   A. Catholics
   B. Jews
   C. Muslims
   D. Protestants

ESSAYS

1. Religion has played a major role in shaping the history and culture of the Middle East. The three major religions in the area are Judaism, Christianity, and Islam.

   A. Explain one idea or belief that all three religions share.
   B. Describe one idea or belief that each one has that is different from the other two.
   C. Name one person who was extremely important for the growth of each religion.

2. Explain the following statements in regard to the Middle East: "Most Arabs are Muslims, but not all Muslims are Arabs."

IV. HISTORY AND POLITICAL GEOGRAPHY OF THE MIDDLE EAST

Overview

The Middle East has the longest recorded history of any region on the globe. The people who have influenced this history and who have been affected by it are of diverse backgrounds. Some of these people can trace their roots to the area itself, while others migrated to the Middle East from elsewhere. There are many patterns and periods in Middle Eastern history, and often they overlap; that is, different patterns and movements frequently occurred at the same time in various parts of the area.

The Historical Setting (Pre-History–600 A.D.)

Early Civilizations. The earliest known people in the Middle East settled in the river valleys of the Nile and the Tigris and Euphrates and built what we call river valley civilizations (see Section I of this unit, "Physical Geography"). These two civilizations—Egyptian, centered in the Nile River Valley, and Mesopotamian, in the Tigris-Euphrates River Valley—had many important achievements that influenced human history throughout the world. For this reason, historians call them "cradles of civilization." (Two other "cradles of civilization" developed in the river valleys of the Indus River in South Asia and the Huanghe, or Yellow, River in East Asia.) Several of these early societies conquered territory and grew into empires.

GLOBAL CONCEPTS

Environment

CONCEPTS GLOBAL

Society	General Area	Achievements
EGYPTIANS	Egypt	Pyramids, mathematics, control of Nile River waters, hieroglyphics, order maintained by a pharaoh, calendar, medicine, mummification
SUMERIANS	Mesopotamia	Cities, cuneiform, geometry, use of vehicles
BABYLONIANS	Mesopotamia	Hammurabi's code of law, hanging gardens of Babylon
HITTITES	Turkey and Syria	Iron weapons
LYDIANS	Turkey	Coined money
PHOENICIANS	Lebanon	Navigators, traders, alphabet
HEBREWS	Palestine	Monotheism, Ten Commandments, Old Testament
CALDEANS	Mesopotamia	Astronomy
PERSIANS	Iran	Roads, unified diverse people in a wide empire

All these societies were developed by people who were native to the Middle East. However, starting in the 4th century B.C., powerful civilizations from outside the Middle East began to make conquests in the area. They had a strong influence on the areas they conquered.

1. After Alexander the Great united the Greek city-states, he swept eastward into Asia Minor, Syria, Palestine, and Egypt. Alexander brought Greek culture to the Middle East and therefore Hellenized the area. The Hellenistic period (the period when Greek culture was brought to the Middle East) lasted from 333 B.C. to 90 B.C.

2. The area called Palestine comes from the word "Philistine." The Philistines controlled a small strip of land along the eastern Mediterranean coast in 1200 B.C. This land was first called Palestine by the Romans. Palestine describes a geographic region and has never been the name of a nation. The present-day nation of Israel is located in most of the land that was called Palestine. Israelite kingdoms existed in Palestine from approximately 1000 B.C. to 70 A.D.

3. By 30 B.C. the Roman Empire controlled most of the Mediterranean region. Its power, laws, and culture extended into all the former Hellenized lands in the Middle East. Christianity began during the Roman period with the birth of Jesus.

It started as a reform movement among Jews and gained converts under the leadership of Paul, a Hellenized Jew. Christianity spread throughout the Middle East and other parts of the Roman Empire, although its followers were persecuted by Rome's emperors. By 313 A.D. Christianity had become so widespread that the Emperor Constantine issued the Edict of Milan, which granted freedom of worship to all Christians in the empire—in both the western part, ruled from Rome, and the eastern part, ruled from the city of Byzantium on the Bosporus. With the decline of the western part of the Roman Empire, the Emperor Constantine moved to Byzantium, where he built a larger city, known as Constantinople (now Istanbul), in Turkey. Constantinople became the capital of the Eastern Roman Empire, also known as the Byzantine Empire.

4. The Byzantine Empire was at its height from 527 to 565, under the Emperor Justinian and his wife Theodora. It included present-day Greece, Turkey, Israel, Egypt, Jordan, and Syria. The Justinian Code set up a legal system based on Roman laws. The beautiful church Hagia Sophia was built under Justinian. Christians in the empire called their church Eastern Orthodox to distinguish it from the Catholic church in Rome. In the years after 600, the Byzantine Empire declined as it was subject to attacks from many outsiders. In 1453 the Ottoman Turks, who were Muslims, captured Constantinople and ended Christian dominance in the eastern Mediterranean.

The Rise and Spread of Islam (622–1453)

Islam became a powerful force in the Arabian Peninsula during Muhammad's life and after his death in 632. During the next 100 years Islam spread from the Arabian Peninsula westward to North Africa and Spain, as well as to other parts of the Middle East. In later years it was brought to Asia and Africa, south of the Sahara, and by the last half of the 20th century, Islam was a major religion in many nations of Africa (for example, Morocco, Nigeria) and Asia (for example, Bangladesh, Indonesia). There is also a large Muslim community in the Philippines.

Upon Muhammad's death, Muslims chose a leader who was called caliph. The first caliph was Abu Bakr, the father of Muhammad's wife, Aisha. After his death, control of the caliphate (the Muslim-dominated lands in the Arabian Peninsula and those to the immediate west and north) passed eventually to the Umayyad clan. Under the Caliph Muswiyah, the Umayyads made Damascus the Muslim capital in 661. However, Umayyad leadership was opposed by the followers of Ali (the husband of Fatimah, Muhammad's daughter), who served as caliph from

GLOBAL
CONCEPTS

Culture

CONCEPTS
GLOBAL

GLOBAL
CONCEPTS

Justice

CONCEPTS
GLOBAL

GLOBAL
CONCEPTS

Power

CONCEPTS
GLOBAL

GLOBAL
CONCEPTS

Political Systems

CONCEPTS
GLOBAL

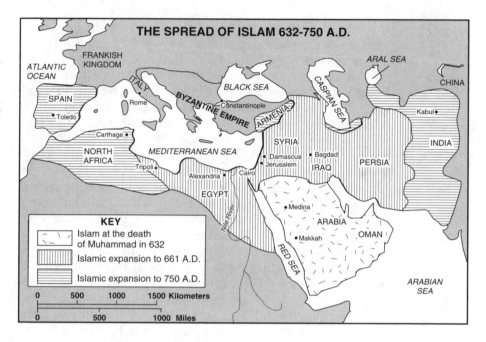

THE SPREAD OF ISLAM 632-750 A.D.

KEY

Islam at the death of Muhammad in 632

Islamic expansion to 661 A.D.

Islamic expansion to 750 A.D.

0   500   1000   1500 Kilometers

0   500   1000 Miles

656 until he was assassinated in 661. Ali's followers eventually formed the Shi'ite branch of Muslims, in opposition to the Sunni branch of Muslims.

Shi'ite Muslims drew up their own ideas about Islam. One was that the correct interpreters of the Quran were the descendants of Ali, especially twelve leaders known as imams. They believe that the twelfth imam, who disappeared about 1,000 years ago, will reappear as the mahdi and save the world. Shi'ite Muslims (from the Arabic phrase *Shi'a Ali,* the party of Ali) currently make up 10 percent of the world's approximately 900 million Muslims. The largest group of Shi'ites is in Iran. Ninety percent of the world's Muslims are Sunnis (from the Arabic word *sunna,* customs), who accept individuals other than Ali's descendants as the true successors to Muhammad. The schism (division, split) into two Muslim branches or sects, which began in the late 600s after Ali's assassination, continues into the 1990s, with the growth of many subsects and small groups.

The Umayyad dynasty lasted from 638 to 750. During that time, its conquests spread Islam throughout three continents.

1. In North Africa and Western Europe (Portugal, Spain, and France) until the Muslims were defeated by Charles Martel in 732 at Tours (in France).

2. In Southwest Asia (in Jerusalem, the Umayyads built a mosque over a holy site; see section on Islam in this unit) and South Asia (people in the Indus River Valley became Muslims; for further information, see Unit II on South and Southeast Asia).

There were many reasons for the successful territorial expansion of the Umayyads and the spread of Islam. One important reason was the Islamic idea that it was necessary to bring Islam to nonbelievers and that to die in a holy war (jihad) guaranteed a place in heaven. Another reason was that the Umayyads were skilled warriors, and they hoped to gain wealth and fertile lands—a contrast to their harsh life in a desert region. In addition, many conquered peoples were willing to convert to Islam, while others were forced to convert. Finally, the conquered Jews and Christians were treated tolerantly (as dhimmis—"people of the book") because some of their ways were similar to those of Muslims.

The Abbasids, another group of Muslims, defeated the Umayyads and created a dynasty that lasted from 750 to 1250. Under the Caliph Mansur, Baghdad became the capital of the new caliphate. The period of the Abbasid caliphate is known as "the Golden Age of Islam" because of the many outstanding cultural achievements at this time.

The achievements in the Muslim world came at a time when much of Europe was experiencing a period known as the Dark Ages. Accomplishments under the Abbasid caliphate reached Europe through trade and commerce and shaped many features of European culture.

After 1200 the Abbasids declined. Several factors brought about the end of the Golden Age of Islam as well as the Abbasid dynasty. First, it was difficult for the Abbasids to keep control over such a large area. Moreover, many Muslim groups, such as the Arabs, Persians, and Turks, did not get along well with each other. Secondly, the Crusades (1095–1291) caused much death and destruction in the Middle East. The Crusades were attempts by Europeans to take over Jerusalem and other Christian holy sites from the Muslims. Eventually, the Seljuk Turks, a Muslim people who had taken over Abbasid territory, were able to defeat the European forces. As a result of the Crusades, however, people from both Europe and the Middle East learned much about each other, and trade and commerce between them increased. This process of cultural diffusion enabled Europe to benefit from the Muslim cultural and scientific advances. Finally, the Abbasids were unable to beat back attacks on their lands by the Turks and the Mongols.

THE GOLDEN AGE OF ISLAM

Subject	Achievement
Science	Manufacture of glass, chemical compounds, laboratory equipment; books on chemistry and optics
Scholarship	Works of Greeks, Persians, and Indians translated into Arabic; House of Learning in Baghdad
Mathematics	Algebra; number system adopted from India and eventually transmitted to Europe as Arabic numerals; same for a decimal system and the concept of zero; a system to calculate square and cube roots of numbers.
Astronomy	Observatories; calculation of distances in space; use of the astrolabe in navigation; estimating the earth's circumference and acknowledging it is shaped like a sphere
Medicine	Advances in surgery and anesthetics; pharmacies; diagnosis and treatment of diseases such as smallpox and measles; medical encyclopedias, hospitals; examinations for physicians
Literature	*The Arabian Nights;* poems of Omar Khayyam; histories written by travelers such as Ibn-Khaldun
Art and architecture	Mosques with elaborate details of trees, flowers, geometric designs, and writing from the Quran; illuminated manuscripts; colorful carpets and textiles

The Ottoman Empire (1453–1918)

GLOBAL
CONCEPTS

Power

CONCEPTS
GLOBAL

The Ottomans were one of several Turkish peoples who eventually took over the territory once held by the Abbasids. They also captured Constantinople in 1453, thereby ending the Byzantine Empire. All this territory, which consisted of land in North Africa, southeastern Europe, and Southwest Asia, formed the Ottoman Empire. The city of Constantinople was now called Istanbul, and it became the center of the empire in what is present-day Turkey. The city's famous Hagia Sophia church was made a mosque.

The name "Ottoman" comes from Osman, a Turkish leader in 1300. However, the most famous Ottoman ruler (called sultan) was Suleiman the Magnificent (1521–1566), under whom the empire reached the height of its power. He was also called "Suleiman the Lawgiver" because of many legal, educational, and military changes he made. For a time, the empire was well organized, functioning basically as a conquering army constantly at war.

GLOBAL
CONCEPTS

Political Systems

CONCEPTS
GLOBAL

The Ottoman Turks developed a good set of administrators, similar to a civil service, to help run the vast territory in the empire. The attempt by the Ottoman Turks to expand their empire farther into Europe was finally stopped at the Battle of Vienna in 1683.

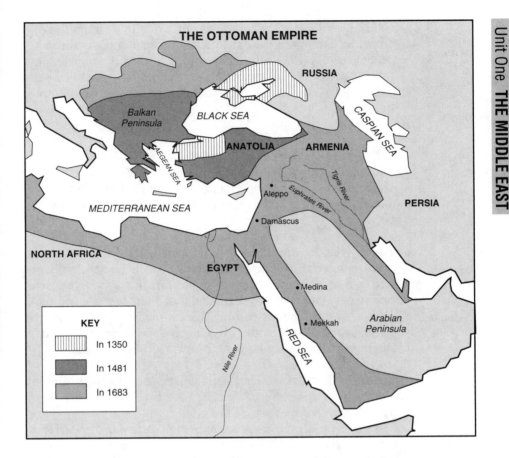

THE OTTOMAN EMPIRE

RUSSIA

Balkan
Peninsula

BLACK SEA

ANATOLIA

ARMENIA

CASPIAN SEA

AEGEAN SEA

MEDITERRANEAN SEA

Aleppo

Euphrates River

Tigris River

• Damascus

PERSIA

NORTH AFRICA

EGYPT

• Medina

• Mekkah

Arabian
Peninsula

RED SEA

Nile River

KEY

In 1350

In 1481

In 1683

During the 1800s, the empire began to decline. Reasons for its decline included corruption and inefficiency on the part of the rulers as well as their inability to hold together so many different peoples. Many of the subject people wished to break free from Ottoman control. Several short wars with other nations weakened Ottoman rule and caused a loss of territory. Finally, the Ottomans failed to modernize and keep up with the growth in industry, technology, learning, science, weapons, and trade that was occurring in Western Europe. As a result, the declining empire became known as "the sick man of Europe."

WORLD ISSUES

War

and

Peace

The final blow to the empire came in 1918 with the end of World War I. The Turks fought on the side of Germany and Austria-Hungary and lost the war. Consequently, the Middle Eastern lands outside Turkey that belonged to the empire were taken away and placed under the control of the newly formed League of Nations. The league created mandates in these lands (Palestine, Iraq, Syria), which were placed under the rule of England

and France. (The mandate gave permission to a nation to govern an area temporarily, until it was considered ready for independence.) By 1923 all that remained of the Ottoman Empire was the nation of Turkey. In that year Turkey was declared a republic under Mustapha Kemal Ataturk, who became the country's first president.

20th-Century Nationalism

The desire of a group of people to establish their own nation in a specific territory can be described as nationalism. Nationalist movements in the 20th century have resulted in many new nations.

Turkey. Under President Ataturk, Turkey tried to break away from traditional Middle Eastern ways and become a modernized and Westernized nation. To do this, many changes were carried out. Among them were: abolition of the fez (a headdress); ending government support of Islam as the official religion; replacing Islamic laws with a civil law code; ordering the Turkish language to be written in Roman letters instead of Arabic.

Arab Nationalism. The nationalistic desires of different groups of Arabs were evident in both the African and Asian parts of the Middle East.

1. *Algeria.* Algeria came under French control in the 19th century. Algerian nationalism grew in the 20th century and posed a problem for France after the end of World War II in 1945. France's refusal to leave Algeria led to a long and bloody war between 1954 and 1962. Peace talks in 1962 finally brought an end to the war, and Algeria became an independent nation. Its first leader was Ahmed Ben Bella.

2. *Lebanon and Syria.* After World War I, France held mandates in Lebanon and Syria. However, after World War II, Lebanon and Syria became free nations when the French left peacefully. Independence came to both nations in 1946.

3. *Iraq and Jordan.* Britain was given mandates over both Iraq and Jordan after World War I. Iraq became independent in 1923, but Britain held on to its mandate in what was then called Trans-Jordan until 1946.

4. *Egypt and Saudi Arabia.* From the late 1800s until 1922, Egypt was a British protectorate. However, in 1922 Egypt became a free constitutional monarchy, although Britain controlled Egypt's foreign affairs. This lasted until 1936, when Egypt gained more self-government. Saudi Arabia, never for-

mally colonized, became a nation in 1927. Its name came from Ibn Saud, the head of a Muslim sect that had established its power in most of the Arabian Peninsula.

Zionism. This term is used for the nationalistic desire of Jews to reestablish a nation of their own. The Zionist goal was achieved in 1948 with the establishment of Israel, which was located in Palestine, with borders somewhat similar to those of the ancient Israelite kingdoms. The territorial goals of Zionists and Arab nationalists conflicted in Palestine, especially while the area was a British mandate from 1920 to 1948. The conflict continues to the present day, with four major wars having been fought between Israel and the Arabs since 1948. (A brief examination of this conflict follows.)

Background of the Arab-Israeli Conflict

The conflict between Israel and the Arab nations is over sovereignty (political control) in the land called Palestine. This small strip of land on the eastern shore of the Mediterranean Sea has been inhabited by Jews and Arabs for thousands of years and, as you read earlier, has been under the dominance of different rulers at many times in history.

1. *Jewish sovereignty* in Palestine existed for about 1,000 years. However, with the Roman conquest in 70 A.D., many Jews were forced to leave what for them was "the holy land." This dispersion of Jews, with many eventually settling in Europe, North Africa, Asia, and later in the Americas, is known as the diaspora. (The word "diaspora" today can mean any place in the world where a people live outside of their original homeland.) Jews in the diaspora generally led difficult lives, especially in Europe. They were often persecuted for their religious beliefs (such persecution against Jews is referred to as anti-Semitism) and were frequently forced to live in separate areas of cities, called ghettoes. The ghettoes as well as village settlements often suffered from violent attacks, called pogroms. By the late 19th century, the majority of Jews lived in the diaspora; yet there was continuous Jewish habitation in Palestine from the Roman conquest into the 19th century. The movement for the restoration of a Jewish nation in Palestine (Zionism) was sparked in the late 1800s by Theodore Herzl, an Austrian Jew and journalist who wrote a book called *The Jewish State.* In the early 1900s, Zionists increased their efforts to help persecuted Jews immigrate to Palestine. At the same time, Zionists tried to get the ruling Ottoman Turks to grant territory for a Jewish state. Jews supported Britain in

WORLD ISSUES

Political and
Economic
Refugees

WORLD ISSUES

War
and
Peace

WORLD ISSUES

Political and
Economic
Refugees

WORLD ISSUES

Human
Rights

33

GLOBAL
CONCEPTS
Identity
CONCEPTS
GLOBAL

GLOBAL
CONCEPTS
Political Systems
CONCEPTS
GLOBAL

WORLD ISSUES

War

and

Peace

WORLD ISSUES

Terrorism

World War I against the Turks; Chaim Weizmann, an English Jewish chemist, contributed to the British war effort with his scientific achievements.

2. *Arab sovereignty* in Palestine can be traced to the Umayyad conquest in 637 A.D., which began a long era of Muslim control that lasted until the end of World War I (1918). Different Arab dynasties held power in Palestine from the 7th to the 15th centuries. From 1453 until World War I, sovereignty was held by the Ottoman Turks, who were not Arabs. However, Arab habitation in Palestine was continuous during the period of Ottoman Turkish rule. The Arabs did not like the Turks and wanted to establish their own nation in the area, as did the Jews. Consequently, the Arabs sided with the British in World War I in the struggle against the Turks. With the end of the war, Britain was given temporary control (the British mandate) over Palestine by the League of Nations.

3. During the period when Palestine was under the British mandate (1920–1948), Jews and Arabs continued to press their nationalistic claims. Britain had made territorial promises to both groups and issued an important document in 1917, while defeating the Turks in Palestine, called the Balfour Declaration. Named after Lord Balfour, the English statesman, the document proposed that Great Britain would view ". . . with favor the establishment in Palestine of a national home for the Jewish people . . . it being . . . understood that nothing shall be done which may prejudice the civil and religious rights of . . . non-Jewish communities . . ." In 1922, acting on their own, the British also carved out over half the mandate area as a separate Arab enclave to be known as Trans-Jordan.

Encouraged by the Balfour Declaration, Jews began to increase their immigration to what remained of Palestine, where they bought land from some Arabs and cultivated areas left unused by the Turks. Arab protests against Jews grew into riots and violent confrontations. Britain found it difficult to maintain peace between the two sides and was further weakened by its involvement in World War II (1939–1945). World War II was also the time when persecution against Jews in Europe reached an unprecedented level, with the killing of 6 million Jews by the Germans in the Holocaust. This tragedy convinced many Jews that the only safe place for them would be their own nation in Palestine.

At the end of World War II, Britain decided to give up its mandate over Palestine and asked the United Nations to resolve the conflict between the Arabs and Jews in Palestine. By a majority vote in 1947 the UN decided to partition Palestine into two states—a Jewish state and an Arab state. The city of Jerusalem, which was holy to both Jews and Muslims, was to be under UN supervision. Jews accepted this decision and declared their state of Israel in 1948. Arabs both in Palestine and in the new Arab nations outside of Palestine rejected the partition plan. In May 1948, six Arab nations—Egypt, Iraq, Trans-Jordan (later to be called Jordan), Syria, Lebanon, and Saudi Arabia—declared war on Israel. Although the combined Arab forces were larger and better equipped, they were unable to accomplish their goal of destroying Israel. A UN-arranged truce in 1949 ended the fighting.

The Four Arab-Israeli Wars

1. *The War for Independence, 1948–1949.* (This was described above.) Even though the Arabs failed in their goal to drive "the Jews into the sea," they still refused to accept the UN Partition Plan of 1947. In addition, they also refused to recognize the state of Israel even though the United States, the Soviet Union, and most of the world recognized the new state.

Israel is the only democracy in the Middle East, and although it was established as a Jewish state, Israel permits religious freedom to all people within its borders. Nevertheless, during the 1948 to 1949 war, over 700,000 Palestinian Arabs fled from Israel to Arab lands, thus becoming refugees. Some of these people fled because they feared the fighting. Many others were urged to leave by Arab armies, who promised to let the Palestinians return once the expected victory over Israel had been achieved.

This first Arab-Israeli war also affected the status of Jerusalem. The Israelis gained control of the western part of the

The holy city of Jerusalem

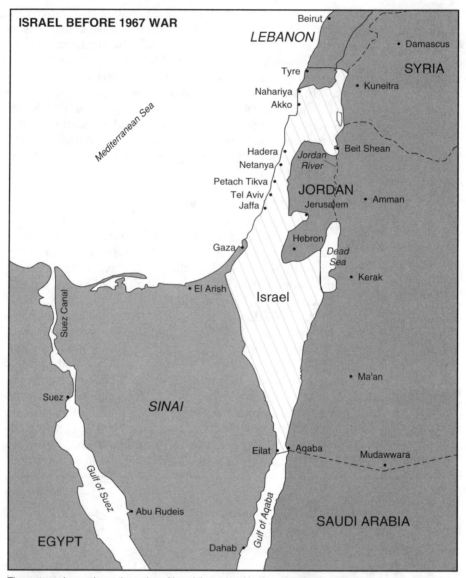

ISRAEL BEFORE 1967 WAR

The patterned area shows the nation of Israel that existed between 1949 and 1967. At its narrowest point, near the city of Netanya, Israel is only 9 miles wide.

WORLD ISSUES

Human
Rights

city, while Jordan seized East Jerusalem, which contained the city's important holy sites. Jordan promised to permit equal access to these holy Christian, Jewish, and Muslim sites for members of the three religions. (However, Jordan never permitted Jews to visit their holy sites.) Jordan also seized and occupied the West Bank. These actions violated the UN Partition

Plan, as this area was supposed to become an independent Palestinian Arab state. The Jordanian occupation received international condemnation and was never recognized by any Arab nation. It lasted for nineteen years, until 1967.

2. *The 1956 War.* Under President Gamal Abdel Nasser, Egypt nationalized (took over) from England the Suez Canal in 1956 and prohibited Israel from using it. Moreover, terrorist raids into Israel by Egypt and other Arab nations caused many deaths. As a result, Egypt and Israel went to war again. However, this time France and England joined with Israel and attacked Egyptian forces along the Suez Canal. Israel defeated the Egyptian army in the Sinai Peninsula and occupied the entire region. The UN arranged a ceasefire ending the second Arab-Israeli war. Egypt kept the Suez Canal and demanded that Israel give back the Sinai Peninsula. Israel agreed to give back the Sinai, hoping that in return Egypt would recognize the state of Israel and agree to peace. A United Nations Emergency Force (UNEF) was sent to keep peace on Israel's borders.

3. *The Six-Day War, 1967.* Egypt and the other Arab nations continued to refuse to recognize Israel and stepped up their terrorist attacks. Egypt built up its forces in the Sinai Desert, forbade Israel to use the Suez Canal, and closed the Gulf of Aqaba to Israeli shipping. It also ordered the UNEF to leave. These measures, along with Egypt's continued threats to destroy Israel, led the Israelis to strike at Egypt in early June 1967. Although Egypt was well supplied with Soviet equipment and was supported by other Arab nations that attacked Israel, Israel was able to defend itself successfully for the third time in 19 years. Arab armies that attacked Israel from the north, east, and south were thrown back, and Israel took over large amounts of land—the Sinai Peninsula and Gaza (from Egypt), the West Bank of the Jordan River and East Jerusalem (from Jordan, which had taken these areas in the 1948 to 1949 war and was asked by Israel not to attack her in 1967), and the Golan Heights (from Syria). The war lasted for six days. Israel annexed East Jerusalem and the Golan Heights, making them part of Israel. Israel offered to negotiate for the other newly won territories if the Arabs would sign a peace treaty and recognize Israel's right to exist.

After the war, Israel held occupied territory, such as the West Bank, that contained a large Arab population. As thousands of people fled, the number of Arab refugees in Arab nations such as Lebanon and Syria increased. Many Arab refugees were forced to live in camps with poor facilities that served as training grounds for terrorist activity against Israel.

WORLD ISSUES

War
and
Peace

WORLD ISSUES

Political and
Economic
Refugees

In November 1967 the UN passed Resolution 242 calling for all warring nations to recognize one another and make peace and for Israel to withdraw from.the occupied lands. The Arab nations continued their refusal to recognize Israel, and Israel refused to return territory until it received recognition.

4. *The Yom Kippur War, 1973.* The fourth Arab-Israeli war began on October 6, 1973 (Yom Kippur, the holiest day of the year to Jews), when Egypt attacked Israel by surprise across the Suez Canal. The war, which the Egyptians call "the October War," lasted almost a month, with Egypt gaining a small amount of land in the Sinai. Syrian troops attacked Israel on the Golan Heights but were beaten back. Several other Arab countries sent troops to fight. The Soviet Union increased its arms shipments to the Arabs, hoping to avoid another victory by Israel. To counter the Soviets, the United States sent help to Israel. Oil-rich Arab nations pressured the United States not to help Israel and began an oil embargo (a refusal to sell oil). Once again, the UN arranged a ceasefire to end the fighting. In 1973 the UN also passed Resolution 338, calling for "negotiations . . . between the parties concerned . . . aimed at establishing . . . peace in the Middle East."

Developments Between 1973 and 1991

1. In 1977 Egyptian President Anwar Sadat visited Israel to begin peace talks. He was the first Arab leader to visit Israel. Later in the year, Israeli Prime Minister Menachem Begin visited Egypt.

2. In 1979, at Camp David near Washington, D.C., an Egyptian-Israeli Peace Treaty was signed by Sadat and Begin. President Jimmy Carter of the United States brought the two leaders together. The peace treaty provided that: (1) Egypt and Israel would recognize each other and exchange ambassadors; (2) the state of war that existed between them from 1949 to 1979 was over; (3) Israel would return the Sinai Peninsula to Egypt in stages between 1979 and 1982, and a UN peacekeeping force would be reestablished on the border; and (4) negotiations would begin on the status of the Palestinian Arabs.

3. Many Arab nations were angry at Egypt's actions and broke off relations. In 1981 Muslim extremists assassinated Sadat, and Hosni Mubarak became the new Egyptian president.

4. In 1982 Israel invaded Lebanon in response to repeated terrorist attacks by the Palestine Liberation Organization (PLO) and the inability of the Lebanese government to control PLO actions. The PLO claimed to speak on behalf of Palestinian Arabs and was so recognized by most Arab nations. By 1984 the PLO

forces had left Lebanon. The Israeli action in Lebanon stirred much controversy among Israelis, and after the 1984 Israeli elections, its army was pulled back from Lebanon except for a small "security zone" in southern Lebanon. While Israel was in Lebanon, it became an ally of a Lebanese Christian militia (a small army). This militia massacred thousands of Palestinians in Sabra and Shatila, two refugee camps in Beirut. Although Israel was not involved in this tragedy, it came under criticism.

5. Also in 1982, Israel, in compliance with the peace treaty with Egypt, withdrew completely from the Sinai Peninsula.

6. In 1987 an uprising by Palestinians in the West Bank and Gaza Strip began. This uprising, called the Intifada, was a protest against continued Israeli occupation of the land it had won in war. Many Palestinians supported the PLO and its leader, Yasir Arafat, in its goals of overthrowing Israel and establishing a Palestinian state. However, the PLO was branded as a terrorist group by Israel, because it was one of several Arab organizations that had carried out murderous actions against civilians in the Middle East and elsewhere in the world. Consequently, the Israeli government refused to negotiate with the PLO over the status of the occupied territories.

Within Israel the question of what to do with the occupied territories has created discussion and divisiveness. Many Israelis want to keep the territories because they view a Palestinian state as a military threat, and some claim that a Palestinian state already exists in Jordan. Others want to meet some of the Palestinian demands. As the 1990s began, the status of the occupied territories was still unresolved and the Intifada continued.

Arab Views of the Conflict

1. The creation of Israel in 1948 was wrong and was another sign of Western imperialism in the Middle East.

2. Israel was established on land that belonged to Arabs.

3. Arabs never accepted the UN Partition Plan of 1947.

4. The majority of people in the Middle East are Arabs. Israeli society and culture represent a threat to Arab values.

5. Israel's creation stemmed from European guilt about what happened to Jews during the Holocaust. It is wrong to take out this guilt on the Arabs. A Jewish state should have been created somewhere, but not in the Middle East.

6. Palestinians deserve a land of their own, as promised in the Balfour Declaration as well as during the British mandate period.

7. The UN has condemned Israeli actions in the occupied territories.

8. Jerusalem is a holy city to Muslims, as it contains the Dome of the Rock and the El Aksa Mosque and is the third holiest city after Makkah and Medina. Jerusalem should be under Muslim authority, not occupied by Israel.

9. Arab sovereignty in Palestine, prior to 1948, was more recent than Jewish sovereignty.

10. Israel seeks to expand beyond its borders.

11. Israel must give back land it gained in wars as a condition for any peace negotiations.

12. The Intifada shows the wrongfulness of Israeli occupation and the need for a Palestinian state.

Israeli Views of the Conflict

GLOBAL
CONCEPTS

Empathy

CONCEPTS
GLOBAL

1. Israel is located on land that was the original homeland of the Jewish people and that was promised to them in the Bible.

2. Arabs sold land to Jews prior to 1948; other Arabs fled from the land in the 1948–1949 war.

3. The UN Partition Plan was approved by a majority of the world's nations.

4. As a small nation of 4 million people, Israel does not represent a threat to the 100 million Arabs in 15 nations in the region. Arabs who still live in Israel have a high standard of living and live in the only democracy in the Middle East.

5. A Jewish state is needed as a safe place and refuge, because of the centuries of anti-Semitism in Europe and in Arab lands.

6. Jordan exists as a state for Palestinians. It was created illegally by the British in 1992 from 77 percent of the land that Britain held as a mandate from the League of Nations. There is no need or obligation to create a second Palestinian state. Most Jordanians today are Palestinians.

7. UN votes condemning Israel are signs of Arab ill-feeling and reflect Arab pressure on oil-poor countries to vote with the Arabs or face oil embargoes.

8. Jerusalem was the capital of Jewish kingdoms in ancient times and is a holy city to Jews, containing the Western Wall and the sites of the first two temples. These areas were restricted to Jews when Jordan ruled Jerusalem from 1948 to 1967. Today the Israeli government permits the Muslim holy sites to be watched over by members of the Israeli Muslim community.

9. Jewish sovereignty in Palestine was earlier in history than that of the Arabs.

10. If Israel had not been attacked so often by the Arabs, it would not have any land other than that given to it under the 1947 Partition Plan. Israel has never intentionally tried to take

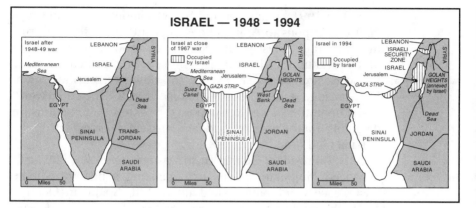

ISRAEL — 1948 – 1994

Israel after 1948-49 war — LEBANON, SYRIA, Mediterranean Sea, ISRAEL, Jerusalem, EGYPT, Dead Sea, SINAI PENINSULA, TRANS-JORDAN, SAUDI ARABIA, 0 Miles 50

Israel at close of 1967 war — LEBANON, SYRIA, Occupied by Israel, ISRAEL, Mediterranean Sea, Jerusalem, GOLAN HEIGHTS, GAZA STRIP, Suez Canal, West Bank, Dead Sea, EGYPT, SINAI PENINSULA, JORDAN, SAUDI ARABIA, 0 Miles 50

Israel in 1994 — LEBANON, ISRAELI SECURITY ZONE, SYRIA, Occupied by Israel, ISRAEL, Jerusalem, GOLAN HEIGHTS (annexed by Israel), GAZA STRIP, EGYPT, Dead Sea, SINAI PENINSULA, JORDAN, SAUDI ARABIA, 0 Miles 50

away land from any Arab nation, whereas the Arabs have tried to take away and destroy Israeli land.

11. Israel is willing to negotiate with the Arabs and return land if the Arabs end the war they have waged since 1948. With the exception of Egypt (since 1979), no Arab nation recognizes Israel's right to exist. Israel has shown that it is willing to exchange land for peace (for example, the return of the Sinai to Egypt).

12. The Intifada is just another phase of the attempt by Arabs since 1948 to destroy Israel. The Intifada would end if the Arabs were to recognize Israel's right to exist.

Other Elements at the Start of the 1990s

1. The Arabs have been worried about the immigration to Israel of thousands of Russian Jews, as well as the growth of Israeli settlements in the occupied territories.

WORLD ISSUES

Determination
of Political
and Economic
Systems

2. The Arab boycott (a refusal to buy goods from someone) against Israel continued as an economic weapon. It operates on two levels: (1) all direct trade between Arab states and Israel is forbidden; and (2) Arab countries will not do business with any company that does business with Israel. Therefore, many companies, afraid of losing business with Arabs, will refrain from having contact with Israel. Israel has repeatedly asked for an end of the boycott.

3. Iraq's threats of nuclear and gas attacks against Israel caused concern about the possibility of a fifth Arab-Israeli war. Iraq's unprovoked firing of Scud missiles on Israel during the 1991 Persian Gulf War almost ignited such a conflict. (Israel was not a participant in the war.)

4. The 1991 breakup of the Soviet Union, a longtime supplier of weapons to Arab nations, meant that the flow of arms into the Middle East would be reduced. Another consequence of the breakup was the increased influence the United States, as the world's chief superpower, could now exert in the region. U.S. prestige also increased in some parts of the Arab world based upon the U.S. role, supported by a few Arab nations, in defeating Iraqi President Saddam Hussein's forces during the Persian Gulf War.

5. U.S. President George Bush was able to use his country's enhanced diplomatic status in organizing a historic Middle East Peace Conference. Held in Madrid, Spain, in October 1991, the conference had representatives from Israel, Egypt, Syria, Lebanon, and a joint Palestinian-Jordanian delegation. It marked the first time that Israelis met formally with PLO officials. (Israel had previously been unwilling to have such contacts.) All the delegations presented their views in Madrid, and many differences were aired. Although no specific progress was made in reaching an overall peace settlement, the mere fact that the delegations met was seen as a hopeful sign for the future. From 1991 through 1994, follow-up talks between the parties were held in Washington, D.C., and Geneva. The most important issues, on which there was little movement, concerned Palestinian self-rule, the status of Jerusalem, and the return of the Golan Heights.

6. A much more dramatic moment in the quest for Middle East peace occurred on September 13, 1993, in Washington, D.C. On that day, with U.S. President Bill Clinton presiding, Israeli Prime Minister Yitzhak Rabin and PLO Chairman Yasir Arafat shook hands and signed a peace agreement. With millions watching on television, the two former adversaries shook hands on the first-ever pact between Jews and Palestinians to end their conflict. Its key features were: (1) Israelis would withdraw from Gaza and the West Bank city of Jericho by April 1994; (2) a five-year period of Palestinian self-rule would begin in these places; and (3) talks on a permanent agreement would start by December 1995, with the agreement to take effect in December 1998.

In the months immediately following the Washington agreement, both sides met often in attempts to work out its various provisions. Many sessions ended in disagreements. Further obstacles to progress could be seen in the protests in Israel and in the occupied territories by those on both sides who were upset with the pact. At times, violence and killings were committed by extremists on both sides.

Jericho and the Gaza Strip came under Palestinian control in 1994.

7. Another historic event affecting the Middle East occurred in 1993. This was the signing in Jerusalem of an agreement between Israel and the Vatican, whereby diplomatic relations would be established for the first time. The Roman Catholic church would now recognize the state of Israel, reversing its prior policy. Both parties anticipated having their respective ambassadors in place by the end of 1994.

8. Peace in the region received another boost in July 1994. At that time, Prime Minister Yitzhak Rabin of Israel and King Hussein of Jordan signed a peace treaty that ended forty years of war between them.

Other Political Developments in the Middle East, 1979–1994

Iran-Islamic Fundamentalism and the War with Iraq. The shah of Iran, Mohammed Reza Pahlavi, introduced many Western and modern practices to his country during the 1960s and 1970s. However, many religious leaders felt that traditional Islamic customs were threatened by Western ideas. These leaders were Islamic fundamentalists, who wanted to keep Islam pure and fundamental, without any "contamination" from the outside world. They opposed the shah and were also upset with the dictatorial manner in which he ruled. Riots

GLOBAL CONCEPTS

Identity

CONCEPTS GLOBAL

THE PALESTINIAN POPULATION

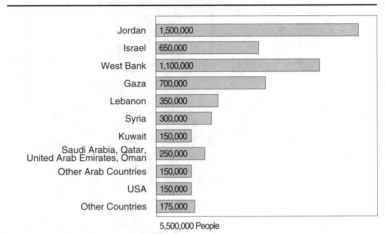

Jordan	1,500,000
Israel	650,000
West Bank	1,100,000
Gaza	700,000
Lebanon	350,000
Syria	300,000
Kuwait	150,000
Saudi Arabia, Qatar, United Arab Emirates, Oman	250,000
Other Arab Countries	150,000
USA	150,000
Other Countries	175,000

5,500,000 People

Source: *N.Y. Times Magazine* May, 1991

and demonstrations against the shah forced him to leave Iran in 1979. In his place the country was run by an Islamic Revolutionary Council, led by Ayatollah Ruhollah Khomeini. This Iranian Revolution, also known as the Islamic Revolution, caused concern in other Muslim nations in the Middle East. The Ayatollah's government was anti-Western and held 52 Americans as hostages from 1979 to 1981. Although Khomeini died in 1989, the new rulers of Iran have followed similar foreign and domestic policies.

In 1980 war between Iran and Iraq broke out when Iraq, under its leader Saddam Hussein, attacked Iran. Known as the Iran-Iraq War, this conflict had several causes. These included: political causes—each nation wanted to dominate the Persian Gulf area; frequent criticism by Hussein and Khomeini of each other; border disputes existed; social causes—Iraq feared the "export" of the Iranian Revolution; there were great religious differences between the Sunni Muslims of Iraq and the Shi'ite Muslims of Iran; and economic causes—the oil fields of the Persian Gulf area are very valuable; the Persian Gulf itself is the most important route for transporting oil from the Middle East. The fighting ended in 1988 under a UN-supervised agreement, but it caused hundreds of thousands of casualties and hurt the economies of both nations. The war ended as a stalemate.

WORLD ISSUES

War
and
Peace

Lebanon—Civil War and Syrian Occupation. A civil war broke out in Lebanon that lasted from 1975 to 1990. It can be explained by examining the country's political and religious

44

history. When the French mandate in Lebanon ended in 1943, a government was created that was supposed to strike a balance between Lebanese Christians and Muslims. Since the Christians were then the majority group, it was decided that most of the top government positions (such as president and armed forces commander) would go to Christians. From the 1940s to the 1970s, Lebanon prospered economically and was peaceful. However, Muslims became the majority group, and they wanted changes in the political structure to give them more power. It was also in this period that Palestinian refugees, including PLO leaders, settled in Lebanon as a result of the Arab-Israeli wars. From these settlements, many Palestinians made terrorist raids into Israel. Frequently, Israeli forces attacked these settlements in retaliation. Lebanese Christians, represented by the Phalange party, were against the Palestinian presence in Lebanon.

In 1975 Muslims and Christians began to fight each other. In addition, different Muslim groups began to fight one another and different Christian groups also began to fight one another. Each of the groups formed its own private army, or militia. In 1976 Syria, under President Hafez el-Assad, sent in troops as requested by the Arab League (an organization of Arab nations in the Middle East). Although Syria's purpose was to restore order, at various times the Syrians supported different militias in Lebanon. By 1990 there were 40,000 Syrian soldiers in Lebanon, and President Assad began to drop hints of incorporating Lebanon into a "greater Syria."

Other Middle Eastern nations, such as Iran and Libya, also supported one or more of the warring groups. Some of these groups, such as the Islamic Jihad, carried out terrorist activities against foreigners and other Lebanese in order to focus world

WORLD ISSUES

Terrorism

attention on their political goals. These terrorist activities included taking citizens of France, the United States, Germany, and the Soviet Union as hostages and sometimes killing them, hijacking a TWA airliner, and killing American and French soldiers in a suicide bomb attack. Tragically, there was no single government in Lebanon acceptable to all its people and able to bring stability to the nation. The civil war resulted in separated enclaves (closed-in areas) in Beirut and elsewhere under the control of whichever militia proved to be the strongest. The Lebanese economy was ruined by the war.

A long series of negotiations led to an agreement that helped bring the war to an end in 1990. This National Reconciliation Pact provided for a new government in which Muslims and Christians would share power equally. The Lebanese army regained control of most of the country, frequently aided by Syrian forces. Many Lebanese now returned to their country, having fled during the long war. Electricity and other basic services were restored, as the economy began to prosper. Yet Syria kept its 40,000 soldiers there and has influenced major Lebanese government policies. A 1991 agreement between both nations spoke of cooperation on political and economic issues. Many Lebanese, especially the Christians, would prefer for Syria to end its occupation. Syria has refused to do this.

War in Afghanistan (1979–1989).

In 1979 a Marxist pro-Soviet government came to power in Afghanistan. It faced opposition by the majority of Afghan people, who began an armed struggle against it. The Soviet Union invaded Afghanistan, claiming that it was reacting to a request by the Afghan government. However, many observers believed that the real reasons for the Soviet actions were to gain access to oil and gas deposits in Afghanistan and possibly to reach through Iran into the Persian Gulf. The Soviets also may have been afraid of the impact of Islamic fundamentalism in Afghanistan and Iran on the Muslim communities in the Soviet Union. The Soviet military action was condemned by nations around the globe and caused controversy in the Soviet Union itself. The Afghan fighters, the Mujahadeen, were supplied by the United States and were able to deny the Soviet Union a victory. In 1989 the Soviets retreated from Afghanistan with severe military and political losses.

Afghanistan was not to have political stability, however, as different religious factions fought each other for control. A coup in 1992 was one sign of this instability.

Libya and State-Supported Terrorism.

WORLD ISSUES

Terrorism

Ever since Colonel Muammar Qaddafi came to power in 1969, Libya has supported terrorist groups. These groups have carried out actions mainly against Israeli and U.S. interests. In 1986 American bombers raided Libya in retaliation for violence directed against Americans in Europe and the Middle East. The worst incident of terrorist violence involving Libya concerned the unspeakable bombing of Pan Am flight 103 as it flew over Lockerbie, Scotland, in 1988. The death toll numbered all 259 passengers and crew members, allegedly due to the work of agents trained in Libya. Libya refused to release the suspects to U.S. authorities, for which the UN imposed sanctions on Libya.

The Libyan government's connection with such bloody unprovoked acts toward people of other nations is an example of "state-supported terrorism." This term refers to a government policy that supports, trains, finances, and protects organizations that engage in terrorist activities. Besides Libya, other Middle Eastern nations that have provided such support are Iran, Syria, Iraq, and Yemen. Examples of groups that have received their assistance have been Islamic Jihad, Hamas, and the PLO. American officials were concerned about any links between Middle East terrorists and the 1993 bombing of the World Trade Center in New York City.

Pan-Arabism. This term refers to the idea of all Arab nations uniting and standing together on political and economic issues. The movement reached a high point while President Nasser ruled Egypt. However, since his death in 1970, and due to several disputes among the Arab nations, the movement has died down. The movement was tied to the idea of Arab socialism (government control of industry and the attempt to improve living conditions for all Arabs).

Operation Desert Storm—The Persian Gulf War of 1991.

This war lasted from January 16, 1991, to February 27, 1991. The conflict, whose chief adversaries were Iraq and the United States, had its roots in the Iraqi invasion of Kuwait in August 1990. Iraq, which wanted to take over Kuwait's rich oil fields and have greater access to the Persian Gulf, would probably have then sought to take over Saudi Arabia. Such actions would have given Iraq control over 40 percent of the world's oil reserves. Saddam Hussein refused to leave Kuwait despite UN requests and its eventual imposition of trade sanctions and threat to use force.

As Iraqi troops killed, tortured, and raped thousands of Kuwaitis, destroyed much property, and were poised for an attack on Saudi Arabia, U.S. President George Bush assembled a multinational force of 500,000 troops from 29 countries. This coalition, under the command of American General Norman Schwarzkopf and containing 450,000 U.S. troops, went into action in January under the authority of a UN Security Council Resolution when Iraq failed to meet a deadline to withdraw its troops from Kuwait. With the use of high-tech weaponry, the U.S.-led coalition defeated the Iraqis and freed Kuwait in five weeks.

The chief consequences of the war for the Middle East were as follows: (1) Saddam Hussein remained in power, still in possession of a large army and many weapons of mass destruction. He frequently failed to cooperate with the UN inspection teams that came to Iraq to check on his weapons program. (2) The

WORLD ISSUES

War
and
Peace

WORLD ISSUES

Human
Rights

WORLD ISSUES

Environmental
Concerns

47

ecology of the Persian Gulf area was severely upset by Iraqi soldiers. They burned oil wells and released great amounts of petroleum into the gulf waters. (3) A large split among Arabs occurred. Egypt, Saudi Arabia, Syria, and Kuwait sided with the U.S. In support of Iraq, although not sending in any fighters, were Jordan, Yemen, Tunisia, Algeria, Yemen, and the PLO. (4) Kurdish people in Iraq were treated very harshly by Saddam Hussein. Their attempt to break away from Iraqi rule was suppressed, and many were killed or forced to become refugees. Thousands were given "safe-haven" areas in northern Iraq under the protection of the United States and the United Nations.

The Future of the Kurds. As an ethnic group of approximately 24 million people, the Kurds have spread out during this century to various parts of Iran, Turkey, and Syria as well as in Iraq. Often suffering persecution, they have long wanted to have a nation of their own—to be called Kurdistan. Such a nation, however, would have to be carved out of land from the previously mentioned four Middle Eastern countries. This is unlikely to happen. Nevertheless, violence associated with Kurdish claims does occur from time to time—most often in Iraq and Turkey.

WORLD ISSUES

Political and
Economic
Refugees

WORLD ISSUES

Human
Rights

REVIEW QUESTIONS

Matching. Match the society in column 1 with the achievement of that society in column 2.

Column 1

_____ 1. Egyptians
_____ 2. Sumerians
_____ 3. Babylonians
_____ 4. Phoenicians
_____ 5. Hittites

Column 2

A. code of justice
B. cuneiform, city-states
C. alphabet, maritime activity
D. iron weapons
E. hieroglyphics

Timeline. For each event below, select the number for the time period in which the event occurred.

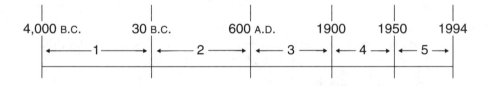

4,000 B.C.   30 B.C.   600 A.D.   1900   1950   1994

←——— 1 ———→ ←— 2 —→ ←— 3 —→ ←— 4 —→ ←— 5 —→

1. Partition of Palestine
2. Conquests of Alexander the Great; Hellenistic influence
3. Balfour Declaration
4. Roman destruction of "the second temple"
5. End of the British mandate in Palestine
6. End of Ottoman sovereignty in Palestine
7. "June (Six-Day) War"
8. Two nations that had previously been at war sign a treaty of peace
9. Iraqi invasion of Kuwait
10. Intifada
11. Israeli-PLO agreement
12. Persian Gulf War

Issues. Each of the statements below refers to one of the four agreements indicated by a letter. For each statement, choose the correct letter.

A. Balfour Declaration
B. Egyptian-Israeli Peace Treaty
C. Partition of Palestine
D. Israeli-PLO Agreement

 1. Israeli sovereignty recognized by an Arab nation
 2. Occurred just before the first Arab-Israeli war
 3. Occurred before all the others
 4. Occurred after the most recent Arab-Israeli war and involved U.S. President Jimmy Carter
 5. Issued before the British mandate went into effect
 6. Occurred after all the others
 7. Decision by the United Nations at the end of the British mandate
 8. Yom Kippur War (October War) occurred six years prior to this agreement
 9. Occurred as a result of face-to-face meetings between nations that once were enemies
10. Signed by Yitzhak Rabin and Yasir Arafat
11. Occurred after the Persian Gulf War

ESSAYS

1. Historical events have both causes and consequences. For each of the following, describe one cause and one consequence:

   A. Partition of Palestine (1947)
   B. Arab oil embargo (1973–1974)
   C. Lebanon civil war (1975–1990)
   D. Overthrow of the shah of Iran (1979)
   E. Egyptian-Israeli Peace Treaty (1979)
   F. Iran-Iraq War (1980–1988)
   G. Intifada (1987–1993)
   H. Iraqi invasion of Kuwait (1990)
    I. Operation Desert Storm (1991)

2. The dispute between Arabs and Israelis has led to several wars since 1948.

   A. Discuss two arguments offered by Arabs on this dispute.
   B. Discuss two arguments offered by Israelis on this dispute.

3. Many individuals have affected the history of the Middle East. Identify each person below by giving his nation or place of origin, the century he lived in, and one way in which he has affected life in the Middle East.

A. Anwar Sadat
B. Alexander the Great
C. Menachem Begin
D. Osman
E. Saddam Hussein
F. Kemal Ataturk
G. Muammar Qaddafi
H. Justinian
I. Theodore Herzl
J. Ibn Saud
K. Ruhollah Khomeini
L. Arthur Balfour
M. Bill Clinton

UNIT TWO

South and Southeast Asia

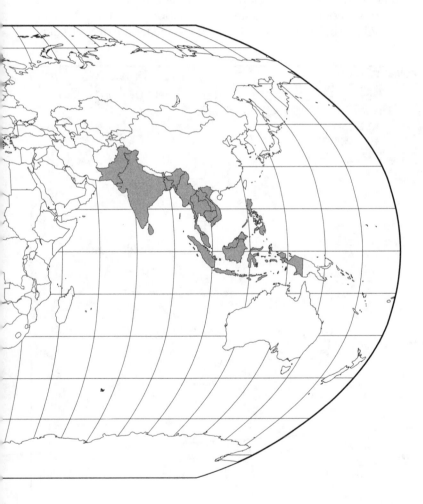

I. PHYSICAL GEOGRAPHY OF SOUTH ASIA

Overview

The region known as South Asia is also called the Indian or Asian subcontinent. It is a very large area, bigger in size and population than all of Western Europe. Consequently, it could be called a continent by itself except for the fact that it is attached to the Asian mainland. The subcontinent is slightly less than half the size of the United States. India, called "Bharat" in that country, is the seventh largest nation in the world in area. The subcontinent contains six nations: India, Pakistan, Bangladesh, Bhutan, Nepal, and the island nation of Sri Lanka.

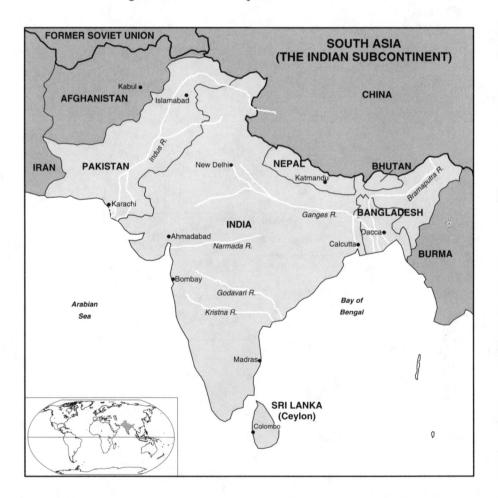

Topography

The region's topography has had a dramatic impact on political, economic, and cultural patterns. Its land features are one reason for the area's being open to greater foreign influences from the west than from the north and east. The Himalaya Mountains in the north contain Mount Everest, the highest peak in the world. The presence of these mountains has acted as a barrier to contact with peoples to the north and northeast of the region, separating the subcontinent from the rest of Asia. In the northwest, openings in the mountains, such as the Khyber Pass, have resulted in the movement of peoples, goods, and ideas. This movement, an example of cultural diffusion, has generally been from west to east and has included the Aryans (2000 B.C.), Alexander the Great (327 B.C.), Muslims (1000 A.D.), and Afghan refugees (1980s). As a result, a traveler to the subcontinent today would find a mixture of many ethnic groups, religions, and languages.

GLOBAL
CONCEPTS

Diversity

CONCEPTS
GLOBAL

South of the Himalaya Mountains lies the Indo-Gangetic Plain, also known as the Hindustan Plain. This is a very fertile area and home to more than half of India's population. Farther south is the Deccan Plateau, lying between the Eastern and Western Ghats. Many mineral resources are found here. Moving farther south, one finds good farm land near the coasts.

The Thar Desert, the main desert in the region, is in the western part of the subcontinent. Its relative flatness and dryness have been barriers to settlement.

Water Bodies

The subcontinent, which is actually a peninsula extending out from the Asian mainland, is surrounded by the Arabian Sea, the Indian Ocean, and the Bay of Bengal. The three chief river systems begin in the Himalayas: the Indus River flows through Pakistan and into the Arabian Sea; the Ganges and Brahmaputra rivers flow through India, converge in Bangladesh, and empty out into the Bay of Bengal. The Indus River Valley was the site of the earliest known civilizations in the subcontinent, which were located at Mohenjo-daro and Harappa in about 3000 B.C. Much flooding occurs in the soil-rich delta region of Bangladesh, due in part to the onrushing waters of the Ganges and Brahmaputra rivers. The heavy monsoon rains and occasional tidal waves are additional factors causing destruction in the delta.

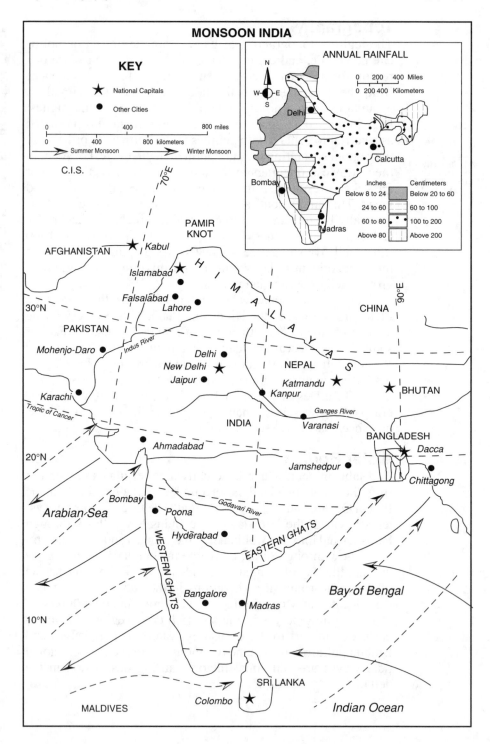

MONSOON INDIA

KEY

★ National Capitals

● Other Cities

0 — 400 — 800 miles
0 — 400 — 800 kilometers

→ Summer Monsoon   → Winter Monsoon

ANNUAL RAINFALL

0 — 200 — 400 Miles
0 — 200 400 — Kilometers

Inches	Centimeters
Below 8 to 24	Below 20 to 60
24 to 60	60 to 100
60 to 80	100 to 200
Above 80	Above 200

Delhi

Bombay

Madras

Calcutta

C.I.S.

70°E

PAMIR KNOT

AFGHANISTAN ★ Kabul

★ Islamabad

Falsalabad ● ● Lahore

30°N

CHINA

90°E

PAKISTAN

H I M A L A Y A S

Mohenjo-Daro ●

Indus River

Delhi ●

New Delhi ★

Jaipur ●

NEPAL

Katmandu ★

Kanpur ●

★ BHUTAN

Karachi ●

Tropic of Cancer

Ganges River

Varanasi ●

INDIA

BANGLADESH

20°N

Ahmadabad ●

★ Dacca

Jamshedpur ●

Chittagong ●

Arabian Sea

Bombay ●

● Poona

Godavari River

Hyderabad ●

EASTERN GHATS

WESTERN GHATS

Bay of Bengal

Bangalore ●

● Madras

10°N

SRI LANKA

MALDIVES

Colombo ★

Indian Ocean

Impact of the Monsoon

WORLD ISSUES

Environmental
Concerns

The monsoon rains occur from June to September, bringing to the subcontinent 90 percent of its annual rainfall. They can be a blessing, bringing crop surpluses, or a curse, bringing famine, flooding, and drought, depending on their timing and the amount of rain that falls. The monsoon's direction is generally northeasterly, coming across the Arabian Sea and affecting mainly northcentral India and Bangladesh.

REVIEW QUESTIONS

Fact or Opinion. If the statement is a fact, write F. If the statement is an opinion, write O.

1. India has been more influenced from the west than from the east.

2. A good monsoon is proof of God's blessings upon the Indian subcontinent.

3. A drought will occur if there is a poor monsoon and little water in reserve in India's dams.

4. The largest nations in physical size on the subcontinent are India and Pakistan.

Modified True-False. Read each statement carefully. If it is true, write TRUE. If it is not true, then write a word or words in place of the underlined word or words that would make the statement true.

1. A drought would occur if the monsoons give <u>little</u> rain.

2. The Ganges and Brahmaputra rivers originate in the <u>Hindu Kush</u> mountains.

3. The Khyber Pass is in the western part of <u>Nepal</u>.

4. The body of water lying to India's west is the <u>Bay of Bengal</u>.

5. The Himalaya Mountains have <u>prevented</u> much cultural diffusion between India and China.

ESSAYS

1. Geography often influences the economy, culture, and history of a nation. Select any two of the following geographic features. For each discuss its influence on the Indian subcontient.

   A. Khyber Pass
   B. Himalaya Mountains
   C. Indus River Valley
   D. Indo-Gangetic Plain

2. The monsoons can be either a "blessing" or a "curse" for the people of South Asia.

   A. Why can the monsoons be a "blessing"? Give two reasons.
   B. Why can the monsoons be a "curse"? Give two reasons.

II. ECONOMIC GEOGRAPHY OF SOUTH ASIA

Agriculture

Over the last ten years, food production in India has increased. Self-sufficiency has been achieved, at least temporarily, despite some bad monsoon years. Consequently, imports from nations such as the United States have declined. Crop production focuses mainly on rice, wheat, cotton, tea, jute, and sugar cane.

Much of this agricultural development has resulted from the Green Revolution, that is, the use of modern science and technology to improve agricultural productivity. Examples of modern technology include laboratory-produced fertilizers, insecticides, and improved seeds, which are high-yielding and drought-resistant, such as IR-8. Scientists involved in these efforts are known as agronomists. A leading figure in this work has been the American agronomist Dr. Norman Borlaugh (winner of a Nobel Peace Prize in 1970). Critics, however, have noted some negative aspects of the Green Revolution:

GLOBAL
CONCEPTS
Technology
CONCEPTS
GLOBAL

1. Resistance among farmers to new planting and landholding patterns.

2. Higher financial costs when using new technology and

AGRICULTURAL PRODUCTION IN INDIA 1972–1984

Commodity	Amount (millions of tons)				
	1989	1984	1975	1974	1972
Wheat	53.4	45.1	25.8	22.0	26.4
Rice	70.8	59.8	70.5	60.0	57.9
Barley	2.1	1.8	2.9	2.3	2.5
Corn	9.4	8.0	5.5	5.0	6.2
Potatoes	10.4	10.1	6.1	4.6	4.8
Bananas	5.3	4.5	—	3.2	3.1
Peanuts	8.0	7.3	6.6	5.2	3.9
Sugar (raw)	10.9	5.5	5.3	4.3	3.3
Jute	2.1	1.6	0.8	1.0	0.8
Cotton	9.0	7.4	5.4	—	—
Number (millions)					
Cattle	193	182	180.3	179.9	176.9
Sheep	51	42	40.0	40.2	43.3
Buffaloes	72	63	—	60.0	55.0
Goats	105	78	—	69.0	69.0
Poultry	164	150	—	118.4	118.0

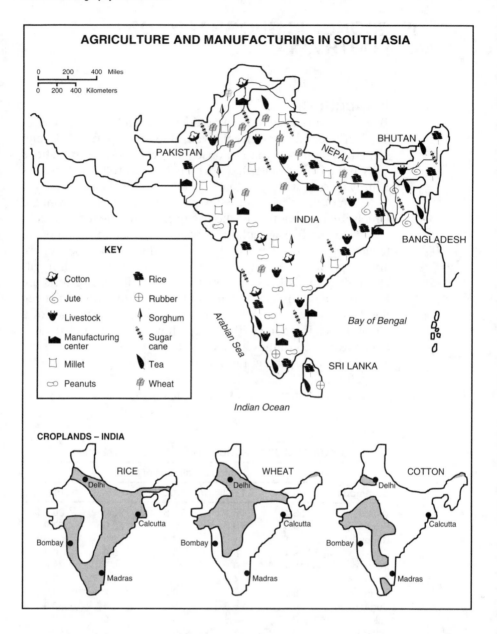

AGRICULTURE AND MANUFACTURING IN SOUTH ASIA

KEY

Cotton
Jute
Livestock
Manufacturing center
Millet
Peanuts
Rice
Rubber
Sorghum
Sugar cane
Tea
Wheat

PAKISTAN
NEPAL
BHUTAN
INDIA
BANGLADESH
Arabian Sea
Bay of Bengal
SRI LANKA
Indian Ocean

CROPLANDS – INDIA

RICE — Delhi, Calcutta, Bombay, Madras

WHEAT — Delhi, Calcutta, Bombay, Madras

COTTON — Delhi, Calcutta, Bombay, Madras

machinery (more readily used by "agribusiness," or large land-holders, rather than small farmers).

3. Need for better nationwide infrastructure, such as storage facilities, dams, and highways.

4. The taste of the food produced is different from traditional crops.

Industrial Production

WORLD ISSUES

Economic
Growth and
Development

India has some of the world's largest steel mills and is a major producer of bauxite. Other major industrial products include textiles, machinery, cement, and scientific instruments. Recently, Indian scientists have made advances in nuclear energy and in developing space satellites. India is the most industrially advanced nation in the subcontinent and has one of the world's ten highest GNPs. Nevertheless, as is true of all industrialized

WORLD ISSUES

Environmental
Concerns

societies around the globe, India must find ways of coping with the environmental consequences of industrialization. The tragic accident involving the Union Carbide Company at Bhopal in 1984 and the destructive effects of air pollution on the Taj Mahal, for example, have been of great concern to India.

Economic Conditions: Decision-Making and Planning

During the British colonial period, basic economic decisions were made by the British, primarily for their own benefit. Since

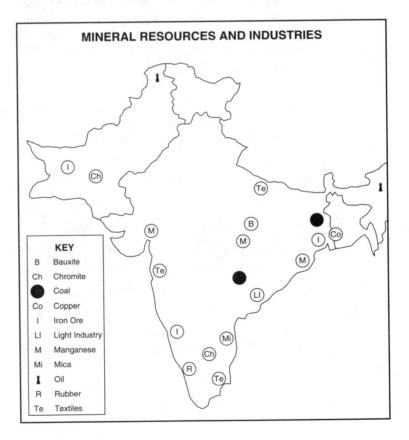

MINERAL RESOURCES AND INDUSTRIES

KEY

B	Bauxite
Ch	Chromite
●	Coal
Co	Copper
I	Iron Ore
LI	Light Industry
M	Manganese
Mi	Mica
☖	Oil
R	Rubber
Te	Textiles

independence, India has adopted elements both of a free enterprise/capitalist system and a socialist system. This combination is called a mixed economy. Although the government controls certain parts of the economy, it tries to develop strategies to benefit all parts. These strategies can be seen in the five-year plans. Disputes have arisen among economic planners, however, in choosing priorities and goals. Key choices involve funds for items such as heavy industry, exportable goods, small-scale cottage industries, and village development schemes. Decision makers must keep in mind two facts about India's population:

1. More than 80 percent of the people live in villages.
2. Population growth can limit economic gains.

Although the standard of living in India and its neighboring countries has generally improved since the departure of the British, severe poverty and malnutrition still exist in many areas. These features are evident in such large cities as Calcutta as well as in the villages.

The attempts by nations such as India to raise sharply the standard of living for all citizens, as well as promote economic growth, have necessitated borrowing money from overseas and importing needed goods. Consequently, India continues to face a large foreign debt and a trade imbalance (where the value of imports exceeds that of exports).

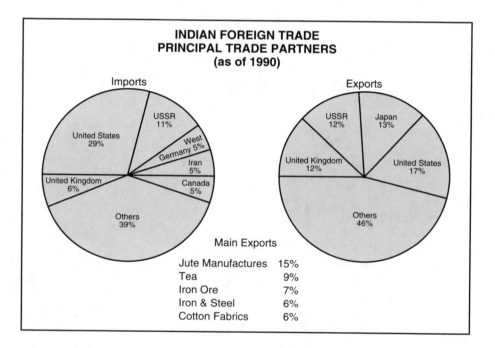

INDIAN FOREIGN TRADE
PRINCIPAL TRADE PARTNERS
(as of 1990)

Imports

- United States 29%
- USSR 11%
- West Germany 5%
- Iran 5%
- Canada 5%
- United Kingdom 6%
- Others 39%

Exports

- USSR 12%
- Japan 13%
- United Kingdom 12%
- United States 17%
- Others 46%

Main Exports

Jute Manufactures	15%
Tea	9%
Iron Ore	7%
Iron & Steel	6%
Cotton Fabrics	6%

In 1991 and 1993 India made significant moves to boost its economy. It attracted Western support by approving more foreign investment projects. It sold off some state-controlled companies, cut interest rates, and raised the ceiling on executive pay. The last move was designed to induce talented Indian managers to stay in India, and thereby reduce India's "brain drain" (migration by one nation's skilled and educated people to another nation, where they hope to gain better positions and more money). The government has also encouraged an import-substitution program. If successful, this would result in India producing for itself those items that it has usually imported. Many observers have noted that the economy would benefit if India could find ways to end the frequent scandals and corruption that have involved some businesspeople and government officials. Another benefit would be a reduction in the vast bureaucracy (large number of offices where permission is needed for commercial ventures). One economist has commented on how this "license-permit-raj" can slow down investment and invite bribery.

WORLD ISSUES

Economic
Growth and
Development

REVIEW QUESTIONS

Multiple Choice. Select the letter of the answer that correctly completes each statement.

1. An agronomist would be most concerned with news of an increase in
   A. cars
   B. food
   C. population
   D. tractors

2. Which of the following has the greatest effect on limiting/decreasing per capita food consumption in India?
   A. monsoons
   B. inadequate funds
   C. population increase
   D. government spending

3. To say that India is self-sufficient in agriculture means that it
   A. needs foreign aid
   B. can pay back other nations for food shipments
   C. grows enough food for its people
   D. can avoid famines

4. Norman Borlaugh would be most pleased with India's added production of
   A. space satellites
   B. steel
   C. fertilizer
   D. airplanes

5. In the 1980s, which condition was probably most responsible for stimulating economic growth in India?
   A. a small urban population
   B. an increasing infant mortality rate
   C. a diversity of languages
   D. an increased investment of capital

1. The Green Revolution has been important in South Asia's agricultural development.

    A. Define the term "Green Revolution."
    B. Describe two features necessary to make this "revolution" successful.
    C. Describe two negative aspects of the Green Revolution.

2. Briefly define each of the following:

    A. mixed economy
    B. trade imbalance
    C. agribusiness
    D. infrastructure

III. HUMAN AND CULTURAL GEOGRAPHY OF SOUTH ASIA

Overview

The most important human feature of South Asia, and in particular of India, is the size of the population. With over 800 million people, India ranks as the second largest nation on earth and is the world's most populous democracy. Pakistan and Bangladesh, after Indonesia, are the second and third largest Muslim nations in the world. The study of population patterns in these and other nations is what demography is all about. The ways in which a population views itself and practices certain lifestyles, along with the human values it holds to be important, may be thought of as its culture.

Demography

India's population is three times that of the United States; yet India is only about one-third the physical size of the United States. Consequently, India has a higher population density (population density is determined by dividing a nation's population by its area). This greater crowding can be seen in such large cities as Bombay, Calcutta, Madras, and New Delhi. However, most of India's people live in rural areas. Over 80 percent of the population lives in the hundreds of thousands of villages. To "know the village," therefore, is to know India. (See below for more data about villages.)

1. *Growth rates.* A nation's annual population growth rate tells us about how fast the nation's population grows each year. The rate is expressed as a percentage and is determined by subtracting the number of deaths per thousand in a given year from the number of births per thousand in the same year. For example, India's birth rate in 1985 was 33.3 per thousand; subtract from this figure the death rate of 12.5 per thousand to arrive at a growth rate of 20.8 per thousand, or 2.08 percent. (The growth rate in the United States at the same time was less than .7 percent.) The growth-rate figure for India is very high and is crucial in that it adds to already existing problems of housing, food, and employment. Indian government officials are very concerned about the high growth rate and try, therefore, to determine ways of reducing it. Their problems stem from the fact that the high growth rate is caused by a birth rate that is increasing and a death rate that is decreasing. What are the reasons for these patterns?

POPULATION GROWTH IN INDIA

1948—345 million
1957—392 million
1961—439 million
1967—501 million
1971—548 million
1977—615 million   Growth rate: 2.1% a year
1989—835 million
1993—897 million (estimated)

2. *Birth rate.* The reasons for a high birth rate in India are generally the same as those for high rates in Pakistan, Bangladesh, and other developing nations that are predominantly rural and agricultural. An agrarian society requires much manual labor, and therefore families tend to have many children to help work the land. Additional factors contributing to a high birth rate include: arranged marriages at an early age; a high infant-mortality rate; children seen as a form of "social security" for their parents in old age; desire for sons to pass on the family name and caste; the low status of women; religious motivations; joint/ extended family patterns; and failure to use birth control measures.

3. *Death rate.* The reasons for a decreasing death rate in India are generally the same as those for decreasing death rates throughout the world. These include: increase in food production; better hygienic and sanitary conditions; and the introduction of modern medicine. (A dramatic and welcome example of the last was the declared eradication of smallpox in India. This disease had long been a leading cause of death among Indians.) The result of a lower death rate means an increase in life expectancy. This has special significance for India, in light of the fact that 36.8 percent of its current population is under 14 years of age. A tragic exception to health improvement was a severe outbreak of pneumonic plague in September and October of 1994. Thousands died in the village of Surat and elsewhere, before this malady was brought under control.

4. *Attempts to lower the growth rate.* The Indian government has been moderately successful in some regions with the introduction of family-planning programs. These include birth-control clinics, monetary incentives for sterilization, and "Madison Avenue" advertising campaigns advocating the advantages of having a small family. (The few instances of government-mandated birth-control tactics have met with controversy and were considered undemocratic.) Additional national strategies involve improving literacy and education rates, improving employment opportunities for women, and implementation of the Hindu Marriage Act. (This act requires a minimum age of

GLOBAL
CONCEPTS
Culture
CONCEPTS
GLOBAL

GLOBAL
CONCEPTS
Choice
CONCEPTS
GLOBAL

GLOBAL
CONCEPTS
Citizenship
CONCEPTS
GLOBAL

18 for men and of 15 for women to marry.) As India becomes more industrialized and urbanized, its birth rate may decline. Such reduction would follow a pattern that has occurred in other nations in the 20th century, such as in Japan, the United States, and Germany.

Languages of South Asia

GLOBAL
CONCEPTS

Diversity

CONCEPTS
GLOBAL

A great diversity of languages is found in India. Sixteen languages are recognized. Of these, the one spoken by the largest number of Indians is Hindi. However, it is spoken by less than half of the population, and mainly in the north. Southern Indians have local languages, such as Tamil, and have objected to any imposition of a uniform national language. Disputes over language have harmful political effects, and in many cases they have fostered stronger ties to people's locality than to their national government. Other principal languages in South Asia include Bengali (Bangladesh), Urdu (Pakistan), and Sinhalese (in Sri Lanka). English is understood by small numbers of people, mainly in urban areas, throughout all nations in South Asia. Among educated people it is a unifying focus. However, many people are wary of using it as an official language because of its link to the age of imperialism.

GLOBAL
CONCEPTS

Identity

CONCEPTS
GLOBAL

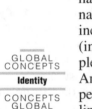

PRINCIPAL LANGUAGES OF INDIA AND PAKISTAN

India		Pakistan	
Language	Number of People Speaking (millions)	Language	Number of People Speaking (millions)
Hindi	331	Punjabi	72
Telugu	68	Pushto	16
Bengali	64	Sindhi	14
Marathi	62	Saraiki	12
Tamil	56	Urdu	9
Urdu	44	Other	12
Gugerati	41		
Kannada	33		
Malayalam	32		
Oriya	28		
Punjabi	23		
Rajasthani	16		
Assamese	10		
Kashmiri	4		

The Village

GLOBAL
CONCEPTS

Empathy

CONCEPTS
GLOBAL

The village is central in understanding India's social structure, as villages contain such a high proportion of India's population. A council of elders in each village, called the panchayat, usually makes rules for the people about local issues, such as sanitation, streets, and family disputes. Families arrange marriages so that young people will marry within their own social group, or caste. This practice is called endogamy. Another village practice is seen in sons' assuming the occupations held by their fathers. This custom, along with the jajmani system, has created self-sufficient communities. (Under the jajmani system, an economic pattern was followed whereby a jajman—a landowner—and members of a caste group would inherit the service relationships and mutual obligations that their immediate ancestors had.)

These customs, along with other traditional practices such as the limited, designated household roles for women, may undergo change as the villages become less isolated from the outside world. Historically, this isolation was the result of poor transportation and communication links. However, the increase in paved roads, electricity, and schools and the introduction of radio and television are making villagers more aware of the world around them and of modern 20th-century cultural patterns. The social changes in village life that these forces have brought about are proceeding slowly. It is uncertain as to which traditional cultural patterns will remain the same, which will be modified, and which will be changed completely.

Hinduism: The Main Religion in India

As with all the world's great religions, Hinduism is a system of beliefs that provide answers to some of the perennial questions humans have asked. These questions concern the origins and meaning of life and proper conduct toward others.

GLOBAL CONCEPTS

Identity

CONCEPTS GLOBAL

Over 80 percent of the people of India consider themselves Hindus. Even though there are differences in some beliefs and practices among Hindus, certain basic ideas are accepted.

1. Each human being occupies a place on the wheel of life (mandala). A person's place on the mandala is determined by the law of karma. According to this law, what happened to a person's soul in a previous life (incarnation) will affect the person's current status. The soul undergoes a process of rebirth, or reincarnation (samsara). Whether reincarnation results in the soul's moving "up" or "down" depends on how a person performed his or her dharma (obligation and behavior based on family and caste).

2. The goal of a Hindu is to achieve moksha (release of the soul from the cycle of birth and rebirth on the mandala).

3. There are many gods and goddesses in Hinduism. However, it could be said that each of these deities is but one form or manifestation of a single God. From its origin in about 3000 B.C. until now, the three chief Hindu deities have been Brahma (associated with creation), Vishnu (associated with preservation), and

Shiva (associated with destruction). The most popularly worshiped today are Vishnu and Shiva, either in their own form or in the different male and female forms they take. For example, Vishnu is often worshiped in the form of Rama or Krishna; Shiva is sometimes worshiped as an ascetic doing yoga (a form of meditation) or in the form of Kali or Durga.

4. There is no one specific holy text or bible in Hinduism. Rather, there are several writings that are looked to for guidance and inspiration. The *Vedas* were written somewhere between 1500 B.C. and 800 B.C., and they contain hymns dealing with creation and reverence for nature. The Upanishads were written about 500 B.C., and they include discussions about the soul and proper ways of behavior. The Ramayana, a very popular long epic poem written between 400 B.C. and 100 B.C., is about Prince Rama (an incarnation of Vishnu) and his wife Sita. The story is performed and read throughout India and Indian communities all over the world. It is viewed as a guide for dharma, love, and devotion. The Mahabharata, which contains the Bhagavad Gita, is one of the longest and best-known poems in the world. It describes the conflict between related families and kingdoms, involving exile, wars, and conquest. It is revered for its pronouncements on morality and proper behavior.

5. The caste system evolved as a hierarchy or ranking of social groups based on heredity and occupation. There have been four major groupings, more accurately referred to as varnas than as castes: Brahmans (priests), Kashatriyas (soldiers), Vaishyas (merchants), and Shudras (laborers). The Untouchables were considered to be outside of and beneath the caste system. In the 20th century, a Hindu is more likely to describe himself or herself as belonging to a jati (subcaste) rather than simply to one of the larger varna groupings. A varna may contain dozens of jatis. With the growth in educational opportunities and of newer and more technological occupations, especially in urban areas, the link between varna and occupation is disappearing. For example, someone whose ancestry has been in a jati within Shudras may become educated and hold down a job as a computer engineer.

GLOBAL
CONCEPTS

Identity

CONCEPTS
GLOBAL

Additional things to remember about the caste system are:

1. Ritual purity and avoidance of pollution, endogamy, and observance of religious taboos are the elements that keep one attached to his or her jati.

2. The Indian constitution prohibits discrimination against a person because of his or her jati. Nevertheless, in many villages, tensions between people of different jatis still exists.

GLOBAL
CONCEPTS

Justice

CONCEPTS
GLOBAL

3. A jati lower in social ranking may rise in status by adopting more pure ideals, such as becoming vegetarian. This

70

process is called sanskritization. Another example would be for a lower-ranking jati to refrain from making leather items from a cow. Because of cow reverence in India among Hindus, working with leather is considered a polluting activity.

Islam as a Major Religion in South Asia

Islam is the major religion of Pakistan and Bangladesh, the next two most populous nations in South Asia after India. The Islamic community in India, although in the minority, is very large. Muslims in India number over 80 million, constituting about 11 percent of the total population. This figure is larger than that of any Muslim nation in the Middle East and would be sufficient to rank among the four largest Islamic populations in the world if the Muslims in India were to make up a nation. Islam came to South Asia from its birthplace in the Middle East and has had a profound impact. For example, even though India is primarily a Hindu nation, its most famous building, the Taj Mahal, was built by a Muslim ruler in the 17th century. (For a discussion of Islam, see Unit One on the Middle East. For more information on Islam in South Asia, refer to the next section on history and political geography.)

The history of Hindu-Muslim relations in South Asia has been at times peaceful and at times violent. The term communalism describes those instances when serious tensions have arisen between the two groups. Respect by each group for the other begins with an appreciation of basic beliefs, practices, and differences. It also includes shared concepts. A checklist of some of these appears in the table below:

	Hinduism	Islam
Holy sites	Benares (Varanasi) Ganges River	Makkah, Medina, Jerusalem (No holy rivers)
Buildings	Carved images of deities, ornate and decorative	Carved images of Allah and Muhammad are not permitted; writings from the Quran
Holy books	Vedas, Upanishad, Ramayana, Mahabharata	Quran
Dietary taboos	Beef	Pork
Obligations	Dharma	Five Pillars
Deity beliefs	Belief in different gods is acceptable	Monotheistic
Life after death	Reincarnation, moksha, depending on karma	Heaven for true believers and those who act righteously

71

cont.	Hinduism	Islam
Divisions	Stratification/hierarchy based on caste	Equality of all before Allah; schism between Sunni and Shi'ite sects
Attitude on life	Ahimsa—doctrine of nonviolence	Jihad—concept of holy wars
Political attitudes	Democratic; separation between civil and religious authority	Theocratic—Quran as basis for laws in society

Buddhism in South Asia

Buddhism grew out of Hinduism as a result of the teachings of the Buddha, born as Siddhartha Gautama. Gautama was born as a high-caste Hindu in 560 B.C. However, he and his disciples

GLOBAL CONCEPTS

Change

CONCEPTS GLOBAL

wished to keep some ideas (such as the mandala) of Hinduism while seeking to change other ideas (such as end the caste system). Buddhism became popular in India during the rule of Ashoka (250 B.C.). However, its influence gradually diminished because some of its ideas were accepted by Hindus and became part of the Hindu religion and also because of the destructive impact of Muslim invasions after 800 A.D. It is estimated that there are about one million Buddhists today in India. However, the population of Sri Lanka is mostly Buddhist. Buddhism became much more popular in Southeast Asia and in East Asia. (See these sections for more information on Buddhism.)

Sikhism

Sikhs form about 2 percent of India's population and are concentrated in the northwestern region known as the Punjab. The

GLOBAL CONCEPTS

Identity

CONCEPTS GLOBAL

religion was founded around 1500 by the guru (teacher) Nanak, born as a Hindu but raised with Islamic ideas. The Sikh (disciple) faith has aspects of both Hinduism and Islam. However, it has no caste system. Sikhs have a reputation as successful businesspeople and good soldiers. Sikhs vow never to cut their hair or beards and to carry a dagger or saber with them at all times. Their attempt to break away from India and form a separate state has led to conflicts with the Indian government in this century. (See the next section on history and political geography).

Jainism

Jains, who make up less than 1 percent of India's population, follow the beliefs set down by the guru Mahavira in about 500 B.C. He was born a Hindu, as were Gautama and Nanak, and also rejected certain Hindu doctrines while accepting others.

The main Jain doctrine is that all of nature is alive. This belief led to the refusal to kill any living thing and to a strict notion of nonviolence, the ideal of ahimsa. This idea was gradually incorporated into Hinduism.

Christians, Jews, and Parsees are also found in India. Their total numbers are very few, and they make up no more than 3 percent of the population.

REVIEW QUESTIONS

Multiple Choice. Select the letter of the answer that correctly completes each statement.

1. In India the traditional role of women has changed during the 20th century mainly because of the
   A. impact of increased urbanization
   B. growth of political unrest
   C. use of passive resistance
   D. effects of religious persecution

2. Demographers are most concerned with studying trends in
   A. religion
   B. culture
   C. dress
   D. population

3. The most widely spoken language in India is
   A. Tamil
   B. Hindi
   C. Bengali
   D. Urdu

4. The practice of endogamy results in married couples who
   A. will have many children
   B. have come from village communities
   C. have had their marriage arranged by their families
   D. come from different castes

5. Which does NOT belong with the others?
   A. Krishna
   B. Vishnu
   C. Shiva
   D. Mandala

6. The duties and obligations of a caste member are known as his or her
   A. dharma
   B. karma
   C. moksha
   D. reincarnation

7. The Bhagavad Gita is the name of a famous
   A. battle
   B. family
   C. poem
   D. city

ESSAYS

1. Explain three basic teachings or ideas of Hinduism.

2. Explain two ways in which Hinduism differs from Islam.

3. Population growth has been an important issue in India.

   A. Explain two reasons for the increasing birth rate in India.
   B. Describe two ways in which the government has tried to limit the birth rate.

IV. HISTORY AND POLITICAL GEOGRAPHY OF SOUTH ASIA

The Historical Setting (3500 B.C.–1200 A.D.)

Early Civilizations. Among the earliest peoples to settle in South Asia were the Dravidians. It is thought that in about 2500 B.C., along the Indus River in what is now Pakistan, two major cities grew—Mohenjo-Daro and Harappa. These settlements were several hundred miles apart and were similar to other early river valley civilizations in the world. Between 1500 B.C. and 500 B.C. the Dravidians were conquered by a people from Central Asia, the Aryans. Aryan settlements grew in what is currently Pakistan, India, and Bangladesh. The blend of Aryan and Dravidian cultures led to some of the major developments in South Asian culture, such as the Sanskrit language and the Hindu religion. The years from 1500 B.C. to 1200 A.D. can be described as the Hindu period.

As did the Aryans, the next significant group of invaders came to the subcontinent from the northwest. Under the leadership of Alexander the Great in 327 B.C., Greeks came through the Khyber Pass and other openings in the western Hindu Kush Mountains. The Greek impact was limited and short-lived, affecting mostly the north, and had its greatest effect on Indian art. For example, images of Buddha began to take on certain Greco-Roman features.

Early Empires. Two dynastic empires soon emerged in South Asia; these were the Mauryas (325 B.C.) and the Guptas (350 A.D.).

Chandragupta Maurya founded the Maurya dynasty, took many of the areas formerly held by Alexander the Great, and established an empire in northern India. His grandson, Ashoka (d. 232 B.C.), became one of the greatest Indian rulers in history. He did not seek to extend his empire and permitted different religions to exist. He was very much influenced by Buddhism. (Remember that Buddhism arose from the teachings of the first Buddha, Siddhartha Gautama, who was born in 560 B.C.). Although Ashoka failed in his attempt to spread Buddhism in India, many Buddhist beliefs became incorporated into Hinduism. The Maurya empire crumbled after the death of Ashoka.

The Guptas controlled much of northern India for approximately 200 years, between 350 and 550. During this period, notable achievements were made in such fields as mathematics (the idea of zero and a decimal system), literature, surgery, art, architecture, and religion (the expansion of Hinduism). As a result, this period under the Gupta emperors became known as India's "Golden Age." Eventually, however, the Gupta empire was unable to withstand attacks by outsiders, such as the Mongols and Turks, and became disunited. Disunity in the subcontinent was to remain until the period of Muslim rule.

The Islamic Period (1200–1760)

The Delhi Sultanate (1206–1526). The 34 different kings who ruled during the history of this kingdom, or sultanate, held power in northern and central India. However, the earliest Muslim takeover in the subcontinent began in the 8th century with the conquest of part of what is now Pakistan. Muslim invaders, such as Mahmud of Ghazni, continued to come from the west (Afghanistan), to spread Islam, and gain more territory. Their successors established the Delhi sultanate. During the last years of the sultanate, the south of India was exposed to European contact and settlement. Vasco da Gama of Portugal landed in 1498 in Calicut. Soon thereafter, Spanish, French, Dutch, and English traders began to appear and established trading posts.

The Mughal (Mogul) Dynasty (1526–1760). This dynasty emerged as a result of military victories by Babur over the Delhi sultan. Babur was a Turkish-Mongol prince, a Muslim, and a descendant of Genghis Khan. Babur's grandson, Akbar, became a very popular ruler, particularly because he won the respect of his Hindu subjects. His rule (1555–1605) was also known for political stability and cultural achievements.

One of Akbar's successors was Shah Jahan (1628–1658). He continued many of Akbar's policies and was responsible for building the Taj Mahal. This great building was a memorial to his wife, Mumtaz Mahal.

Another Mughal ruler was Aurangzeb (1658–1707), who was a harsh and unpopular leader. A very strict Muslim who wanted to spread Islam, he carried out policies that angered Hindus, Sikhs, and other groups. This was one factor leading to the breakdown of the Mughal empire. Other factors included corrupt administration, wasteful spending of money, and excessive military campaigns. Although the empire did not end until 1857, the Mughal rulers after Aurangzeb had very little influence in India. The weakness and disunity of the Mughals was one reason Britain was able to gain control in India.

The British Raj (Rule) (1760–1947)

The British involvement in India, an example of imperialism, grew from economic contact to direct political control. Britain was able to outmaneuver its European rivals, build alliances with some Indian rulers of small areas, and inflict military defeat on other rulers.

The British East India Company. Granted a charter from Queen Elizabeth I in 1600, the British East India Company received permission from the Mughals to trade in India as early as 1613. From this time until 1858, the company exercised powers usually associated with a government. It had, for example, its own private army. One of its employees, Robert Clive, led military forces to victories over both French and native Indian armies. As a result of the most important of these victories, at Plassey in 1757, the British became the dominant economic and unofficial political power in the subcontinent.

The Sepoy Mutiny and Direct Rule by Britain. The Sepoy Mutiny of 1857 was fought against the British for both religious and political reasons. It began when Indians in the British army (sepoys) suspected that the grease used on bullet cartridges came from cows and pigs. If so, to bite into these cartridges would have violated Hindu and Muslim beliefs. These suspicions led to a rebellion that gradually spread beyond the military and became an anti-Western movement. (In fact, some Indian historians view the Sepoy Mutiny as a war of independence.) Eventually it was severely crushed. Nevertheless, the East India Company was abolished and replaced as a governing body by the British Crown. In 1876 Queen Victoria was proclaimed Empress of India. What was now called the Crown Colony of India actually included present-day Pakistan, India, and Bangladesh.

Rule by Britain brought some benefits to the colonized people, such as improved transportation and communication, health services, education, and political unity. However, colonial rule was more beneficial for the British, allowing them to exploit Indian resources and provide employment for many English people. In addition, Indians felt that their cultural values, beliefs, and practices were threatened because they clashed with those of the British. British ethnocentrism stirred bad feelings.

Growth of an Indian Nationalist Movement. The movement for Indian independence grew from distrust of British economic, cultural, and political practices. In addition, Indians felt it was wrong for Britain to preach democratic ideals while denying Indians democratic rights, such as the right of self-determination. The Sepoy Mutiny could be viewed as the first major step in an Indian nationalist movement. Other important developments included:

1. In 1885 the Indian National Congress was founded, initially to promote a gradual relaxation of British economic and political control. It eventually became known as the Congress party. In the 20th century, leading political figures associated with the Congress party were Mohandas Gandhi, Jawaharlal Nehru, and Indira Gandhi.

2. In 1906 the Muslim League was created by those Muslims who feared that the Congress party was becoming too strongly dominated by Hindus. One of its founders was Mohammed Ali Jinnah.

WORLD ISSUES

War
and
Peace

3. From 1914 to 1918 British participation in World War I adversely affected Britain in the colony of India. Indian soldiers fought in Europe and gained military distinction. However, they soon began to question for whose interests they were really fighting. Also, they came to realize that the terrible tragedies associated with the war cast doubt on the British claim of the superiority of European culture and civilization.

4. In 1919 the Amritsar Massacre occurred when British troops fired on unarmed Indians attending a political rally. The death of hundreds of people in this town in the Punjab infuriated Indians.

5. In 1921 the Montagu-Chelmsford Reforms provided for a limited amount of self-government. This included a two-house legislature with limited powers that would have more members elected by Indians than appointed by the British.

6. In 1935 the Government of India Act extended the policy of limited self-government by letting Indian provinces have more control over their own affairs. It was intended to set the groundwork for India to become a self-governing dominion within the British Empire, like Canada.

7. Gandhi's nonviolent movement. Known as Mahatma ("the great soul"), Mohandas K. Gandhi organized boycotts and other nonviolent activities, such as a march to the sea to protest a salt tax, in an attempt to shame the British and achieve swaraj (self-rule). Gandhi also went on frequent hunger strikes. His nonviolent actions stemmed from the Hindu idea of "ahimsa." His tactics were described as examples of passive resistance and civil disobedience.

World War II, Partition, and Independence. With the end of World War II in 1945, Britain moved to seek a peaceful transition for Indian independence. Britain was exhausted after the war and did not want to spend the money or use the personnel needed to maintain the colony. It also wanted to adhere to the principles of the United Nations charter concerning self-determination for all people. However, even though the British had hoped to leave behind them one united country, there was much tension between Hindus and Muslims. The Congress party, led by Jawaharlal Nehru, and the Muslim League, led by Mohammed Ali Jinnah, were unable to resolve all their differences. These differences led to much bloodshed and threatened to bring on a civil war if no agreement was reached on a partition plan. Eventually, on August 15, 1947, independence came with the creation of two independent nations, India and Pakistan, formed by a partition of the subcontinent.

Independence Period (1947 to the Present)

Political Structure in India. India has existed since independence as the world's largest democracy. It has a parliamentary form of government similar to that of Britain but different from that of the United States.

Important Leaders

India has had several important political leaders.

1. Jawaharlal Nehru, the first prime minister (1947–1964). Nehru brought some stability to the new nation and tried to achieve a sense of "unity in diversity." He hoped to build a spirit of nationalism, in spite of the many differences among India's population, including religion, language, and varying loyalties to local states and regions.

2. Indira Gandhi, prime minister (1966–1977, 1980–1984). Mrs. Gandhi, the daughter of Nehru, held power longer than any Indian leader. Although popular when she first took office, she gradually began to govern with an "iron fist" in order to pursue her policies concerning economics, birth control, and other issues. Her proclamation of a "state of emergency" in the 1970s was seen as harming India's democracy and led to her downfall in the 1977 elections. From 1977 to 1980, her successors, Morarji Desai and then Charan Singh, proved unable to achieve their goals. Mrs. Gandhi returned to power in 1980, faced with severe internal problems such as persistent poverty and the desire by

A COMPARISON OF TWO DEMOCRACIES

	United States	India
Basic form	Federal republic; one central government and 50 state governments	Federal republic; one central government and 17 state governments
Legislature	A bicameral system: Congress consists of the Senate and House of Representatives	A bicameral system: Parliament is composed of the Council of States (Rajya Sabha) and House of the People (Lok Sabha)
Executive	A president indirectly elected by the public (presidential form)	A prime minister elected by the legislature (parliamentary form; the prime minister usually is head of the majority party in the Parliament)
Governing document	Constitution of 1787 with subsequent amendments	Constitution of 1950 with subsequent amendments
	Both documents describe the political structure, protect civil rights and liberties, and were influenced by British legal traditions.	
Political parties	Two main parties: Democrat and Republican	Several parties: Congress, Janata Dal, Bharatiya Janata

Sikhs to have their own nation in the Punjab region. Her strong actions against Sikh militants provoked a harsh reaction and led to her assassination by two Sikhs in 1984.

3. Rajiv Gandhi, prime minister (1984–1989). The son of Indira Gandhi, Rajiv Gandhi tried to obtain foreign help for India in meetings with American President Reagan and Soviet Premier Gorbachev. Although he began his term of office amid much sympathy due to his mother's death, Rajiv proved to be a weak and unpopular leader. He made little progress in solving domestic problems (poverty, Sikh dissension). His administration was criticized for being corrupt. An Indian politician in an opposition party claimed that the mood of the people was "one of extreme disenchantment." Consequently, in the elections of November 1989, Mr. Gandhi and his Congress party were voted out of office.

4. Vishwanath Pratap Singh, prime minister (1989–1990). V. P. Singh's Janata Dal party won 141 of the 525 seats up for election in the Lok Sabha in 1989. Other parties supported the Janata Dal and joined with it to form a coalition (a combination formed of different political parties to run a government when no single party has a majority of seats). The coalition was called the National Front and was headed by V. P. Singh, India's eighth prime minister. Yet he found it very hard to keep this coalition together. One reason was his support of the Mandal report. This report recommended that up to 49 percent of jobs in government and public works be reserved for untouchables and members of low-ranking castes. Singh's decision to carry out the recommendations led to riots and to the withdrawal of the BJP (Bharatiya Janata party) from his governing coalition. The BJP is a right-wing party that is supported mostly by upper-caste Hindus. As opposition to Singh increased, the coalition government fell apart and new elections were scheduled for 1991.

5. P. V. Narasimha Rao, prime minister (1991–). Although six political parties entered the 1991 elections, most people believed that the Congress party would emerge as the winner, with its leader, Rajiv Gandhi, regaining the prime minister post. However, Gandhi was assassinated in May 1991. The assassin was a Tamil woman who was angered by his actions as prime minister in helping Sri Lanka put down a Tamil rebellion there. (See the section below in this unit for information about trouble in Sri Lanka.) The Congress party won the election, and one of its members, P. V. Narasimha Rao became prime minister. However, since the Congress party did not win a majority of seats, Mr. Rao had to form a coalition government to run the country. The government has made some progress in boosting India's economy by creating more of a free-market system. In political matters, it has searched for ways to end critical domestic problems as well as to mend relations with neighboring nations. (See the section below in this unit for more information.)

Political Structure in Pakistan and Bangladesh

Although Pakistan today can be described as a parliamentary democracy with a constitution, its first years after partition were very unstable. Under British rule, the Muslims had had very little experience in politics. Therefore, it is not surprising to find frequent instances of divisiveness and "strong-man" rule in Pakistan since independence in 1947.

GLOBAL CONCEPTS

Justice

CONCEPTS GLOBAL

WORLD ISSUES

Determination of Political and Economic Systems

Mohammed Ali Jinnah's death in 1948 was a severe blow to the young nation. The ineffective political struggles for power by civilians ended when the military suspended the constitution in 1958 and declared martial law. General Mohammed Ayub Khan ruled the country until 1969. Another example of dictatorial rule by the military occurred in 1977, when General Mohammed Zia took power away from the civilian-elected prime minister, Zulfikar Ali Bhutto. General Zia's rule ended with his death in a plane crash in August 1988. In that year, voters put into power the Pakistan People's party and its leader, Benazir Bhutto. As the daughter of a former prime minister, Ms. Bhutto became the second woman to head a government in the subcontinent and the only woman ever to govern a Muslim nation. In August 1990 the president of Pakistan dismissed the government of Ms. Bhutto, accusing it of corruption and nepotism (favoring relatives for jobs). Ms. Bhutto claimed, however, that democratic reforms that she tried to institute had angered many army officials. It was they who supposedly caused her downfall.

In October 1990 Mian Nawaz Sharif became prime minister of Pakistan. He helped to boost the nation's economy but was unsuccessful in foreign dealings with India and the United States. Antigovernment demonstrations increased, leading to new elections in 1993, and Benazir Bhutto returned to power as prime minister. Her chief problems involve poverty, corruption, education, and Islamic fundamentalism.

Bangladesh came into existence in 1971. Previously it had been the part of Pakistan known as East Pakistan. It was separated from the western part of Pakistan by 1,000 miles. Political, religious, and economic tensions led to a rebellion by East Pakistan in 1971. A war broke out in which India sided with the East Pakistanis. By December the rebellion was a success and the nation of Bangladesh was declared.

Bangladesh's first prime minister, Sheik Mujibur Rahman, had led the struggle for independence. His inability to deal with food riots and a growing population as well as a growing perception of corruption were some of the reasons for his assassination. After his death, the country experienced several coups. One of these was led by Lt. General Hussain Mohammed Ershad, who ruled as a military dictator from 1982 to 1990. His resignation was brought on by a series of protests and demonstrations and was followed by elections in February, 1991. Begum Khaleda Zia became prime minister, as her BNP party (Bangladesh Nationalist party) emerged victorious. A change in the nation's constitution gave her greater power than that of any former prime minister. However, she has faced enormous problems in

GLOBAL
CONCEPTS
Power
CONCEPTS
GLOBAL

GLOBAL
CONCEPTS
Change
CONCEPTS
GLOBAL

governing a country plagued by overpopulation, severe natural diasters such as floods, and a declining world market for jute—the country's chief product.

Current Political Issues in South Asia

Separatist (secessionist) movements are the most dangerous political issues facing India and Sri Lanka in the 1990s. Different groups in both nations have grievances against the national governments and want to break away.

In India's Punjab state, Sikhs want to form their own nation—Khalistan. Resentment against the central government in New Delhi was fueled in 1984 when Mrs. Gandhi sent troops to attack Sikh militant separatists in the Golden Temple at Amritsar, the holiest shrine to Sikhs. Continued violence by both Sikh terrorists and government forces resulted in many deaths, with over 5,000 people killed in 1991. With an increased police and military presence by the Indian government and a diminished desire for independence, the Sikh rebellion seemed to be over by 1994.

India is concerned about growing unrest by the Muslim majority in the northern state of Kashmir. Kashmir is the larger part of an area that was taken over by India after the 1947 partition. However, Pakistan challenges India's claims to the state, especially as Muslims are in the majority. Early in 1990, efforts by the Jammu and the Kashmir Liberation Front to secede from India led to riots and violence. India claims that Pakistan has been behind these activities. India has also been bothered by antigovernment activity by tribal groups, such as the Assamese in the northeast.

In Sri Lanka, the Tamil people, who are of Indian origin, want to have their own state. The Sri Lankan government has had difficulty in putting down terrorist actions by Tamils against members of the majority Sinhalese community. Many Sri Lankans think that people in South India are helping the terrorists. The Colombo government nevertheless welcomed the presence of Indian troops to help keep the peace from 1987 to 1989. Since that time, several cease-fire agreements between the Sri Lankan government and the Tamil Tigers (the leading revolutionary group) have broken down.

Communalism (ethnic tension between Hindus and Muslims) has been a frequent source of irritation in India. Part of this tension stems from the partition of the subcontinent in 1947. Much bloodshed broke out between the two groups, as some Muslims in India wished to migrate to Pakistan, while some Hindus in Pakistan wished to migrate to India. Religious differences between the two groups have been another source of friction. The worst case of communalism in recent years occurred in late 1992 and early 1993, and stemmed from an incident in Ayodhya. Located in north India, this site contained a mosque built in the sixteenth century by a Mogul ruler. Hindus have claimed, however, that the site is the birthplace of Lord Rama and that the mosque should be replaced with a Hindu temple. After unsuccessful marches on the site in 1989 and 1990, Hindu extremists tore down the mosque in 1992. This led to terrible Hindu-Muslim riots in Bombay and elsewhere in India. Within two months over 3,000 people had been killed and many homes destroyed.

Wars have been fought three times between India and Pakistan. While the two nations are now at peace, it remains to be seen whether they can permanently overcome problems over borders, distrust, communalism, and nuclear arms.

During the cold war between the United States and the Soviet Union, India tried to follow a policy of nonalignment. In doing so, India hoped to establish itself as a leader of the so-called Third World nations. This policy has come into question, however, since India fought a war with China over a border dispute and had been more friendly toward the former Soviet Union than toward the United States. India was not as alarmed as was Pakistan during 1979–1989, when Russian soldiers were fighting rebels in Afghanistan. Today, however, with the Soviet Union gone, India realizes the importance of establishing better relations with the United States.

The history of South Asia has been carved by its native inhabitants as well as by outsiders. The British dream of having the colony of India become one united nation upon independence did not materialize. The internal (national) and external (international) problems facing South Asian nations will take time to overcome. It should be remembered, nevertheless, that they have done much to improve themselves since independence.

REVIEW QUESTIONS

Matching. Match the people in column 1 with the correct description in Column 2.

Column 1

_____ 1. Ashoka
_____ 2. Indira Gandhi
_____ 3. Mahatma Gandhi
_____ 4. Mohammad Ali Jinnah
_____ 5. Shah Jahan
_____ 6. Jawaharlal Nehru

Column 2

A. India's first prime minister
B. Pakistan's first prime minister
C. Leader killed by Sikh militants
D. Spread Buddhism in India
E. Builder of Taj Majal
F. Nonviolent protester of British policies

Multiple Choice. Select the letter of the answer that correctly completes each statement.

1. The partition of the Indian subcontinent into India and Pakistan after World War II was based largely on
   A. political and religious factors
   B. economic concerns
   C. military strategies
   D. health and medical problems

2. The Muslim League was primarily responsible for creating the nation of
   A. Nepal
   B. Sri Lanka
   C. Bangladesh
   D. Pakistan

3. Which of the following was most upset with the political goals of the Indian National Congress?
   A. Nehru
   B. Jinnah
   C. Mahatma Gandhi
   D. Indira Gandhi

ESSAY

At various times in the 20th century, the Indian subcontinent has been faced with severe political issues. For each of the following, explain what the problem was, and give either one reason for it or one result of it:

1. Amritsar Massacre
2. communalism
3. partition
4. civil war in Sri Lanka
5. Sikh militance
6. status of Kashmir
7. Ayodhya dispute

I. PHYSICAL GEOGRAPHY OF SOUTHEAST ASIA

Overview

The region known as Southeast Asia consists of ten nations. Six are on the Asian mainland: Cambodia (Kampuchea), Laos, Malaysia, Myanmar (Burma), Thailand, and Vietnam. The other four are island nations: Brunei, Indonesia, the Philippines, and Singapore. In the past, parts of the region have been known by other names, such as the Spice Islands, the East Indies, and Indochina. The land portions of this region total about half the area of the United States.

Topography

GLOBAL
CONCEPTS

Environment

CONCEPTS
GLOBAL

Most of mainland Southeast Asia is located on two peninsulas—the Indochina Peninsula and the Malay Peninsula. The island nations of Indonesia and the Philippines form archipelagoes. The soil found on these islands, much of it from volcanic ash, is very rich. Mountain chains on the mainland divide the land area into river valleys, in which most of the population lives. Many tropical jungles and swamps exist here. Geography has tended to isolate some peoples from others and is partially responsible for the great diversity of cultures found in Southeast Asia.

Water Bodies

The two oceans that sandwich the region, the Indian and Pacific, have acted as "highways," bringing foreigners from

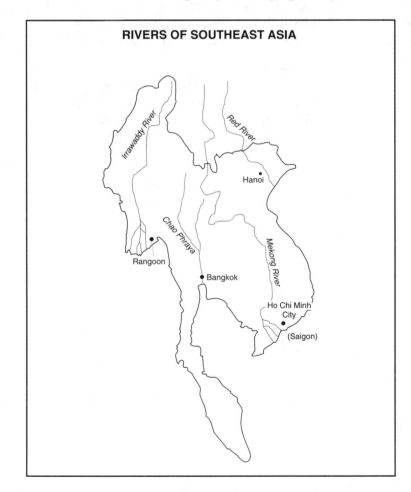

RIVERS OF SOUTHEAST ASIA

South Asia, East Asia, Europe, and the United States. This foreign contact has continued for over 500 years and has contributed to the "patchwork quilt" of cultures found in the ten Southeast Asian nations. The Strait of Malacca, lying between Indonesia, Malaysia, and Singapore, is a vital strategic and economic link between the Indian and Pacific oceans, in the way that the Panama Canal is a link between the Pacific and Atlantic oceans. The major rivers are the Irawaddy, Chao Phraya (Menam), Mekong, and Red. They flow southward, forming fertile river valleys and providing transportation routes for the movement of goods and people. The largest lake in Southeast Asia is the Tonle Sap (Great Lake) located in Cambodia. The rivers and straits in the area, along with the major seas, including the Java Sea and the South China Sea, make up half the size of the region. As a result, it is easy to see why water bodies have had such an enormous effect on the diet, commerce, transportation, and history of Southeast Asia. It is also estimated that Indonesia and the Philippines together contain over 20,000 islands.

Climate

The climate is tropical, characterized by much humidity and heavy rainfalls, especially in the summer. These features are similar to those found in the Caribbean Sea area in the West Indies, Haiti, the Dominican Republic, and Puerto Rico. The winds that cause the heavy rainfall are referred to as the summer monsoons. As in South Asia, the monsoons can make the difference between a good or a bad harvest.

II. ECONOMIC GEOGRAPHY OF SOUTHEAST ASIA

Agriculture

GLOBAL
CONCEPTS

Environment

CONCEPTS
GLOBAL

Due to the amount of rainfall and kind of soil, rice is the major crop grown in Southeast Asia. For many years, in fact, Myanmar was the world's largest exporter of rice. From the rich forest lands come teak and ebony. Farming is the occupation of well over half the people of the region. Although famine has never been a problem, nations of the region still look for ways to increase food production. Increases can come from using more modern farming methods as well as from the Green Revolution. Much hope also rests with the Mekong River development project. This project includes the construction of several dams along the Mekong River. It is expected that these dams will control floods, provide water for irrigation, and be a source of electricity.

Industrial Production

WORLD ISSUES

Economic
Growth and
Development

The region is rich in natural resources. Chief among these are tin, iron ore, and petroleum. Rubber is also the basis of a major industry. Nevertheless, Southeast Asian nations lack sufficient technology, money, and a skilled, educated labor force to exploit the many natural resources.

ASEAN

The Association of Southeast Asian Nations, which is made up of Brunei, Malaysia, Thailand, the Philippines, Indonesia, and Singapore, was formed in 1967 to promote cooperative economic advancement. It seeks to increase exports and gain more help from nations such as Japan.

Economic Decision-Making

Different economic systems are found in the countries of Southeast Asia. Capitalist features predominate in Singapore, Malaysia, and the Philippines. Greater centralized control of the economy is found in Indonesia, Cambodia, and Vietnam.

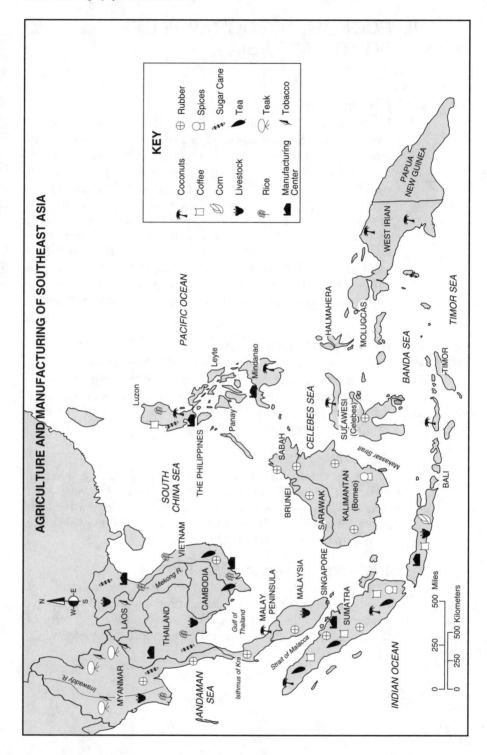

AGRICULTURE AND MANUFACTURING OF SOUTHEAST ASIA

KEY

Coconuts · Rubber
Coffee · Spices
Corn · Sugar Cane
Livestock · Tea
Rice · Teak
Manufacturing Center · Tobacco

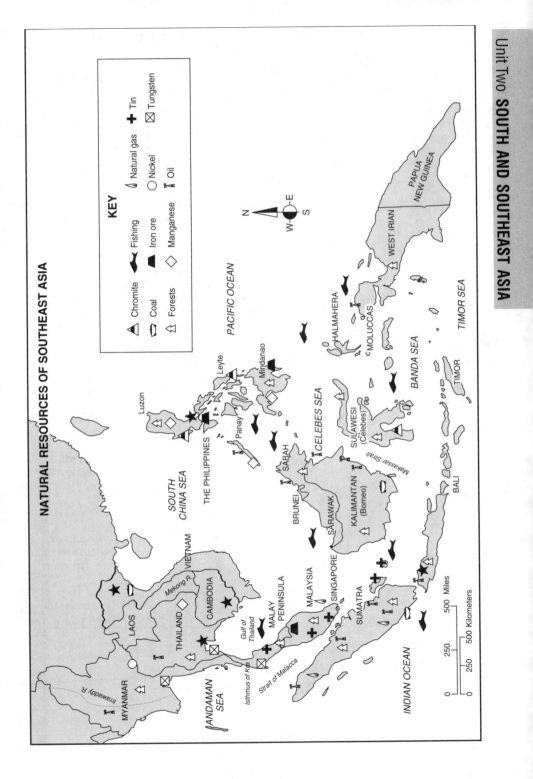

NATURAL RESOURCES OF SOUTHEAST ASIA

KEY

Chromite
Coal
Forests

Fishing
Iron ore
Manganese

Tin
Tungsten
Natural gas
Nickel
Oil

PACIFIC OCEAN

THE PHILIPPINES
Luzon
Panay
Leyte
Mindanao

SOUTH CHINA SEA

VIETNAM
LAOS
Mekong R.
CAMBODIA
THAILAND
Gulf of Thailand
MYANMAR
Irrawaddy R.
ANDAMAN SEA
Isthmus of Kra
MALAY PENINSULA
Strait of Malacca
MALAYSIA
SINGAPORE
SUMATRA
INDIAN OCEAN

BRUNEI
SABAH
SARAWAK
KALIMANTAN (Borneo)
CELEBES SEA
SULAWESI (Celebes)
Makassar Strait
BALI

MOLUCCAS
HALMAHERA
BANDA SEA
TIMOR
TIMOR SEA

WEST IRIAN
PAPUA NEW GUINEA

N
W E
S

0   250   500 Miles
0   250   500 Kilometers

93

TRADE AND COMMERCE IN SOUTHEAST ASIA (SELECTED COUNTRIES)

Country	Percent of Trade		Leading Trade Partners		Major Exports (%)
	To U.S.	From U.S.	Exports (%)	Imports (%)	
Myanmar (formerly Burma) (1988–89)	1	5	Southeast Asia (23)	Japan (40)	Rice (32) Teak (43)
Cambodia (1988)	3	0	Former Soviet Union (88)	Former Soviet Union (93)	Rubber (83)
Indonesia (1989)	16	14	Japan (42) USA (16)	Japan (23) USA (14)	Oil (23) Natural gas (12)
Laos (1988)	0	0	China (16) Former Soviet Union (5)	Thailand (11) Former Soviet Union (53)	Timber (33) Coffee (9)
Malaysia (1988)	17	18	Japan (17) Singapore (19)	Japan (23) USA (17)	Petroleum (11) Rubber, palm oil, timber (25)
The Philippines (1988)	34	21	USA (34) Japan (20)	Japan (17) USA (21)	Electrical equipment and parts (21) Textiles (18)
Singapore (1989)	23	17	Malaysia (14) USA (23)	Japan (21) USA (17)	Petroleum products (13) Office machines and electrical equipment (27)
Thailand (1988)	20	14	Japan (16) USA (20)	Japan (29) USA (14)	Food and live animals (34) Basic manufactured goods and machinery (34)
Vietnam (1988)	—	—	Former Soviet Union (51) Hong Kong (14)	Japan (8) Former Soviet Union (69)	Fuel and raw materials (45) Machinery (23)

REVIEW QUESTIONS

Multiple Choice. Select the letter of the answer that correctly completes each statement.

1. Geographically, the nations of Southeast Asia are
   A. part of mainland Asia
   B. island nations
   C. mostly archipelagoes
   D. both island and mainland nations

2. A leading rubber-producing nation in Southeast Asia is
   A. Singapore
   B. Malaysia
   C. Indonesia
   D. Thailand

3. What do Indonesia and the Philippines have in common? They both
   A. border China
   B. are island nations
   C. have gone to war over trade routes
   D. have peninsulas

4. The word "Indochina" refers to a
   A. river
   B. nation
   C. region
   D. mountain

5. Which would not be considered an island nation?
   A. Malaysia
   B. Indonesia
   C. Laos
   D. the Philippines

6. In Southeast Asia, the continued importance of the monsoon cycle shows that this region is
   A. becoming a major exporter of oil
   B. developing heavy industry
   C. opposed to the use of nuclear power
   D. dependent on traditional farming methods

ESSAY

Read the following statements carefully. Give two reasons to explain each of the following:

1. Southeast Asia is more of a supplier of raw materials than a manufacturer of finished goods.
2. Southeast Asia has been known by many names throughout the course of history.

III. HUMAN AND CULTURAL GEOGRAPHY OF SOUTHEAST ASIA

Overview

The most striking feature of Southeast Asia's population is its variety. This variety can be seen in the different languages, religions, and ethnic groups. Therefore, the region can be described as a "patchwork quilt" of peoples. With a total population of slightly over 400 million, the ten nations have more people than in all of North America. Indonesia, with 195 million people, is the fourth largest nation in the world.

Demography

Although the majority of people live in the villages and the mountains, there are several large cities in Southeast Asia. The population density is uneven. The Indonesian island of Java, for example, has over 1,500 people per square mile, while the whole nation of Indonesia has 225 people per square mile. Most other areas have less than 125 people per square mile.

Language

The many languages spoken in Southeast Asia are primarily a reflection of the area's history. Several of these can be traced to nations from outside that have had great influence here. French is spoken in Cambodia, Laos, and Vietnam; Spanish in the Philippines; English in the Philippines, Myanmar, Malaysia, and Singapore; and Dutch in Indonesia. Migration of people from India and China have brought Tamil and Chinese to parts of mainland Southeast Asia. Languages native to the region are Thai, Vietnamese, Burmese, Lao, Malay, Pilipino and Tagalog.

Religion

A diversity of religions exists, basically for the same historical reasons that a variety of languages exists. Animism, a form of nature worship, is native to the region. The five major "outside" faiths include Buddhism, Confucianism, Christanity, Hinduism, and Islam. The number of Muslims in Indonesia make it the largest Islamic nation in the world. However, the religion with the greatest number of followers in the mainland nations is Buddhism. Buddhism began in India. Some of the main ideas about Buddhism are:

1. Siddhartha Gautama became the Buddha or the "Enlightened One."

2. The Four Noble Truths are from Gautama's teachings: Suffering is part of life; Selfish desires cause suffering; To end suffering, one must give up these desires; To end these desires, one must follow the Eightfold Path.

The Eightfold Path consists of a series of words and acts, such as right speech, right occupation, right thought, and right conduct; following the "middle way" between extremes, such as denial or indulgence.

3. The goal of Buddhists is to reach enlightenment and then nirvana. Nirvana results in a release from the mandalas (wheel of life) and extinction of the soul.

4. Two major schools, or sects, of Buddhism are found in Southeast Asia. The Hinayana ("Little Vehicle") Buddhists are found in Myanmar and follow a more strict and traditional form of practice. The Mahayana ("Greater Vehicle") practitioners are more liberal and have adopted certain ideas such as that of the bodhissatva. (A bodhissatva is someone who has achieved buddhahood but has given up this status to return to earth and be of help to human beings.)

Ethnic Groups

GLOBAL CONCEPTS
Diversity
CONCEPTS GLOBAL

There is a great variety of ethnic groups in Southeast Asia. These include both those native to the region and those that have ancestral ties to foreign areas. Among the ethnic groups native to Southeast Asia are the Khmers (Cambodia), Chams (Vietnam), and Malays (Indonesia, Malaysia, Philippines). "Outside" groups include Europeans, Indians, and Chinese. Of these, the Chinese are the most numerous. Referred to as the hua-chiao ("overseas Chinese"), they have usually settled in urban areas and have had a major economic impact in several nations, such as Singapore.

WORLD ISSUES

Economic
Growth and
Development

However, they have also been the target of prejudice on occasion, especially in Indonesia and Malaysia. The various ethnic groups have slowly made progress in learning to live with each other and in adapting traditional customs to modernization and to Westernization.

REVIEW QUESTIONS

Multiple Choice. Select the letter of the answer that correctly completes each statement.

1. The "hua-chiao" are Chinese who
   A. control Singapore
   B. live outside of China
   C. live in coastal areas of Southeast Asia
   D. fought the Indonesian government

2. The word "buddha" can be translated as meaning the
   A. middle way
   B. enlightened one
   C. eightfold path
   D. noble truth

3. The most populous nation in Southeast Asia is
   A. Indonesia
   B. Cambodia
   C. Vietnam
   D. Myanmar

4. Mahayana Buddhism differs from Hinayana Buddhism in its emphasis on the concept of
   A. nirvana
   B. the bodhissatva
   C. enlightenment
   D. four noble truths

ESSAYS

1. The region of Southeast Asia, in terms of its people and culture, has been described as a "patchwork quilt." Discuss the validity of this description by giving four specific examples.

2. Buddhism has played a major role in shaping the history and culture of Southeast Asia.
   A. Explain two basic teachings or ideas of Buddhism.
   B. Name one person associated with the development of Buddhism.
   C. Discuss the impact of this person on the religion.
   D. Describe one impact of Buddhism on Southeast Asia.

IV. HISTORY AND POLITICAL GEOGRAPHY OF SOUTHEAST ASIA

The Historical Setting (1500 B.C.–1500 A.D.)

Early Civilizations. Little is known about the earliest inhabitants of Southeast Asia. They were most likely people who grew rice and worked with bronze. Migrations from the Indian subcontinent and China added to the native populations. (To this day, China refers to the entire region as "nanyang," lands of the southern ocean.) The Indian cultural diffusion included its ancient language, Sanskrit, as well as the spread of Hinduism, Buddhism, and Islam. Chinese influence was seen in the adoption of the Confucian cultural patterns and in the racial similarities between ethnic Malays and Chinese. China also controlled Vietnam for almost 1,000 years, up until 939 A.D. In other parts of Southeast Asia, several kingdoms emerged and grew into large empires.

The Funan empire, 100 A.D., was located in Cambodia and southeast Vietnam. It controlled trade routes with India and China. The Khmer empire, 800 A.D., located in Cambodia, based its wealth on agriculture and was known for the impressive capital at Angkor. The temple at Angkor (Angkor Wat) is an example of cultural diffusion from India; its sculpture shows both Hindu and Buddhist influences. The Srivijaya empire, 800 A.D., located in Indonesia, became powerful by securing the Strait of Malacca as a key link in the trade between India and China. It was known for a magnificent Buddhist structure, Borobodur, on the island of Java.

The Colonial Period (1500–1963)

When the Portuguese took control of the Strait of Malacca in 1511 and the Spanish landed at Cebu Island (part of the present-day Philippines) in 1521, the period of European colonialism began. Eventually, four other nations—England, France, Holland, and the United States—established colonies in Southeast Asia. With the exception of the present-day nation of Thailand, every part of the region was colonized at one point in its history. By 1963, when the British left Malaysia and Singapore, nearly all the entire region had become independent nations. (Technically, the colonial period did not end until 1983; in that year, England gave up its protectorate in Brunei.)

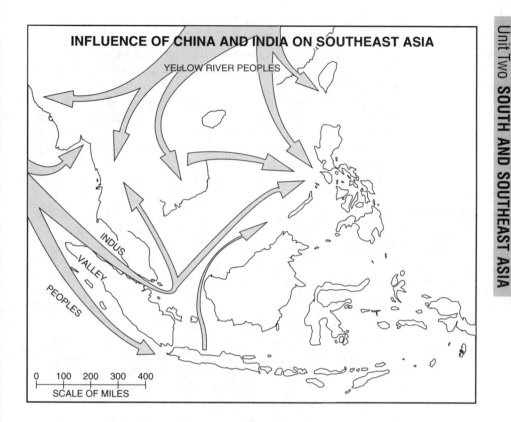

INFLUENCE OF CHINA AND INDIA ON SOUTHEAST ASIA

YELLOW RIVER PEOPLES

INDUS

VALLEY

PEOPLES

0 100 200 300 400
SCALE OF MILES

What were the main reasons for colonialism? European nations were interested in the spices from the region. The aim of Christopher Columbus in 1492 was to reach the "spice islands" in the "Indies." In later years, European interest in the area was focused on its mineral deposits, its agricultural products (see the sections on physical and economic geography), and political control of territory.

Nationalistic, anticolonial movements began in Southeast Asia in the 19th century and gained strength after World War II. The war was of importance for these nationalistic movements for several reasons: (1) Between 1942 and 1945, the European colonial powers lost much of their territorial control to the Japanese. (2) The Japanese, who took over the colonies, were hated as much as the European colonial powers, and the Southeast Asian people rose up to fight for independence. (3) At the war's end, some of the former European colonial powers took back control of their colonies, but they were weary and drained from the war. They sought to comply with the aims of the

WORLD ISSUES

War
and
Peace

United Nations charter, and therefore were willing to grant independence. (4) Other colonial powers who took back control of their former colonies were unwilling to grant independence, and they were confronted by native leaders who had fought against the Japanese.

A peaceful transition to independence occurred in these nations: Myanmar (then Burma), Malaysia, Singapore, and Brunei—from England; the Philippines—from the United States. (The United States gained control from Spain in 1898, after the Spanish-American War.)

Bloody transitions to independence occurred in Indonesia, Cambodia, Laos, and North and South Vietnam. Indonesia, under the nationalist leader Ahmed Sukarno, fought against the Dutch from 1945 to 1949. Cambodia, Laos, and North and South Vietnam were created in 1954, after these nations fought the French for eight years. The major forces defeating France were the Vietnamese Communists, led by Ho Chi Minh. After the French defeat in the battle at Dien Bien Phu, the Geneva Accords were signed. They brought the war to an end and provided for French withdrawal from Indochina.

In the early 1960s fighting broke out in South Vietnam, as North Vietnam attempted to establish one unified nation of Vietnam. Fighting against the South Vietnamese government were the Viet Cong (South Vietnamese Communists) and ultimately the army of North Vietnam. The Viet Cong and North Vietnamese received material assistance from China and the Soviet Union. South Vietnam received help from the United States in the form of material as well as over 500,000 combat troops. In 1973 President Richard Nixon withdrew U.S. forces in the hope that both North and South Vietnam could work out their differences peacefully. The South Vietnamese government, under President Nguyen Van Thieu, grew weak and very unpopular. Fighting resumed, resulting in a North Vietnamese takeover in 1975 and the proclamation in 1976 of a united country. Hanoi became the country's capital, while Saigon, the former capital of South Vietnam, had its name changed to Ho Chi Minh City.

WORLD ISSUES

Determination
of Political
and Economic
Systems

WORLD ISSUES

War
and
Peace

Independence Period (1963–the Present)

The political structures that have evolved since independence reflect the varied backgrounds of the nations in Southeast Asia. Therefore, it is not surprising to find different forms of government.

Nation	Form of Government	Current Leader*
Brunei	Monarchy	Sultan Sir Bolkiah Hassanal
Cambodia	Monarchy	King Norodom Sihanouk
Indonesia	Military government, republic	President General Suharto
Laos	Communist dictatorship	Chairman Kaysone Phomvihan
Malaysia	Constitutional monarchy	Prime Minister Mahathir bin Mohammad
Myanmar (Burma)	Military dictatorship	General Than Shwe
Philippines	Federal republic	President Fidel Ramos
Singapore	Parliamentary government	Prime Minister Goh Chok Tong
Thailand	Constitutional monarchy	Prime Minister Likphai Chuan
Vietnam	Communist state	Chairman Non Duk Manh

*Given the instability in Southeast Asian politics, these leaders may hold office only for a short time. Each was his nation's leader in 1994.

Key Issues Since Independence

Local versus central control is a problem in Myanmar, where local tribal groups (Karens) in rural remote areas refuse to obey decisions of the national government in Yangon (Rangoon). In the 1990 elections, Aung San Suu Kyi and her National League for Democracy party emerged as victors. However, these results were nullified by the military leaders of the State Law and Order Restoration Council (SLORC). Although Aung San Suu Kyi was awarded the 1991 Nobel Peace Prize, she was placed under house arrest.

Civil war and invasions have plagued Cambodia since Prince Norodom Sihanouk was overthrown in 1970. The military rulers who took over were unable to defeat the Khmer Rouge, a Communist force backed by Vietnam. By 1976 the Khmer Rouge, under its leader Pol Pot, controlled the nation and changed the official name to Kampuchea. (However, the country today is commonly referred to as Cambodia.) The Pol Pot government proved to be harsh and genocidal, killing thousands of people. It tried to impose a drastic social and economic restructure of society between 1975 and 1978. Its actions were the basis for a feature movie titled *The Killing Fields*. The Pol Pot government angered Vietnam, which had long wished to take over the territory. (Historically, the people of Kampuchea and Vietnam have been enemies.) With Soviet encouragement and material aid, Vietnam conquered Cambodia in 1978 and installed a government headed by a native figure, Hun Sen. This

103

government faced a rebellion by Khmer Rouge forces, backed by China. With Vietnamese forces withdrawing in 1989, a coalition government was established that sought to bring together the Khmer Rouge and other warring groups.

A UN-supervised ceasefire agreement was signed in 1991, providing for a UN peacekeeping force and UN-sponsored elections. The elections, held in May 1993, produced a 120-member National Assembly, which promptly drew up a new constitution and provided for the return of Norodom Sihanouk as king. In September 1993, Sihanouk ascended to the throne in an elaborate ceremony. His new government was immediately recognized by the United States. His biggest political problem has been trying to put down the armed resistance of the Khmer Rouge. Although they were a party to the 1991 agreement, the Khmer Rouge boycotted the 1993 elections and have been upset with some of Sihanouk's political actions since he became king.

Instability and corruption are features in many parts of Southeast Asia. However, they erupted into a striking change of government in the Philippines in 1986. Ferdinand Marcos, who had ruled with strong military backing since 1965, was an unpopular ruler who enriched himself and did little to help the masses of people. Widespread demonstrations, a controversial election, and a declining military enabled Corazon Aquino to come to power in 1986, as Marcos fled into exile. He died in 1989, while in Hawaii. As president from 1986 to 1992, Mrs. Aquino was unsuccessful in dealing with problems concerning hostility from Communist and Muslim groups, corruption in government, and a declining economy. A significant foreign policy decision of her government was to refuse to renew the lease on the naval base at Subic Bay. She did not run for reelection in 1992. Fidel Ramos was the winner in that election, decisively defeating former Filipino first lady Imelda Marcos.

There are other tensions that have existed in the region in the post-independence period. They include:

1. Indonesia has had disagreements with Malaysia. It also had riots that caused the death of many Chinese in 1965 in the midst of a strong anti-Communist policy and scattered anti-Chinese prejudice. Indonesia has been condemned for its human rights violations, based upon its actions in dealing with protests in East Timor.

2. Chinese and Vietnamese antagonism surfaced in 1979 with a short-lived border war.

3. Thailand has been worried about the spread of communism from Vietnam, as well as the problem of coping with

refugees from the fighting in Cambodia. Instability caused by corruption and political infighting led to a military-dominated government from 1990 to 1992. In October 1992 a civilian-led government was installed in Thailand for the first time in sixty years. In recent years, it has been concerned with an alarming spread of HIV/AIDS among the urban population.

4. Singapore, which is inhabited mostly by Chinese, strives to maintain good relations with its two large Malay-dominated neighbors, Indonesia and Malaysia. (The Malays are the majority ethnic groups in these nations.)

Developments in Vietnam in the 1990s

Severe economic conditions in Vietnam brought about significant changes in government policy. (1) Many years of fighting within and without the country had drained the treasury. (2) The collapse of the Soviet Union in 1991 led to a drastic reduction in the foreign aid that had long maintained the Vietnamese economy. (3) Centralized planning and a refusal to make needed changes hurt productivity.

High-level contacts with the United States were begun in 1990, stemming mostly from the economic factors described above. Americans have agreed to talks based upon Vietnam's willingness to seek peace with its neighbors and to account more fully for U.S. MIA/POWs (missing-in-action/prisoner-of-war servicemen and women). In 1993 and 1994 American businesspeople and politicians visited Vietnam, amid talk of normalizing relations between the two former enemies.

REVIEW QUESTIONS

Multiple Choice. Select the letter of the answer that correctly completes each statement.

1. In the 20th century, most nations of Southeast Asia have been characterized by
   A. struggles for independence
   B. a high standard of living
   C. political stability
   D. tolerance of ethnic minorities

2. Which of the following pairs of colonial power and colony are correct?
   A. England-Thailand
   B. Holland-Indonesia
   C. Spain-Malaysia
   D. France-Singapore

3. Former French Indochina was divided in 1954 into how many parts?
   A. two
   B. three
   C. four
   D. five

4. This division came about at a meeting in
   A. Bangkok
   B. Ho Chi Minh City
   C. Paris
   D. Phnom Penh

5. As a result of the Spanish-American War of 1898, the United States came into control of
   A. Vietnam
   B. the Philippines
   C. Laos
   D. Malaysia

ESSAYS

Since World War II, several Southeast Asian nations have faced various political problems. Among these nations have been the following:

Vietnam
Cambodia
The Philippines

For each of these nations, do the following:

1. State the capital city.
2. Describe one political problem it faced.
3. Name one person or group connected with this problem.
4. Discuss the role played by this person or group.
5. Explain whether or not the problem exists today.

2. Study this 1994 cartoon carefully, and then answer these questions:

A. Explain the caption of the cartoon.
B. Write your own caption for the cartoon.
C. Based upon the cartoon and your knowledge about Vietnam, explain whether you agree or disagree with each of the following statements:
   (1) Americans would like to do business in Vietnam.
   (2) Vietnamese would welcome the American presence in their country.

Tribune Media Services

UNIT THREE

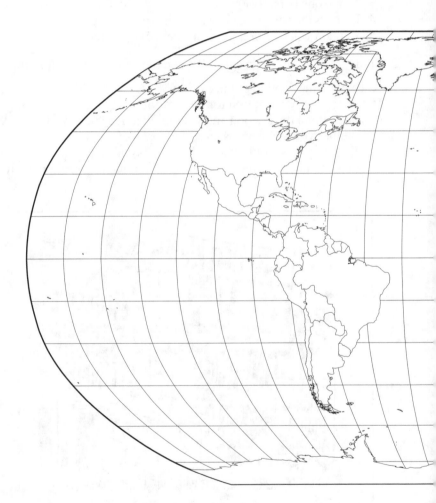

East Asia

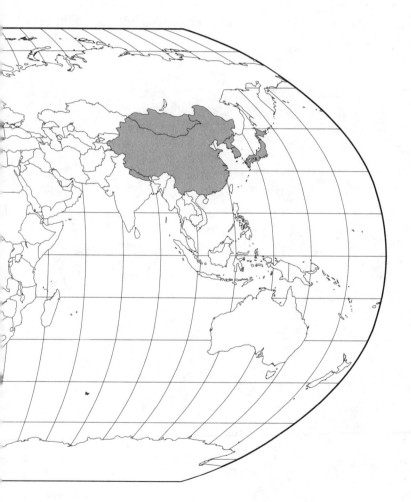

I. PHYSICAL GEOGRAPHY OF CHINA

Overview

Until the age of exploration in the 1500s, China was largely isolated from other regions of the world by the ocean, the deserts, and the mountains along its borders. For the most part, Chinese civilization developed independent of external influences and in a unique Chinese fashion. As a result, the Chinese developed a strong ethnocentric attitude, believing that their civilization was superior to all others and that China was the Middle Kingdom, the center of the universe. This attitude was reinforced by the fact that most cultures China came into contact with in the area (Japan, Korea, Vietnam) adapted elements of Chinese culture.

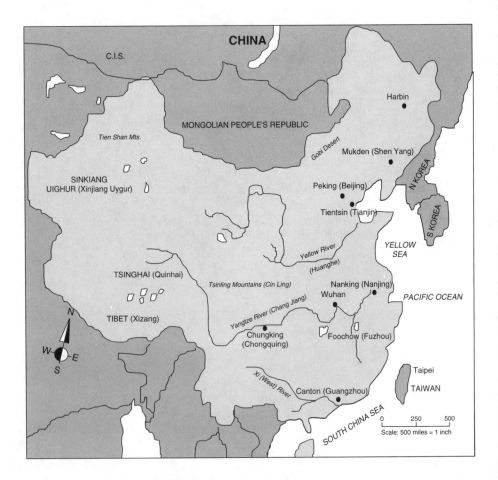

110

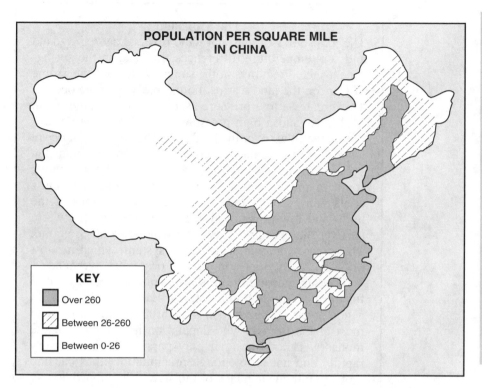

POPULATION PER SQUARE MILE IN CHINA

KEY

Over 260

Between 26-260

Between 0-26

WORLD ISSUES

Population

Land Area and Climate

China is the third largest country in physical size in the world and contains the world's largest population. Its population, estimated at approximately 1 billion 170 million in 1992, is concentrated in China Proper, the eastern third of the country.

The land area of China is over 3 million square miles. Its long, irregular coastline provides China with many excellent harbors. Latitude, altitude, wind patterns, and distance from the sea determine the varied climates of China. In general, the farther north a region lies, the cooler it will be; the farther west a region lies, the drier it will be because it is farther from the source of the summer monsoon. Chinese farmers depend on the summer monsoon rains for their crops, but the monsoons are not dependable. Sometimes the rains fail and the crops suffer drought. Sometimes the rains are excessively heavy and the crops suffer floods.

GLOBAL
CONCEPTS

Environment

CONCEPTS
GLOBAL

The Monsoon

The monsoon is a seasonal wind reversal caused by land and sea temperature differences. In Asia, in the springtime, as the direct rays of the sun move toward the Tropic of Cancer, the land warms more rapidly than the oceans. This creates a low-pressure system over the huge Asian land mass and a high-pressure system over the oceans. As the warm air over the land rises, the cool, moist ocean air rushes in to replace it, creating the summer monsoon system. In the fall, as the direct rays of the sun move south to the Tropic of Capricorn, the Asian land mass cools more rapidly than the water, the positions of the high- and low-pressure systems are reversed, the warm air over the ocean rises, and the winds reverse direction. This creates the winter monsoon system, which in most of Asia is a dry monsoon, since it originates over land.

The summer monsoon is the major source of rainfall for most of South, Southeast, and East Asian farmers. In a good year, the monsoon may bring adequate rains to most of the farmers who depend on it. However, if the monsoon is too strong it may pass over an area very rapidly and not drop enough precipitation, thus causing crops to fail due to a lack of moisture. The monsoon may continue carrying an excessive amount of moisture; thus, when it hits a mountain wall farther inland, it creates a flood problem in that area. A weak monsoon may stall in an area fairly near the coast and create terrible flooding there, while at the same time a drought may occur in areas farther inland because the moisture has fallen elsewhere. In general, the average amount of rainfall a region receives is determined by its nearness to the sea and its location in relation to hills and mountains, which will cause the winds to rise and precipitation to fall. Areas on the windward side of hills and mountains receive higher amounts of precipitation than other regions.

For most of Asia, the winter monsoon is dry. It originates over the lands to the north of India and China, and therefore the only regions that receive significant amounts of rainfall are those that lie on the northern and western coasts and slopes of mountains.

The summer monsoon is the southeast or southwest monsoon, and the winter monsoon is the northwest monsoon. The systems are named, like other winds, for the region in which they originate.

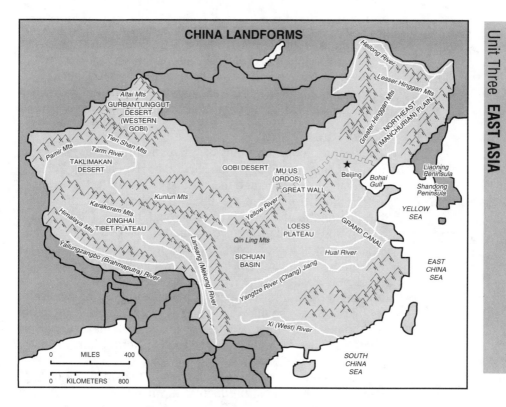

CHINA LANDFORMS

China has five major geographic and climatic regions:

1. Southern China, which is warm and moist year-round, is a major rice-growing region and contains the southern hills region and the Xi and Chang (Yangtze) river valleys.

2. North China, a cold, relatively dry region, is a major wheat-growing region and contains the Huanghe (Yellow) River Valley and the North China Plain.

3. Manchuria, in northeast China, is a large region of low-land plains, and contains vast mineral resources.

4. Inner Mongolia and Xinjiang (Sinkiang), in northcentral and western China, are largely desert and dry steppe.

5. Tibet, in the southwest, is a vast, cold plateau with an average elevation of 15,000 feet.

Mountains and Deserts

The Gobi Desert stretches across most of northcentral China (Inner Mongolia). Some of the world's highest mountains are located in and adjacent to the borders of China. To the northwest are the Altai and Tien Shan and to the southwest the Himalayas, the highest mountains in the world. The Qinling (Tsinling), in central-eastern China, separate the dry, cold

113

northern region from the wet, warm southern region and serve as a cultural dividing line in China.

GLOBAL CONCEPTS
Environment
CONCEPTS GLOBAL

The difficult terrain (hills, plateaus, mountains, and deserts) has resulted in sparse population in both north and west China. However, the eastern third of China, known as China Proper, is very heavily populated, containing about 90 percent of China's people.

The River Valleys

The heaviest concentrations of population in China Proper are in the great river valleys—the Huanghe (Hwang-ho or Yellow), the Chang (Yangtze), and the Xi (Hsi or West).

WORLD ISSUES

Environmental
Concerns

The northernmost of the three, the Huanghe, is the major farming region of China. It flows through the great loess (fertile yellow soil) region of northern China and picks up and carries a vast amount of topsoil, which is deposited in the bed of the river and on the flood plains of the North China Plain. The river carries so much silt that the riverbed has been built up to an elevation higher than the surrounding plains and must be controlled by dikes. When the dikes fail, the river floods, destroying crops and homes and killing people. For this reason, the river has become known as "China's sorrow" and the North China Plain, the "famine region of China."

The Chang (Yangtze), China's longest river, flows through some of China's most productive farmland. The rich deposits of topsoil from floods encourage farming, and many of China's most important industrial cities, such as Nanjing (Nanking), Wuhan, Hankow, Chongqing (Chungking), and Shanghai, are located along it.

The Xi (Hsi or West) River, in the far south of China, is an important source of irrigation, and at its mouth lies the city of Guangzhou (Canton) and, nearby, the British colony of Hong Kong.

REVIEW QUESTIONS

Multiple Choice. Select the letter of the answer that correctly completes each statement.

1. The majority of China's over 1 billion people live in the
   A. Manchurian Plains
   B. river valleys of eastern China
   C. Kweichow Plateau
   D. Takla Makan of western China

2. A population density map shows us the
   A. distribution of ethnic groups in China
   B. location of villages in a region
   C. approximate number of people per square mile
   D. location of industrial centers in a given nation

3. The direction of the flow of China's major rivers indicates that
   A. eastern China is cooler than western China
   B. western China is at a higher elevation than eastern China
   C. northern China receives more rainfall than southern China
   D. the monsoons originate in the southwest

4. North China raises large crops of wheat. South China raises large crops of rice. This is largely because of a difference in
   A. elevation
   B. rainfall
   C. cultural development
   D. technological development

5. Chinese farmers use terracing because they
   A. fear technological change
   B. must use all available land to feed the people
   C. prefer farming on the hills and plateaus
   D. can farm without irrigation

6. Over 90 percent of China's people live on less than half the land. The major reason for this is
   A. fear of the "barbarians" in the border regions
   B. the other half is disputed territory
   C. the rain forest prevents human habitation
   D. most of China's arable land is found in the east

7. Physical geography and history combined to give the early Chinese
   A. a deeply religious attitude
   B. an ethnocentric view
   C. a desire for modernization
   D. motivation to establish trade to gain knowledge

8. As one travels from eastern to western China, one is less likely to find
   A. sparse population
   B. mountains
   C. deserts
   D. agricultural centers

9. The most important influence on farming in China is
   A. the diurnal temperature change
   B. the availability of heavy machinery
   C. the winter monsoon
   D. the summer monsoon

10. The Yellow River is also known as the
    A. Chang
    B. Xi
    C. Huanghe
    D. Amur

ESSAY

Geography often plays a strong role in the economic and social development of a nation. Choose three different geographic features of China. For each, explain how it has affected the economic or social development of China.

II. ECONOMIC GEOGRAPHY OF CHINA

Resource Potential

China has adequate supplies of coal, iron ore, petroleum, natural gas, tin, antimony, tungsten, uranium, and many other minerals. It also has enormous hydroelectric-power potential, and China has constructed some dams and hydroelectric power plants. Most of China's petroleum reserves are located in the sparsely populated western regions, but pipelines transport crude oil to refineries and the densely inhabited eastern areas. Enough oil is produced for export. Most of the exported oil goes to Japan. China has major deposits of iron ore and coal in Manchuria. This iron has made possible the development of a sizable steel industry and has also made Manchuria a center of other types of heavy industry, such as locomotive production.

Agriculture, however, is still China's major source of income. The majority of the Chinese people are still engaged in agriculture, and the capital for investment in developing industries must come from the sale of agricultural products. Since only one third of China's land is arable, peasants must overproduce to feed the vast Chinese population and also have products to sell abroad. The intensive agriculture employed by the Chinese farmers (hand labor, terracing, irrigation, and so on) and the new incentives under the "responsibility system" have increased production, but the growing population demands ever more goods and services. To modernize China, its agricultural economy must be transformed into an industrial economy. To achieve this goal, the Chinese are using technology to overcome the scarcity of both food and consumer goods.

Changes in the Economic System Under Mao Zedong

For generations, China was an agrarian nation. The majority of the people were tenant farmers who rented their land from the landed gentry, who made up 10 percent of the population but owned 70 percent of the land. Rent and taxes kept the vast majority of tenant farmers impoverished. They lived on a subsistence level, providing their families with the necessities of life—food, clothing, and shelter—unless the monsoons failed them, and then many of them starved. The peasants were constantly faced with the threat of famine, starvation, and exploitation by the landlords and the government.

WORLD ISSUES

Energy:
Resources and
Allocations

GLOBAL
CONCEPTS

Agriculture

CONCEPTS
GLOBAL

WORLD ISSUES

Determination
of Political
and Economic
Systems

WORLD ISSUES

Hunger
and
Poverty

WORLD ISSUES

Determination
of Political
and Economic
Systems

After the establishment of the People's Republic of China in 1949, Mao Zedong made drastic changes in China's economy. Those changes included:

1. Foreign-owned industries were almost immediately nationalized, and Chinese-owned industries were also gradually nationalized.

2. Banks, transportation, and mining also came under government control.

3. Production goals and methods to meet China's economic goals were set by Communist leaders through five-year plans.

4. The Communists carried out land reform, and the peasants were given small plots of land of their own.

GLOBAL
CONCEPTS

Choice

CONCEPTS
GLOBAL

Under Mao's leadership, the Communists were determined to industrialize China. The capital for investment had to come from the sale of agricultural products. However, since the peasants on their small plots simply were not producing enough to provide that capital, the communist government began to take control of the land and agricultural production.

Cooperative farms were formed where individual farmers still owned the land but shared the ownership of machinery, tools, and work animals, and the farmers worked the land collectively. However, cooperatives also did not provide the desired increase in production.

WORLD ISSUES

Determination
of Political
and Economic
Systems

The next step was the collective farm, where the land, the tools, machinery, and animals belonged to the collective (the state) and decisions on production were made by government officials. Individuals were paid wages, and the goods produced and the profit from that production now belonged to the state. Individuals were still allowed to own their homes, and they still enjoyed a private family life.

During the Second Five-Year Plan (1958–1962), called the Great Leap Forward, all the country's resources were to be directed toward greater industrialization. Communes—huge state-owned farms which were economic, political, and social units—were formed. The commune managed local schools, hospitals, power plants, radio stations. Agricultural planning was done by Communist party members, as was the planning for the industry the commune was engaged in. Ownership of private property ended. The communes had communal dining halls, nurseries, and dormitories. The plan called for increasing grain production by 100 percent in one year. Instead, it decreased by 20 percent in two years. Drought, peasant resistance, and inefficient central planning caused the failure of the Great Leap Forward. As a result, the government divided the communes into production brigades to set goals and production teams to perform the labor. Most of the decisions were made by the commune members themselves. The government gave them quotas, but they decided how to meet those quotas and what to do with any surplus. Although production increased, it did not meet the needs of the growing Chinese population.

Economic Development Under Deng Xiaoping

Deng Xiaoping has been the most powerful figure in China since the death of Mao in 1976. In 1978 he began a program known as the Four Modernizations in agriculture, industry, defense, and science and technology, which made significant changes in China. Deng believed there should be less government control and planning. To carry out this program, Deng introduced elements of capitalism (free enterprise), and as a result China now has a mixed economy rather than a strict command economy. (In a command economy, the government makes all the basic economic decisions.)

Beginning in 1979, the communes were dismantled and the "responsibility system" was started, under which the land still belongs to the state but individual families lease plots. The peasants decide what to raise on the land and how to raise it. They contract with the state for a certain amount of their produce. Anything produced above that amount belongs to the peasant, who can choose what to do with the surplus. Free markets were established to sell the extra produce. Production has increased considerably. Estimates are that the average peasant's income has more than doubled and production has grown by over 7 percent per year.

The responsibility system was extended to state-owned industries in 1984. Managers are now allowed to make production decisions. They must still meet quotas set by the state but can decide what to do with surplus production. The factories and the machinery belong to the state, and the state still controls raw materials, but managers are free to obtain raw materials themselves. The industries pay a tax on the profit of sales of surplus goods, but the rest of the income can be used for reinvestment or to reward workers.

Some private enterprise has also been encouraged. The government offered tax breaks and low-interest loans to people to organize small businesses, such as fast food, beauty shops, brick-making, carpentry, and so on. The number of workers who can be employed in these private enterprises is limited by the government.

The production of consumer goods has also been stressed. There has been a push to raise the standard of living of the average Chinese, and there has been much greater production of radios, bicycles, cameras, TVs, and other consumer goods. Other major economic changes have been the encouragement of foreign investment in Chinese industries and allowing foreign industries to locate in China.

Joint ventures between Chinese and foreign businesses have been encouraged, but, in addition, foreign companies have been encouraged to locate in Special Economic Zones (SEZ) located in coastal southeastern China. Here almost none of the restrictions placed on Chinese businesses apply, and private enterprise is the order of business. The foreign businesses receive tax benefits, raw materials can be imported, workers can be hired and fired at will, and profits can be kept. These Special Economic Zones are capitalist enclaves in China. The Chinese have also reached agreements with several foreign countries for scientific and technological exchange. The major foreign investments are from Britain, the United States, Germany, France, and Japan.

WORLD ISSUES

| World |
| Trade and |
| Finance |

New Educational and Cultural Policies

As part of the Four Modernizations program, the government tried to improve education. The closing of schools during the Cultural Revolution and the persecution of teachers caused a major weakness in scientific and technical skills in China. To bridge this gap the government began to allow Chinese students to study abroad, and there were several thousand foreign advisers and many foreign students studying in China.

GLOBAL
CONCEPTS

Change

CONCEPTS
GLOBAL

There was less emphasis on the use of art to further socialist ideals. During the Cultural Revolution (see page 145) artistic expression was severely restricted. Under Deng, Western television and music were allowed into China.

Many leaders of the Chinese Communist party believed Deng went too far in allowing capitalism into the Chinese economy. They feared corruption and the exploitation of workers. They also feared that the party would lose social and political control. The new freedom in education and culture was also seen by many government leaders as dangerous. But Deng and his supporters felt it was essential in order to advance science and technology. Indeed, the student "democracy" movement of May and June 1989 indicated that those who foresaw danger were right, and Western influences were blamed for the student rebellion that began in Beijing. Deng ordered a military crackdown on the democracy movement.

Conditions Posing Problems in Achieving Goals

WORLD ISSUES

Economic
Growth and
Development

In spite of the many hindrances to development in China, progress has been made and the majority of the Chinese people enjoy a higher standard of living than before the Communist Revolution. Nonetheless, several factors make it difficult for the Communists to achieve their economic goals.

Since China's economy still has an agricultural base, most of the capital for investment still must come from agriculture. Secondly, economic development has been uneven since regional differences present problems for development. Southeast China has excellent conditions for agriculture and has made economic gains. However, the North China Plain suffers recurring floods and drought, and much of the western regions are desert. North-

WORLD ISSUES

Population

eastern China (Manchuria), with its major iron and coal resources, has seen major industrial development. Uneven regional economic development creates another problem. The regions are inhabited by diverse ethnic groups, and the economic development, or lack of it, serves to prolong ethnic differences and conflicts. Moreover, attempting to provide at least an elementary education for the Chinese people has put enormous strains on the economic resources of the state. China's large population and level of education are both important factors in determining the level of development in the country and, for the time being, serve to hinder that development.

REVIEW QUESTIONS

Multiple Choice. Select the letter of the answer that correctly completes each statement.

1. The Great Leap Forward was expected to produce gains in China's
   A. imports
   B. birth rate
   C. army
   D. gross national product

2. An example of government-organized collectivist and group ideology was seen in China's
   A. foreign relations
   B. military
   C. commune system
   D. maritime trade

3. Since World War II Manchuria has become important as a center of
   A. heavy industry
   B. rice cultivation
   C. nomadic herding
   D. mining for gold

4. Arable land can be described as land that is
   A. dry and windblown
   B. composed of loess
   C. affected by earthquakes
   D. fertile and can be farmed

5. The best example of a command economy is
   A. China under Mao during the 1950s
   B. the responsibility system in China
   C. tenant farming in pre-civil war China
   D. subsistence farming in ancient China

6. Many nations have mixed economies. This means they have
   A. combined elements of democracy and dictatorship
   B. adopted both socialist and capitalist elements
   C. government ownership of all mines
   D. individual ownership of all industries, resulting in monopolies

7. Five-year plans in China have been used primarily to
   A. set economic production goals
   B. limit population growth
   C. increase adult literacy
   D. decrease infant mortality

8. The nationalization of industry refers to
   A. employing only native inhabitants
   B. government takeover of private industry
   C. government subsidies for industries
   D. providing government contracts to defense industries

9. The Four Modernizations program of Deng Xiaoping was designed to make specific changes in all of the following except
   A. agriculture
   B. industry
   C. science and technology
   D. family structure

10. The student rebellion and demonstration in Tiananmen Square in 1989 led to
    A. the establishment of a democratic government
    B. a military crackdown on the participants
    C. greater emphasis on individual rights
    D. decreased government restraint on political freedom

ESSAYS

1. The economic policies of both Mao Zedong and Deng Xiaoping were designed to increase agricultural and industrial production in China. However, each man chose very different ways to achieve those goals.

   Using specific information, describe three major ways in which the policies of Mao and Deng differed. Explain the specific outcome each hoped to achieve by using those particular methods.

2. Under the leadership of Mao, China's goal was to increase agricultural production to gain capital investment funds for industry. In so doing, the peasants gradually lost all control of the land and agricultural decision-making.

   Describe the chief characteristics of the three major types of agricultural organizations used under Mao in the effort to increase agricultural production.

III. HUMAN AND CULTURAL GEOGRAPHY OF CHINA

Confucianism

Confucian thought, the foundation of Chinese civilization, influenced social organization, political structure, and the educational system. Confucius, or Kung Fu-tzu (551 B.C.–479 B.C.), lived during a time of great turmoil in China, marked by constant civil war. Confucius believed he knew how to bring about peace and harmony. His teachings became the basis of Chinese society during the Han dynasty (202 B.C.–220 A.D.).

GLOBAL CONCEPTS

Culture

CONCEPTS GLOBAL

Confucius was not concerned with religion and did not teach about a divine being or salvation. He taught ethics (good and bad conduct), or moral precepts. A conservative, he believed the Chinese should follow ancient ways that had worked well in the past. Confucius taught that one should *not* do to others what one would *not* want done to oneself, stressing actions *not* to be taken against others.

GLOBAL CONCEPTS

Identity

CONCEPTS GLOBAL

Confucius believed there was a basic order to the universe and that people must live in society to fulfill their potential. To achieve a peaceful and harmonious relationship in society, Confucius taught five basic relationships. All the relationships were based on the principle of reciprocity. Each person, according to Confucius, had a place in society, and if each person accepted the duties and obligations of his or her role, society would function properly. In each relationship there is a superior and an inferior. The superior shows love for and responsibility for the inferior. The inferior owes loyalty and obedience to the superior.

Five Relationships:

1. **Ruler and subject**
2. **Father and son**
3. **Husband and wife**
4. **Older brother and younger brother**
5. **Friend and friend.** This is the only relationship not based on a superior/inferior foundation. Friends were to respect and honor each other.

For many centuries China was ruled by imperial dynasties. Confucianists believed that the ruler held the mandate of heaven (the right to rule granted by the will of heaven). If he was a just ruler and cared for his subjects, he and his family would continue to hold the mandate. But if he was not, the people had the right to rebel and overthrow the ruler and the dynasty. The success of their rebellion would be proof that the ruler had lost the mandate.

The Traditional Chinese Family System

The extended, patriarchal, and patrilineal family was the traditional ideal in China and was the basic social unit, although usually only the wealthy could actually afford to live in such large households. A person gained his position in society as a member of his family. To be without family was to be without position. The family was also the basic economic unit. Most families lived on farms. Domestic handicraft was the major type of manufacturing. With few exceptions a son learned the trade of his father. There was a single family budget. Upon his death, a man's property would be divided equally among his sons, who would begin to build their own extended families.

Two well-defined, unwritten rules determined relationships within the family. Those rules were:

1. The superiority of males over females.
2. The superiority of the old over the young.

Strong-willed, older females were likely to exercise considerable influence over family decisions, although most females were reluctant to do so, simply because they had learned to accept their inferiority as a matter of custom and tradition.

The most important virtue in China was filial piety, which might be defined as reverence, love, and devotion to family and respect and obedience to parents. Individuals had a lifelong obligation to their parents, and were expected to serve them during their worship. Ancestor worship actually reduced the mobility of Chinese families. One had to remain near the graves and the spirits of one's ancestors, so that the proper sacrifices could be made to the spirits at the appropriate times. It was believed that the spirits of the ancestors watched over the activities of the living, and that the spirits were to a large degree responsible for the prosperity or lack or prosperity experienced by the living. Ancestor worship was practiced by nearly everyone in China.

The individual was subordinate to the family. What was good for the family was allowed; what was not good for the family was not allowed. The success or failure of the individual

GLOBAL CONCEPTS
Power
CONCEPTS GLOBAL

GLOBAL CONCEPTS
Citizenship
CONCEPTS GLOBAL

GLOBAL CONCEPTS
Identity
CONCEPTS GLOBAL

reflected on the family, and vice versa. The head of the family was expected to punish infractions of societal mores and values to save "face" and preserve the family's good name. Government officials often dealt with the head of the family rather than with the individual who had committed crimes. The patriarchal clan cared for the aged and orphans. If a person had family, they would always be cared for.

The oldest living male was the head of the family and the chief authority figure. He was responsible for the actions of all members of the family, and, ideally, his authority was unquestioned.

GLOBAL
CONCEPTS
Human Rights
CONCEPTS
GLOBAL

The traditional inferiority of the female made the female role in China unenviable, particularly for young women. A woman's role was to provide her husband with sons to carry on the family name, and she had virtually no position in her husband's family until this was accomplished. Indeed, failure to produce sons was one of the most shameful things for a woman. The feet of upper-class females were bound because small feet were considered necessary for making "good" arrangements for marriage. Female children were often abandoned to die (female infanticide) during times of famine so that older members of the family might survive.

Marriages were arranged, and were considered social and economic arrangements between families. It was common for the couple not to see each other until the marriage actually took place. It was an important means of maintaining the existing social order. Arrangements were made between families with the assistance of a go-between who researched the background of the families and the two being married, including horoscopes and astrology. Most important were the family's social and economic status. The marriages were made to enhance the standing of the two families, not to satisfy the couple. The most important product of the marriage would be sons to carry on the family name and the family business, and to care for the parents when they were too old to care for themselves.

The rules worked because they were based on the principle of reciprocity derived from Confucianism, on mutual responsibilities and obligations. The head of the family had a duty to care for and protect the other members of the family, and the young and the females had a duty to respect and obey the head of the family in return. The subordinate members of the family trusted in the impartiality of the head of the family and in the belief that he would do what was best for the family (the group) and, therefore, what was best for the individual.

The system provided psychological and economic security. It created a sense of lifelong belonging. As long as the family existed and one did not shame the family, one would always be cared for. In a nation where political conflict and economic insecurity were common, the family provided an ongoing sense of social security. These were the advantages of the system. The disadvantages included: spreading the family income very thin, jealousy in the extended family, particularly if there were joint households; in-law problems; mistreatment of young wives by mothers-in-law, who were finally superior to someone and whose sons were duty bound to support them in disagreements, during times of famine, sacrifice of young for the old.

The Four Chinese Social Classes

1. Scholars, who made up a very small portion of society, held the highest position in Chinese society. They were the only ones eligible to take the civil service examinations and serve in government.

2. Peasants, who made up the largest portion of society, were the second highest class because they were the primary producers, providing the grains and textiles necessary for food and clothing.

3. Artisans, or craftspeople, were skilled workers who made up the third group. They were secondary producers.

4. Merchants, the lowest socially, though often the wealthiest, made their profits from the labor of others.

The nobility were above the class system. Soldiers and a group called "chien-min" (barbers, entertainers, etc.) were below the system.

Taoism (Daoism)

Taoism, a Chinese philosophy traditionally attributed to Lao-tzu ("old master"), originated in the 6th century B.C., about the same time as Confucianism. Taoism teaches the necessity of the individual's having a sense of nature, understanding his or her part in it and adapting to it.

The Taoists believed there was a natural order to existence and that people should do as little as possible to change that natural order. By accepting things as they are, people could live in harmony with the natural laws. Taoists opposed the existence of a large bureaucratic government and many governmental laws. Individuals should seek to find their own nature and place in the natural world and act according to instinct, since human instincts are good, and it is learning and custom that have taught them to be bad. Once people rid themselves of the burden of unnatural laws and customs, they could find the tao (or way) of the universe.

Like Confucianism, Taoism was not immediately widely accepted. However, over the years it underwent major changes. It borrowed heavily from old Chinese folk religions and became a religion with a priesthood, ceremonies, and elaborate rituals. Some Taoists practiced alchemy (trying to change inferior metals to gold), some practiced magic, and others did ritual exercises.

Legalism

The Legalist philosophy originated in the same period as Confucianism and Taoism. The Legalists assumed that human nature was evil and that people must be restricted by laws. They believed that through harsh punishment people would be forced to obey those laws. They taught that a strong central government was essential to maintain peace and order, and that the ruler should have unquestioned authority. They also believed that only two occupations should be allowed: farmer (to provide sustenance) and soldier (to support the ruler).

Buddhism

GLOBAL
CONCEPTS

Change

CONCEPTS
GLOBAL

Buddhism originated in India in the 6th century B.C. and was carried to China by Indian merchants during the 1st century A.D. (See unit on Southeast Asia for a discussion of Buddhism.)

The first Chinese converts were from the upper class. The complex philosophy and elaborate rituals appealed to them. Buddhism was greatly changed by the Chinese, who translated difficult Buddhist concepts into traditional Confucian ethics. They stressed the obligations of children to parents. They interpreted nirvana not as a place empty of human thought and desire but as a continuation of life on earth, without the usual

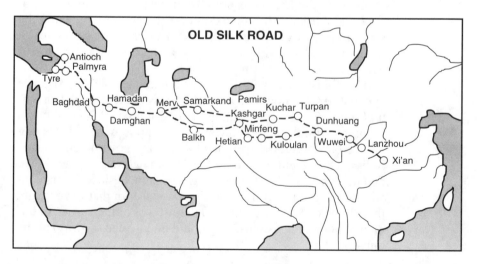

suffering. In the period of disorder after the fall of the Han dynasty, many Chinese began to accept Buddhist beliefs. Buddhist temples and monasteries became centers of education, and monasteries became economically and socially powerful.

The Chinese saw no contradiction in being a Buddhist-Confucianist-Taoist-Legalist. Buddhism offered optimism and hope for a better existence; Confucianism offered order and harmony and strong family relationships; Taoism offered rituals and ceremonies; and Legalism offered control. So a Chinese could be all these things.

Chinese Contributions

Historically, China was one of the world's leading civilizations in technological development. The Chinese contributed much to the world: silk, tea, porcelain (china), paper, block printing, gunpowder, the mariner's compass, and many plants and plant products. Most of these early Chinese inventions and products were diffused to the West (Europe) between 200 B.C. and 1800 A.D. by one of two routes—the Old Silk Road, which led from China through Central Asia into the Middle East and from there to Europe, or by the southern sea route, from China to India and onward to the Middle East and again from there to Europe.

Chinese Influence upon Other Peoples in East Asia

The original Chinese writing was a system of pictographs. Each symbol was a recognizable picture of an object. Eventually the Chinese developed a system of ideographs—symbols used for expressing ideas. The writing system includes more than fifty thousand symbols. This elaborate system of writing spread to Korea, Japan, and Vietnam.

Buddhism was adapted to the Chinese civilization, and Chinese Buddhism spread from China to Korea, Japan, and Vietnam. The Zen Buddhism practiced in Japan is said to have originated in China and entered Japan by way of Korea.

The Confucian tradition of ancient China also influenced the cultures of Korea, Japan, and Vietnam. Confucian influence can be seen in their family systems, ethical systems, and class systems, which are adaptations from the Chinese. Confucianism can also be seen in the dominance of the idea that there should be harmony between the individual and nature and in the importance given to the peasant in all three societies. Japanese and Korean art also reflect Confucian influence.

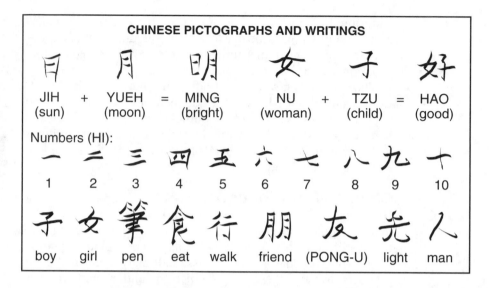

CHINESE PICTOGRAPHS AND WRITINGS

JIH (sun) + YUEH (moon) = MING (bright)   NU (woman) + TZU (child) = HAO (good)

Numbers (HI):

1   2   3   4   5   6   7   8   9   10

boy   girl   pen   eat   walk   friend   (PONG-U)   light   man

China's Population

WORLD ISSUES

Population

GLOBAL
CONCEPTS

Scarcity

CONCEPTS
GLOBAL

A large population requires large amounts of resources for subsistence and therefore makes development difficult. China has a huge population and a limited amount of arable land. The people themselves are perhaps China's most important resource and the cheapest factor in production, but their numbers are one of its greatest problems. To counteract this population problem, the Chinese government encourages a "one-child policy." This policy is relatively ineffective in the countryside but has had success in urban areas. China's goal is not just to decrease the birth rate but to actually decrease the population growth rate. The government also encourages late marriage.

REVIEW QUESTIONS

Multiple Choice. Select the letter of the answer that correctly completes each statement.

1. On which Asian nation did Chinese culture have the greatest impact?
   A. India
   B. Thailand
   C. Japan
   D. Pakistan

2. A goal common to Confucianism, Taoism, and Buddhism is to
   A. establish peace and harmony
   B. provide the basis for democratic government
   C. return the power of emperors
   D. promote individual artistic activity

3. The traditional Chinese writing system makes use of
   A. letters
   B. ideographs
   C. phonetics
   D. an alphabet

4. The "Five Relationships" were part of the philosophy of
   A. Lao-tzu
   B. Confucius
   C. Sun Yat-sen
   D. Mao Zedong

5. Of the world's total population, China contains about
   A. one half
   B. one third
   C. one fourth
   D. one fifth

6. The one word that would best describe five relationships of Confucius
   A. manorial
   B. ethnic
   C. disorderly
   D. reciprocal

7. The two groups in China whose social and economic positions most improved since the Communist victory in 1949 are
   A. students and government workers
   B. the aged and industrial employees
   C. factory managers and soldiers
   D. women and peasants

8. A Chinese emperor ruled through the "Mandate of Heaven." This meant he was
   A. chosen by the gods to rule
   B. descended from the gods
   C. a god himself
   D. able to communicate directly with the gods

9. Which Chinese philosophy contains ideas most like those found in Machiavelli's *The Prince*?
   A. Confucianism
   B. Taoism
   C. Mencius
   D. Legalism

10. The major purpose of China's one-child policy is to
    A. lower the infant mortality rate
    B. increase the amount of agricultural production
    C. decrease the population growth rate
    D. improve the literacy rate

ESSAYS

1. Chinese culture has been influenced by each of these philosophies:

   Taoism
   Buddhism
   Confucianism
   Legalism

Select any three of these and do the following:

   A. Explain one idea of this philosophy that is not found in the other two.
   B. Describe one way in which this philosophy has affected Chinese culture.

2. China faces a serious population explosion.

   A. Describe two reasons for this explosion.
   B. Explain why China is so concerned about the increasing growth rate of the population.
   C. Describe two ways in which the Chinese government is attempting to limit the population growth.

MAJOR CHINESE DYNASTIES

Dynasty	Achievements
Xia (ca. 2000–1500 B.C.)	Written language, pictographs
	Development of agriculture: domestication of animals, cultivation of plants
Shang (ca. 1523–1028 B.C.)	Production of bronze jewelry, ritual vessels, and weapons
	Sericulture (silk production)
Zhou (ca. 1028–256 B.C.)	Iron tools, iron plow
	Fine bronzes
	Irrigation canals dug
	Confucianism, Taoism, Legalism, and numerous other philosophies develop
Qin (221–206 B.C.)	First empire
	Great Wall begun
	Canals and roads improved
	Standardized writing system, system of weights and measures
Han (206 B.C–220 A.D.)	Extended control to Central Asia
	Established tribute system
	Development of civil service exams
	Paper, calendar, ceramics
Tang (618–907)	Poetry, literature, art
	Movable block print
	Porcelain
	Golden Age
Song (960–1279)	Compass, gunpowder
	Improved ceramic processes
	Paper money
	Landscape paintings
	Golden Age
Yuan (1279–1368)	Marco Polo visited and wrote chronicles of China
	Attempted invasions of Japan
Ming (1368–1644)	Sea trade with Arabian peninsula, Africa, and Southeast Asia
	Painting, porcelain
	Imperial palace built in Beijing
	First European traders (Portuguese)
Qing (1644–1912)	Opium Wars
	Unequal Treaties
	Taiping Rebellion
	Sino-Japanese War
	Development of industries, mines, communications, and military

IV. HISTORY AND POLITICAL GEOGRAPHY OF CHINA

Historical Development

Until 1912 Chinese history was divided into periods of dynastic rule, characterized by periods of stability and strong central government followed by periods of civil war and chaos. According to Chinese tradition, the ruler was responsible for setting a moral example and caring for his subjects. If he failed, the people had the right of rebellion. Dynasties were usually strong when first established, but weakness and corruption became common as time went on. When natural disasters such as flood and drought created famine or when China was invaded, it was a sign from heaven (the emperor, the "son of heaven," ruled through the will of heaven), and rebellion would break out. After a period of civil war and chaos, a winner would emerge, whose success indicated that the new ruler had gained the mandate of heaven, and a new dynasty would begin.

Changes in the Dynastic Order Result in Changes in Chinese Civilization

Chinese civilization originated in the Yellow River Valley about 4,000 years ago. According to legend, the Xia (Hsia) dynasty ruled for about 500 years, from about 2000–1500 B.C. During this period the Chinese developed a written language and agriculture. By the time of the Shang dynasty (1523–1028 B.C.), most Chinese were farmers, but there were also skilled craftspeople, who produced bronze jewelry and weapons.

The Zhou (Chou) dynasty (1028–256 B.C.), the longest in Chinese history, followed the Shang. The Zhou kings ruled over a feudal system. The last four hundred years of their rule was a period of conflict and led to the development of such philosophies as Confucianism, Taoism, and Legalism. It is known as the time of Warring States and also of a Hundred Schools of Thought. Despite the turmoil, China made great strides during this time. Iron tools and the iron-tipped plow were introduced, fine bronzes were produced, irrigation canals were dug, and agriculture was improved.

The conflict was ended by Qin Shi Huang (Ch'in Shih-Huang-ti), the first emperor of China, who established the Qin (Ch'in) dynasty (221–206 B.C.), the shortest dynasty in Chinese history. The first Chinese empire was organized along Legalist lines. Qin Shi Huang required that books supporting other philosophies be destroyed. He sent hundreds of thousands of laborers to work on the Great Wall, which ran approximately 2,000 miles across northern China. The various laws of the different feudal states were replaced with imperial law; roads were built for armies to move on; canals were dug; Chinese script (writing) was made standard, and weights and measures were standardized. Forced labor and harshness led to the downfall of the dynasty.

The Great Wall of China is actually a series of walls built over many centuries.

GLOBAL
CONCEPTS

Citizenship

CONCEPTS
GLOBAL

The centralized state begun during the Qin dynasty was continued during the Han dynasty (206 B.C.–220 A.D.). The Han rulers united the Chinese people and extended both the territory and the influence of the empire into central Asia and Tibet. Parts of Korea and Vietnam came under Chinese influence as tribute states. The structure of government, which continued to exist in China until 1912, was established. China was divided into administrative units, with governors responsible to the emperor. Legalist rule was relaxed, and Confucianism became the official state philosophy. A civil service examination system was established. To serve in government, an individual had to be trained in the Confucian classics and pass a series of civil service exams based on them. Education became important, and scholars became highly respected. Major cultural achievements were made during the Han dynasty. The Chinese learned to make paper, invented a calendar, improved pottery-making, and began the production of ceramics.

The fall of the Han dynasty began another period of conflict, but China was united again by the Tang dynasty (618–907). Tang rulers expanded their control to include nearly all of modern-day China. The arts flourished. China's greatest poets lived during the Tang dynasty. Chinese Buddhists invented movable block printing about 800 years before Gutenberg in Europe. Porcelain was first made. Because of the great achievements of the Tang dynasty, it is often referred to as China's Golden Age.

GLOBAL
CONCEPTS

Technology

CONCEPTS
GLOBAL

The next great dynasty, the Song (Sung), lasted from 960 to 1279, and this period is also considered a golden age. Chinese culture and trade continued to flourish. The Chinese invented the compass, improved ceramic techniques, developed gunpowder, began the use of paper money in trade, and produced some of China's greatest landscape paintings. The Song were defeated by the Mongols in 1279, and so began the Yuan dynasty, one of only two foreign dynasties to rule China. The Mongols ruled China from 1279 to 1368. Mongol rule was established by Kublai Khan, but the size of the Mongol empire made it difficult to rule. The Mongols left Chinese officials in office in the provinces, and China was ruled through its own political institutions. However, the Chinese resented foreign rule and rebellions broke out.

GLOBAL
CONCEPTS

Political Systems

CONCEPTS
GLOBAL

The Tribute or Tributary System

The nations that participated in the tribute system recognized China as their superior, and the relationship between China and these nations was much like any one of the five reciprocal relationships of Confucius. The tribute nations brought tribute (or gifts) to the Chinese emperor once a year, and in return the emperor promised protection in case of outside attacks. The Chinese emperor was regarded as the head of a family of nations, and his subordinates owed him respect and obedience. Any nation not willing to accept subordinate (or inferior) status would have no official way of dealing with the Chinese. In the eyes of the Chinese, they would forever remain barbarians.

In 1368 the Mongols were replaced by the Ming dynasty (1368–1644). The Ming dynasty is most famous for the production of fine porcelain and for the sea voyages carried out during the Ming rule. China sent ships to South and Southeast Asia and carried out extensive trade with areas as far away as the Red Sea and East Africa. Beautiful palaces were constructed in Beijing, including the Imperial City with the residence of the emperor, the Forbidden City, at its center. The first Europeans to arrive were the Portuguese, who founded a colony at Macao in 1557.

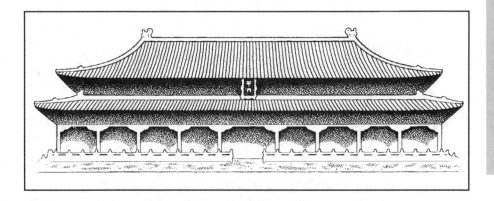

To repel Mongol invasions, the Ming called on the Manchu, a people to the northeast, for assistance. However, the Manchus conquered China and established the second foreign-ruled dynasty, the Qing (Ch'ing) (1644–1912).

The Manchus ruled an empire in which they were greatly outnumbered by the Chinese people they ruled. To facilitate their rule, they distanced themselves from the Chinese. Chinese were forbidden to emigrate to Manchuria in the northeast, Manchus and Chinese were not allowed to intermarry, and the Manchus retained their own language. Most of the key positions in government and the military were held by Manchus.

GLOBAL
CONCEPTS

Human Rights

CONCEPTS
GLOBAL

China's Relationships with the West

WORLD ISSUES

World

Trade and

Finance

Westerners became interested in opening relations with China for a number of reasons. Western missionaries wished to convert the Chinese to Christianity. Western traders were interested in obtaining Chinese silks, tea, ceramics, spices, and other luxury goods and in selling Western goods to the Chinese. In the 19th century, during the period of European imperialism, the Europeans sought to conquer Chinese territory and exploit its resources.

Chinese interest in Christianity and foreign trade was limited, however. The government, in an effort to limit foreign influence, restricted the activities of the missionaries. European trade with China was restricted to the port of Guangzhou (Canton) in 1757, and severe restrictions were placed on that trade. Foreign relations with the Chinese could only be conducted through the tributary system. The Chinese considered themselves superior to all other nations, and all non-Chinese were considered "barbarians."

The Tribute System and Trade

The Chinese applied the idea of the tribute system to trade with the Europeans. As long as trade didn't interfere with the Chinese way of life and economy, and as long as the Westerners "knew their place," the Chinese would allow trade, but they believed they controlled that trade. The Europeans sought trade, not the Chinese. The Chinese believed that they produced everything they needed, and they saw trade as a favor extended to the Europeans. They were willing to sell to the Europeans, because they could understand that Europeans would want fine Chinese products. However, they did not believe that there was anything they might want from the Europeans. They did not wish to purchase European products, and the Europeans must therefore accept all the Chinese restrictions on trade or no trade would be allowed.

The West Carves Up China in the 19th Century

The Chinese enjoyed a favorable balance of trade with the Europeans for many years. However, in opium, the Europeans finally found a product that turned the balance of trade in their favor. By 1839 the British were making enormous profits from the opium trade, and the Chinese government took steps to end the trade. British opium was confiscated and destroyed, and the British were informed they could no longer trade with China. In 1840 the British sent warships to China and the Opium War began. In 1842 the Chinese were defeated because of the superior technology of the West.

The treaty ending the war, the Treaty of Nanjing (Nanking) (1842), was the first of the unequal treaties forced upon China. The Chinese were forced to open five ports to trade; Hong Kong was ceded to the British; China was to pay a $21 million indemnity to Britain; foreign merchants were to be allowed to reside in the treaty ports; and the Chinese were not allowed to set tariffs (taxes on imports) in the treaty ports. Other nations,

WORLD ISSUES

War
and
Peace

Causes of the Opium War

Background Causes

Chinese:

1. British imported opium from India into China; addiction became a problem in China, upsetting society.
2. As demand for opium increased, silver was drained from China to pay for it, upsetting the economy and resulting in an unfavorable balance of trade.
3. Chinese law made opium trade illegal, British continued the trade.

British:

1. British resented being treated as inferiors under the tribute system.
2. Chinese put such a high tariff on British products most Chinese couldn't buy them.
3. British resented being restricted to Canton.
4. Chinese refused to import British textiles, one of Britain's most important industries.
5. Chinese law was applied to British citizens in China, and Chinese law was harsh.
6. British wanted free trade but did not want to trade through guilds or trade associations called cohongs, which was required in China.

Immediate Cause:

Chinese officials burned British opium.

including the United States, Germany, Russia, and France, quickly followed suit, and China was forced to agree to more demands. Western diplomats were allowed to live in Beijing (Peking), Christian missionaries were able to establish churches, foreign powers were granted concessions in Chinese ports, and foreigners gained the right of extraterritoriality.

Furthermore, China was carved into spheres of influence, areas of China where only one imperialist Western power was allowed to dominate, with exclusive rights to trade. In 1894 China and Japan went to war over their interests in Korea, a Chinese tributary state. The Japanese, who had instituted rapid industrialization and militarization in the 1860s to prevent Western nations from carving up Japan, defeated China. China

WORLD ISSUES

Economic
Growth and
Development

was forced to cede Taiwan and the Pescadores Islands to Japan, and Chinese influence in Korea was ended. Within a few years, Japan annexed Korea. China was being whittled away, but the Chinese, because of their lack of technological progress, were powerless to stop it. In 1899, in order to prevent its exclusion from the China trade, the United States encouraged Western nations to adopt the Open Door Policy: all nations would have equal trading rights in China and would recognize the territorial integrity of China.

Treaty of Nanjing (Nanking): The First Unequal Treaty

Britain Gained:

1. Payment for the opium
2. Control of Hong Kong
3. Freedom to trade in five cities
4. Abolition of the tariff on British goods or the right to set the tariff low
5. Extraterritoriality
6. Most-favored nation clause

China Lost:

1. The right to control the British in China
2. Control over parts of Chinese territory and the Chinese people in it
3. The right to control their own infant industries with the tariff
4. Control of trade
5. Prestige—they were defeated by the "barbarians" and couldn't compete with them

---

Chinese Response to Foreign Imperialism

Although the scholar-bureaucrats of China were resistant to change, some attempts at reform were made. The tributary system was replaced by a government office to deal with foreign representatives as diplomatic equals. Those in the government who favored reform wished to adopt Western technology without making any major changes in China's government or society. These reformers believed that the Chinese had been defeated only because of the superior armaments of the West. Western experts were employed to create and train a modern army and navy. A small effort was also made at industrialization. Coal mines were opened, arsenals and dockyards were built, and railroads and telegraph lines were constructed.

The real power in China between 1861 and 1908 was the Empress Dowager Tzu-hsi (Cixi), who ruled as regent for her son and then her nephew. In 1898 Kuang Hsu (Guang-xu) took control of the government from his aunt and issued daily edicts calling for reforms. This period was called the Hundred Days Reform. Kuang Hsu's edicts called for changes in government, in education, foreign policy, agriculture, technology, and the military. These reforms threatened the interests of Confucian scholars, government officials, Tzu-hsi, and also foreign interests in China. Tzu-hsi regained control of the government within three months and ended the reform movement. In 1900 anti-foreigner Chinese called "Boxers," with the secret support of the Empress Dowager, attacked the foreign delegations in Beijing, hoping to expel the foreigners (Westerners) from China. The Boxers were defeated by combined foreign forces after 55 days.

Overthrow of the Emperor (1911–1912)

Revolts against the Manchu Qing (Ch'ing) dynasty began in the late 1700s. However, most of the rebellions were limited and easy to suppress. One of the strongest uprisings against the Manchu was the Taiping Rebellion, which spread across southern and central China from 1850 to 1864.

GLOBAL
CONCEPTS

Change

CONCEPTS
GLOBAL

A successful rebellion against the Manchus began on October 10, 1911. The revolutionaries declared a republic and elected Sun Yat-sen as the provisional president. His program for China was known as the Three Principles of the People, and the party to carry it out was the Kuomintang, the National People's party, or the Nationalist party.

Three Principles of the People

1. Nationalism meant restoring the pride of the Chinese people and Chinese rule, and removing the foreigners, their concessions, and their spheres of influence.

2. Democracy meant popular sovereignty, but it was to be approached in three stages: first, a military government to remove the Manchu dynasty and defeat the Westerners; second, rule of the Kuomintang; and third, constitutional government, with popularly elected executive, judicial, and legislative branches called yuans.

3. Livelihood meant a program of land reform, the redistribution of land to the peasants, and the elimination of the system

of tenant farming. The government was to control transportation, communication, and heavy industry.

The Manchus turned to Yuan Shih-kai (a former general in the Manchu army) to defeat the revolution. Instead, Yuan reached an agreement with the revolutionaries and used his power to force the abdication of the Manchu emperor. In return, Sun Yat-sen resigned as president of the republic and was replaced by Yuan. Yuan became a military dictator and eliminated the democratic reforms instituted by Sun and the Kuomintang. Sun and his followers tried to overthrow him, but Sun was forced into exile. Yuan died in 1916, and Sun returned to China. However, warlords who had been building up their own power in the provinces began to struggle against each other to gain control of the country. China fell into a decade of total chaos, with warlords fighting each other.

The Nationalist Period

Sun Yat-sen died in 1925, and after a brief power struggle, Chiang Kai-shek emerged as the new leader of the Kuomintang. In 1926 Nationalist forces, led by Chiang Kai-shek, began a military campaign called the Northern Expedition to overthrow the warlords and gain control of Beijing. It was interrupted in 1927 when Chiang, fearing that the Communists in the Kuomintang were about to seize control, turned on them. Some were executed and many arrested and imprisoned. When the Communist threat had been eliminated, the expedition continued and Beijing was captured in 1928. The Nationalists were recognized as the official government of China, even though the north, west, and much of the south were still in the hands of warlords. Chiang made attempts at reform, but his major efforts were to consolidate his power over the warlords and the Communists and to prevent Japanese aggression in China.

Appeal of Marxism

Marxism appealed to many Chinese for a number of reasons. The Communists predicted the end of imperialism worldwide and called for a government made up of peasants, the proletariat, and the scholars, appealing to nearly all levels of Chinese society.

Marxism promised a program of land reform to end tenant farming. Through government ownership of the means of production and the equal distribution of wealth, poverty in the cities would be eliminated. The Russian (Bolshevik) Revolution in 1917 had overthrown a corrupt, despotic government much like their own, and it appeared that the Communist government there was making strides toward equal distribution of wealth and industrialization. Marxism promised the development of industrialization in China which would make it possible for China to compete with the West. Moreover, Marxism seemed to be the exact opposite of the old Confucian order that had kept so many people poverty-stricken and without political power. Finally the Communists had a charismatic leader, Mao Zedong.

Japanese Invasions

In 1931 the Japanese invaded the Chinese province of Manchuria. Chiang Kai-shek's forces were not powerful enough to resist those of the Japanese. The last emperor of the Qing (Ch'ing, Manchu) dynasty of China was installed as a puppet ruler, with the Japanese maintaining real control, and they began to develop iron and steel industries in Manchuria.

In July 1937 the Japanese invaded the Chinese mainland, and World War II in Asia began. Japan captured approximately the eastern third of China, but the Nationalists and their armies stubbornly held out from their new capital at Chungking.

The damage done to China during World War II was tremendous. Chinese cities were reduced to rubble, peasants' crops were destroyed, industries were destroyed, millions of Chinese were displaced, and many Chinese died. When the war ended in 1945, the Nationalists were war-weary, for they had been fighting since 1911.

WORLD ISSUES

War
and
Peace

Long March of the Communist Forces

After Chiang's purge of the Communists in 1927, Mao Zedong, one of the founders of the Chinese Communist party in 1921, escaped to southeastern China. Mao built up a following among the peasants and organized a guerrilla force called the Red Army.

In 1931, the same year Japan conquered Manchuria, Chiang decided to eliminate the Communists. Finally, in 1934 Chiang's Nationalist Army had the Communists surrounded and blockaded. Mao, however, organized his Communist followers, broke through the Nationalist lines, and began the "Long March." Approximately 100,000 Communists marched 5,000 to 6,000 miles across some of the most rugged terrain in China. Twenty thousand reached northern China in 1935.

The Communist Victory

With the Japanese attack in 1937, both the Communists and Nationalists found themselves resisting further Japanese aggression. From 1940 on, however, as the Nationalists fought the Japanese, the Communists extended their influence in

China. Mao concentrated on building up the Red Army and extending its control. In the areas of China under Communist control, economic and social reforms were introduced. Land rentals were reduced and education programs were begun.

When World War II ended, both the Nationalists and Communists tried to regain control of the areas in eastern China that had been under Japanese control.

In 1947 the Communists and Nationalists battled for control of Manchuria. After the Communists won, they began to push the Nationalists southward. In 1949 the Nationalists could no longer hold the country, and they fled to Taiwan, an island off the coast of mainland China. They established a government called the Republic of China, with Chiang Kai-shek as president, and claimed that the mainland, which they still considered part of their country, was actually in rebellion.

On October 1, 1949, the Communists established the People's Republic of China, with Mao Zedong as the chairman of the Chinese Communist party and Zhou Enlai (Chou En-lai) as premier. The capital was established at Peiping, and the city was renamed Peking.

Why the Nationalists Lost the Civil War

One of the most important reasons the Nationalists lost the war was that the Communists were supported by the peasants. When the Nationalists ruled, they did little to relieve the burden of the Chinese peasants (80 percent of the population). Mao and the Communists promised an extensive program of land reform and reduced land rents in the areas under their control.

The Communist forces did little actual fighting against the Japanese during World War II. Instead, they used the war to spread their influence throughout northern and central China. When the war ended, the Communist forces were strong, fresh, and ready. The Nationalist Army, on the other hand, was war-weary and demoralized. The Communist leaders who survived the Long March had suffered with their people and were seen as popular folk heroes. They were hardened and disciplined. Moreover, the leaders of the Communists—Mao Zedong, Chu Teh (Zhu De), and Zhou En-lai—knew how to appeal to the Chinese people, who were tired of inflation, war, and corruption and blamed Chiang and the Nationalists.

Goals of the People's Republic of China in 1949

The three major goals of the Communists in 1949 were to reestablish China's world prominence, to push economic development, and to improve life for the Chinese people. To reestablish their prominence, the Chinese had to control China ; remove the foreign imperialists. Industries owned and by foreigners were nationalized, Christianity was banned, and Christian missionaries were expelled from China. The Communists brought border areas under Chinese control that had at one time been part of the Chinese empire or tributary states. Such areas included Sinkiang (Xinjiang), Manchuria, Inner Mongolia, and Tibet (Xizang).

To achieve world prominence, the Communists realized that China must be capable of competing with the Western powers both economically and militarily. Consequently, their early economic goal was to industrialize China as rapidly as possible. They employed five-year plans, which stressed industrial production at the expense of agriculture.

To achieve their goals, the Communists had to transform Chinese society and win the loyalty of the Chinese people. To suppress Confucianism and turn the Chinese into supporters of the Communist state, the Communists were determined to replace family loyalty with loyalty to the state and party. The Communists used the education system to do this. The legal system was used to improve the position of women. New marriage laws prevented families from forcing girls to accept arranged marriages. Divorce laws gave women equal rights. Women were employed in all occupations. The Communists also undertook mass campaigns to improve health and sanitation. Rural "doctors" were trained in the combined use of traditional Chinese medicine and Western medical practices.

A thought-reform movement was established to eradicate the influence of traditional Chinese ideas and replace them with socialist ideology and the cult of Maoism. Former owners of industries, the intelligentsia, businesspeople, and others were subjected to stringent retraining sessions and indoctrinated in socialist ideology. Mao's "Red Book"—*The Thought of Mao Zedong*—became required reading in schools, in factory study sessions, peasant study sessions, and so on.

The Cultural Revolution

In the late 1950s, Mao's almost complete control of events in China was challenged for the first time. Conservative party leaders questioned Mao's revolutionary domestic and foreign policies. Mao's opponents, called reactionaries or counter-revolutionaries, were led by Liu Shaoqi (Liu Hsao Ch'i). In 1965 their differences became an actual power struggle. Because the conflict was over economic, educational, scientific, political, and social programs, it became known as the Cultural Revolution.

Mao closed the schools and sent high school and college students into the streets to rout out reactionaries. The students, who were known as Red Guards, attacked, intimidated, and humiliated Mao's opponents and anyone they suspected of being reactionary or influenced by Western ideas. They plunged China into chaos. Factories closed, industrial production fell, and transportation facilities were disrupted. Estimates of the number of people who died ran into the hundreds of thousands. The chaos eventually led to a military crackdown, and by 1969 the Cultural Revolution was over. Mao appeared to have won the struggle.

GLOBAL
CONCEPTS
Human Rights
CONCEPTS
GLOBAL

Policies Pursued Since Mao's Death

Following the Cultural Revolution, a power struggle emerged between the moderates led by Zhou Enlai, premier of the People's Republic since 1949, and the radicals, led by Jiang Qing (Chiang Ch'ing), Mao's wife.

After Mao's death in 1976, Jiang Qing and three of her strongest allies, who became known as the Gang of Four, tried to take power. However, they were arrested, charged with plotting to seize power as well as crimes against the people and the party during the Cultural Revolution. In 1980 they were tried. All four were found guilty, and Jiang was given the death penalty (which was commuted to life imprisonment in 1983). One of the purposes of the trial was to punish the Gang of Four for the way they treated members of the Chinese leadership during the Cultural Revolution. Another was to decrease the esteem in which Mao was held by the Chinese people. Deng Xiaoping, the real ruler of China since Mao's death, felt it was necessary to remove the cult of Mao to effectively carry out his policies. Mao's support for the Gang of Four was revealed during the trial, and it showed the Chinese people that Mao's policies in his old age were in error.

United States-China Relations, 1949 to the Present

In 1949 the United States refused to recognize the People's Republic of China as the legitimate government of China. Instead, it recognized the Nationalist Chinese government on Taiwan, under the leadership of Chiang Kai-shek. In 1950 the Communists seized U.S. consular buildings in China, and all direct diplomatic ties were broken off.

The Korean War broke out in June 1950 when North Korean troops invaded South Korea. UN forces were rushed to Korea to support the South Koreans. By autumn of 1950,

United Nations and South Korean forces had pushed north to the Yalu River, the boundary between North Korea and China. Fearing an invasion of Manchuria, Mao sent Chinese forces across the Yalu, and fighting raged until 1953, when an armistice was finally signed reestablishing the Korean border along the 38th parallel. United States troops fought under the UN command.

As a result of the Korean War, the United States recognized Nationalist China (Taiwan) as the legitimate government of all China and resisted all attempts to seat representatives of the Chinese Communist government in the United Nations. The Taiwan policy of the United States was considered by Mao as another humiliating blow from a Western imperialist power.

GLOBAL CONCEPTS

Change

CONCEPTS GLOBAL

In October 1971 the United States ended its objection to seating the People's Republic in the UN, arguing instead that both Chinas should be seated. However, Communist China was seated and Nationalist China was expelled from the world organization in 1971. The People's Republic of China was given the permanent seat on the UN Security Council previously held by Taiwan.

Another region in Asia that caused friction between the United States and Communist China was Vietnam. When the Communists began to make inroads in South Vietnam through the activities of guerrillas known as Viet Cong, the United States increased its military aid and sent military advisers. In 1965 the United States began to send combat forces to Vietnam. The Viet Cong were assisted and reinforced by the North Vietnamese, who in turn received aid from the former Soviet Union and Communist China. China objected strenuously to the U.S. role in Vietnam and its invasions of Cambodia and Laos.

GLOBAL CONCEPTS

Change

CONCEPTS GLOBAL

In 1971 relations between the United States and Communist China improved when an American ping-pong team was invited to China. This was the first time in over twenty years that an American group had been invited to China. In 1972 President Richard Nixon made a state trip to China, and the two nations agreed to reciprocal contact and exchange, and they also agreed to expand trade. In 1973 missions of the two nations were established, and in January 1979 full diplomatic relations were established.

Taiwan continues to be an area of discord. The United States withdrew its diplomatic representation from Taiwan when it recognized the People's Republic. However, the United States still maintains unofficial representation in Taiwan through an American Institute. Both Taiwan and China consider Taiwan a part of China. Their disagreement is over who actually should control China. In recent years, the relationship between the two countries has seen some improvement, in spite of the fact that Taiwan refuses to consider any suggestions from China concerning reunification.

Trade relations between the United States and China were expanded considerably after diplomatic recognition in the 1970s. In fact, Hong Kong, Japan, and the United States rank as China's top three trading partners. Diplomatic and trade relations between the United States and China were strained by the government's brutal crackdown on the democracy demonstra-

tors in Tiananmen Square in 1989. The United States objected to both the actual crackdown and the arrest and subsequent incarceration of thousands of young Chinese. China now enjoys most favored nation (MFN) status with the United States. However, in 1994 the Clinton administration was considering tying the renewal of that status to the question of human rights abuses in China. The United States demanded that China stop exporting goods produced by prison inmates who were used as forced labor, that an agreement of some sort be reached concerning political prisoners, and that the Chinese adhere to the UN Universal Declaration of Human Rights, among other things. Although China made only some minor concessions in these areas, President Clinton decided to renew China's MFN status. He felt that the continuation of this status would help the American economy and would ultimately improve human rights conditions in China. His actions, however, were criticized by many U.S. Congresspersons and Chinese human rights activists. There are indications China has been selling nuclear weapons technology to some Third World nations. The United States has also voiced very strong objections to these actions.

Relations Between the People's Republic and the Third World

Communist China saw itself as the example of revolutionary change for the former colonies of Western powers and also as the leader of the Third World nations. It supported Marxist revolutions in Third World nations, provided technical and financial assistance, and set up cultural exchanges with nations in Africa and Asia.

Sino-Soviet Relations

The Sino-Soviet Treaty of Friendship of 1950 seemed to indicate that a long-lasting supportive relationship between China and the Soviet Union had begun. The Soviet Union agreed to assist China against aggressive attacks and provide economic and military assistance. By 1960, however, the Soviet Union had cut off its assistance.

Reasons for the split between China and the Soviet Union included:

1. *Khrushchev's attacks on Stalin.* Mao was a great admirer of Stalin.

2. *Peaceful coexistence.* Khrushchev believed that through peaceful coexistence, the world's people would see the superiority of the Communist system, and Communism would spread worldwide. Mao believed war and revolution were necessary.

3. *Leadership.* The Soviet Union considered itself the leader of the world Communist movement. Mao disputed its claim to leadership.

4. *Soviet support for India.* In 1962, when Indian and Chinese forces clashed over territory, the Soviet Union assisted India.

5. *Border disputes.* The Soviets held territory in Central Asia and northeastern China that China claims. There have been occasional outbreaks of fighting between troops stationed on the borders.

6. *Afghanistan.* China objected to the Soviet invasion in 1979.

Mikhail Gorbachev's trip to China in May 1989 was intended to normalize relations, but his visit was upstaged by the student rebellion in Tiananmen Square.

China's New Status in the Pacific

Chinese diplomatic relations with Japan were reestablished following President Nixon's trip to China in 1972. Since then, the two countries have signed trade agreements, and Japan has become one of China's largest trading partners. Japan imports China's agricultural products and petroleum, and China imports Japanese machinery and technology. Japan has given China millions of dollars in loans for development.

GLOBAL
CONCEPTS
Interdependence
CONCEPTS
GLOBAL

In 1984 Great Britain and China reached an agreement to return the island of Hong Kong to Chinese control in 1997. Hong Kong's economy will continue to be based on private enterprise for at least fifty years, until 2047. Its social and legal systems will remain, and it will be allowed a great deal of control over its own affairs. China will be in charge of defense and foreign affairs.

China After Tiananmen

GLOBAL
CONCEPTS
Human Rights
CONCEPTS
GLOBAL

In the aftermath of the pro-democracy movement and the military crackdown in 1989, the Chinese government reverted to many policies that seemed to be a reminder of the more authoritarian times of Mao. There were more restrictions on the press, there were political study sessions for workers, films and music were banned, and so on. But these restrictions seem to be loosening again. It appears that the economic changes that the government deems necessary to maintain growth and prosperity cannot be achieved under the social and political restrictions that the hard-liners would like to impose.

REVIEW QUESTIONS

Multiple Choice. Select the letter of the answer that correctly completes each statement.

1. The unequal treaties were the result of a war fought against
   A. Japan
   B. Britain
   C. Russia
   D. Vietnam

2. Which of the following required a high degree of knowledge and education?
   A. the tribute system
   B. the civil service
   C. the foreign service
   D. the military

3. The Chinese considered foreigners to be barbarians. This attitude was an example of
   A. ethnocentrism
   B. cultural diffusion
   C. empathy
   D. interdependence

4. During the 19th century, Western nations were able to gain control over parts of China mainly because
   A. the Chinese had a strong tradition of nonviolence
   B. China lacked the military technology needed to stop these ventures
   C. China was promised aid for its industries
   D. the Chinese lacked a strong cultural identity

5. During the Communist Revolution in China, many farmers supported the Communists because they promised
   A. land reform
   B. a peace treaty with Japan
   C. a federal republic
   D. aid from the industrial nations

6. After gaining control of the Kuomintang (Nationalist party), Chiang Kai-shek's most important goal in the 1920s was
   A. land reform to assist the peasants
   B. destruction of the Communists
   C. the invasion of Korea
   D. assisting Ho Chi Minh in overthrowing the French

7. Hong Kong
   A. is a British Crown Colony
   B. will be returned to the Chinese in 1997
   C. has an economy based on agriculture
   D. was won by the Japanese in the Sino-Japanese War

8. The Communist victory in the Chinese Civil War was a result of all the following except
   A. the inability of the Nationalists to stabilize the economy
   B. the lack of U.S. aid to the Communists
   C. peasant dissatisfaction with the Nationalist regime
   D. the effective use of propaganda and guerrilla warfare by the Communists

9. A study of the history of China would reveal that
   A. there has always been strong central government in China
   B. until modern times a single dynasty ruled China
   C. periods of strong central government alternated with periods of internal disturbance, foreign invasion, and government corruption
   D. foreigners ruled China for far longer periods than native Chinese

10. During the early 1800s the relationship between China and the Western nations was strained because
   A. the Western nations did not wish to purchase Chinese goods
   B. China insisted it be dealt with through the tribute system
   C. the Western nations wished to purchase opium and the Chinese refused
   D. China wished to buy Western armaments and other manufactured goods and was rebuffed

11. A country with an unfavorable balance of trade
   A. exports goods of greater value than it imports
   B. imports goods of greater value than it exports
   C. exports natural resources and imports manufactured goods
   D. imports manufactured goods and exports textiles

12. The very existence of the Yuan dynasty supports the fact that China's least effective geographic barrier was the
   A. Himalayan Mountains
   B. Great Wall
   C. Gobi Desert
   D. Tien Shan Mountains

13. Which form of government is most likely to suppress human rights?
   A. constitutional monarchy
   B. democratic republic
   C. parliamentary system
   D. totalitarian regime

14. The ethnocentric attitude of the Chinese
    A. resulted in a reluctance to adopt aspects of other cultures
    B. led to periods of internal strife during famine
    C. prevented the Chinese from expanding their territory
    D. caused student rebellions in the 1980s

15. China's earliest civilizations originated in the
    A. Tibetan Plateau
    B. region of Xinjiang
    C. Huanghe River Valley
    D. Canton delta region

16. The 19th century was China's Age of Humiliation for all the following
    reasons *except*
    A. China was conquered by the Mongols
    B. the unequal treaties
    C. China's defeat in the Opium War
    D. the granting of spheres of influence to Western nations

17. In the late 1880s Confucian scholars resisted government reform and
    economic change because
    A. the Empress Dowager wished to hand the reins of government to the
       peasants
    B. they feared it would erode their own political influence
    C. the Russians threatened to withdraw financial aid if the changes took
       place
    D. Japan had agreed to help them maintain an isolationist policy

18. During the Manchu dynasty in China the tribute or tributary system
    A. required foreigners to bring gifts to the Chinese emperor and
       recognize China's superiority
    B. was used to build irrigation systems in the North China Plain
    C. allowed the Chinese to assimilate the culture of the Manchus
    D. granted extraterritorial rights to the European traders in Hong Kong

19. Sun Yat-sen's Three Principles of the People were designed to do all the
    following *except*
    A. rid China of foreign influence
    B. establish democratic government
    C. break up large estates and provide peasants with land
    D. bring all industry and mining under government monopoly

20. The Tang dynasty was known as a Golden Age because of achievements in all the following areas *except*
    A. poetry
    B. porcelain
    C. printing
    D. armaments

ESSAYS

1. Select any three of the following leaders and discuss how each one played an important role in China's history in this century.

   Sun Yat-sen
   Chiang Kai-shek
   Mao Zedong
   Zhou Enlai
   Deng Xiaoping

2. Many events have had profound significance in China's history. Among these have been the following:

   Opium War (1840s)
   Taiping Rebellion (1864)
   Civil War (1927–1949)
   Cultural Revolution (1966–1970)
   Tiananmen Square Massacre (1989)

   Select any three of these and do the following for each one:

   A. Explain one reason why it occurred.
   B. Explain one result of this event for China.

I. PHYSICAL GEOGRAPHY OF JAPAN

Location and Size

GLOBAL
CONCEPTS

Identity

CONCEPTS
GLOBAL

Japan is a chain of islands (archipelago) lying off the east coast of the Asian mainland in the northern Pacific Ocean, separated from the mainland by the Sea of Japan and the Korean Strait. Because it has no land borders with the rest of Asia, Japan has been able to maintain its insular (separate) quality, develop a sense of identity, and borrow selectively from the cultures of

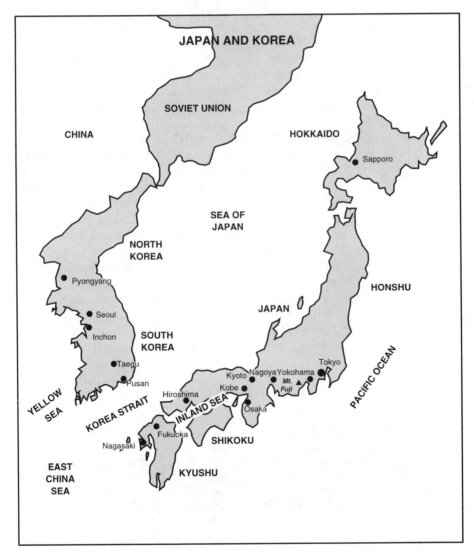

155

the nations near it. Through the processes of cultural borrowing, adaptation, and assimilation, Japan has created a uniquely Japanese society. Korea (a "land bridge" to Japan) served as a cultural bridge between Japan and China.

Japan's land area is approximately 143,000 square miles, and it has a coastline of over 16,000 miles, with many excellent harbors. The four main islands of Japan are Hokkaido, Honshu, Shikoku, and Kyushu. Hokkaido, the northernmost and second largest of the islands, has a difficult terrain, a somewhat severe winter climate, and the smallest population. Hokkaido is Japan's frontier. Honshu, the largest island, contains 60 percent of Japan's total land area and the vast majority of Japan's 123 million people. Most of Japan's best farmland, its major cities, and its industry are located here. The island of Kyushu is second in importance to Honshu. Across the Inland Sea lies Shikoku. These three southern islands were the region where Japanese civilization developed. Japan also contains some 3,400 smaller islands, many of which are uninhabited.

Topography, Climate, and Resources

GLOBAL
CONCEPTS

Environment

CONCEPTS
GLOBAL

Because 85 percent of the total land area of Japan is mountainous, only 11 percent of the land is arable. The highest mountain, Mount Fuji, or Fujiyama (over 12,000 feet), is an extinct volcano, conical in shape and snow-covered year round. To overcome the shortage of arable land, the Japanese have practiced intensive agriculture for generations—reclaiming land from the sea, terracing hillsides, building irrigation canal systems, and employing human labor to make the best possible use of the land.

Japan has only a few small areas of plains squeezed between the seacoast and the foothills of the mountains. The most important plains region is the Kanto, which is located on the island of Honshu in the region of Tokyo-Yokohama.

Japan has many rivers. They are of very limited use in navigation, but they do provide a source of hydroelectric power and irrigation.

The most important factors in determining the climate of Japan are its island location (ocean currents), latitude, nearness to the Asian continent, and elevation. The climate is similar to that of the United States along the Atlantic Coast, as it lies in much the same latitude zone, and the Japanese enjoy four seasons. The northern Japan summers are warm, and winters long, snowy, and cold. Most of the rest of Japan enjoys a mild winter with little or no snow. Summers, with the exception of the subtropical southeast, are generally warm, with adequate rainfall. In fact, nearly all of Japan receives at least 40 inches of rain per year.

Japan lies at the northern edge of monsoon Asia. In summer the moist, cool winds bring rains to the southeastern coasts of Japan. The winter monsoon drops heavy snowfall on the northwestern slopes of Honshu and Hokkaido. September and October in Japan can be a dangerous time as it is the season of typhoons (tropical wind storms much like hurricanes). Typhoons can cause severe damage to buildings, crops, and people and very often result in flooding and tidal waves, which do even more damage.

GLOBAL
CONCEPTS

Scarcity

CONCEPTS
GLOBAL

Japan's resource base, like its arable land, is severely limited. Deposits of iron ore and petroleum are limited. Deposits of coal are extensive, but the coal is low grade. The Japanese must import the raw materials needed for industrial production.

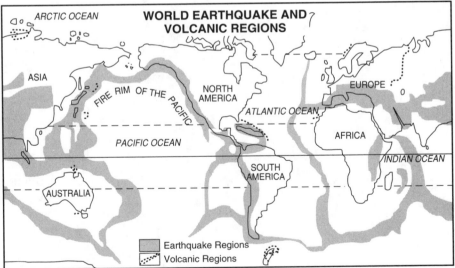

Japan is located in a volcano and earthquake-prone area known as the "Fire Rim of the Pacific."

Japan lies in what is often referred to as the fire rim of the Pacific, or the ring of fire, an earthquake and volcano zone. More than half the world's active volcanoes lie in this zone. Most of Japan's volcanoes are inactive, though there is an occasional eruption. Earthquakes occur much more frequently. An average of four earthquakes a day strike Japan. Most are slight tremors, but every few years a major quake occurs.

The sea plays an enormous role in the lives of the Japanese. They depend on it as a source of livelihood, food, transportation, and in recent years, commerce. For many years the sea also served as an effective barrier to invasion by other countries.

Multiple Choice. Select the letter of the answer that correctly completes
each statement.

1. Which statement best characterizes Japan?
   A. part of the Asian mainland
   B. the longest archipelago in the world
   C. an island nation
   D. flat topography

2. Which part of Japan is larger than the other three?
   A. Kyushu
   B. Honshu
   C. Shikoku
   D. Hokkaido

3. The most important plains region in Japan is the
   A. Kyushu plain
   B. Kanto plain
   C. Great plain
   D. Shikari plain

4. The Japanese must use their land carefully and wisely because
   A. very little is arable
   B. most of it is desert
   C. the topography is uneven
   D. much flooding occurs

5. Which Japanese industry would be most severely affected by a
   maritime disaster such as a typhoon?
   A. coal mining
   B. electronics
   C. cameras
   D. fishing

6. A nation like Japan, consisting of a chain of islands, is
   A. a peninsula
   B. an isthmus
   C. an archipelago
   D. a promontory

7. The most important geographic influence of the cultural development of Japan was
   A. the mountainous nature of the islands
   B. the shortness of the rivers
   C. the frequent occurrence of flood and drought
   D. its location in relation to the Asian mainland

8. The best description of Japan's climate is
   A. tropical
   B. desert
   C. variable
   D. polar

9. Which of the following types of natural disasters is *not* common in Japan?
   A. earthquake
   B. typhoon
   C. drought
   D. flood

10. Which phrase would best describe the resource base of Japan?
    A. adequate for heavy industry
    B. much like that of the U.S.
    C. severely limited
    D. equal to that of China

ESSAYS

1. Japan has been greatly influenced by its geography. Discuss three ways in which Japanese cultural, economic, political, or social development has been affected by Japan's geography.

2. Japan has a severe shortage of arable land. Describe three things the Japanese have done in an effort to overcome this shortage.

II. ECONOMIC GEOGRAPHY OF JAPAN

Economic Recovery after World War II

At the close of World War II, Japan lay in ruins. More than 3 million people had been killed; 10 million were homeless. One fourth of Japan's industry and manufacturing facilities had been destroyed. Communications and transportation lines had been badly damaged. Nearly the whole maritime fleet had been destroyed, and harbor and port facilities were in ruins. The Japanese empire had been reduced to the four main islands, and as a result it had lost its source of raw materials.

The leaders of the occupation (see the part of Section IV on the United States occupation of Japan, 1945–1952) realized that to build a democratic nation, there would also have to be

WORLD ISSUES

Economic
Growth and
Development

economic reform. A program of land reform to increase food production by providing greater incentives to farmers, who now owned the land, was the most successful and long-lasting program. A second step in economic reform was to destroy the zaibatsu (monopolies). However, since the financial resources of the zaibatsu could help rebuild Japan, the effort to break them up was eventually dropped. The zaibatsu still exist in Japan today (for example, Mitsui, Mitsubishi, Fuji, Sumitomo). A third effort at economic reform was to organize and encourage the organization of labor unions.

Characteristics of the Japanese Economy

There has been tremendous growth in the Japanese economy since 1950. Today its GDP is over $2,300 billion, second only to the United States. Per capita income in 1991 was over $19,000, and the unemployment rate is less than 3 percent. (GDP, Gross Domestic Product, is the dollar amount of all goods and services in a nation in a given year.)

Japan's unemployment rate is likely to rise in the near future, unless steps are taken to improve economic conditions in the nation. Japan has been in a recession since 1992. Efforts by major Japanese companies to maintain their policy of lifetime employment may eventually give way to the necessity to cut back costs so that some industries survive. If this occurs, some employees will have to be laid off, and the unemployment rate will rise. There are two reasons the rate has not already risen in Japan: companies have not been replacing retiring workers, and they have been moving managerial workers into blue-collar jobs. Because of the recession, it is probably inevitable that many more young people will face unemployment in Japan in the near future. College graduates will find themselves competing for fewer and fewer job openings.

Japan is the world's leading shipbuilding nation. It is a leader in producing textiles, cameras, microscopes, and electronic goods. By the 1980s it had become one of the leading producers of cars and trucks. It exports steel and machinery. It is second only to the United States in the manufacture of computers. In 1992 its trade surplus was over $100 billion.

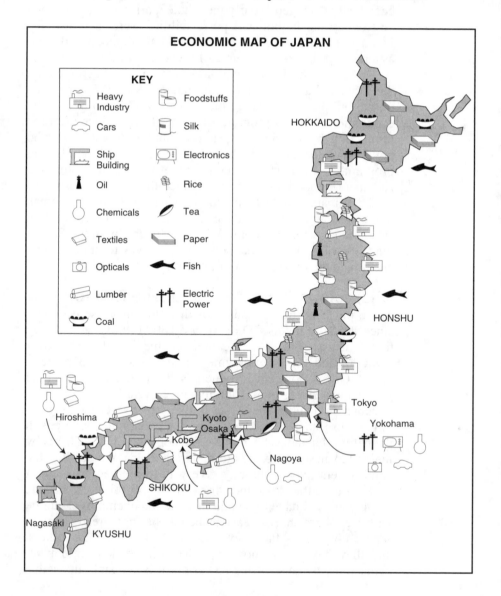

ECONOMIC MAP OF JAPAN

KEY

- Heavy Industry
- Cars
- Ship Building
- Oil
- Chemicals
- Textiles
- Opticals
- Lumber
- Coal
- Foodstuffs
- Silk
- Electronics
- Rice
- Tea
- Paper
- Fish
- Electric Power

HOKKAIDO
HONSHU
Hiroshima
Kyoto
Osaka
Kobe
Tokyo
Yokohama
Nagoya
SHIKOKU
Nagasaki
KYUSHU

How did the Japanese make such incredible economic gains after the almost total destruction of World War II?

Japan's economic recovery was aided by:

1. *Its people.* The Japanese people were disciplined and hard-working. The labor force was highly skilled, receptive to on-the-job training, and well educated. For many years they accepted low wages, which gave Japanese industry a competitive edge in the world market.

GLOBAL CONCEPTS

Technology

CONCEPTS GLOBAL

2. *Technology.* When industry was rebuilt after World War II, the latest in technology was used. This allowed the Japanese to use more efficient methods than countries with older factories and gave it a competitive edge.

3. *U.S. assistance.* The United States provided Japan with millions of dollars of aid, assistance, and loans to rebuild its economy because it wanted a strong democratic ally in Asia.

4. *Restrictions on the military.* Japan does not have the enormous cost of maintaining military forces. Instead, the United States is committed to defending Japan. Japan spends less than 1 percent of its GDP on the military, while the United States spends nearly 6 percent.

5. *Government assistance.* Business in Japan is assisted by the government through low-interest loans, subsidies for new businesses, favorable trade agreements with other nations, and tariffs to protect Japanese industries.

Japan Must Import to Live			
Wool	100%	Wheat	91.7%
Cotton	100%	Sugar	86%
Crude Oil	99.7%	Coal	65%
Iron Ore	99.3%	Lumber	47%
Soy Beans	96.4%		

Continuing Needs and Problems Facing the Japanese Economy

Japan's scarcity of raw materials and oil has affected its pattern of economic development. Japan must import almost all the minerals it needs for industry, such as copper, iron ore, lead, coal, and zinc, and all its petroleum. Until the 1970s most petroleum came from the Middle East. When OPEC embargoed oil in 1973, Japanese industry suffered from energy shortages and unemployment rose. Since then, the Japanese have found a

GLOBAL CONCEPTS

Scarcity

CONCEPTS GLOBAL

new source of oil in China, although they are still highly dependent on Middle Eastern oil. Japan's economic life depends on its ability to import raw materials and its capacity to maintain and expand its exports to pay for those raw materials.

Although arable land in Japan is scarce, by making use of the advanced farming technology of the Green Revolution, Japanese farmers provide about 70 percent of the nation's food supply. Most of the rest comes from the United States, China, Australia, and Canada.

United States-Japanese Economic Interactions

GLOBAL
CONCEPTS

Interdependence

CONCEPTS
GLOBAL

Since the 1970s the balance of trade between the United States and Japan has run heavily in favor of Japan. The United States buys about 33 percent of Japanese exports. The United States feels that the Japanese government's restrictions on the import of foreign goods is largely responsible and that Japanese tariffs keep U.S. goods from selling in Japan. Japanese investments are welcomed in the United States, but the Japanese government restricts foreign investments in Japan. The U.S. government has accused Japan of employing unfair trade practices.

Japan needs to maintain its high level of exports to pay for imported raw materials, and the United States needs to increase its exports to Japan to decrease its trade deficit. Consequently, the United States has asked Japan to voluntarily decrease some exports to the United States, to open their markets to more American goods, and to allow American companies to operate in Japan on an equal basis with Japanese companies. The United States has threatened to increase tariffs and place import quotas on Japanese goods unless Japan ends its unfair trade practices. Japan has promised to increase its defense spending, relax trade barriers, and export less. Some concessions have been made, but American policy makers continue to demand further concessions. In 1992 Japan agreed to concessions in the areas of paper, computers, auto sales and parts, and so on. In 1993 they agreed to open construction contracts to American bidding. Since then, Japanese prime ministers have been expected to attempt to improve trade relations, but they have found themselves pressured by entrenched financial interests in Japan. Most Japanese in a position to influence government decisions do not really wish to allow Americans free access to the Japanese market, and American businesspeople and politicians will continue to demand that Japanese markets be more open to foreign competition.

WORLD ISSUES

World
Trade and
Finance

Japan's Role in the Global Economic Picture

While Japan may be dependent on other countries for resources, its economic strength gives it power in international relations. While it has not played an international political role consistent with its economic strength, its influence has been felt through its trade policies. Beginning in the 1980s Japan has participated in a series of economic summits with the world's leading non-Communist economic powers. The Japanese have promised to increase foreign access to Japan's domestic markets at these economic summits, but so far no major changes have been made. Also in recent years, there has been a large increase in Japanese economic investment in the United States.

REVIEW QUESTIONS

Multiple Choice. Select the letter of the answer that correctly completes each statement.

1. Japan has overcome its shortage of mineral resources by relying on
   A. Shinto spirits
   B. allies
   C. imports
   D. the United Nations

2. The word yen refers to
   A. transistors
   B. money
   C. sushi
   D. architecture

3. Japan is considered an "economic giant" for all the following reasons *except*
   A. most of its labor force is engaged in agriculture
   B. Japan makes use of scientific management and innovation
   C. Japan has one of the highest GDPs in the world
   D. most of its labor force is engaged in industrial production

4. Japanese-American interdependence is characterized most by
   A. America's wish for Japan's goods and Japan's need for American markets
   B. America's need for foreign investment and Japan's need for American surplus goods
   C. America's dependence on agricultural imports and Japan's need for electronics
   D. America's need for nuclear arms and Japan's ability to supply material for that need

5. Japan's economic recovery after World War II was due to all of the following *except*
   A. the Japanese people were willing to sacrifice for Japan's recovery
   B. the latest technology was used to replace factories destroyed during World War II
   C. the Soviet Union provided assistance in an effort to build a strong Asian ally
   D. the Japanese Government created trade barriers to protect Japanese industries

6. Japanese farmers today
   A. are very efficient
   B. are mainly subsistence farmers
   C. are mostly tenant farmers
   D. use no artificial fertilizers

7. Japanese tariffs
   A. are considered unfair trade barriers by many of its trading partners
   B. are the only reason Japan has had such economic success since World War II
   C. have protected Japanese defense industries from competition
   D. have made Japan the largest producer of petroleum products in the world today

8. The zaibatsu in Japan
   A. were ancient warriors
   B. are industrial monopolies
   C. were emperors
   D. were labor unions

9. Japan is a leading producer of all the following *except*
   A. cars
   B. electronics
   C. oil
   D. ships

10. All the following were part of the U.S. occupation reforms *except*
    A. land reform
    B. creation of labor unions
    C. discouraging the zaibatsu
    D. rearming the military

ESSAYS

1. The following statements are about Japan's economy.

   A. Japan is more of a producer of finished goods than a supplier of raw materials.
   B. Japan is considered the Great Britain of the Orient.
   C. Japan's GDP has grown enormously since World War II.
   D. Japan must import in order to survive.
   E. Government economic policies in Japan have placed a strain on its relationships with other nations.

Choose any three of these statements. For each one, describe at least two specific facts that prove the validity of the statement.

2. Japan's economic recovery after World War II is one of the most incredible success stories every told.

   List three of the major reasons for Japan's success. For each reason listed, explain specifically its contribution.

III. HUMAN AND CULTURAL GEOGRAPHY OF JAPAN

The Japanese People

The early inhabitants of Japan migrated from northern Asia, Korea, China, and Southeast Asia over hundreds of years. These peoples gradually intermingled and intermarried and became the Japanese people we know today. The Japanese people are ethnically homogeneous (alike), and the only really distinct group of people who remained were the Ainu (the original inhabitants of Japan), who were pushed northward to the island of Hokkaido by the people we call Japanese.

GLOBAL
CONCEPTS

Identity

CONCEPTS
GLOBAL

The Japanese tend to think of themselves as a racially pure people. As a result, they seldom accept foreigners as full members of their society. Japan's strong sense of cultural unity is a result of Japan's relative isolation from foreign influence for many centuries and its cultural homogeneity for at least 1,000 years.

Shinto, the "Way of the Gods"

GLOBAL
CONCEPTS

Culture

CONCEPTS
GLOBAL

Shinto, the native religion of Japan, began as a simple form of nature worship. The Shintoist believed that all natural things—trees, rocks, storms, ocean waves—contained *kami* (the spirits of the gods). Later on, Shinto came to include hero, ancestor, and emperor worship.

Shinto teaches no moral precepts, no ethical code. It teaches that the Japanese should be thankful for and reverent to all aspects of nature; grateful for life, birth, fertility. Shinto teaches that physical purity, not moral, is of the utmost importance. Shinto therefore is an example of a type of religion called animism.

Because Shinto has no concept of a single god and no moral precepts, it has been relatively easy for the Japanese to accept other religious teachings. Buddhism and Shinto have existed side by side for over 1,000 years.

Buddhism

Buddhism was introduced from Korea in 552 A.D. At first, it was popular only among the nobility and upper classes. Buddhist teachings were too complicated and its outlook too pessimistic to appeal to the common people. During the Kamakura period, Buddhism in Japan underwent basic changes, however, and its teachings were made easier to understand and accept.

Consequently, Buddhism began to be accepted by the lower classes, who combined Shinto and Buddhism. Happy events such as birth and marriage were observed with Shinto ceremonies and funerals with Buddhist rites.

One of the Buddhist sects, which became especially popular with the samurai (warriors), is Zen. Zen teaches that each person must seek enlightenment individually through meditation and that no others can help an individual achieve enlightenment. The meditation requires great self-discipline and the ability to conquer oneself. The self-discipline learned in Zen was later applied to the code of the warrior, Bushido. The simplicity taught by Zen is revealed in Japanese painting, poetry, and the tea ceremony.

Chinese Influence

The first contacts between the Japanese and Chinese took place through Korea. Chinese civilization was much more advanced

GLOBAL
CONCEPTS

Change

CONCEPTS
GLOBAL

GLOBAL
CONCEPTS

Political Systems

CONCEPTS
GLOBAL

GLOBAL
CONCEPTS

Culture

CONCEPTS
GLOBAL

than that of the Japanese, and some powerful Japanese determined that elements of Chinese civilization should be introduced in Japan. By the 10th century, Japan had been transformed, but it was not just an imitation of China. Chinese culture was adapted to suit Japanese needs.

During the rule of Prince Shotoku in the late 6th and early 7th centuries, Japanese students were sent to China to study religion, philosophy, art, architecture, and government administration. The greatest flowering of Chinese culture in Japan occurred during the Nara period (710–794). The Yamato rulers established a central government based on that of the Chinese, and officials were appointed to govern administrative units, but no civil service was established. Japanese officials were chosen, instead, because of their connections and families. The Chinese emperor ruled by the mandate of heaven, but the Japanese emperor held the throne because he was considered divine.

The traditional Japanese family was much like the traditional Chinese family. The Japanese had been strongly influenced by Confucianism from China. The ideal family in Japan was the extended patriarchal and patrilineal family. The eldest male was the head of the household, and was legally responsible for every member of the household. Women and the young were subordinate, and marriages were arranged. Filial piety determined relationships within the family.

The family was the basic social and economic unit, and the individual existed only as a member of this socially accepted group. Children were officially registered with the local authorities, and a family could disown a member by removing his or her name from the register. If this happened, the person was no longer socially accepted, and they might just as well be dead. Everything an individual did was supposed to be considered in light of how it would reflect on the family.

The Chinese writing system was adopted, but it presented problems, so the Japanese eventually developed a writing system of their own based on the Chinese. It is a mixture of Chinese characters for words and symbols that stand for sounds. The phonetic (for sound) symbols are called kana; there are fifty of them.

In 708 the Japanese built their first permanent capital city, Nara, modeled after the Chinese capital. Later in the 8th century, a new capital city was built at Heian (now Kyoto), which remained the imperial capital until 1868.

During the Heian period (794–1185), contact with China was decreased. Japan stopped sending students and envoys to China to study. They believed that they had advanced to the point where they could develop their own arts and culture without Chinese influence. Japanese art and literature blossomed. The world's first novel, *The Tale of Genji,* describing Heian court life, was written by Lady Murasaki about 1000 A.D. Painting, sculpture, poetry, architecture, and landscape gardening flourished. The literacy rate increased considerably. During their long period of isolation, the Japanese developed a strong feeling of their own uniqueness.

Cultural Developments During the Feudal Period

Zen Buddhism was introduced to Japan at about the same time the first shogunate was established. Zen influenced the development of chanoyu (tea ceremony), ikebana (flower arranging), and landscape gardening. Literature and poetry flourished. Haiku poetry was developed and refined during shogunal rule. Japanese Noh drama, Bunraku (puppet plays), and Kabuki drama developed. Landscape painting achieved remarkable refinement. Japanese arts reflected cultural refinement (haiku, landscape painting, tea ceremony). Their art also reflected the times, with drama often depicting their present way of life as well as the conflict of the changing times.

Population Characteristics of Japan Today

Japan's population in 1992 was estimated at about 124 million. The country itself is slightly smaller than California.

Haiku is the simplest form of poetry. It consists of one verse with seventeen syllables, spaced over three lines in a 5-7-5 pattern. A good haiku sets a mood, then flashes a sudden understanding of life—all in three lines.

The Pond
The ancient pond
A frog leaps in
The sound of water

BASHO

Mist
Above the veil
of mist, from time to time
there lifts a sail . . .

GAKOKU

A Remembrance
Show that we two
looked at together—this yew
Is it fallen anew?

BASHO

The Crow
On a leafless branch
a crow has settled:
autumn nightfall.

BASHO

WORLD ISSUES

Population

With a population density of about 850 people per square mile, Japan is one of the most crowded nations in the world, and living space for urban Japanese is incredibly limited. About 97 percent of the Japanese people are employed in manufacturing, mining, and service industries. Approximately another 3 percent are engaged in agriculture. The birth rate has decreased in recent years, but because of improved health care and increased life expectancy, the population continues to grow slowly. By the year 2030, Japan's population is expected to stabilize, or cease to grow.

The Japanese population is one of the most homogeneous in the world. Over 99 percent of the people are ethnic Japanese. The largest minority group are the Koreans. Only one major language, Japanese, is spoken in the country, and over 80 percent of the people belong to the same religious grouping—a blend of Shinto and Buddhism.

Education System

The importance of education in Japan is unmatched in any other country. Entrance to the top-ranking universities is highly competitive. Only one of six applicants is accepted. As a result, the pressure on a Japanese student to achieve is incredible.

Education is compulsory through junior high school. Entrance exams must be passed to enter high school and university. Some of the better schools even have entrance exams for kindergarten. Since good jobs and the right education are so closely linked, the competition in schools is fierce.

The school day, the school week, and the school year are longer in Japan than in the United States. Discipline is strict, and all the students are expected to study a foreign language. Most students receive outside tutoring and/or attend "cram" schools, even during vacations. Teachers are considered responsible for students' behavior both inside and outside the school.

Urban Issues and Problems

WORLD ISSUES

Environmental
Concerns

Many of Japan's cities are clustered together in a megalopolis (one city blends into the edges of another). Because of the size of Japan's urban areas and its industries, Japan has one of the highest rates of pollution in the world. Smog is a serious problem. Rivers and coastal waters are being polluted by industrial wastes. The increasing use of insecticides and chemical fertilizers by farmers adds to the pollution problem.

Japan's cities are terribly overcrowded. There is a severe housing shortage. Transportation, while among the best in the world, is inadequate to meet the needs of the enormous urban populations.

Evolving Role of Women

Since the end of World War II, the roles and status of women have changed. Much of this is due to the constitution, which gave women equal rights. They were allowed to vote, to own property, to hold political office, and to seek divorce. They must receive an education, and more and more of them go on to receive a university education. Nearly 40 percent of the Japanese work force is female, though the majority of them have low-status, service-oriented jobs. Many of them earn less money than men doing the same job. The man's authority as head of the family has decreased somewhat. In addition, about six of ten working women are married. They share not only economic responsibility but authority as well. Arranged marriages are still common, however.

Treatment of Minorities

There are only a few non-Japanese people in the country. About 12,000 Ainu, the original inhabitants of Japan, live on the northern island of Hokkaido. Most of them have been integrated into rural life on Hokkaido.

GLOBAL
CONCEPTS

Human Rights

CONCEPTS
GLOBAL

The second major group of non-Japanese people are the Koreans, most of whom came during World War II to work in wartime industries. Koreans are discriminated against in employment, housing, and social life. They were not allowed to become Japanese citizens until 1985.

A third minority group are the burakumin people, descendants of people who did jobs considered unclean by the Japanese, such as butchering. They used to live separately in small villages and were considered outcasts. Today they live in segregated slums in the cities and are discriminated against in housing, employment, education, and social life. There may be as many as 3 million burakumin.

Social and Work Relations

The Japanese share an intense loyalty to groups, such as the family or the company. Group loyalty means putting the interests of the group before one's own interests, being willing to accept the decisions of the group, and avoiding situations that might shame the group. This loyalty concept extends to the workplace. Employers provide many benefits to their employees and expect loyal service in return. Japanese employees take great pride in their company and do not change jobs often because it would be disloyal to the company.

GLOBAL
CONCEPTS

Identity

CONCEPTS
GLOBAL

GLOBAL
CONCEPTS
Culture
CONCEPTS
GLOBAL

The Japanese do not like emotional confrontations and blunt speech, which might hurt feelings or cause one to lose "face" (pride). They reach decisions in business as they do in government, by consensus; they negotiate until everyone agrees on a decision. Consensus may take a long time, but for the Japanese it means that everyone is satisfied with a decision.

GLOBAL
CONCEPTS
Environment
CONCEPTS
GLOBAL

Most probably the great emphasis on conformity grew out of the problem of accommodating too many people on too little land. People had to learn to cooperate and restrain themselves because the Japanese have had to live uncomfortably close to each other physically. Only harmony in human relationships would make such close physical proximity bearable.

Impact of Japan's Aesthetic Ideas

GLOBAL
CONCEPTS
Identity
CONCEPTS
GLOBAL

The Japanese still maintain their identity through traditional values and activities. They have a strong love of nature, which is expressed in activities such as hiking and skiing and in landscape gardens and flower arranging. The Japanese still use haiku as a creative medium. Millions of Japanese write haiku, and there are national poetry contests each year. Most Japanese are skilled in at least one of the traditional arts: music, dance, drama, painting, calligraphy.

REVIEW QUESTIONS

Multiple Choice. Select the letter of the answer that correctly completes each statement.

1. The most populated part of Japan is
   A. Honshu
   B. Kyushu
   C. Hokkaido
   D. Shikoku

2. Even though Japan has few natural resources, it has a high standard of living mainly because it has
   A. developed technology that can be exchanged for the resources it needs
   B. printed more money whenever living standards have started to decline
   C. imported manufactured goods
   D. produced goods and services without obtaining resources

3. Which statement best describes Japan today?
   A. Japan has become an urban society that has adopted Western values in nearly every aspect of life.
   B. Japan has continued to rely on China and Korea for its cultural values and technological development.
   C. Japan has remained primarily an agrarian society with an emphasis on maintaining traditional values.
   D. Japan has adopted modern technological advances while maintaining aspects of the traditional culture.

4. Birth and marriage ceremonies are celebrated with rituals associated with
   A. Zen
   B. Bushido
   C. Shintoism
   D. Buddhism

5. Nara, Kyoto, and Tokyo are cities that have all been
   A. centers of heavy industry
   B. conquered by the Chinese
   C. capitals of Japan
   D. populated by the Ainu

6. Haiku is a form of
   A. painting
   B. poetry
   C. furniture
   D. architecture

7. An example of the type of religion called animism is
   A. Judaism
   B. Christianity
   C. Shinto
   D. Islam

8. As a result of cultural diffusion, many aspects of Japanese culture were adapted from the Chinese. An example of this is
   A. the Japanese writing system
   B. Shinto
   C. the tea ceremony
   D. ikebana

9. Which of the following statements about the people of Japan is *not* true?
   A. The people of Japan are ethnically homogeneous.
   B. Most Japanese practice a mixture of Shinto and other religions.
   C. Most Japanese are not well educated.
   D. Japanese people feel strong group loyalties.

10. Which of the following is *not* associated with Zen?
    A. ikebana
    B. landscape gardening
    C. the tea ceremony
    D. zaibatsu

11. Buddhism in Japan is an example of
    A. imperialism
    B. cultural diffusion
    C. isolationism
    D. nativism

12. The strongest example of Chinese influence in Japan can be seen in
    A. Bushido
    B. Shinto
    C. Noh drama
    D. the written language

13. The Japanese constitution
    A. guarantees equal rights for minorities
    B. gives women the right to vote
    C. guarantees equal education for all
    D. establishes a totalitarian government

14. Education in Japan
    A. is available only to the upper classes
    B. is highly competitive
    C. does not include technical skills
    D. has failed to decrease the illiteracy rate since 1945

ESSAY

The following statements are about Japan.

    A. Japanese culture has been greatly influenced by China.
    B. Japan's population is generally homogeneous.
    C. Japan's educational system requires great motivation and dedication.
    D. Geography has had a profound effect on the social life of the Japanese.
    E. Industrialization has created some problems in Japan.

Choose any three of these statements and, for each one, discuss three specific facts that prove the validity of the statement.

IV. HISTORY AND POLITICAL GEOGRAPHY OF JAPAN

Early History

One of the major sources of information on early Japanese history is contained in the chronicles of Chinese and Korean visitors to Japan as early as the 3rd century A.D. Another source of information is found in archeological discoveries, indicating that Stone Age people lived in Japan perhaps as long as 200,000 years ago. The third major source of information is contained in the myths, legends, and traditions of the Japanese, which were first written down in the 8th century A.D. in the Kojiki (Record of Ancient Matters) in 712 and the Nihongi (Chronicles of Japan) in 720.

The Jomon culture in Japan dates from about 3000 to 300 B.C. The people of this culture maintained themselves by hunting and gathering and represent Mesolithic culture in Japan. From 300 B.C. to 300 A.D. a new wave of migrants from the mainland introduced wet-rice cultivation, bronze working, and finally iron-working. This new culture was called Yayoi.

GLOBAL CONCEPTS

Culture

CONCEPTS GLOBAL

The Tomb period (300–650), so-called because of burial mounds or tombs created during this period, was the most advanced culture of prehistoric Japan. During the Tomb period, references to Japan show up in Chinese chronicles and indicate that Japan was organized along clan lines. Toward the end of the Tomb period, the Yamato clan gained ascendancy and became the most powerful of the warring clans in Japan.

The Yamato clan leaders were the first emperors of Japan. In 645 nobles who favored the adoption of Chinese culture began a program known as the Taika Reforms (Great Reforms) that made political, social, and economic changes. They proclaimed the Yamato ruler emperor of all Japan, abolished private ownership of land, and declared that all territory was the property of the imperial government. To justify and solidify this claim, they called for the writing of an official history of Japan. According to the official histories (Kojiki and Nihongi), the rulers of Yamato were descended from Amaterasu, the sun goddess, who was descended from Izanagi and Izanami, the creators of Japan. Since the emperor is considered divine, the Japanese have never questioned the imperial family's right to the throne.

GLOBAL CONCEPTS

Political Systems

CONCEPTS GLOBAL

Often the emperor has been a ruler in name only, and a strong noble or warrior (samurai) family or, in modern times, military leaders have ruled Japan. The emperor's most significant role has been as high priest of the Shinto religion and intermediary between the people and the gods. Japanese history is filled with the names of the families who ruled Japan and who used the emperor to legitimize their authority, but they never attempted to take the throne.

IMPORTANT DATES IN JAPANESE HISTORY

300 B.C.–250 A.D.	Legendary period
3000–300 B.C.	Jomon culture
250 B.C.–250 A.D.	Yayoi culture
250–645	Tomb culture
552	Introduction of Buddhism to Japan
604	Shotoku Taishi's *Seventeen Article Constitution*
645	Taika Reforms
702	Taiho Code
710–784	Nara period
794–1185	Heian period
858–1156	Fujiwara period
1192–1333	Kamakura (or Minamoto shogunate) period
1274, 1281	Mongol invasions
1338–1568	Ashikaga (shogunate) period
1549	Arrival of Francis Xavier and Christianity
1603–1868	Tokugawa (shogunate) period
1868–1912	Meiji Restoration

The Feudal Period (1185–1600)

During Japan's feudal period, power rested in the hands of a military ruler rather than in those of the emperor. Feudalism was a political, economic, and social system based on land rights and individualized bonds of loyalty.

In the period from 794 to 1185, called the Heian period, a single family, the Fujiwara, came to dominate the imperial court and government by marrying their daughters to the emperors. During this period the power of the central government declined, allowing clans in the countryside to claim land belonging to the emperor. As a result, the economic strength of the imperial government decreased, as did its ability to protect the outlying regions of the empire. The noble families in the countryside became more powerful, as peasants who could not protect themselves from roving bands of robbers and the Ainu gave up their land, which became part of the noble's estate. In return, the peasant was entitled to the protection of the noble and his samurai (warriors on horseback). The daimyo (the more powerful lords) built palaces, collected taxes from the peasants, and increased the size of their military. The military and the peasants built up a loyalty system to the daimyo, who protected and employed them. The daimyo and the samurai became

GLOBAL
CONCEPTS

Power

CONCEPTS
GLOBAL

the real rulers of Japan. A feudal system similar to Europe's during the Middle Ages was the result. The daimyo controlled their own land, collected taxes, created armies, built castle headquarters, and through the peasants encouraged economic self-sufficiency. This feudal system lasted for approximately five hundred years.

As the power of the Fujiwara declined, two daimyo families, the Taira and the Minamoto, struggled for power. The Minamoto, under the leadership of Yoritomo, won this struggle. Yoritomo forced the emperor to grant him the title of shogun (military ruler or general), and the daimyo and samurai gained control of Japanese government. This control would last until the Tokugawa shogunate. The shoguns were the real heads of government until the Meiji Restoration in 1867, although the imperial family continued to occupy the throne. The imperial family was used to legitimize the power of the shoguns by the granting of the shogun title.

WORLD ISSUES

Determination
of Political
and Economic
Systems

Bushido

During the feudal period a warrior code developed, which drew on the military discipline of the samurai, Confucian ethics, Shinto, and Zen Buddhism. Bushido (the way of the warrior) was a code of conduct that stressed the importance of superior-inferior relationships and the unswerving loyalty of the samurai to their lords and through them, to the lord's superiors, including the emperor. Family loyalty was important, though it was expected that a loyal samurai would sacrifice his family for the good of his lord. The samurai subordinated individual desires for the good of the group or society. Self-discipline and self-control were stressed, as was complete indifference to death. It was considered glorious to die in battle and absolutely unacceptable to surrender. To avoid surrender or capture, a samurai was expected to commit harakiri or seppuku (ritual suicide involving disembowelment). Samurai also committed suicide in this way to atone for behavior unworthy of a samurai, for example, disloyalty to a feudal lord, if that disloyalty was discovered. According to the code of bushido, a samurai must be brave, honorable, loyal to lord and emperor, and able to subordinate his emotions.

GLOBAL
CONCEPTS

Identity

CONCEPTS
GLOBAL

Mongol Invasion

In 1270 Kublai Khan demanded that the Japanese pay tribute, but the Minamoto shogun refused. The Khan sent a Mongol force of 40,000 to Kyushu in 1274. The Japanese samurai were no match for the Mongol force, but they received assistance in

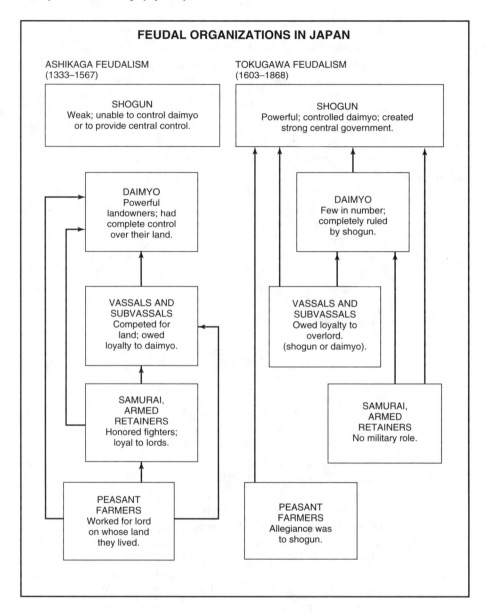

FEUDAL ORGANIZATIONS IN JAPAN

ASHIKAGA FEUDALISM
(1333–1567)

TOKUGAWA FEUDALISM
(1603–1868)

SHOGUN
Weak; unable to control daimyo
or to provide central control.

SHOGUN
Powerful; controlled daimyo; created
strong central government.

DAIMYO
Powerful
landowners; had
complete control
over their land.

DAIMYO
Few in number;
completely ruled
by shogun.

**VASSALS AND
SUBVASSALS**
Competed for
land; owed
loyalty to daimyo.

**VASSALS AND
SUBVASSALS**
Owed loyalty to
overlord.
(shogun or daimyo).

**SAMURAI,
ARMED
RETAINERS**
Honored fighters;
loyal to lords.

**SAMURAI,
ARMED
RETAINERS**
No military role.

**PEASANT
FARMERS**
Worked for lord
on whose land
they lived.

**PEASANT
FARMERS**
Allegiance was
to shogun.

the form of a typhoon, which destroyed much of the Mongol
fleet. The Mongols were forced to abandon their invasion. To
the Japanese, the typhoons were divine winds, kamikaze
(*kami*-gods; *kaze*-winds) sent by the gods to protect Japan. A
similar storm destroyed much of the Mongol fleet when they
attempted a second invasion in 1281.

The Tokugawa Shogunate

During the Ashikaga shogunate (1338–1568), there was much civil strife and little central control. By the late 15th century, Japan fell into the hands of local warlords. Three of the most important were Nobunaga, Hideyoshi, and Ieyasu. Nobunaga began to reunify Japan. He conquered other local warlords and eventually brought about twenty provinces under his control.

Nobunaga was followed by Hideyoshi, who within a few years had gained control of all Japan. After his death, the struggle for control was won by Ieyasu, who gained the title of shogun and created Japan's last shogunate, the Tokugawa.

GLOBAL
CONCEPTS
Political Systems
CONCEPTS
GLOBAL

A strong bureaucratic central government was established, with a new capital at Edo (Tokyo), from which the Tokugawa ruled over a 250-year period of peace and stability. They did this by imposing controls designed to preserve the social and economic order as it existed in 1600. These controls included:

1. *The system of sankin-kotai (alternate attendance).* Each of the daimyo was required to spend every other year in Edo, and his family was required to reside in Edo at all times as hostages.

2. *The class system of the nation became a caste system.* Membership in a class was made hereditary, and the classes were ranked according to their value to society. At the top of the system were the samurai; the second class were the peasants; the third class were the skilled workers, the craftspeople; and the fourth class were the merchants.

3. *Japan was isolated.* Portuguese traders came in the 16th century and were followed by Christian missionaries. Fearing the foreign influences that came with Christianity, the Tokugawa persecuted Christians and eventually crushed the religion. The Tokugawa feared all foreign influence. A small contingent of Dutch and Chinese were confined to a small island in Nagasaki harbor. All other foreign traders were expelled from the country. Japanese were forbidden to go abroad, and Japanese in other countries were forbidden to return.

GLOBAL
CONCEPTS
Identity
CONCEPTS
GLOBAL

Although the Tokugawa controls were designed to prevent change in Japan, change did take place. The 250 years of imposed peace and isolation led to an increase in internal commerce, the development of cities, and the strengthening of the economic power of merchants. Most of the samurai, with no wars to fight, fell on hard times and often married daughters of merchants to improve their fortunes. Many of the samurai became scholars and teachers, and the literacy rate increased considerably. During their long period of isolation, the Japanese developed a strong feeling of their own uniqueness.

Americans Arrive in Japan

On July 14, 1853, Commodore Matthew Perry, in command of four U.S. ships, sailed into Tokyo Bay. The Japanese had never seen steamships before and were astonished at the fire power of the warships. Perry carried with him a letter from U.S. President Millard Fillmore, demanding that Japan open its ports to American trade and ships, and that the government guarantee fair treatment of American sailors (shipwrecked sailors were badly treated).

The Japanese were opposed to the American demands, but the government of the shogun realized that the Japanese could not defend themselves against American technology. In 1854 the shogun's government signed a treaty opening two Japanese ports to American ships to take on supplies, and an American consulate was opened. Within four years, the United States had been granted full trade rights in several other ports, extraterritoriality, and limitations on the Japanese right to impose tariffs on American goods. Soon the European powers were demanding the same rights. The Japanese believed that Japan would be cut up into spheres of influence, as China had been, unless they took steps to prevent it.

GLOBAL
CONCEPTS

Change

CONCEPTS
GLOBAL

Meiji Restoration (1868–1912)

Many Japanese blamed the shogunate for failing to defend Japan against foreign interference and believed that the Tokugawa could not resist the foreigners. In 1868 samurai forces overthrew the shogunate and restored the emperor's rule. This so-called Meiji Restoration brought to the throne Emperor Matshuhito, who was only fifteen years old.

Changes by 1912

The Japanese who led the overthrow of the shogun and the restoration of the emperor believed that the only way to remove the threat of the Western powers was a rapid program of modernization to enable Japan to compete with the West. Japan already had a high literacy rate, a high degree of urbanization, a large pool of skilled labor, and channels for mass training of citizens. What stood in the way of full-scale modernization was the feudal system, which the leaders of the restoration set about to destroy.

The daimyo (feudal lords) were persuaded to give up their estates, and Japan was divided into prefectures under the direct control of the government in Tokyo (the new name for Edo). Class divisions and restrictions were abolished, and equality of all people was declared. The samurai lost all their special privileges, and universal military service was adopted. An education system was established.

The leaders of the restoration created a highly centralized bureaucratic government, which was an oligarchy (a small group controlling the government and allowing little opposition). In 1889 the Japanese were presented with a written constitution, a "gift from the emperor." The new constitution established a two-house legislature, called the Diet. This was a severely limited democracy, and the small elite group who took control of the government in 1868 remained in control. The Western powers recognized Japan's efforts to provide at least a limited democracy.

A program of rapid modernization was begun. The government constructed railroads, highways, and telegraph lines and also built industries—textile mills, armaments factories, ship-building facilities—and opened mines. Later these industries were sold to private enterprise, thereby sponsoring the development of the zaibatsu (Japanese industrial monopolies that controlled all aspects of an industry). Japanese students were sent to Western nations to study, and Western advisers were employed. Western experts were hired to assist the Japanese in developing a modern army and navy. By the close of the 19th century, the foundations of a truly modern state had been laid.

Japanese Expansion Prior to World War II

Japanese aggression against weaker neighbors resulted from its need to acquire raw materials for its industrialization. Such aggression was modeled after imperialist actions of the Western powers in the late 19th and early 20th centuries. By the late 19th century, Japan's rulers were concerned that Korea, "a dagger pointed at the heart of Japan," would fall into the hands of an imperialist Western power because the Manchu dynasty in China could not defend it. This led to the Sino-Japanese War (Sino means Chinese) of 1894 to 1895, which was won by Japan. The Treaty of Shimonoseki granted Japan control of Taiwan, the Pescadores, and China's Liaotung Peninsula, plus an indemnity of several hundred million dollars and trade concessions in China. Korea was declared to be independent of China, and Japan began to seek control of the region.

Japan's chief rival in Korea was Russia, and the Japanese launched an attack in 1904 against the Russian fleet based at Port Arthur in China, beginning the Russo-Japanese War. The Russians were driven out of Korea and southern Manchuria, and Japan captured Port Arthur. In 1905 U.S. President Theodore Roosevelt negotiated peace between the two belligerents. The

Treaty of Portsmouth gave Russia's lease on Port Arthur and its concessions in southern Manchuria to Japan. By 1910 Korea had been annexed by Japan.

World War I gave Japan the opportunity to further expand its interests in Asia. Declaring itself at war with Germany and an ally of Great Britain, Japan seized German-held territories in China. It also gained control of German-held islands in the northern Pacific—the Marshall, the Caroline, and the Mariana islands.

In 1915 the Japanese secretly presented the Chinese with the Twenty-One Demands, which called for political, economic, and military concessions. However, China made these demands public. The United States objected, as did many Japanese who opposed their government's imperialist policies, and Japan dropped the demands. By the end of World War I, Japan had become the dominant military and economic power in Asia.

GLOBAL
CONCEPTS
Interdependence
CONCEPTS
GLOBAL

Japan's success led to a program known as the Greater East Asia Co-Prosperity Sphere, in which Japan tried to persuade all East Asian nations that economic cooperation with Japan was to everyone's best interest. Japan would provide technical services and manufactured products, and other nations would provide raw materials and agricultural products. It was little more than the application of the old mercantilist colonial policy by Japan in East Asia.

The 1920s were a period of social, political, and economic unrest in Japan. There was conflict between the modernized, younger elements of society and the tradition-bound society of the countryside and the older generation. A rapid population increase (in fact, population doubled from 1868 to 1925) resulted in a high unemployment rate. Most of Japan's farmers were reduced to tenant status.

WORLD ISSUES

World
Trade and
Finance

The worldwide depression of the 1930s hurt Japan's foreign trade. Extreme nationalist groups in Japan believed that their problems could be solved through military expansion, and they encouraged the nationalist fervor of the Japanese. Japanese expansion began in Manchuria. It had rich deposits of coal and iron ore, fertile agricultural plains, raw materials, and space for Japan's excess population. In 1931 Japanese military forces invaded Manchuria (the Manchurian Incident), and Japan established a puppet state called Manchukuo. The League of Nations objected to the invasion, but Japan merely withdrew from the League.

In 1937 Japan invaded China, and World War II in Asia began. World War II in Europe broke out in 1939, and in 1940 Japan,

WORLD ISSUES

War
and
Peace

Germany, and Italy signed the Tripartite Pact, more commonly called the Rome-Berlin-Tokyo Axis. In 1941 Japan invaded Southeast Asia to gain control of vital oil, tin, and rubber resources. The United States placed an embargo on trade with Japan.

For several months in 1941 the United States and Japan were engaged in talks to resolve their differences. On December 7, 1941, Japan launched an invasion of the Dutch East Indies and an attack on the American naval base at Pearl Harbor, Hawaii. The following day the United States declared war on Japan.

Within a few months, Japanese forces had extended their control over a region stretching from Japan to Australia on the south and to the borders of India on the west. The American victory at the Battle of Midway in 1942 was the turning point of the war, and the United States began a campaign of island hopping (conquering important Japanese-held islands while bypassing others and leaving the Japanese forces cut off from communication and supplies) to push its way toward the Japanese homeland. President Harry Truman, in the summer of 1945, ordered the use of the first atomic bomb, which was dropped on the city of Hiroshima on August 6, 1945. After a second atomic bomb was dropped on Nagasaki on August 9, Japanese Emperor Hirohito announced Japan's surrender. For the first time in its history, Japan was conquered, and was about to be occupied, by a foreign power.

United States Occupation of Japan (1945–1952)

U.S. occupation of Japan led to the diffusion of some American ideas and practices into Japanese culture. United States armed forces, under the leadership of General Douglas MacArthur, the Supreme Commander of the Allied Powers (SCAP), occupied Japan from 1945 to 1952. Japan was stripped of its military conquests, and its territory was restricted to the four main islands. Its armed forces were disbanded and weapons factories were closed. Government and military leaders accused of war crimes were brought to trial, and those who had played a role in Japan's military expansion were removed from positions of power. The emperor renounced his divinity. Nationalistic organizations were banned. MacArthur had a new constitution written for Japan, which went into effect in 1947. It is one of the world's most democratic documents.

GLOBAL
CONCEPTS

Change

CONCEPTS
GLOBAL

The American occupation of Japan also brought a number of economic and social reforms. The zaibatsu were broken up; a land-reform program required landlords to sell land cheaply to their tenants; all titles of nobility were abolished; the legal authority of the head of the family over other family members was abolished; and compulsory education was extended for three more years.

The Impact of the Atomic Bombs of 1945

Japan, the only nation in the world ever to have been attacked by nuclear weapons, is opposed to their development and stockpiling. Major demonstrations have occurred in Japan protesting American storage of missiles and the arrival of American nuclear submarines. Similarly, the Japanese protest the testing of nuclear weapons by all nations.

To allay Japanese fears, the United States-Japanese Mutual Security Pact was revised in 1960 to include a clause stating that the United States could not bring nuclear weapons into Japan without the knowledge of the Japanese government, nor could it use its forces based in Japan in military action without the approval of the Japanese government. Japan has developed the peaceful use of nuclear power, but many Japanese also protest the opening of nuclear power plants.

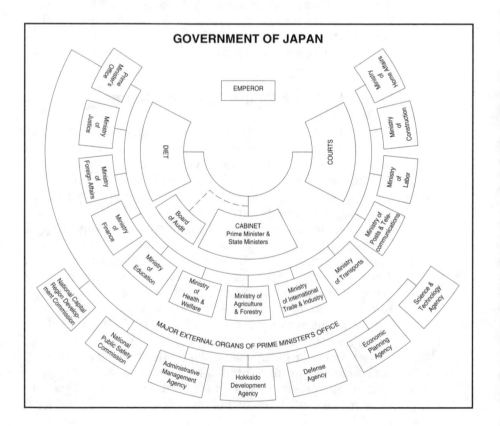

GOVERNMENT OF JAPAN

Democratic System of Government

GLOBAL
CONCEPTS

Political Systems

CONCEPTS
GLOBAL

GLOBAL
CONCEPTS

Human Rights

CONCEPTS
GLOBAL

GLOBAL
CONCEPTS

Citizenship

CONCEPTS
GLOBAL

The 1947 constitution created a parliamentary system with a two-house parliament called the National Diet. The lower house, the House of Representatives, is the more important. The prime minister is elected by the House and is responsible to it. The prime minister and his cabinet can be removed by a "no-confidence" vote, in which case elections will be held for a new House, which then elects a new prime minister. The constitution lists the rights of the Japanese people, which are much like the rights contained in the U.S. Bill of Rights but also include equal rights of women, collective bargaining, equal education, and so on. The right to vote was granted to all citizens over the age of twenty. One of the most well-known provisions of the constitution is Article IX, which renounces the use of war and the "maintenance of land, sea and air forces, as well as other war potential." It does allow the maintenance of defense forces or forces necessary to maintain internal peace.

According to the constitution the emperor is the symbolic head of state and a symbol of the unity of the Japanese people. His is a ceremonial, not a governing, role. The present emperor, Akihito, came to the throne in 1989 upon the death of his father, Hirohito.

Politics in Japan since World War II has been dominated by the Liberal Democratic party (LDP). The LDP is closely allied with big business and receives much of its support from rural villages, towns, and small cities. The LDP's major opposition comes from the Socialists, the Democratic Socialists, and the Communists. Supporters of these parties tend to be concentrated in the major urban areas. Their major disagreements with the LDP have been over Japanese-United States relations. Trade unions tend to support these parties.

National politics centers on factions of the LDP within the parliament, with each faction having a leader in the Diet. Legislation is usually passed by consensus, with compromises having been worked out before a bill is actually presented for passage. Until 1993 the LDP managed to maintain political control by forming coalitions with minority parties when necessary. In August 1993 a new coalition of seven minority parties was formed with Morihiro Hosokawa as its leader, and for the first time since the LDP was formed in 1955 it lost control of the government. Hosokawa and the coalition promised an end to corruption and scandal in the government and changes in Japan's trade policies. In January 1994 the political reform bill that Hosokawa presented to the parliament was voted down, and he was forced to compromise with leaders of the LDP and present a new reform bill. Later that year he resigned as a result of a financial scandal. The present prime minister, Tomiichi Marayama, is a socialist.

Present Military Status of Japan

In spite of the provisions of Article IX of the constitution, Japan does maintain forces for the defense of the Japanese islands. These self-defense forces originated in 1950 when U.S. occupation forces were withdrawn from Japan. They were limited to 250,000 men, and service was voluntary.

Treaty of Mutual Cooperation and Security Between the United States and Japan

According to the terms of the mutual security treaty between the United States and Japan, the United States agrees to take the major responsibility for defending Japan against aggressors. Many Japanese oppose this treaty because they fear that Japan could be drawn into a United States war against its will and that the presence of U.S. forces in Japan might even provoke an attack on Japan. Japan's military forces have been steadily built up since 1954, but the government maintains that they are only for purposes of self-defense. In recent years Japan has been pressured by the United States to spend more on its own defense. The Japanese people remain opposed to more spending.

Japan's Role in World Organizations

Japan's role in the United Nations was affected by the Soviet bloc's distrust of Japanese-American defense arrangements.

ECONOMIC AND SOCIAL PROFILES OF SELECTED COUNTRIES—EAST ASIA

	Population Millions 1976	(est.) 1990	Per Capita Income 1989	GNP (billions of dollars) 1989	Literacy Rate % 1976	1992	Doubling Population Time
Japan	113	124	23,730	2920	99	100	exceeds 100 years
Korea (South)	36	43.2	4400	186.5	88.5	96	70 years
Korea (North)	16	21.8	1240	28	NA	95	38 years
China (Peoples Republic)	852	1150	360	393	40	73	48 years
Taiwan (Republic of China)	16.3	20.5	7480	150	86	94	61 years

Source: *Encyclopedia Britannica Book of the Year 1992*

Relations between the Soviet Union and Japan were sometimes strained by the presence of American bases in Japan and the close military alliance of the United States with Japan. A dispute over the southern portion of the Kurile Islands and the uneasiness the Soviets felt over Japan's close military alliance with the United States caused the Soviet Union to block Japan's admission to the United Nations from 1952 to 1956. In 1956 the two nations resumed diplomatic relations, and Japan was admitted to the world organization in 1956.

GLOBAL
CONCEPTS

Change

CONCEPTS
GLOBAL

Japanese Relations with Other Asian Nations

Many of the nations of Southeast Asia have found it difficult to throw off the image of Japan as the militaristic/imperialist nation that invaded, conquered, and exploited their territories during World War II. Some of the nations feel Japan is still exploiting them economically through trade. To create goodwill in Southeast Asia, Japan paid war reparations to the countries that suffered from Japanese aggression. Japan has also provided economic and technical assistance to developing nations and has contributed large amounts to the Asian Development Bank. Japanese industries have been developed in many areas.

WORLD ISSUES

War
and
Peace

In 1972 the People's Republic of China and Japan signed an agreement. Japan recognized the People's Republic as the official government of China and cut its diplomatic ties with Taiwan. This led to a treaty ending World War II between China and Japan and also to trade agreements.

Increasingly, other Asian nations (South Korea, Taiwan, Singapore, China) are competing with Japan in the world market in such areas as textiles, cameras, electronics, and even cars. But Japan is still by far the leading industrial and economic power in Asia.

REVIEW QUESTIONS

Multiple Choice. Select the letter of the answer that correctly completes each statement.

1. After World War II, Japan was occupied by and aided in its recovery by
   A. China
   B. Russia
   C. Korea
   D. the United States

2. The Tokugawa shogunate was best known for its policy of
   A. isolation
   B. interdependence
   C. education
   D. imperialism

3. The Meiji Restoration was significant for its
   A. military conquest of Korea
   B. enlightened approach to modernization
   C. victory over Russia
   D. return to a policy of feudalism

4. The Kojiki and Nihongi are books dealing with Japan's
   A. economy
   B. politics
   C. history
   D. military

5. Since the early 1970s, Japan's foreign policy has become more independent of U.S. policies because
   A. Japan opposes the U.S. policy of ending the cold war with Russia
   B. Japan has grown as an economic superpower
   C. the United States has failed to honor its commitments to Japan
   D. Japan is so strong militarily that it no longer needs the United States to protect it

6. The Diet is Japan's
   A. royal family
   B. legislature
   C. economic control board
   D. army

7. The real power of the Japanese emperors has often been usurped by others, but the imperial family has never been dethroned. A major reason for this has been
   A. the Japanese emperor was revered as a god
   B. the military was controlled by the imperial family
   C. shoguns never remained in power long enough to make important decisions
   D. the strong cultural influence of the Chinese

8. During the 1930s and 1940s Japan practiced a policy of imperialism in order to gain control of the resources necessary to support its industrialization. An example of this was the
   A. opening of trade with the United States
   B. invasion of Manchuria in 1931
   C. signing of the Portsmouth Treaty
   D. expansion of the zaibatsu

9. Japan's feudal period was marked by the
   A. dominance of the samurai
   B. expansion of foreign trade
   C. destruction of the imperial family
   D. weakening of the traditional extended family

10. Real political power in Japan during the feudal period from 1185–1600 was actually held by the
    A. emperor
    B. priesthood
    C. shogun
    D. middle class

11. Which of the following statements about the Japanese imperial family is true?
    A. They have most often ruled in name only.
    B. They gained their legitimacy from the shogun.
    C. They control politics in Japan today.
    D. They still claim descent from the gods.

12. Japan's long period of isolation was ended in the 1850s
    A. by the expedition of Commodore Matthew Perry
    B. because the Japanese wanted to renew contact with the European colonial powers
    C. by the occupation by the Allied Powers
    D. in order to gain international relief for earthquake victims in Tokyo

13. The Tokugawa shogunate isolated Japan because it
    A. feared the Mongols would invade Japan
    B. saw European contact as a threat to its control
    C. wanted to end Chinese influence in Japan
    D. was located so close to the Korean peninsula

14. After the Japanese occupation of Manchuria in 1931
    A. the United States placed an embargo on trade with Japan
    B. the League of Nations condemned the attack
    C. China surrendered to Japan
    D. American and British objections forced the Japanese to withdraw
       from the Asian mainland

15. Japan adopted imperialist policies in the 20th century in order to
    A. control the East Asian sea lanes
    B. gain resources for industrialization and militarization
    C. free the Filipinos from U.S. control
    D. maintain its policy of isolation begun under the Tokugawa shoguns

ESSAYS

1. From 1894 to 1945 Japan followed an imperialist policy designed to increase its military and economic power. Describe three steps taken by Japan to increase its military and economic power, and explain how each step added to its power.

2. Describe three of the policies designed to prevent social and economic change that were followed by the Tokugawa shoguns.

I. PHYSICAL GEOGRAPHY OF KOREA

The Korean peninsula, bordered by the Yellow Sea, the Sea of Japan, and the Korea Strait, lies between China and historic Russia, and Japan. (See map on page 155.) Its strategic location between these three regions has had a profound effect on its history. China has often seen fit to extend its influence into the region in order to maintain some control over what it has seen as a strategic outpost on its northeastern borders. Indeed, for many years, Korea was one of the Chinese tribute states. Russia's interest was mainly in the warm water ports to be found in Korea. And Japan often used Korea as a launching point for invasions of the Asian continent.

Korea, known as "the land of the morning calm," is a peninsula approximately half the size of California, and is home to over 67 million people and the site of two countries, the Democratic Republic of Korea, and the Republic of Korea. The division of the peninsula following World War II deprived each region of the other's resources, therefore limiting the economic future of each. Much of the peninsula is hilly and mountainous, limiting the amount of arable land to approximately one fifth of the land area. The most extensive farming regions are found in the southwest and in the coastal plains throughout the peninsula. The Republic of Korea, or South Korea, contains the largest amount of arable land, but the Democratic Republic, or North Korea, has the most extensive deposits of natural resources, including coal, iron, tungsten, copper, and zinc.

II. ECONOMIC GEOGRAPHY OF KOREA

Traditionally, agriculture was the chief economic activity in Korea. Industrial activity was on a low level and was severely hurt during the Korean War (1950–1953).

However, since the war, both North and South Korea have made significant economic strides. Since the early 1960s South Korea has seen a spectacular increase in its GNP and per capita income. GNP has increased from just over $2 billion to over $270 billion. Per capita income in 1990 was over $6,000.

Major industrial products include clothing, textiles, automobiles, electronics equipment, and steel, much of which is exported to the United States and Japan. Approximately 74 percent of the population is urban. North Korea's GNP is over $23 billion, and its per capita income over $1,000. Its major trading partners are China, the Commonwealth of Independent States, and Japan. The government has concentrated on the development of heavy industry rather than on consumer products. Its major industrial products include machines, textiles, and petrochemicals. Approximately 60 percent of the North Korean population is urban.

III. HUMAN AND CULTURAL GEOGRAPHY OF KOREA

GLOBAL
CONCEPTS

Identity

CONCEPTS
GLOBAL

GLOBAL
CONCEPTS

Choice

CONCEPTS
GLOBAL

GLOBAL
CONCEPTS

Environment

CONCEPTS
GLOBAL

GLOBAL
CONCEPTS

Diversity

CONCEPTS
GLOBAL

The Korean people are of Mongoloid origin, probably originating in Siberia, Manchuria, and northeastern China and migrating to the peninsula in prehistoric times. These people mingled and intermarried, and the resultant people are the Koreans. The Koreans are a homogeneous grouping, speaking a single language. Their written script, hangul, originated in the 15th century, and replaced many Chinese characters that had been used previously. Hangul consists of 10 vowels and 14 consonants, which are combined to form syllables. It is perhaps one of the most scientific writing systems in the world and because it is also one of the simplest it helps to account for the high literacy rates in both North and South Korea. Koreans also still use some Chinese characters.

As a result of its geographic location, Korea has been strongly influenced by Chinese culture. The Chinese influence can be seen in the traditional family, social and government systems which indicate diffusion of Confucian philosophy. Buddhism, architecture, ceramics, painting, sculpture, and historical writing also reflect Chinese influence. Korea served as a cultural bridge between China and Japan. The Koreans, much like the Japanese after them, would adapt the Chinese cultural contributions to their own system, making them their own before passing them on to Japan.

The oldest religious belief is Shamanism. It is a form of nature worship, or animism. A key figure is the shaman, a person who is believed to act as an intermediary with the spiritual world. A shaman may be called upon to perform a kut, a ritual to get rid of evil spirits. In South Korea the major religions are Buddhism (47% of the population) and Christianity (Protestantism—38%, Catholicism—11%). North Korea discourages adherence to religious beliefs.

IV. HISTORY AND POLITICAL GEOGRAPHY OF KOREA

The Koreans were politically united by the kingdom of Silla in 668 A.D. The kingdom maintained control until the year 935, and ruled during a Golden Age. The arts, architecture, ceramics, and literature all flourished. The writing system was invented and the Koreans developed movable metal type. Silla was replaced by a new kingdom called Koryo, which was subjected to the Mongol invasions in the 13th century. In 1392, Koryo was replaced by the Choson Kingdom (more commonly referred to as the Yi dynasty in the west), which would maintain control until 1910.

The Yi dynasty experienced Japanese and Manchu invasion in the late 16th and 17th centuries and in a defensive measure closed itself to the outside world for approximately 250 years. As a result, it became known as the "Hermit Kingdom." In 1876, the Japanese forced Korea to sign a treaty allowing diplomatic and trade relations, and the "opening" of Korea was begun. The United States and European nations followed suit, and Korea was forced to sign more treaties granting trade and diplomatic relations to other nations. China saw these treaties as a threat to her control of a tributary state, and attempted to halt the foreign intrusion in Korea. The Sino-Japanese War (1894–1895) occurred as a result of China's attempt to reassert her influence in Korea. The results were devastating for Korea. The Chinese and the Japanese battled over Korean territory. Japan emerged the winner and Chinese influence in Korea was ended. The Russo-Japanese War (1904–1905) was a result of the conflicting interests of Japan and Russia in Manchuria and Korea. Again, the war and its results were devastating for Korea. Both nations agreed to recognize the independence of Korea, but by 1910 the country had been annexed by Japan.

WORLD ISSUES

War
and
Peace

Japan proceeded to develop a transportation system in Korea designed to grant them easier access to Korean natural resources. They opened mines, developed industries, and sent Japanese to farm in Korea. Rice was exported to Japan while people in Korea went hungry. Attempts were made to eliminate Korean culture. Education in Korea was offered in the Japanese language. The Japanese policy of assimilation provoked Korean nationalism. A nationalist rebellion in 1919 was brutally put down by the Japanese. Called the Mansei Uprising, it led to the arrest of thousands, and beatings, imprisonment, and

WORLD ISSUES

Human
Rights

torture of many of those arrested. Following the Mansei Uprising, the Japanese instituted even more repressive rule in Korea and remained in control of the peninsula until the close of World War II.

At the close of World War II, according to an agreement worked out at the Potsdam Conference, the Soviet Union accepted surrender from Japanese troops north of the 38th parallel in Korea, and the United States accepted surrender south of the 38th parallel. Elections for a government of a united Korea were supposed to be held, but efforts to hold the elections were resisted by the Soviet Union, and in 1948 a communist regime was declared in the north with Kim Il-Sung at its helm, and a republic was established in the south with Syngman Rhee as the elected president.

The Korean War

On June 25, 1950, the North Koreans, led by Kim Il-Sung launched an unprovoked attack on the South. The South Koreans suffered terrible losses. Seoul fell in three days. Almost all of Korea, except for a small area in the southeast, called the Pusan perimeter, was overrun in a month. The UN General Assembly decided to send troops to help the South, under the command of U.S. General Douglas MacArthur. They soon forced North Korean soldiers northward, near the Chinese border. China now intervened with her own forces compelling the UN soldiers to retreat. An armistice was signed in July 1953, near the 38th parallel, in Panmunjom. A demilitarized zone (DMZ) separates the two Koreas to this day.

The war led to mistrust and hatred between people on both sides. The division of the peninsula has increased political and cultural differences. Millions of people became refugees, separated from their families. In the last 15 years, contact between the two Koreas have been rare. Some family exchanges have occurred; a joint South-North Korean women's ping-pong team captured the world title in the 1980s. However, North Korea refused to send athletes to the 1988 Olympic Games in Seoul. Unification has been a controversial issue. The first round of high-level talks between both Koreas on this issue was held in Seoul in 1990.

Recent Political Developments

In September 1987 South Korea's constitution was amended to provide for the direct election of a president. In December 1987 the first civilian president of South Korea, Roh Tae Woo, was elected, and he took office in 1988. A second peaceful, democratic election took place in 1992, where Kim Young Sam was chosen president.

In 1993 North Korea threatened to withdraw from the nuclear nonproliferation treaty it had signed nearly ten years before and refused to allow inspection of its nuclear facilities. In mid-February 1994 North Korea agreed to the inspection of its facilities by the International Atomic Energy Agency, but refused to let them inspect the facility at Yongbyon, which has the capacity to produce the enriched plutonium that can be used in the production of nuclear weapons. North Korea maintained that it should establish the boundaries of the inspections. In inspections in other countries, the United Nations has established the boundaries. A CIA report in April 1994 indicated that North Korea might already have at least two nuclear weapons. The United States wished to prevent further development of any nuclear weapons on the Korean Peninsula, and called for a UN resolution threatening sanctions against North Korea. China's plan called for issuing a statement encouraging North Korea to allow inspection of its nuclear sites instead, with the possible use of sanctions later. The Chinese plan had the support of other UN members, even South Korea.

In late March and early April of 1994 the armies of both North and South Korea were put on alert, and the United States offered to deploy Patriot missile launchers to help South Korea defend against possible North Korean attack. Kim Il Sung, who had led North Korea since 1946, threatened that the peninsula was "on the brink of war."

South Korea maintains a military defense treaty with the United States, and the U.S. military has over 36,000 troops stationed in South Korea. In March 1994 the United States and South Korea announced that they would resume joint military exercises, but as of April 1994, the decision to carry out the exercises had been postponed.

The most dramatic event to occur in Korea in mid-1994 was the death of North Korean leader Kim Il Sung. Known as the "Great Leader," he designated his son Kim Jong Il, known as the "Dear Leader," as his successor.

REVIEW QUESTIONS

Multiple Choice. Select the letter of the answer that correctly completes
each statement.

1. South Korea
   A. has a Communist government
   B. has more natural resources than North Korea
   C. has had greater economic success than North Korea
   D. signed a mutual defense treaty with China

2. Korea is
   A. a peninsula
   B. an island
   C. a subcontinent
   D. an archipelago

3. The man who controlled North Korea from 1946 to 1994 was
   A. Kim Jong Il
   B. Kim Young Sam
   C. Kim Il Sung
   D. Chu Chang Chun

4. Korea has been divided at the 38th parallel since
   A. World War I
   B. World War II
   C. the Korean War
   D. the Russo-Japanese War

5. Today the majority of Koreans make their living in
   A. agriculture
   B. fishing
   C. manufacturing
   D. lumbering

ESSAYS

1. Discuss one way Korean history has been influenced by each of the
   following nations.

   A. United States
   B. China
   C. Japan

2. Explain how the cultural, economic, and political development of
   Korea have been affected by its geographic location.

UNIT FOUR

Africa

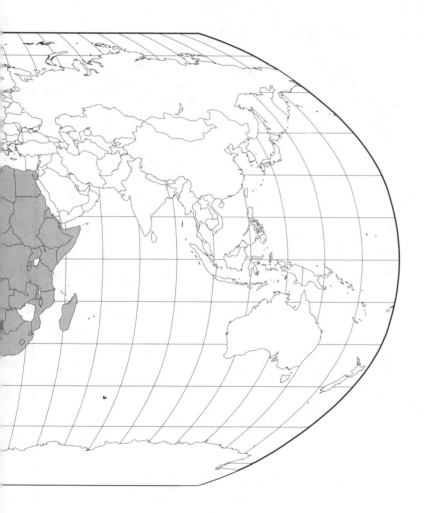

I. PHYSICAL GEOGRAPHY OF AFRICA

Overview

The geography and climate of Africa have played an important role in its historical, economic, and cultural development. For many years Africa was known as the "Dark Continent" because Western Europeans and Americans knew so little about it. The

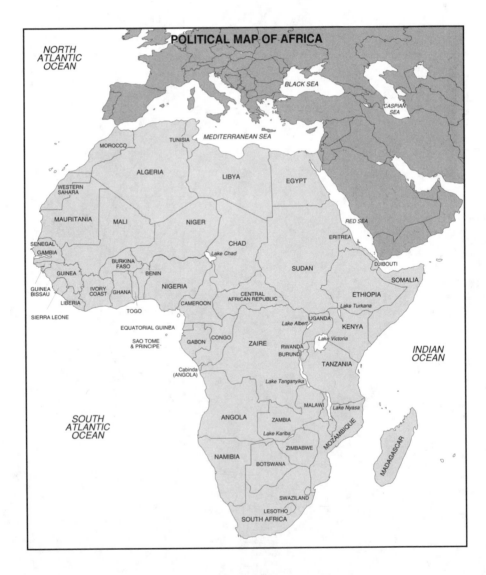

POLITICAL MAP OF AFRICA

smooth coastline with few natural harbors, the falls and rapids near the mouths of rivers that made interior navigation difficult, and the deserts isolated Africa south of the Sahara. It was not until modern times that Westerners began to learn of Africa's early civilizations and its many diverse cultures.

Size and Location

The African continent is the second largest in the world. Stretching nearly 5,000 miles north to south and 4,500 miles east to west, the continent contains 11,700,000 square miles. The total land area is approximately three times the size of the continental United States. Africa contains 20 percent of the world's land surface, but only 12 percent of the total world population.

The African continent is divided nearly in half by the equator, and it stretches from approximately 38° north latitude to

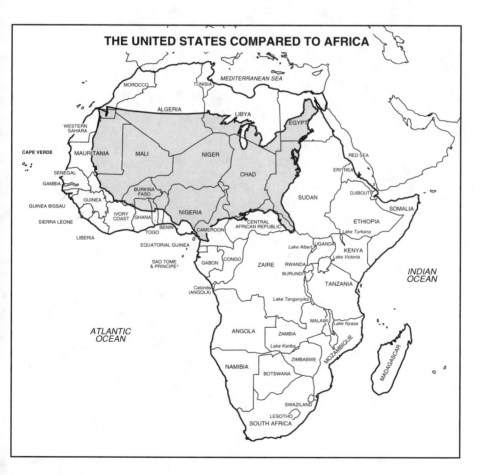

THE UNITED STATES COMPARED TO AFRICA

about 35° south latitude. Because of this, the central portion of Africa lies within the tropics.

The Mediterranean Sea lies to the north and has served as a link between Africa and European culture. To the west is the Atlantic Ocean, and to the east lies the Indian Ocean, which served as a trade route between Africa and India, Southeast Asia, and China. On the east coast is the Red Sea, which served as a trade route between Africa and Arabia and as a route for cultural diffusion, especially the diffusion of Islam. In the northeast is the

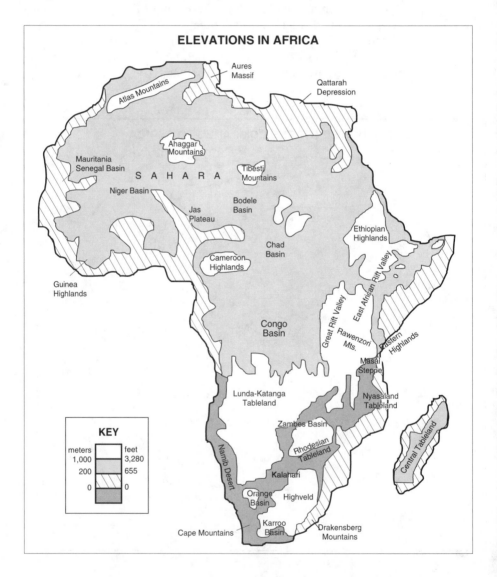

ELEVATIONS IN AFRICA

Suez Canal, which is a major route for the transport of crude oil between the Persian Gulf nations and Europe.

Mountains

Much of Africa is a great plateau or a series of plateaus interspersed with many great river basins. The central plateau makes the average elevation of Africa higher than that of any other continent. About 90 percent of sub-Saharan Africa (Africa south of the Sahara) is over 500 feet in elevation. The plateau is interrupted by various mountain ranges. The Atlas Mountains are located in the northwest. The Ethiopian Highlands in the northeast contain Lake Tana, the source of the Blue Nile. In the central region are the Ruwenzori (Mountains of the Moon) Mountains. Africa's highest mountain is Mt. Kilimanjaro (19,340 feet), and Mt. Kenya (17,040 feet) is the second highest. The Drakensberg Mountains are found in South Africa. The Tibesti Mountains, the Ahaggar Mountains, and the Tassili-N-Ajjer are in the Sahara Desert.

Great Rift Valley

In the east the plateau is sliced by the Great Rift Valley, a great trough, or canyon, created by upheavals and disturbances in the earth's surface millions of years ago. The Eastern Rift Valley is

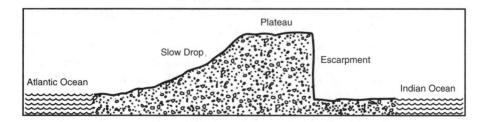

about 4,000 miles long, while the Western Rift is about 1,000 miles long. The sides of the rift are as much as 100 miles apart and the depth of the valley varies from hundreds of feet to a mile. The rift influenced migration in East Africa, forcing people to move in a north-south direction.

Rivers

The great central plateau region drops sharply near the coast, creating a series of waterfalls and rapids on most of Africa's great rivers. As a result, Africa has a narrow coastal plain, and interior navigation is difficult. However, many of the rivers are navigable once the falls and rapids have been traversed. For example, the Congo (Zaire) River is navigable from the Atlantic Ocean for only 85 miles, but beyond the falls and rapids it becomes a major transportation route for Central Africa, with nearly 8,000 miles of navigable waters. The falls and rapids mean that Africa has great hydroelectric power potential. Much of this potential, however, goes untapped because of a lack of capital as well as little call for electricity in the villages.

The Nile River, at over 4,100 miles long, is the longest river in the world. The White Nile, which has its source in Lake Victoria, joins the Blue Nile, which has its source in Lake Tana in Ethiopia, at Khartoum in Sudan. The river flows north and empties into the Mediterranean Sea at Alexandria in Egypt, where it forms the Nile delta, an important agricultural area. Egypt is desert except for a strip, approximately ten miles wide, along the Nile. The predictable Nile flood provided a fresh deposit of alluvial soil each year and the river makes irrigation, transportation, and communication possible. In Sudan aquatic vegetation creates a region known as the Sudd, where the vegetation is so thick that travel becomes difficult and channels must be cut through the vegetation. Lake Nasser, created by the construction of the Aswan High Dam, is located in Egypt on the Nile.

The second longest river in Africa is the Congo (Zaire). With its tributaries it drains an area of 1.4 million square miles. The Zambezi River contains Victoria Falls. Below the falls, a dam and lake (Lake Kariba) have been created to provide hydroelectric power. The Niger River rises in the Guinea Highlands, flows northeast through Mali, turns to the southeast and joins the Benue in Central Nigeria, then flows south to empty into the Gulf of Guinea in Nigeria, where it forms the Niger delta. The Niger, like the Nile, flows through a desert region, and many of the early West African kingdoms or civilizations developed along the Niger.

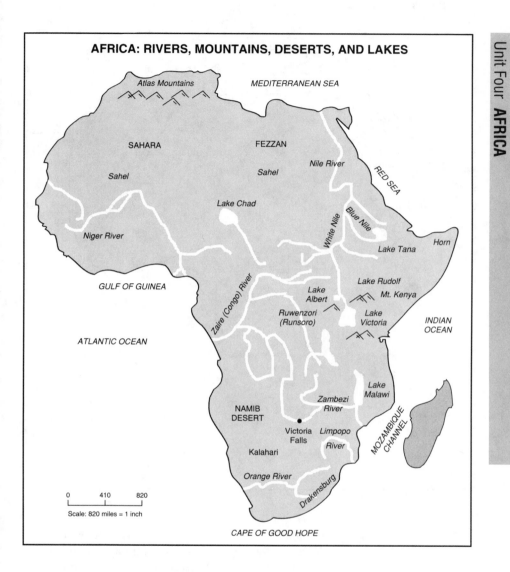

AFRICA: RIVERS, MOUNTAINS, DESERTS, AND LAKES

Atlas Mountains

MEDITERRANEAN SEA

SAHARA

FEZZAN

RED SEA

Sahel

Sahel

Nile River

Lake Chad

White Nile

Blue Nile

Niger River

Lake Tana

Horn

GULF OF GUINEA

Lake Rudolf

Mt. Kenya

Zaire (Congo) River

Lake Albert

Ruwenzori (Runsoro)

Lake Victoria

INDIAN OCEAN

ATLANTIC OCEAN

Lake Malawi

Zambezi River

NAMIB DESERT

Victoria Falls

Limpopo River

MOZAMBIQUE CHANNEL

Kalahari

Orange River

Drakensburg

0   410   820

Scale: 820 miles = 1 inch

CAPE OF GOOD HOPE

The Deserts

The Sahara, the largest desert in the world, covering 3.5 million square miles, was not a total barrier to migration and trade. Arab traders set up camel caravan routes in the west, while the Nile River and coastal waters in the north and east provided routes of trade and cultural diffusion.

The Sahara was not always a vast wasteland. Archeological discoveries indicate that at one time it was a well-watered grassland and that streams, lakes, and animals abounded. Climate changes, resulting from the Ice Age, are largely responsible for the changes.

Today the Sahara is largely uninhabited, with heavier population settlements in the areas where oases (places in the desert where there is enough ground water to make cultivation possible) or rivers are found, such as the Nile River Valley. The Niger River in the western Sahara made the development of the early kingdoms of Ghana, Mali, and Songhai possible.

The Sahara is inhabited mainly by two groups—by nomadic peoples (those who move from place to place searching for grazing land for their animals) and seminomadic peoples and by people who have settled in the oases and are engaged in agriculture, raising date palms, vegetables, and grains. In recent years, mineral deposits, such as petroleum, natural gas, iron, phosphates, manganese, and copper, have been discovered in the desert.

The southern edge of the Sahara is bordered by a region known as the Sahel. It is a region of steppe, a marginal zone between the deserts to the north and the savanna to the south. The Sahel has long been inhabited by animal grazers and farmers. As long as the number of inhabitants remained relatively small, the Sahel could support human population. However, as the numbers of both people and animals have increased, the strain on the land and its water resources has increased. As a result, the process of desertification (the process by which arable land becomes a desert) is taking place, and the Sahara is inching slowly southward into the Sahel.

Other major desert regions in Africa include the Namib, the Kalahari, and the deserts of southeastern Ethiopia and Somalia. The Kalahari has been inhabited by the Bushmen (Khoisan peoples) for hundreds of years.

The Lakes

East Africa and the area of the Great Rift Valley are often referred to as the lakes region since many of Africa's great lakes are located there. Lake Victoria, the largest lake in Africa, the world's second largest fresh water body, and the world's third largest lake, is located between the two rift valleys and is very shallow. Lake Tanganyika in the Western Rift Valley, one of the deepest lakes in the world, reaching a depth of about 4,800 feet, is the second largest lake in Africa and the seventh largest in the world. The third largest lake in Africa is Lake Malawi (Nyasa). Lake Chad is located on the southern edge of the Sahara and in the Sahel, making it a very important source of water. Unfortunately, the lake is prone to evaporation and varies in size and volume throughout the year. Africa's lakes are an important source of fish, one of the major sources of protein in Africa.

Climate and Vegetation Zones

The three most important factors in determining the climate of Africa are latitude, altitude, and wind patterns. Since the equator divides Africa nearly in half, climatic zones are similar in the north and south.

Extending north and south of the equator in Central or Equatorial Africa and in West Africa is a rain forest region, which makes up about 15 percent of Africa. It is characterized by high humidity, daily rainfall (60 to 80 inches average per year), and high temperatures (90°F) year round. Vegetation is basically on three levels. The ground cover consists of ferns and creeping plants. There is a second level of middle-growth trees and a third layer of tall trees. The last layer forms what is known as a canopy and prevents sunlight from reaching the rain forest floor.

The rain forest region is inhabited by some settled farmers, by some people who practice shifting cultivation, and by hunting-and-gathering groups such as the Pygmies. It is sparsely populated in Central (Equatorial) Africa and heavily populated in the coastal regions of Nigeria, Benin, Togo, and Ghana. The characteristics of the rain forest region discouraged European settlement.

GLOBAL
CONCEPTS
Environment
CONCEPTS
GLOBAL

North and south of the rain forest are the savanna zones, which cover about 40 percent of Africa. In the north the region is called the Sudan, and in the south, the Veldt. The savanna is characterized by a distinct wet season and a dry season. Rainfall varies from 20 to 60 inches per year. Vegetation consists of

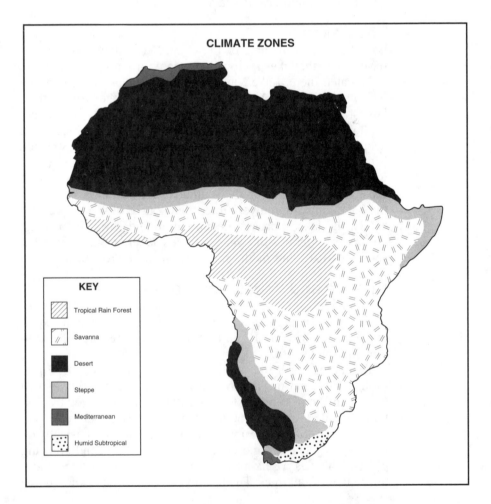

CLIMATE ZONES

KEY

Tropical Rain Forest

Savanna

Desert

Steppe

Mediterranean

Humid Subtropical

tall grasses, brush, and scattered trees. It is useful for grazing livestock and for shifting cultivation, and it is the home of much of Africa's wildlife. For the most part, the savanna is sparsely populated and did not attract European settlers. However, Zambia and Zimbabwe were heavily settled by Europeans because the winds and altitude moderated the climate.

North and south of the savannas are the steppe regions, the so-called marginal lands. Rainfall here varies from 10 to 20 inches per year. Vegetation consists of short, scattered grasses. Grazing and some settled agriculture and shifting cultivation are possible. In general, this region is sparsely inhabited and did not attract European settlement.

GLOBAL
CONCEPTS

Scarcity

CONCEPTS
GLOBAL

North and south of the steppes are the desert regions, which receive less than 10 inches of rain per year. The desert regions make up another 40 percent of Africa. The Sahara lies to the north and the Namib and Kalahari to the southwest. Vegetation in the Sahara is mostly scattered desert grasses, often called cram-cram. These regions are very sparsely inhabited.

North and south of the deserts, in the northwest and southeast coastal regions, is a Mediterranean climate zone. There the summers are warm and dry; winters are cool and moist. Settled agriculture is possible, and olives and citrus fruits are raised. This is one of the climate zones that Europeans found attractive.

In the highlands of southern and eastern Africa, there is a vertical climate—that is, within a relatively short distance, because of changes in elevation, several climate types are found. These highlands attracted European settlement because of the fertile soils and more moderate temperatures.

WORLD ISSUES

Hunger
and
Poverty

Many regions of Africa suffer from shortages of water. Twenty inches of rain may fall one year, none the next year, and 40 inches the next. Farmers, who rely on rainfall for their livelihood, have a very uncertain existence in Africa.

REVIEW QUESTIONS

Multiple Choice. Select the letter of the answer that correctly completes each statement.

1. What part of Africa are the rift valleys in?
   A. northern
   B. southern
   C. eastern
   D. western

2. Which is the most valid description of Africa's topography?
   A. a relatively tilted plateau
   B. all rivers navigable for their entire lengths
   C. mountain ranges extending east and west
   D. savanna areas unfit for human habitation

3. The famine conditions in the Sahel region of Africa have been worsened by all the following *except*
   A. desertification
   B. overpopulation
   C. overgrazing
   D. international relief efforts

4. The Sahara
   A. prevented cultural diffusion in North Africa
   B. is a major source of agricultural products
   C. is home to many nomadic groups
   D. prevented migration in North Africa

5. Africa was once known as the Dark Continent, largely because of its
   A. nearness to the equator
   B. people
   C. geography
   D. lack of resources

6. A major reason for the north/south migration trend in East Africa is the location of the
   A. Atlas Mountains and Zaire Basin
   B. Atlantic Ocean and Orange River
   C. Mediterranean Sea and Lake Chad
   D. Great Rift Valley and Nile River

7. European settlers in Africa tended to claim areas
   A. in the equatorial zone
   B. along the upper reaches of the Nile River
   C. adjacent to the Great Rift Valley
   D. in the cool highlands

8. Africa's geography
   A. helped to ensure cultural uniformity on the continent
   B. helped to create cultural diversity on the continent
   C. prevented foreign contact until the 19th century
   D. created insurmountable barriers to north/south migration

9. The Sahara Desert was not a total barrier to communication between North Africa and the West African kingdoms because of the existence of
   A   several north-/south-flowing rivers
   B. an early railroad system
   C. trans-Saharan camel trade routes
   D. a paved highway system

10. The most urgent problem in the Sahel of Africa is the
    A. process of desertification
    B. loss of the rain forest
    C. lack of farm machinery
    D. annual flooding of rivers

11. Africa's smooth coastline
    A. forced the Africans to develop deepwater fishing
    B. limits the number of good natural harbors
    C. prevented European conquest of the interior of the continent
    D. is caused by river runoff and deposits

12. Europeans who settled in Africa chose the highlands of the east largely because
    A. the people there were culturally similar to the Europeans
    B. natives of the area were mostly Christian
    C. the languages spoken there were similar to European languages
    D. the climate was similar to what they were used to in Europe

13. Egypt has been called the Gift of the Nile because
    A. transportation on the Nile made building the pyramids possible
    B. the Nile provides water for irrigation and deposits of alluvial soil
    C. the falls and rapids of the Nile prevented foreign invasion of Egypt
    D. the water of the Nile provide hydroelectric power for industry

14. The Great Rift Valley
    A. improved east/west travel in Africa
    B. is the location of many of Africa's great lakes
    C. was a major avenue of trade in ancient Africa
    D. contains Africa's richest farmland

ESSAYS

1. One of the greatest environmental problems in Africa is the process of desertification in the Sahel.

   Write an essay describing three of the causes of desertification and attempts to resolve the problem.

2. For many years Europeans referred to Africa as the Dark Continent.

   A. Explain why Europeans referred to Africa as the Dark Continent.
   B. Explain two reasons why Europeans remained ignorant of much of Africa for such a long period of time.

II. ECONOMIC GEOGRAPHY OF AFRICA

Resources

The soils of Africa are generally poor, oxidized, and hard. Much of the soil contains laterite, which is not useful for agriculture. The soil of the tropical rain forest appears to be rich but is not. It is leached; the heavy rainfall forces the minerals so deep into the ground that plant roots cannot reach them, and the heavy vegetation is actually supported by the decay of humus on the forest floor. When the rain forest is cut down, heavy erosion occurs and desertification begins.

Africa is rich in mineral resources. In the countries of the Sahara and Nigeria, petroleum is an important source of revenue. Zaire, Zambia, and Zimbabwe have enormous copper deposits. South Africa is a leading producer of gold and the world's major source of diamonds. The continent produces about 80 percent of the world's diamond supply. Other important minerals found in Africa include bauxite, uranium, tungsten, cobalt, tin, and zinc.

WORLD ISSUES

World
Trade and
Finance

Barriers to African Development

Because of geographic, climatic, and economic factors, Africans have had to make major adjustments to suit the environment. In the process, distinct hunting, farming, herding, and fishing societies have developed in various regions of Africa. These groups have long traded with one another, making them interdependent.

Many factors combined to slow development in Africa and to limit the Africans' ability to live in certain regions and provide enough food. One factor is that about 75 percent of the region south of the Sahara is short of water. This is a result of the unpredictability of rainfall, the few great river systems for a continent of this size, and the concentration of lakes in the rift valleys. A lack of capital has made it difficult for many African nations to construct major irrigation projects.

GLOBAL
CONCEPTS

Scarcity

CONCEPTS
GLOBAL

The Africans have made limited use of available natural resources. Historically, the major reason was that resources were located far from market centers. Today they lack the technology to develop these resources, and they also lack the capital for investment in mining and processing industries. Since the resources are located far from market centers, the lack of capital makes it difficult to construct new transportation facilities and to maintain existing ones. Moreover, rivers are not navigable

GLOBAL
CONCEPTS

Technology

CONCEPTS
GLOBAL

all the way to the trade centers because of falls and rapids, and certain climate zones (desert, rain forest) also make it difficult to construct transportation routes.

In sub-Saharan Africa the tsetse fly, which attacks livestock, made the use of horses and oxen impossible, so the Africans developed farming techniques that relied on human labor. Reliance on traditional methods of agriculture and a lack of agricultural equipment make the exploitation of soils, trees, and minerals difficult.

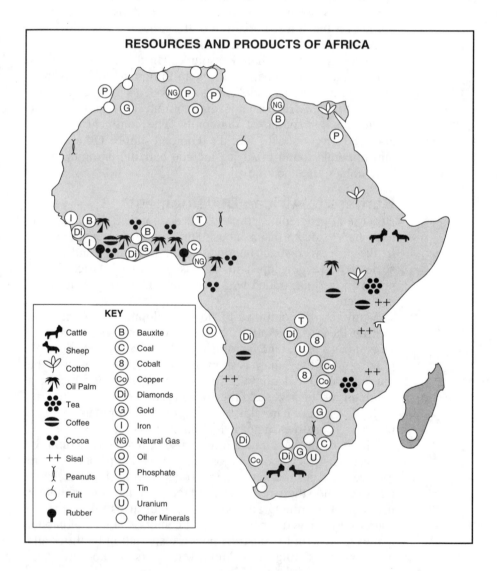

RESOURCES AND PRODUCTS OF AFRICA

Economic Development Since Independence

WORLD ISSUES

Economic
Growth and
Development

The colonial powers followed a policy of mercantilism (colonial powers required their colonies to buy and sell only to them, thus enabling them to export more than they imported and build up economic profit). As a result, some of Africa's resources were developed, but the profits went to the colonial powers. Since Africans were encouraged to raise cash crops and forced to buy more expensive finished products from the mother country, most African nations did not accumulate any capital reserves.

When the African nations became independent, they needed capital to continue the development of their resources and to build industries and modernize. As a result, African nations were forced to borrow heavily from the superpowers (the United States and the Soviet Union) and from their former colonial rulers. They also turned to international organizations such as the World Bank. However, they have borrowed so heavily from such organizations that, with their current economic problems, these organizations are reluctant to lend them more.

WORLD ISSUES

World
Trade and
Finance

Current economic problems of African nations are a result of many factors:

1. With the capital from international loans, some gains were made, but often local conditions were not considered. Factories have been built in areas where the climate makes work difficult, both for people and machines. Dams that were built to supply hydroelectric power sometimes ruin the ecological balance of a region and are therefore harmful to farmers.

2. Capital investment in most countries has been concentrated in the industrial sector. Since most of Africa is still rural, this has not given Africans greater purchasing power, and there is little domestic market for manufactured products.

3. Africa lacks skilled workers. Colonial education was designed to provide lower-level government workers, and those who can afford higher education today are more interested in law, medicine, and so on—education that provides prestige or entry into politics and government.

4. Transportation and communications systems in Africa are still inadequate. Roads are difficult to build and maintain in the tropical climates. It is difficult to transport resources to the sites of manufacturing plants.

5. To achieve progress, people must work together, and this is difficult in nations where ethnic rivalries are prevalent.

GLOBAL
CONCEPTS
Choice
CONCEPTS
GLOBAL

6. Much of the money from international loans and foreign aid has been squandered in schemes designed to promote national pride (such as huge government buildings, statues, and so on) or simply confiscated by corrupt leaders.

7. World economic conditions have also affected Africa. During the 1970s many African nations were forced to pay high prices for petroleum. During the 1980s countries like Nigeria, which export oil, suffered from low oil prices. Prices for many of Africa's cash crops have dropped in the world market.

WORLD ISSUES
Determination
of Political
and Economic
Systems

The heavy debt burden and the export of cash crops create an economic dependency for trade, capital, and food, which is deeply resented by many African peoples and interpreted as neo-colonialism (establishing colonial-type political and economic control in independent developing nations). Many countries in Africa have nationalized (placed under state control) industries, and the presence of multinational corporations (companies with branches in several nations) has been encouraged, even though many Africans resent the foreign ownership and fear a loss of control.

Various attempts at economic development have included the introduction of socialism or mixed economic activities. When Julius Nyerere became president of Tanzania with Tanzania's independence in the 1960s, he introduced a socialist system called ujamaa (familyhood, sharing). In 1967 a program of nationalizing industries and plantations and creating cooperative farms began. Villages in the rural areas were formed into cooperatives, schools and clinics were established, and new farm machinery and techniques were introduced. In the 1970s the rising cost of petroleum products hurt Tanzania, and there were some problems with ujamaa. Hit by drought in 1980 to 1984, Tanzania had to appeal for international aid. Nyerere was replaced in 1985.

WORLD ISSUES
Economic
Growth and
Development

Nigeria has a mixed economy—major industries and oil production are nationalized, while small industries and agriculture remain in private hands. Multinational corporations are required to serve local needs as well as their own interests. Nigeria has experienced success in industrial and petroleum output, but agricultural production still lags, and food must be imported. Many other nations have a mixed economy, such as Kenya, Angola, Zambia, Uganda, Algeria, and Egypt.

WORLD ISSUES
Political and
Economic
Refugees

The trend has been to invest in the urban, industrialized areas and to neglect the rural sector of the economy, and most Africans still live at or near the poverty level. So many Africans have moved to the cities in search of work that the cities are overcrowded, and shantytowns have sprouted up on their outskirts. The unemployment rate is high since there are not enough jobs for all the Africans who have migrated to the cities. City services have proven inadequate to handle the needs of the rapidly expanding population, and pollution and unsanitary conditions are a problem. There is also a notable difference between the "haves" (the rising middle class) and the "have nots" (unemployed rural immigrants), which emphasizes the inequality that still exists in Africa.

Agriculture

Over 70 percent of the African people are still engaged in agriculture. Most African farmers are subsistence farmers, raising just enough to support their families. Many of these farmers use a method known as bush-fallow (the same crop is planted until the land loses its fertility, and then the land is allowed to lie fallow until the fertility is naturally renewed). In order to gain capital, many governments have encouraged the raising of cash crops, such as coffee, peanuts, cotton, cocoa, and palm products, for export. Major food products include maize, cassava, and yams. Because of the demand for cash crops, African farmers do not raise enough food for themselves, and many food products must be imported. In addition, food production is unable to keep up because the population is increasing so rapidly. But there are other reasons:

WORLD ISSUES
Economic
Growth and
Development

1. *Deforestation and erosion.* Most Africans still use wood as a source of fuel, and forests are being destroyed. The loss of forest cover leads to soil erosion and loss of topsoil.

2. *Lack of government encouragement and assistance.* Many African governments are interested in the export of cash crops and accumulation of capital and have failed to provide programs to encourage greater food production.

3. *Desertification.* Overgrazing and overcultivation in the marginal lands (particularly in the Sahel) have increased the rate at which the desert is advancing into what was once agricultural land.

4. *Scarcity of water and erratic rainfall.* African farmers, without government assistance, simply cannot afford the high cost of sinking wells and building irrigation systems.

5. *Failure to fertilize the land.* Many Africans use natural fertilizer for fuel. Most farmers cannot afford artificial fertilizers, and African soils are not naturally rich.

6. *Civil wars.* Civil wars in some countries (notably Ethiopia, Sudan, Mozambique, Chad, Somalia) have resulted in a great decrease in food production and contributed to famine in those countries.

WORLD ISSUES

Environmental
Concerns

7. Drought in the 1970s and 1980s. Over twenty countries in Africa suffered drought in the 1970s and 1980s. The drought was particularly severe in the countries of the Sahel (though drought has affected Tanzania, Mozambique, Kenya, Somalia, and others). Food production dropped and millions of people died.

WORLD ISSUES

Population

The birth rate in Africa remains high because people in rural areas have little access to education and health services. Rural Africans have many children because children can assist in the fields, provide social security (eventual care for their elders), and assure continuance of the family lineage. At the same time, better medical care has decreased the death rate and increased life expectancy.

GLOBAL
CONCEPTS

Change

CONCEPTS
GLOBAL

The Green Revolution, with its hybrid seed and new fertilizers and methods, promises great hope. However, African farmers need government encouragement and assistance to benefit from the Green Revolution. They must be convinced that the new technology is better than traditional methods, and they need financial assistance to purchase the expensive new seeds and fertilizers.

Multiple Choice. Select the letter of the answer that correctly completes each statement.

1. South Africa is one of the world's greatest sources of
   A. oil
   B. gold
   C. iron
   D. timber

2. Which factor of production do poorer African nations need from the World Bank?
   A. labor
   B. capital
   C. land
   D. management

3. An increase in cash crops would directly increase a nation's
   A. imports
   B. exports
   C. population
   D. territory

4. A family that grows only enough food to feed itself is engaged in farming that is known as
   A. single crop
   B. cash crop
   C. subsistence
   D. modernized

5. A country with a one-crop economy is
   A. self-sufficient
   B. economically dependent on others
   C. unaffected by world market fluctuations
   D. independent of international economic trends

6. Europeans colonized Africa for all the following reasons *except*
   A. to provide markets for their own industrial products
   B. to gain control of natural resources
   C. to expand their own empires
   D. to study the languages and religions of the Africans

7. Which of the following beneficial results of colonial rule has actually helped to create one of the major modern problems in emerging African nations?
   A. European technology led to the development of new African industries.
   B. European settlers introduced modern farming methods in Kenya.
   C. Missionaries established elementary schools in the Congo.
   D. New medicines increased life expectancy and decreased the infant mortality rate.

8. Which type of nation is most dependent on world economic trends?
   A. one with a cash-crop economy
   B. one with a subsistence economy
   C. one with a command economy
   D. one with a capitalist economy

9. Vegetation zones in Africa
   A. have strongly influenced regional land use
   B. are much like those in North America
   C. run parallel to the prime meridian
   D. have not affected cultural development

10. Africa is best known for its
    A. mineral resources
    B. food surpluses
    C. democratic governments
    D. health care facilities

11. Leached soil
    A. has high levels of minerals and nutrients
    B. does not support profitable agriculture
    C. results from overgrazing
    D. occurs in desert regions

12. European powers required their colonies to buy from and sell to only them. This practice is known as
    A. imperialism
    B. nationalism
    C. mercantilism
    D. nationalization

13. A country in which the government owns mines and rail lines and private citizens own major industries and the land has an economy known as
    A. communism
    B. utopian
    C. mixed economy
    D. traditional

14. All the following have contributed to famine conditions in Africa *except*
    A. civil disturbances and warfare
    B. erosion
    C. desertification
    D. excess rainfall

15. Many early sub-Saharan societies did not use horse and oxen power because
    A. the tsetse fly and sleeping sickness were present
    B. they made use of the camel as a source of labor instead
    C. they had no domesticated animals
    D. their animistic beliefs denied them the use of animal power

16. The majority of sub-Saharan nations do not have the necessary capital to invest in industrial development largely because
    A. colonial powers made no efforts to develop African resources
    B. they are spending most of their money cleaning up the environment
    C. too much is spent providing social services for rural inhabitants
    D. the majority of sub-Saharan Africans are subsistence farmers with little or no cash income

17. Which of the following is a result of the fact that approximately 70 percent of all Africans live in rural areas and depend on agriculture for a living?
    A. Africa has one of the most rapidly growing populations of any of the continents.
    B. There is a problem of unemployment in African urban areas.
    C. Most African governments have concentrated on building roads and electric plants in rural areas.
    D. The increase in population growth has been matched by increasing food production.

ESSAYS

1. Many African nations face barriers to economic development. Discuss three barriers, including both natural and manmade problems.

2. Food production is inadequate in many parts of Africa. Describe three reasons for this situation and specific steps being taken to solve each one.

III. HUMAN AND CULTURAL GEOGRAPHY OF AFRICA

The People of Africa

A 1991 estimate of Africa's population puts it at 817 million, approximately 15 percent of the world's population. The people of Africa may be more diverse than the people of any other continent. They differ from one another both culturally and physically for two main reasons. First, Africans have intermingled and intermarried with others for generations. Second, because of geography many African groups developed in relative isolation. In fact, there are over 2,000 distinct cultural or ethnic groups.

Anthropologists seem to agree that most of the people of sub-Saharan Africa reveal physical characteristics of the Negroid race. Physical characteristics vary from group to group, however. Skin color ranges from very dark to light, hair texture varies, and the world's tallest as well as the shortest peoples are found in Africa. The people of North Africa reflect Caucasian characteristics. Many Europeans have settled in South Africa, Kenya, and Zimbabwe. East Africa and the Republic of South Africa also have many Asian peoples.

GLOBAL
CONCEPTS
Diversity
CONCEPTS
GLOBAL

African Languages

Somewhere between 800 and 1,000 different languages are spoken on the African continent. The Bantu languages of sub-Saharan Africa are the most widely spoken. Swahili, a mixture of Arabic and Bantu, is spoken in East Africa. The Khoisan (click) languages are spoken by the Bushmen and Hottentots. Hausa is common in West Africa, and Arabic is common in North Africa. In addition, many European languages are spoken and reflect the colonial heritage. For example, in many African countries, English and French were the colonial European languages widely spoken there before independence. Today they are used as official languages.

GLOBAL
CONCEPTS
Change
CONCEPTS
GLOBAL

Religion in Africa

Most Africans still believe in their traditional religions, although many are Christians and Muslims.

Traditional Beliefs

Traditional African religions were as varied as the ethnic groups that created them, and there are over 2,000 ethnic groups on the African continent. In spite of this, there are certain beliefs that most of the traditional African religions have in common. These include belief in ancestral spirits, belief in continuity of the clan and ethnic group, and belief that the land is held in ancestral trust. Traditional religions developed a philosophy of the individual's relation to the natural world and of the individual's place in that world. It helped to provide each clan and ethnic group with an identity.

In traditional Africa the individual was a member of a family, which was a part of a clan, which in turn was part of an ethnic group or tribe. It is common belief that the African is part of an unbroken chain that includes dead ancestors, living relatives, and unborn relatives, and that a person's spirit lives as long as he or she is remembered by future generations.

Also common in sub-Saharan traditional religious belief is the idea that ancestral spirits are involved in the lives of the present generation. It is believed that the ancestral spirits watch over the living. The spirits of ancestors are helpful as long as they are respected, but when they are not, they will bring harm to their descendants. As a result, prayers, ceremonial rites, and even sacrifices are necessary to show respect for ancestors.

According to tradition, the land was held in trust by the ancestors and could not be owned. The African only had the right to use it. The land belonged to the family, the clan, and the ethnic group, and the right to work or use it was handed down from generation to generation.

Also common in traditional African religion is belief in a supreme God who created the world and then withdrew and in lesser gods whose spirits inhabit natural things (animism). These spirits determine everything that happens; they control life and death, good and evil. Most Africans do not worship rivers, trees, animals, and so on; instead, they worship the spirits they represent.

Among some traditional African groups, there was also a belief that the chiefs or kings were divine. In others, the chief was considered the custodian of the land, and he could assign the right to use it.

Islam in Africa

Islam, the religion of the prophet Muhammad, originated in the deserts of the Arabian Peninsula in the 7th century. Shortly thereafter, Muslim conquerors swept across North Africa in search of converts to Islam and also arable land. They offered the conquered peoples three choices: fight, convert, or pay tribute. Conversion to Islam was the easiest and most practical response. Many of the teachings of Islam were similar to those of traditional African beliefs and were liberal enough to allow an African to become a

Muslim and still retain many traditional beliefs and customs (see the unit on the Middle East for a discussion of Islam).

Islam spread to West Africa as a result of the trade carried along the trans-Saharan trade routes by the Arabs. In time, Islam spread to the kingdoms of Ghana, Mali, and Songhai, which became theocracies (where religious leaders are also government leaders). Muslims established universities, religious centers of learning, and research that enriched the lives of the people of West African kingdoms. In the eastern coastal regions of Africa, Islam was spread by Arab traders, who controlled the trade between Africa and the Far East and who settled in coastal cities and towns.

In a region of great ethnic diversity, Islam has provided a focus for unity, and in some of the North and West African

GLOBAL
CONCEPTS

Change

CONCEPTS
GLOBAL

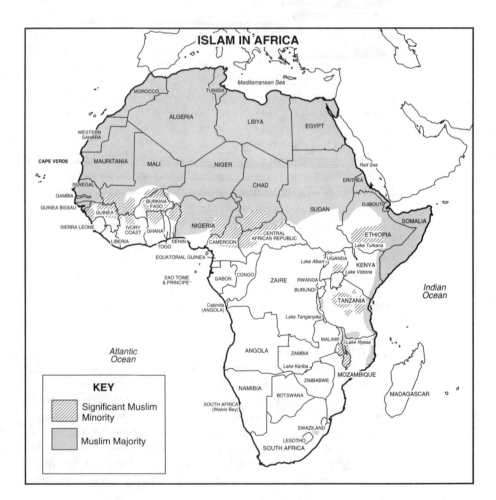

ISLAM IN AFRICA

KEY

Significant Muslim Minority

Muslim Majority

GLOBAL
CONCEPTS

Identity

CONCEPTS
GLOBAL

GLOBAL
CONCEPTS

Justice

CONCEPTS
GLOBAL

WORLD ISSUES

Terrorism

GLOBAL
CONCEPTS

Change

CONCEPTS
GLOBAL

GLOBAL
CONCEPTS

Culture

CONCEPTS
GLOBAL

countries, it was used as a rallying point for independence movements. The Arabic language also provided unity and in many areas, the first written language. Koranic (Quran, the holy book of Islam) studies led to a new class of educated leaders. Islamic law (which exists along with traditional African law) and laws established during the colonial period in most of North Africa provided a uniform system of justice, while Muslim traders increased the amount of trade and market activity.

Fundamentalist Islamic movements in some African countries have created tension and violence in the 20th century. The assassination of Egyptian President Anwar Sadat in 1981 is one example. The political unrest in Sudan as a result of an attempt to institute Islamic law in the 1980s is another.

Christianity in Africa

The Coptic Christian church was established in Egypt in the 1st century A.D. as a result of Greek influence. Coptic Christianity was brought to the Sudan or Nubia by Egyptian missionaries and made its way to Axum in the 4th century, where it was adopted as the official religion.

In the 1400s and 1500s, Portuguese and Spanish explorers who came to Africa were accompanied by Christian missionaries. Numerous missions were established along the west coast, but not many Africans converted to Christianity. In the late 19th century, missionaries followed the explorers into the interior of Africa, where they established schools to teach the doctrines of Christianity. By the end of the 19th century, Europeans had carved Africa into colonial empires, and Christianity came to be associated with colonial regimes. Nevertheless, millions of Africans converted to Christianity, both for spiritual and practical reasons. As with Islam, there were certain similarities between Christianity and traditional African beliefs, such as the African belief in a supreme God and the Christian belief in a single God, that enabled many Africans to adopt Christianity. Moreover, Africans soon learned that training at the mission schools was necessary if they wanted to take part in the economic activities and administration of government under their colonial rulers. Many of them used the knowledge of scientific theory, human rights, and self-determination they learned in the mission schools to become leaders of independence movements in their nations. There have been movements to establish independent African Christian churches and to make Christianity more African in form. Many Africans believe that Christianity can be adapted to African life and tradition without sacrificing its major teachings.

Role and Expression of Traditional African Art

GLOBAL CONCEPTS

Identity

CONCEPTS GLOBAL

Two of the dominant and most famous of the traditional African art forms are sculpture and masks. African sculpture served ritual purposes and was often designed with the intent of social control. African sculpture includes figurines, fetishes (objects thought to have magical powers to bring good or evil and protect the owner from evil forces), and stools. A piece of sculpture was not designed to be looked at and enjoyed as a beautiful creation. Instead, it was designed for use in ceremonies, to represent spirits of ancestors or gods, or even to house spirits of unborn babies. Some, usually those of animals, were carved to represent admirable qualities, such as strength, speed, or endurance. Some represented fertility. Since these sculptures were often representations, it was not considered proper for them to be too realistic. As a result, African art was often abstract or exaggerated. The most favored material for sculpture was wood, but bronze, brass, gold, clay, ivory, and soapstone were also used.

GLOBAL CONCEPTS

Culture

CONCEPTS GLOBAL

African masks, which can be considered a form of sculpture, were worn in ceremonies of ritual dance. The mask, which was often worn with a costume, was part of a spiritual disguise. Often the masks were hidden, except when the ceremonies took place. When used in ceremonial rites, worn by rapidly whirling and swaying dancers, the masks became powerful representations of the spirits and gods.

African dance is generally symbolic and has strong ties to traditional religions. Dance was used at initiation ceremonies, funerals, and before going into conflict with other groups. There are dances for a good harvest, a successful hunt, and so on. There are dances to thank, appease, and make requests from the spirits. Dance is also performed for entertainment. Dance is most often accompanied by music. Instruments include drums, gourd rattles, horns, flutes, stringed instruments, and xylophones, depending on the region. African music is polyrhythmic, consisting of as many as five rhythms being played at the same time.

African Cultural and Social Institutions

GLOBAL CONCEPTS

Change

CONCEPTS GLOBAL

The diffusion of Western ideas and institutions resulted in significant changes in African lifestyles and world views of Africans.

Perhaps the most significant change taking place in Africa is the development of many major urban areas. With its rapidly growing population, there isn't enough arable land to support the people, causing many young Africans to migrate to urban areas in search of jobs. Here their lives undergo dramatic change.

In traditional Africa and in the rural areas even today, an African is a member of an extended family, a clan, a lineage, and an ethnic group. As members of an extended family and clan, Africans have social security and are assured of support. In the cities, the extended family becomes a luxury young people can no longer enjoy. Also, in urban life arranged marriages become less and less common. Moreover, since urban Africans no longer depend on the land, the old ethnic authority structure is breaking down. The influence and authority of chiefs or elders is no longer so strong and is seldom felt in the cities.

In much of traditional Africa and in some rural areas today, polygamy was (or is) practiced. In urban areas this is no longer practical for most Africans, and more and more Africans practice monogamy. However, some urban dwellers, who can afford to, still practice polygamy.

African women have traditionally played an important role in society. Among many ethnic groups, division of labor meant that men were hunters and or warriors; among most herders, men were responsible for the herds. This left women to tend the fields, and they were often responsible for marketing the produce. Several ethnic groups practiced matrilineal descent, in which inheritance is carried through the mother's family line. Urban African females are active today in politics, law, medicine, and other professions. In rural areas, the traditional female role is still strong, though more and more men engage in cultivating the fields.

The majority of Africans still live in rural areas and depend on the land for subsistence. The rural areas retain traditional values, attitudes, and practices. There is strong loyalty to the ethnic group and the traditional authority system. The influence of the council of elders is strong, and there is a strong community spirit. Women are largely engaged in traditional roles, and the birth rate is high.

These traditional values and the traditional morality are often in conflict with the changing attitudes of the urban dwellers. The conflict is compounded by the increasing role played by the media and education. Through the mass media and the education process, Africans gain knowledge of Western ideas of mass democracy, socialism, majority rule, and minority rights, and they wish to adopt these concepts. Industrialization and modernization are bringing new technology to Africa, which in turn requires some change in traditional roles and relationships. Women who are wage earners are no longer willing to accept subordinate roles, for example.

GLOBAL CONCEPTS
Choice
CONCEPTS GLOBAL

GLOBAL CONCEPTS
Identity
CONCEPTS GLOBAL

GLOBAL CONCEPTS
Change
CONCEPTS GLOBAL

Although there have been major changes in the lifestyles of many Africans, tradition still has a strong hold in Africa. Many urban Africans return to the rural areas for ceremonies such as marriage, birth, death, and circumcision. In urban areas, members of ethnic groups often band together to provide support.

REVIEW QUESTIONS

Multiple Choice. Select the letter of the answer that correctly completes each statement.

1. The largest language group in Africa is
   A. Swahili
   B. Bantu
   C. Arabian
   D. Hausa

2. Which of these groups has African society been organized around for thousands of years?
   A. occupational
   B. ethnic
   C. economic
   D. national

3. The spread of Islam throughout Africa is an example of
   A. national security
   B. socialism
   C. self-determination
   D. cultural diffusion

4. Animistic beliefs emphasize
   A. monotheism
   B. ancestor worship
   C. nature worship
   D. patriotism

5. The influence of traditional African cultures is best seen today in Western
   A. art forms
   B. technological advances
   C. family patterns
   D. political ideas

6. Racial and family patterns have been studied mostly by
   A. economists
   B. biologists
   C. anthropologists
   D. archeologists

7. Cultural change will occur most rapidly in a region that is
   A. geographically isolated
   B. ethnocentric
   C. industrializing
   D. self-sufficient

8. The greatest advantage for the Africans of the colonial period was that
   A. natives who received a Western education shared a common language
   B. African resources were exploited
   C. through mercantilism the natives had a market for their industrial products
   D. the European countries sold manufactured products to the Africans

9. The effects of urbanization and industrialization on the traditional family include
   A. the strengthening of patriarchal authority
   B. increase in family size
   C. the loss of the eldest male's authoritative control
   D. increased subordination of women

10. The introduction of Western education during the colonial period in Africa
    A. led to the development of nationalist movements in the colonies
    B. insured that the emerging African nations would have a surplus of technically trained workers
    C. resulted in democratic governments in all the former colonies
    D. resulted in equality of the sexes in the independent African countries

11. Young Africans who move to the city seeking employment are likely to find
    A. they miss the sense of security they had as members of a rural community
    B. their lack of education is not a problem because African industry already has plenty of skilled workers
    C. housing in the cities is readily available and fairly cheap
    D. other recently arrived workers are eager to help them adapt to urban living

12. As African nations become more urbanized
    A. traditional ties to the family become stronger
    B. clan and family loyalties weaken
    C. nuclear families become less popular
    D. ancestor worship becomes increasingly important

13. The term Bantu refers to
    A. a tribal grouping in Africa
    B. a linguistic group
    C. religious groups
    D. village organization in Tanzania

14. In which of the following areas would one find the people most strongly
    affected by traditional attitudes and values?
    A. suburban area with many middle-class factory workers
    B. an urban, upper-class neighborhood inhabited by doctors and lawyers
    C. a rural area where the majority have always been subsistence farmers
    D. a lower-class city neighborhood inhabited by people from many dif-
    ferent ethnic backgrounds

ESSAY

There is a great human diversity in Africa. Discuss the validity of this
statement with regard to these items:

1. religion
2. race
3. language

Give specific information in your answers.

I. HISTORY AND POLITICAL GEOGRAPHY OF AFRICA

Discovering Africa's Past

Recent archeological finds in eastern Africa indicate that humans originated in Africa. Evidence indicates that there were humanlike creatures in Africa as much as 5 million years ago, and that humans may have developed there 1.75 million years ago. Basic technology first occurred in Africa. Africa enjoyed a long and rich history before the era of European exploration, conquest, and colonization.

Sources of African History. Our knowledge of early African history is gained in many ways.

1. Archeological evidence is one important source of information. Archeologists working in digs have discovered many fossils (remains of living things) and artifacts (remains of things made by humans) which tell us much about life in Africa millions of years ago. Radiocarbon dating, which determines the age of organic matter by measuring its carbon 14 emission, is used to date the fossils.

2. African oral tradition is another important source of information. African oral tradition consists of myths, legends, fables, and histories passed without a written record from generation to generation. The myths and legends of the Africans are vital clues to the African past. They tell us much about the African perception of themselves (identity), their respect for ancestors, and their relationship to the natural world. The oral tradition has provided continuity of culture and customs in much of sub-Saharan Africa and has enabled many African Americans to trace their lineage.

3. A third important source of knowledge is provided by the writings of the Arab traders and scholars who traveled in Africa and chronicled their visits as early as the 8th century.

4. A fourth important source of knowledge consists of studies done by anthropologists (scientists who study the origin and development of humans and their culture). Some anthropologists, such as the members of the Leakey family (Louis, Mary, and Richard), work on archeological digs to unearth finds relating to early humans. In 1959, Dr. Mary Leakey and her husband, Dr. Louis Leakey, found a skull from a humanlike creature that lived about 1.75 million years ago.

GLOBAL
CONCEPTS

Identity

CONCEPTS
GLOBAL

The Beginnings of Agriculture and Iron Age Technology

It appears that agriculture was practiced in the Nile delta as early as 4000 B.C. Some experts believe that at the same time the cultivation of sorghum and millet began in West Africa.

Agriculture made permanent settlements possible and led to the development of villages, governments, specialization, and increased population. Iron Age technology and the production of iron tools and weapons made possible the increase of food production needed for the growing population.

Iron Age technology began in Africa in the kingdom of Kush in East Africa about 500 B.C. The technology of iron production may have been brought to Kush from a Middle Eastern people known as Assyrians. The technology of iron-making first appeared in West Africa among the Nok peoples of northern Nigeria about 300 B.C. It is believed that Iron Age technology spread southward throughout Africa with the Bantu migrations about 100 A.D.

Various groups of Africans traded with one another. Eventually market towns emerged. There was trade with places as distant as India, Rome, Southeast Asia, and China. The trade with Southeast Asia had a longlasting effect in that the cultivation of certain Southeast Asian crops (rice, yams, bananas) was brought to Africa.

WORLD ISSUES

Economic
Growth and
Development

GLOBAL
CONCEPTS
Technology
CONCEPTS
GLOBAL

GLOBAL
CONCEPTS
Interdependence
CONCEPTS
GLOBAL

Early African Civilizations

Early civilizations other than the Egyptian civilization, which arose along the Nile River, developed in Africa. Two major civilizations that developed in northeastern Africa were Kush and Axum.

Kush civilization developed as early as 2000 B.C. At times, Kush was a province of Egypt. Consequently, Egyptian civilization influenced Kush. For example, in the Kush capital of Napata, there was a religious center dedicated to an Egyptian god. About 700 B.C. Kush invaded and conquered Upper Egypt, and eventually the Kush kings ruled as pharaohs over an empire stretching from the Mediterranean to modern Ethiopia. The Kushites were driven out of Egypt by the Assyrians in about 600 B.C., and the Kush capital was moved from Napata to Meroë in about 540 B.C. The reasons for this move were probably economic. The wealth of Kush was based on the trade of much sought-after African goods, such as ivory, gold, and ebony, with areas to the north and east. As Kush declined it was eventually succeeded by Axum in about 350 A.D.

GLOBAL
CONCEPTS

Interdependence

CONCEPTS
GLOBAL

Axum originated in the coastal region of modern-day Ethiopia about 300 B.C. and evolved into the modern Ethiopian state. The Axumites were Semitic, and they developed a written language of their own. The wealth of Axum was based on the control of northeast African and Red Sea trade routes, which brought them into contact with both the Mediterranean and Arabian worlds. The capital of Axum, Adulis, was a cosmopolitan area with peoples from Greece, Egypt, Rome, Persia, and India. Iron was traded to other Africans, and the goods received in exchange (ivory, gold, slaves, and so forth) were in turn traded with Greece, Egypt, Arabia, and other countries.

Axum extended its control over Meroë in about 350 A.D. and also conquered areas on the Arabian Peninsula. Axum adopted Coptic Christianity in about 100 A.D. Persia invaded the Arabian provinces of Axum in the late 6th century, gaining control of some of Axum's more important trade routes, and the power of Axum began to decline. Muslim invasions in the 7th and 8th centuries also lessened the trading power of Axum, but the kingdom continued and eventually extended its borders to those of present-day Ethiopia.

In West Africa the kingdoms of Ghana, Mali, and Songhai developed along the Niger. All three kingdoms were powerful for several reasons. First, they controlled the trans-Saharan trade routes in West Africa. Second, they were located between the salt mines to the north and the gold mines to the south. Third, they had developed agriculture. Fourth, they had strong central governments. Fifth, they all used iron. Sixth, they all had large armies.

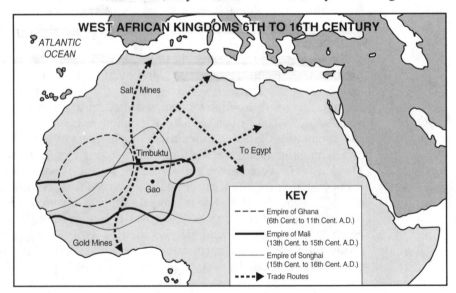

WEST AFRICAN KINGDOMS 6TH TO 16TH CENTURY

ATLANTIC OCEAN

Salt Mines

Timbuktu

To Egypt

Gao

Gold Mines

KEY

- - - - Empire of Ghana
(6th Cent. to 11th Cent. A.D.)

——— Empire of Mali
(13th Cent. to 15th Cent. A.D.)

——— Empire of Songhai
(15th Cent. to 16th Cent. A.D.)

- - -▶ Trade Routes

Ghana developed in about 300 A.D. The people to the north wanted gold, and the people to the south who had the gold needed salt from the people in the north. Their trade routes passed through Ghana, and the king taxed the trade in both directions and became very wealthy. He also claimed title to all gold in the kingdom and controlled the amount of gold on the market. The tax money was used to support the government and army. Iron tools made the farmers of Ghana more efficient, and iron weapons made it possible for them to subdue enemies and expand territory. In the 11th century, Ghana was attacked by Muslims. The warfare disrupted the trade routes and interfered with agricultural production, and Ghana went into a state of decline. By 1235 it no longer existed.

Mali originated in 1200, replacing the kingdom of Ghana. Its power was based on the use of iron, its wealthy farming region, its control of the trans-Saharan trade routes, and the salt and gold mines. Like Ghana, Mali taxed all goods transported through the kingdom and became extremely prosperous. Income from taxes was used to support the government and military and to build enormous mosques and palaces. Timbuktu became an important center of Arab learning. Mali was a Muslim kingdom, and its most famous ruler, Mansa Musa, on his pilgrimage to Mecca scattered so much gold in North Africa that it took years for the gold market to recover. In the early 15th century, people from the north and south attacked, and people within the kingdom revolted. Mali went into a state of decline, from which it did not recover.

Songhai, a Muslim kingdom, began to expand into an empire in the 15th century under Sunni Ali. The empire of Songhai was greater in extent than either Ghana or Mali (at its height it contained an area about equal to the continental United States) and also controlled the trans-Saharan trade routes and sources of gold and salt. Both imports and exports were taxed. Cities grew up around commercial and religious centers. In the late 16th century Songhai was invaded by armies from Morocco equipped with guns and cannons. The spears and arrows of the larger Songhai army were no match for them, and they were defeated. The Songhai empire disappeared.

The kingdom of Kongo originated in Central Africa in the coastal region in the late 14th century. Trade and agriculture were the basis of Kongo's economy. The king was considered divine and absolute. The Portuguese appeared in Kongo in 1482 and were interested in obtaining slaves. The divisions caused by disagreements over European influence and the sale of the Kongolese as slaves caused serious problems, and the kingdom disintegrated.

In southeastern Africa a kingdom called Zimbabwe originated perhaps as early as the 6th century. The people of Zimbabwe engaged in agriculture, iron-making, and trade. They
constructed massive stone walls and buildings of stone without
the use of mortar. Trade was carried on with regions as far
away as India and China. It is not known what happened to the
people of Zimbabwe. Perhaps they migrated in search of grass-
lands for their cattle.

Slavery and the Slave Trade in Africa

Slavery has existed in the world since the development of civilization. It existed in ancient Greece, Rome, and China and Africa
long before the arrival of the Europeans. However, slavery in
Africa was quite different from the slavery that developed later,
especially in the Americas. Slaves were captives taken in warfare or criminals and debtors. Slavery was not necessarily hereditary, and it was not seen as total ownership of another human

GLOBAL
CONCEPTS

Human Rights

CONCEPTS
GLOBAL

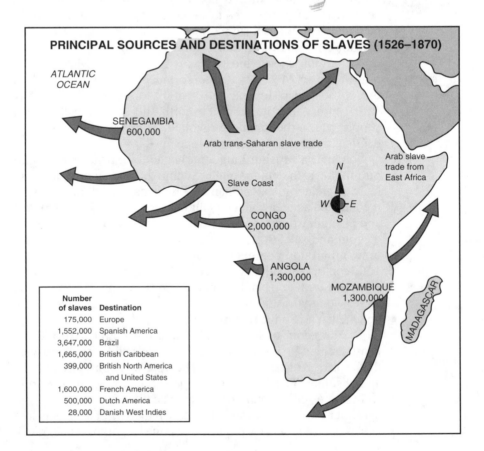

PRINCIPAL SOURCES AND DESTINATIONS OF SLAVES (1526–1870)

ATLANTIC
OCEAN

SENEGAMBIA
600,000

Arab trans-Saharan slave trade

Arab slave
trade from
East Africa

Slave Coast

N

W—E

S

CONGO
2,000,000

ANGOLA
1,300,000

MOZAMBIQUE
1,300,000

MADAGASCAR

Number of slaves	Destination
175,000	Europe
1,552,000	Spanish America
3,647,000	Brazil
1,665,000	British Caribbean
399,000	British North America and United States
1,600,000	French America
500,000	Dutch America
28,000	Danish West Indies

being. Slaves had certain rights and might even be allowed to purchase freedom and own property. The slave trade also existed in Africa before the Europeans arrived. Arabs captured slaves or took them in exchange for other goods and sold them in India, Egypt, Persia, and other places.

The first African slaves to be transported to Europe were taken by the Portuguese in the 15th century. There was no great need for slaves in Europe, however, and they did not become an important item of trade until after the development of plantation agriculture in the Caribbean and North America. In order to raise sugar and tobacco on large plantations, many workers were needed. The native peoples of America did not survive the labor. Indentured servants eventually gained their freedom. Africans, accustomed to hard labor in the tropics, seemed a suitable replacement, and the slave trade increased greatly by the mid-16th century. The Europeans were involved in the highly destructive slave trade from the 16th to the 19th centuries, and their primary interest in Africa was in acquiring slaves.

A triangular trade developed. Cheap European goods, usually cloth and trinkets, were shipped from Europe to Africa (the outward passage), where they were traded for African captives. The Africans were transported to the Americas (the middle passage), where they were traded for sugar and tobacco. These were transported back to Europe (the inward passage), where they could be sold for considerable profit. The profits from this triangular trade in large part provided the capital investment that made the Industrial Revolution in England and America possible.

GLOBAL
CONCEPTS

Interdependence

CONCEPTS
GLOBAL

For the most part, the Europeans did not go into the interior and take their own captives. They established stockades (slave factories) in the coastal regions and purchased captives from the Africans or from Arab slave raiders. However, to provide the vast numbers of captives the slave traders demanded, it became necessary to raid other villages and groups, and this required guns. As a result, one of the most important articles of trade to the Africans became guns.

Effects of the Slave Trade

GLOBAL
CONCEPTS

Change

CONCEPTS
GLOBAL

1. *Depopulation.* An estimate of the number of Africans lost to the slave trade might approach 50 million. Many were killed in tribal warfare. Many died of disease in overpacked slave ships.

2. *Increased tribal warfare.* Villages and crops were destroyed in the warfare to provide captives for the slave trade. Bitterness among Africans themselves developed that still affects relations between ethnic groups in the modern African nations.

3. *Insecurity and fear.* Africans fearing the slave raids sometimes abandoned their villages and moved farther into the interior. Others lived in a constant state of fear, more interested in avoiding capture than in the development of their own society. Arts and crafts declined.

4. *Economic disruption and decay.* Some African states abandoned their traditional ways of making a living and took part in the slave trade. While the slave trade lasted, they were wealthy and powerful, but when it ended, their economies were ruined and the states disappeared. Benin is an example.

5. *The trans-Saharan trade was destroyed.* Because of the huge profits in the slave trade, the trans-Saharan routes of trade lost importance, and the kingdoms in the interior of West Africa declined.

6. *Racism.* To justify the slave trade, those involved nurtured the belief that black Africans, because of their color, were inferior. This belief was accepted by Europeans and Americans, who knew nothing of Africa and its cultures. The resulting prejudice and bias were later used to excuse the imperialist expansion of European nations into African territories.

GLOBAL
CONCEPTS

Human Rights

CONCEPTS
GLOBAL

The Era of Discovery and Chartered Companies

In the late 15th century, the European nations became rivals for the rich trade of the Indies and other parts of Asia. European monarchs granted monopolies on trade to chartered companies such as the British East Africa Company, Dutch East Indies Company, and French East India Company. The trading companies established trading posts and stopovers (way stations) along the coast of Africa, which were located on the route to Asia. Until the 19th century, the European presence was limited to the coastal areas and the trade in gold, ivory, and slaves.

European Imperialism

In the late 19th century, the Europeans began to explore the interior of Africa and to expand their control. This imperialist expansion was made possible by their technological superiority. As the Europeans expanded in Africa, they dominated the African people as well as their territory. They used the excuse of "the white man's burden," a legacy of the slave trade, to justify this expansion, claiming that it was their duty to bring civilization, progress, and Christianity to the less developed regions of the world. In reality, their major goal was to accumulate

GLOBAL
CONCEPTS

Power

CONCEPTS
GLOBAL

profit and power. This period of European imperialism was influenced by industrial capitalism and the increasing demands for raw materials for European factories and for markets for European manufactured goods. The Europeans needed African resources—mineral, land, forest products. They also desired greater power and prestige. The more territory they controlled, the more powerful and important they became, and European nations became rivals for African territory.

The Africans resisted the intrusion of Europeans and felt they were defending themselves against invasion. The Zulu fought the British and Boers in South Africa. The Sudanese fought the British. The Mandingo fought the French in West Africa. The Germans were forced to fight in East Africa. The Africans fought conventionally and also used guerrilla tactics, but their weapons were no match for those of the Europeans. Some of the African peoples used passive resistance. The Bushmen and Hottentots in South Africa simply disappeared into the bush.

In 1875, European holdings in Africa were fairly small, but by 1914 all of Africa except Ethiopia and Liberia were under European control. The scramble for Africa began after King Leopold of Belgium announced he was taking control of the vast Congo Free State in Central Africa in 1879. In 1885, at the Berlin Conference, the European nations reached agreement on how Africa should be divided into colonial territories.

GLOBAL
CONCEPTS

Political Systems

CONCEPTS
GLOBAL

Some Africans served as mercenaries in the European armies or worked with the colonial governments. The British used a colonial policy known as indirect rule. They left tribal leaders in charge, but the Africans were actually puppet rulers who followed directions from the British colonial administrators.

GLOBAL
CONCEPTS

Change

CONCEPTS
GLOBAL

The French practiced a policy of assimilation. Their hope was to make the Africans "French" by changing their culture and traditions. The French ruled more directly than the British and removed the traditional rulers.

The Belgians used a policy of paternalism, treating the indigenous peoples as children who needed to be cared and provided for.

The Portuguese at first believed the Africans needed to be taught discipline and obedience. In the 20th century, however, this attitude changed, and they adopted a policy of assimilation intended to eventually make the Africans citizens of Portugal.

German rule in Africa was different in different colonies. In some they used forced labor. In others they tried the indirect rule approach.

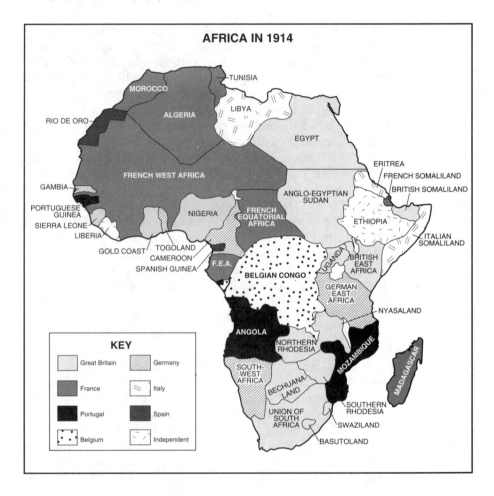

AFRICA IN 1914

KEY
- Great Britain
- France
- Portugal
- Belgium
- Germany
- Italy
- Spain
- Independent

For additional information on European imperialism, see Unit 6.

Effects of European Rule on Africa

GLOBAL CONCEPTS

Identity

CONCEPTS GLOBAL

1. *Establishment of boundaries.* When the Europeans divided Africa, they drew up boundaries that had nothing to do with physical features or ethnic boundaries. As a result, ethnic groups found their territories divided among more than one colony; some were within boundaries with traditional enemies. Because the colonies were granted independence based on the European-drawn boundaries, the problems created by dividing ethnic territories or expecting enemies to coexist remain in modern Africa.

2. *Changes in agriculture.* To provide raw materials for their industries, the Europeans encouraged the development of plantations and the cultivation of cash crops such as cocoa, cotton, coffee, peanuts, and palm oil. Many Africans concentrated on the cultivation of these cash crops, and they had to import food crops to feed themselves. In areas of heavy European settlement, such as South Africa and the Kenya highlands, the best farmland was reserved for Europeans.

WORLD ISSUES

Economic
Growth and
Development

3. *Transition from barter to money economy.* Taxes such as the head tax or the hut tax had to be paid in cash. To pay the tax, many Africans were forced to work for Europeans. They had to move to the city, sometimes with their families, sometimes leaving the family in the countryside to work the land, thereby destabilizing the family system. In addition, the money economy created greater disparities in wealth. Some Africans accumulated capital, while others did not. As a result, social tension was created between the haves and the have nots.

4. *Changes in the landholding system.* Europeans introduced the idea of individual ownership of land. This weakened tribal ties and also meant that for some, there was no land, thus destroying the Africans' traditional way of making a living.

5. *Exploitation of resources.* The Europeans needed raw materials for their factories, so they developed the resources of Africa by opening mines and plantations. The benefits of this development went to the Europeans, not the Africans.

6. *Improved transportation and communications.* In order to exploit the resources of Africa, the Europeans had to build railroads and communications systems. These improvements benefited the Africans by assisting in the development of national unity and opening remote regions of the interior to economic development. However, they also accelerated the migration of African labor to areas where work could be found, further weakening tribal and family ties.

WORLD ISSUES

Determination
of Political
and Economic
Systems

7. *New legal and judicial systems.* The European nations introduced their own ideas of law and justice in the colonies. Secular law and religious law were separated, while traditional law was changed or abolished, again weakening group ties and eroding traditional authority systems.

8. *Education.* Although education was not freely available to all Africans, some education was provided. Through European education, Africans learned of democracy and natural human rights and again began to reject traditional authority systems. Traditional African culture was downgraded and European culture upheld as the example of how things should be. Educated

Africans became the core of the nationalist movements in Africa and led the struggle for political independence from colonial domination.

9. *Preventive medicine and improved nutrition.* Because of Western medicines and medical practices, the infant mortality rate and overall death rate dropped dramatically. As a result, Africa has the most rapidly increasing population growth rate (about 3 percent) of any of the continents.

African Nationalism and Pan-Africanism

The nationalist movements in Africa varied from region to region and colony to colony. However, for Africans of all colonies, nationalism meant that they wanted to rule themselves and to decide what form that rule would take.

During World War II, many Africans served in the armies of their colonial rulers in Asia, Europe, and Africa. Many others moved to the cities to work in wartime industries for comparatively high wages. In the cities they acquired new skills, learned about life in other parts of the world, joined labor unions and political organizations, and came into contact with the ideas of young nationalists. They began to see that a unified nation might be built and began to transfer their loyalties from traditional groups and authority to these new groups and the idea of a modern nation state.

When the war ended, many of the colonies in Asia achieved independence. Successful independence movements in Asia encouraged the Africans to seek their own independence. Some African nationalists employed the nonviolent methods of Mahatma Gandhi and used passive resistance. Others employed guerrilla tactics. The Europeans, struggling to repair their own economies, industries, and societies, could not afford a prolonged struggle in Africa. They began to prepare their colonies for independence.

In 1957 the Gold Coast gained its independence from Great Britain. It changed its name to Ghana. Guinea gained its independence from France the following year. By 1977 there were more than 40 independent nations in Africa. The era of African colonialism was over.

The colonial legacy left a major problem for the newly independent African nations to deal with—rivalries among the many ethnic groups inhabiting their nations. The new African nations must try to unite people with diverse languages, religions, and customs. Many African leaders have met this challenge by outlawing all but one political party and creating single-party

WORLD ISSUES

Determination
of Political
and Economic
Systems

states. Most leaders do not see this as undemocratic, because membership in the one party is open to all, and they feel that a single party will ensure a more stable government. Some African nations have approached the problem by not holding elections. In others, elections are so corrupt that they are meaningless.

In many African nations, the military staged a coup d'etat (overthrow of the government). Sometimes the coup was to overthrow leaders who were thought to be bad, ineffective, or corrupt. Sometimes it was in an effort to improve economic conditions or to subdue rival political factions that had built up their own military. Sometimes it was simply the desire of military leaders for more power.

In about 1960 there was a call for pan-Africanism, a joining together of African nations to improve conditions for all African peoples. The goals of pan-Africanism are to improve economic, political, and social conditions for all Africans. Nationalist feelings in the various African nations have been a stumbling block to pan-Africanism, however.

GLOBAL
CONCEPTS
Identity
CONCEPTS
GLOBAL

In 1963 the Organization of African Unity was created to try to foster cooperation and unity in order to achieve progress. It has had success in solving some problems but has no real authority to force its decisions on any nation.

South Africa

The Dutch established a supply station at the Cape of Good Hope in 1652. Before long, Dutch settlers began to arrive, and the supply station became Cape Colony. (The Dutch settlers and their descendants are known as Afrikaaners. The Dutch farmers were known as Boers.) The Hottentots and Bushmen were pushed north as the settlers took more land for farms. The farmers (Boers) employed black slave labor.

In the late 18th century, the British came to establish their own supply stations, and in 1806 they seized the Cape Colony. In 1836 several thousand Boers began the "great trek" northeastward to escape British rule and preserve their Afrikaaner culture. They were resisted by the Zulu (Bantus), who were defeated at the Battle of Blood River in 1838. By the 1850s the Boers had established two republics in the interior: the Transvaal and the Orange Free State. However, when diamonds were discovered in the Orange Free State in 1871 and gold in the Transvaal in 1886, British miners and businesspeople began to arrive.

Hostilities between the Afrikaaners and the British increased until the Boer War of 1899 to 1902, in which the Afrikaaners were defeated. In 1910 the British united the two Boer republics, Cape Colony and Natal, into the Union of South Africa, which became a self-governing country of the British Empire in 1934.

African and Asian (mostly from the British colony in India) workers were recruited for work in the mines and associated industries. Many Afrikaaners believed in the superiority of the white race and its culture, and the British did little to prevent this attitude or the resulting discrimination and segregation.

In 1948 the Afrikaaner Nationalist party gained control of the government and began the policy of apartheid (Afrikaans word meaning "separateness"). This policy rigidly defined four racial groups: white, black, Asian, and colored. Under this policy each group was to have its own living areas and develop its own political institutions. Black Africans had to carry passbooks containing information on where they lived and worked and where they could travel. Intermarriage was forbidden, separate education was provided, strikes by black workers were outlawed, jobs were restricted to racial groups, separate facilities had to be maintained, and blacks could not own land outside black homelands. Blacks had no vote and no representation in government. They were denied basic human rights. The Bantu Authorities Act of 1951 established ten Bantustans (homelands) for the blacks. Until 1985 a policy of forced relocation of unemployed blacks to the homelands was followed. The blacks were to be allowed "separate but equal" development on these homelands. They were to become independent countries with their own governments and economies.

POPULATION OF SOUTH AFRICA

Official Category	Number of People (millions)	% of Total Population
Black	23.9	67.7
White	4.8	18.3
Colored	3	10.6
Asian	1	3.4

In 1912 the African National Congress (ANC), an organization to unite the South African blacks, to end segregation and to work for the right to take part in government, was created. The ANC was originally a nonviolent organization. They used strikes and employed many of the same methods used by Mahatma Gandhi. After the Sharpeville Massacre in 1960, the

ANC turned to the use of sabotage. They blew up power lines and refineries to undermine confidence in the government, disrupt the economy, and bring international attention to their plight. The government banned the ANC and arrested its leaders, including Nelson Mandela.

Beginning with the Soweto riots in 1976, activity against the policy of apartheid increased in South Africa. As more and more nations condemned the policy, some restrictions were relaxed. Petty apartheid (separate facilities) was largely dropped, though some beaches remained restricted. Blacks were allowed to form labor unions, but they still had no voice in government.

As protests and violence escalated, international pressure on South Africa to change its policies increased. The government, under the leadership of P. W. Botha, repealed the pass laws and the Mixed Marriages Act. Many black prisoners were released.

WORLD ISSUES

World

Trade and

Finance

In 1974 South Africa lost its voting privileges in the United Nations. In 1986 the U.S. Congress passed sanctions against South Africa. Most American companies sold their interests and left South Africa. The British Commonwealth nations also voted for sanctions.

F. W. de Klerk became president of South Africa in 1989. In 1990 he lifted the ban on the ANC and released Nelson Mandela from prison. By June 1991 the last of the apartheid laws, the race registration law, was repealed, and talks between the white government and representatives of the ANC—including, of course, Nelson Mandela—were begun. In June 1993 the representatives agreed on a date in April 1994 for the first election, in which all people in South Africa would be eligible to vote for a legislature, which would write a new constitution for the country. In September 1993 Nelson Mandela told world leaders that enough progress had been made with the government in South Africa and that the economic sanctions imposed by other nations could and should be lifted.

GLOBAL
CONCEPTS

Citizenship

CONCEPTS
GLOBAL

Proposals for the new constitution include guarantees of freedom of speech and fair trial, freedom to choose where to live, freedom from torture, limits on the president's power to declare a state of emergency, and guarantees against the loss of citizenship. In addition, it has been agreed that the homelands will be abolished immediately after the elections.

There were a number of groups that condemned the agreements. They included conservative Afrikaaners who did not wish to see any change in the government at all and other white groups that demanded that territory be set aside as a white homeland that would no longer be part of South Africa. There were also black groups that were against the agreements. They

included the Inkhatha Freedom party, which represents the Zulu ethnic group, numbering more than 8 million. The leader of Inkhatha is Mangosuthu Gatsha Buthelezi, who did not wish to cede his political power to Nelson Mandela, who went on to win the presidential election in April 1994. Lucas Mangope, the leader in Bophuthatswana, the homeland of the Tswana people (2.5 million residents), also objected to the new agreements.

In spite of all the objections, enormous steps have been taken to end the system of apartheid in South Africa and to finally provide political representation for the majority of its people.

In December 1993 Nelson Mandela and F. W. de Klerk jointly received the Nobel Peace Prize for their efforts to work out a plan for the peaceful transition to majority rule and to bring about the end of apartheid in South Africa. The 1994 elections were generally peaceful, and resulted in a multi-party legislature. Nelson Mandela became the nation's new leader in an historic inauguration.

Kenya

In the late 19th century, Kenya came under the control of the British government as part of the East Africa Protectorate. Before long, British settlers came.

The nationalist movement in Kenya began in the early 20th century. Jomo Kenyatta, the leader of the nationalist movement, became president of the Kenya African Union in 1947. Its major goals were to regain control of the land lost to the Europeans, to halt exploitation of Africans by Europeans, and to gain basic civil rights for Africans.

An organization known as the Mau Mau was created in 1952, which used terrorist and guerrilla activities to free Kenya. The British declared a state of emergency and placed thousands in detention camps.

In 1956 the British began gradual reforms and Africans were allowed some participation in government. However, Africans demanded independence, and in 1963 Kenya was granted independence. In 1964 Kenya became a republic in the British Commonwealth of Nations and Jomo Kenyatta its first president.

There were many problems in Kenya as a result of differences among the many ethnic groups (the Kikuyu, the Luo, the Masai, the Kalenjin, and so on). Kenyatta, a Kikuyu, urged his people to forget their ethnic loyalties and accept a principle he called harambee (pulling together). Kenyatta died in 1978 and was succeeded by Daniel Arap Moi.

Because the major political parties in Kenya represented the major ethnic groups and helped prolong the ethnic rivalries,

WORLD ISSUES

Determination
of Political
and Economic
Systems

GLOBAL
CONCEPTS

Human Rights

CONCEPTS
GLOBAL

Kenya was declared a one-party state in 1982. The only legal political party is KANU (Kenya African National Union). In 1991 a constitutional amendment established a multi-party system. Several new parties have emerged since then, but there is much factionalism, and elections have been plagued by electoral fraud. Moi was elected to his fourth term of office December 1992, and in January 1993 he dissolved the multi-party legislature, probably because he feared the legislature would introduce legislation that would limit presidential powers. Kenya is considered one of the top human rights violators in the world, and in recent years American tourists have been cautioned about traveling in Kenya because of the strife and ethnic conflicts.

WORLD ISSUES

Political and
Economic
Refugees

The government began a program to Africanize Kenyan life and economics. Asians were required to obtain work permits and could not be employed unless there were no Kenyans suitable for the job or they had special talents. Many Asians emigrated to Great Britain. In 1968 Britain limited immigration, and the remaining Asians have suffered economically and socially. As part of the program to Africanize Kenya, European ownership of land has also been reduced.

Most of Kenya's people make a living in agriculture, although fertile land is scarce. Kenya has one of the most rapidly increasing populations in the world. The annual per capita income is about $300. Major exports are cash crops such as coffee, tea, and sisal. Industrial development is limited, and the unemployment rate is high. The country has two official languages, English and Swahili, and many ethnic languages are spoken by the groups inhabiting the country.

Nigeria

GLOBAL
CONCEPTS

Diversity

CONCEPTS
GLOBAL

Over 200 different ethnic groups live in Nigeria, but the four largest and most politically dominant are the Hausa and Fulani in the north, the Ibo in the southeast, and the Yoruba in the southwest.

In the mid-19th century, the British began their expansion into Nigeria. By 1914 all of Nigeria was a British colony. After World War I a nationalist movement arose. The British gradually allowed more African participation in government until in 1954 a constitution creating a federal union, ensuring the power of the three major regions—the east, the west, and the north—was accepted. Independence was finally granted in 1960.

Almost immediately, regional differences became obvious. The northern region, with the largest population, controlled the federal government. In 1966 there was a coup led by Ibo military officers, and General Ironsi took control of the government. Later in 1966 violence broke out against Ibo living in the north, and General Ironsi was killed by Hausa soldiers and replaced by Yakuba Gowon, a northerner. General Ojukwu, the leader of the Ibo region, declared eastern Nigeria independent as the Republic of Biafra.

Civil war broke out about two months later. Biafra was unable to hold back the Nigerian troops or to feed its people. An estimated one million Biafrans died as a result of military action or starvation. Early in 1970 Biafra surrendered.

Military coups have occurred frequently in Nigeria since 1970. The country has been under military rule for most of the years since independence. It has been divided into nineteen states, each having its own governor. From 1983 to 1989 all political parties were banned. In 1989 political parties were again allowed to register. Later in 1989 the incumbent president, General Ibrahim Babangida, announced that the government would create two new political parties because, he said, other political parties were linked to discredited groups and had also failed to fulfill registration requirements. Elections were held in the summer of 1993, but the results were voided by Babangida. In August 1993, after much turmoil in the nation, Babangida resigned, and an interim government was named.

Nigeria made a rapid recovery from the civil war, largely because of oil revenues. However, mismanagement and overspending of funds led to an economic decline in the early 1980s. In 1987 the government announced plans for economic austerity, began to encourage a birth-control program, and promised a return to civilian government by 1992. Besides petroleum, exports include cash crops such as rubber, palm products, and timber. The annual per capita income is less than $500. In 1994, labor disputes continued to weaken Nigeria's economy. A military-dominated government remained in power, still refusing to give in to Moshood Abrola, the civilian winner in the 1993 elections.

WORLD ISSUES

Determination
of Political
and Economic
Systems

Africa in the Global Context

For the most part, after independence African nations chose to remain nonaligned (choosing to be neither pro-Soviet nor pro-United States). African leaders also feared neocolonialism. For this reason, many were reluctant to maintain strong relationships with their former colonial rulers or with any industrialized Western nation. Others were economically so weak that they had to allow colonial banks and industries to remain in place. In addition, many nations that avoided foreign involvement immediately following independence have since been forced by economic and political crises to accept the presence of multinational corporations.

WORLD ISSUES

Determination
of Political
and Economic
Systems

International Organizations. Many African nations have joined a number of international organizations to promote African unity, improve economics, and strengthen their influence in world markets and world events.

1. *The United Nations.* The African nations now have the most powerful voting bloc in the United Nations General Assembly, with about 50 members, and can influence UN decisions and policies. African nations have received much aid and assistance through various UN agencies.

2. *The World Bank.* The bank, a specialized agency associated with the UN, provides loans and technical assistance to developing nations.

3. *The International Monetary Fund.* The IMF, another specialized agency of the UN, provides loans to members with balance-of-payments problems and provides technical assistance.

4. *The Commonwealth of Nations.* Many of the former colonies of Great Britain belong. It was organized to promote economic cooperation and to coordinate scientific, military, and educational affairs.

5. *The Lome Convention.* In 1975 a number of African, Caribbean, and Pacific nations voted to associate themselves with the European Economic Community to gain economic benefits through trade and tariff agreements.

6. *Organization of Petroleum Exporting Countries.* OPEC, designed to control world oil prices by coordinating and controlling production, has four African member states: Algeria, Gabon, Libya, Nigeria.

7. *Organization of African Unity.* The OAU was founded in 1963 to promote unity, solidarity, and cooperation among African states. It has little power beyond talking and trying to encourage cooperation. It has enjoyed some success in settling boundary disputes and developing energy sources.

Foreign Intervention. In certain instances African countries or groups within those countries have been forced to ask for, or have been unable to prevent, foreign intervention in their internal affairs.

1. *The Congo (Zaire) in the 1960s.* After the Belgian Congo became independent in June 1960, the Province of Katanga, under the leadership of Moise Tshombe, seceded and declared its independence. Belgium sent troops to end the rebellions. The prime minister (Patrice Lumumba) of the Congo appealed for Soviet aid, and the Soviets sent weapons, transport equipment, technicians, and advisers. Soviet influence alarmed some Congolese and most Western nations, who encouraged the

president of the Congo (Kasavubu) to dismiss Lumumba. An army leader, Joseph Mobutu, ordered the Soviets to leave the country, and in 1961 Lumumba was assassinated. Meanwhile, the Katanga rebellion continued, with Tshombe employing European and South African mercenaries to resist a United Nations peacekeeping force that had been sent into the region. An agreement to end the secessionist movement was finally reached, and UN troops left the Congo in 1964. Tshombe was elected president, but in 1965 he was overthrown in a military coup led by Mobutu. In 1971 Mobutu changed the name of the country to Zaire. Foreign investors have been invited back into the country (most fled during the terrorism of the rebellions), but continued conflict in the country has discouraged them.

2. *French military involvement in Chad.* Chad gained independence from France in 1960. Chad has a sparse population (being located mostly in the regions of the Sahara and the Sahel). The population is divided between the Christian south and the Muslim north, and tribal differences are also a problem. In 1960 a southerner, Francois Tombalbaye, became president. A rebellion broke out in the northern and eastern sections in 1965 and resulted in civil war. In 1975 a military coup overthrew Tombalbaye's government, but another southerner took control of the government. The conflict between the north and south continued, with France supporting the southern government. Northern forces called on Libya for assistance, and Muammar Qaddafi sent Libyan troops. In 1981 foreign troops were withdrawn, but in 1982 civil war broke out again. Libyan forces entered the war in support of the north, and French and Zairian forces entered the war in support of the south. In 1984 France and Libya agreed to remove their forces, but Libyan troops remained in the north in violation of the agreement. In 1987 the government launched an attack against the northern and Libyan forces and regained control of all but a small strip of land where Libya has an air base. In 1990 a Libyan-supported group overthrew the government, and their leader became president.

3. *Superpower rivalry in Ethiopia and Angola.* Except for a short time during World War II when it was occupied by Italian forces, Ethiopia was one of the only two African nations that maintained their independence. Emperor Haille Selassie ruled Ethiopia from 1916 to 1974. The United States provided the emperor with aid and assistance partly because of the country's strategic location on the Red Sea. In 1974 he was overthrown, and the army began making socialist reforms—land was taken from landowners and turned over to peasant associations. In 1976 a military agreement was reached with the Soviet Union,

and United States military advisers were expelled. Ethiopia and Somalia have had border disputes since Somalia became independent in 1960. Because the Soviet Union was supporting Ethiopia, Somalia turned over a military base to the United States.

Angola received its independence in 1975. After independence, three rival groups fought for control and there was a civil war. The MPLA (Popular Movement for the Liberation of Angola) was supported by the Soviet Union and Cuba; the FNLA (National Front for the Liberation of Angola) was supported by the United States, France, and Zaire; and UNITA (National Union for the Total Independence of Angola) was supported by Portugal, China, South Africa, and white Angolans. By 1976 MPLA had achieved victory. The MPLA established a Marxist state with Soviet backing and Cuban support troops. The United States continued to provide assistance to UNITA rebels, so conflict continued. In 1991, according to the terms of an agreement worked out by President Mobutu of Zaire, the last Cuban troops were withdrawn from Angola. Later that same year UNITA signed a treaty with the government to end the civil war that had gone on for 16 years. UNITA rejected election results in 1992, and fighting broke out again. In 1993 the United States recognized the government of Angola for the first time since its independence in 1975.

4. *Ethnic clashes in Rwanda.* Lingering tensions between the Hutus and the Tutsis in Rwanda exploded in 1994 when the country's Hutu president died in a mysterious plane crash. Hutus blamed the Tutsis. The resulting fighting is thought to have caused over 500,000 deaths. Refugees seeking to escape to Zaire were faced with food shortages and outbreaks of cholera and dysentary. France sent troops to try to stop the fighting and to restore political stability.

GLOBAL
CONCEPTS
Change
CONCEPTS
GLOBAL

United States/African Relationships

As part of its policy to contain the spread of communism in the 1960s, the United States began to provide aid and assistance to many African nations.

Americans (government and private citizens) have provided assistance (medical, food, volunteers) to drought-stricken and famine-ridden regions of Africa. Starting in the 1960s, the Peace Corps has helped to develop rural Africa—teaching agricultural techniques, establishing schools, and carrying out many other programs.

WORLD ISSUES

World
Trade and
Finance

The American government has provided millions of dollars in military loans and grants. American multinational corporations have established branches in many African nations, providing employment and infusing some money into the local economy. The United States has on occasion maintained military bases in Kenya, Somalia, and Liberia.

In the past, black African nations have had difficulty reconciling American ideals on human rights with the reality of racial prejudice and inequality in the United States. However, the civil rights gains of the 1960s and the change in American policy from constructive engagement to divestment and sanctions against the government of South Africa did much to improve this situation.

Somalia and the United States

The Somali Republic became independent in 1960. As a result of a coup in 1969 Somalia came under the rule of General Muhammad Siyad Barrah. In 1991 Barrah fled the country, and there was intense fighting between rival clans to gain control of the country. By the late fall of 1992 thousands of people were in peril. Civil war, drought, and famine had already taken the lives of thousands, and the lives of thousands more were threatened. The rival clans interfered with international efforts to relieve the famine by keeping relief supplies from reaching their enemies and also to make the people dependent on them for the supplies. By November 1992 the Bush administration felt that conditions in Somalia had deteriorated to the point where U.S. intervention was necessary. He volunteered U.S. troops for the UN force in Somalia to protect the relief workers, supply routes, and humanitarian-aid distribution points. The UN authorized the U.S. forces to use all means necessary to deliver the relief supplies to the needy. The pressure from the UN and U.S. forces resulted in the signing of a peace treaty by the two most powerful clan leaders in December 1992. Early in 1993, shortly after the agreement was reached, it was broken, and clan fighting broke out again. In June 1993 Pakistani members of the UN peacekeeping forces were killed; General Mohammed Farah Aidid, one of the most powerful clan leaders in Mogadishu, the capital, was considered responsible. Subsequently, several attacks were carried out against Aidid's weapons caches and his supporters' holdings. Aidid was targeted for capture, but he was not caught. In October several members of the peacekeeping forces were killed, including 18 Americans. Another American was taken captive and interrogated by Aidid's forces, and video excerpts from the interrogation were broadcast worldwide. More American forces and equipment were ordered to Somalia, but it was also announced that all American forces would be withdrawn by March 1994. This was done, amidst concern for the future of Somalia.

WORLD ISSUES

War

and

Peace

REVIEW QUESTIONS

Multiple Choice. Select the letter of the answer that correctly completes each statement.

1. During the 19th century, the African continent was affected most by
   A. the French Revolution
   B. the Crusades
   C. European imperialism
   D. the introduction of socialism

2. Which statement is most accurate about the African slave trade from the 15th through the 19th centuries?
   A. The slave trade was limited to East Africa.
   B. The slave traders brought ivory and timber to Africa.
   C. The slave trade involved African, Arab, and European slave traders.
   D. Most slaves were transported from Africa to Europe.

3. Which statement is accurate concerning the policy of apartheid in the republic of South Africa?
   A. It was encouraged by other nations.
   B. It was the result of attempts to improve the conditions of blacks living in homeland areas.
   C. It had its roots in European imperialism in Africa.
   D. It resulted in separate but equal treatment for whites and blacks.

4. Which nation was once controlled by a white minority government?
   A. Nigeria
   B. Zambia
   C. Zimbabwe
   D. Ghana

5. Important archeological finds concerning humans have been made by the Leakey family in the vicinity of
   A. the Niger River
   B. Olduvai Gorge
   C. Victoria Falls
   D. the Horn of Africa

6. Which policy is the Organization of African Unity most interested in developing?
   A. apartheid
   B. Africanization
   C. pan-Africanism
   D. Westernization

7. The Nigerian civil war was primarily due to
   A. ethnic conflicts
   B. water use
   C. failure of cash crops
   D. language differences

8. Many emerging nations preferred a nonaligned foreign policy. This means they
   A. will not trade with communist nations
   B. will not accept aid from the United States
   C. prefer not to accept humanitarian aid in times of crisis
   D. tried not to take sides in the ideological dispute between the United States and the Soviet Union

9. The major goal of African nationalist movements that developed in the years between World War I and World War II was
   A. increased elementary education for African children
   B. the freedom to move from rural to urban areas in search of jobs
   C. the right to serve in the armies of their colonial rulers
   D. the independence of their countries from colonial rule

10. Slave trade in Africa
    A. was started by the Europeans
    B. led to tribal warfare
    C. was limited to the area of the Kongo Basin
    D. depopulated South Africa

11. One of the benefits of colonial rule in Africa was that
    A. population was stabilized at 0 percent growth
    B. Europeans bought natural resources from the Africans
    C. Africans were allowed to maintain political independence
    D. some Africans received a Western education

12. Plantation agriculture
    A. involves the cultivation of a small piece of land
    B. requires the use of slave labor
    C. is commercial agriculture involving the cultivation of cash crops
    D. is a type of subsistence agriculture

13. Nelson Mandela was once given a sentence of life imprisonment because of his activities against
    A. the policy of apartheid
    B. British colonial rule
    C. the Mau Mau movement in Kenya
    D. pan-Africanism

14. An archeologist would be most interested in
    A. studying the way people today make a living
    B. tracing the cultural development of humankind
    C. determining how political leaders are chosen
    D. studying the physical remains of early humans

15. The major achievement of the anti-apartheid movement in South Africa has been
    A. the relocation of the black homelands to areas with more fertile soil
    B. desegregation in major cities
    C. the abandonment of the pass laws
    D. that blacks have gained the right to vote in national elections

16. Nationalism has been a difficult concept to develop in many African nations for all the following reasons *except*
    A. the citizens lack a common native language
    B. the nations contain diverse ethnic groups
    C. no foreign power dominated these regions before World War II
    D. tribalism is often a stronger factor

17. Many African nations have suffered great internal disturbances because
    A. European colonial powers drew up modern boundaries without regard to tribal boundaries
    B. the Israelis claimed African territory as part of the Occupied Territories
    C. Hindu and Sikh factions have been unable to reconcile their differences
    D. the policy of apartheid is widespread throughout the continent

18. The British colonial policy of indirect rule in Africa meant that
    A. tribal chiefs were deposed and replaced with newly elected African officials
    B. traditional rule was immediately replaced with a new civil service
    C. the power of traditional chiefs was preserved under British direction
    D. military rule was imposed on each village in British territory

19. The Great Trek of the Boers was most like
    A. the scorched earth policy of the Russians
    B. the migration westward of American settlers
    C. the Salt March in India
    D. the Long March in China

20. By 1914 the only regions in Africa *not* under European control were
    A. South Africa and Rhodesia
    B. Kenya and Zaire
    C. Nigeria and Algeria
    D. Ethiopia and Liberia

21. The African slave trade from the 16th century to the early 19th century resulted in all the following *except*
    A. the depopulation of some regions of Africa
    B. increased tribal warfare in Africa
    C. the disruption of technological progress in Africa
    · D. greater cooperation among African ethnic groups to stop the trade

22. The end of colonial rule in Africa
    A. was achieved by the end of the 19th century
    B. followed a period of intense nationalism in most African states
    C. saw a smooth transition to stable, native rule
    D. came about as a result of the cold war

23. The major purpose of the Organization of African Unity is to
    A. establish a single socialist state on the African continent
    B. promote economic development and cooperation for the entire continent
    C. attract foreign investors to African mines
    D. preserve African cultural heritage for future generations

24. Anthropologists believe human beings originated in Africa because
    A. the oldest human fossils have been unearthed there
    B. Egyptian written records have revealed that fact
    C. the remains of Mesopotamia were unearthed in Africa
    D. three of the world's major religions originated there

25. Africa's oral tradition is
    A. the only known source of knowledge of African history
    B. a record of African history left by Arab traders
    C. the myths, legends, and history of Africa passed by word of mouth from generation to generation
    D. the history of Africa as revealed in archeological discoveries of fossils and artifacts

26. Africa enjoyed a long and rich history before the era of European exploration and conquest. Which of the following is proof of this?
    A. the discovery of Harappa in the 1920s
    B. the remains of great Zimbabwe
    C. the construction of the Taj Mahal
    D. artifacts of the Yayoi culture

27. Which was a major cause of the increase in the African slave trade beginning in the 16th century?
   A. a strike by European coal miners
   B. not enough skilled laborers for British factories
   C. need for strong, cheap labor for American plantations
   D. need for labor in New England textile mills

28. The relative ease with which Europeans conquered Africa in the 19th century was largely a result of the fact that
   A. European technological development was more advanced
   B. Europeans adopted African lifestyles
   C. the European trading companies combined their forces and worked together
   D. Africans had no experience with armed conflict

29. The main purpose of the policy of apartheid was to
   A. increase the amount of South African exports
   B. improve the quality of education on the secondary level
   C. maintain white supremacy
   D. decrease the spread of disease

30. Government instability in many of the newly independent countries of sub-Saharan Africa in the 1960s and 1970s was a result of all the following *except*
   A. tribal rivalries
   B. corruption and nepotism
   C. military coups d'etat
   D. nationalism

ESSAYS

1. Many important civilizations and kingdoms arose in Africa prior to the coming of the Europeans. Select four of these civilizations or kingdoms. For each one do the following:

   A. Give its name and general geographical location.
   B. Describe one significant accomplishment.

2. The new nations that have emerged since World War II have faced many problems. Describe three of these problems, giving both the reasons for these problems and attempts to resolve them. Give specific references to nations and leaders.

UNIT FIVE

Latin America

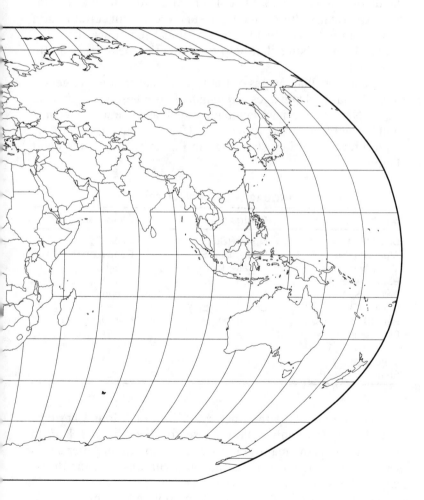

I. PHYSICAL GEOGRAPHY OF LATIN AMERICA

A Definition of Latin America

Latin America refers to the area in the Western Hemisphere that is south and southeast of the United States. Within this area there are nations and other lands that are not really part of the Latin American group of countries or cultures. They are the English-speaking Caribbean basin nations, such as Barbados, Belize, and Jamaica, and the Dutch-speaking islands of Curaçao and Aruba. There are also a number of Native American cultures that have survived within certain Latin American nations. Besides geographical locations, there are other characteristics that help to define the meaning of Latin America.

The national languages of Latin American nations are generally Romance languages—Spanish, Portuguese, and French. Some Native American languages, such as Guarani, Quechua, and Amayra, are also spoken. In Haiti, the use of Creole is widespread, and English is used in Puerto Rico (see the chart below).

LANGUAGES OF LATIN AMERICA

South America	Central America	Caribbean
Brazil (Port.)	Mexico (Sp.)	Cuba (Sp.)
Argentina (Sp.)	Guatemala (Sp.)	Dominican Republic
Uruguay (Sp.)	El Salvador (Sp.)	(Sp.)
Paraguay (Sp.)	Honduras (Sp.)	Haiti (Fr., Creole)
Bolivia (Sp.)	Nicaragua (Sp.)	Puerto Rico
Chile (Sp.)	Costa Rica (Sp.)	(Eng., Sp.)
Peru (Sp.)	Panama (Sp.)	Martinique (Fr.)
Ecuador (Sp.)		Guadeloupe (Fr.)
Colombia (Sp.)		
Venezuela (Sp.)		
French Guiana (Fr.)		

The nations of Latin America all have a colonial heritage that is either Spanish, Portuguese, or French, and Roman Catholicism is the major religion. The term "Latin America" is used to describe the nations, peoples, cultures, and the diversity of this vast and complex area.

The process of cultural diffusion continues to play an important role in shaping society in Latin America. Recent immigration from Asia and the Middle East has had a significant impact. For example, in São Paulo, Brazil, the influence of Japanese immigrants is strongly felt in agriculture. In Costa Rica, increased North American immigration by retired persons seeking a less expensive environment and year-round warmer climate has caused a different kind of cultural diffusion.

LATIN AMERICA POLITICAL MAP

UNITED STATES

NORTH

ATLANTIC OCEAN

MEXICO

Gulf of Mexico

BAHAMAS
Nassau

Havana
CUBA

DOMINICAN REPUBLIC   San Juan
PUERTO RICO
•VIRGIN ISLANDS (U.S. & G.B.)
•ANGUILLA (G.B.)
•ANTIGUA & BARBUDA
•ST. CHRISTOPHER & NEVIS
•MONSERRAT (G.B.)
•GUADELOUPE (Fr.)
•DOMINICA
•MARTINIQUE (Fr.)
•ST. VINCENT & THE GRENADINES
•BARBADOS
•GRENADA   TRINIDAD & TOBAGO
Port-of-Spain

Mexico City

CAYMAN ISLANDS (G.B.)
JAMAICA
Kingston
HAITI
Port-au-Prince
Santo Domingo

Belmopan
BELIZE
GUATEMALA
Guatemala City
Tegucigalpa
HONDURAS

CARIBBEAN SEA

•ARUBA(Neth.)
•NETHERLANDS ANTILLES (Neth.)

EL SALVADOR
San Salvador
Managua   NICARAGUA

San José
COSTA RICA   Panama City
PANAMA

Caracas

VENEZUELA

GUYANA
Georgetown
SURINAME
Paramaribo
FRENCH GUIANA (Fr.)
Cayenne

Bogota
COLOMBIA

Quito
ECUADOR

GALAPAGOS ISLANDS (Ec.)

PERU
Lima

BRAZIL

Brasilia

Lake Titicaca
BOLIVIA
Lake Poopo
Sucre

PACIFIC OCEAN

CHILE
PARAGUAY
Asunción

URUGUAY

Santiago
Buenos Aires
ARGENTINA   Montevideo

FALKLAND ISLANDS (G.B.)
Stanley

Strait of Magellan
TIERRA DEL FUEGO

S. GEORGIA ISLAND (G.B.)

Political Geography

Latin America can be divided into three geopolitical regions. South America, Middle (Meso) America (Mexico and Central America), and the Caribbean Sea islands that are classified as Latin American. There are a total of 24 nations and dependent lands.

Physical Geography

Latin America, which has one sixth of the earth's land surface, is approximately 8 million square miles. From the northern border of Mexico to the southern tip of Chile, it is 6,000 miles. The nations of Latin America range in size from Brazil, the world's fifth largest country (larger than the continental United States), to the small Caribbean islands of Martinique and Guadeloupe.

GLOBAL
CONCEPTS
Environment
CONCEPTS
GLOBAL

Latin America lies between latitudes 33° north and 56° south. The geographical location of most of Latin America within the tropics and subtropics determines its climate, rainfall, and vegetation. Other geographical factors also influence the climate, rainfall, and agriculture and help determine the political, economic, and social patterns of Latin America.

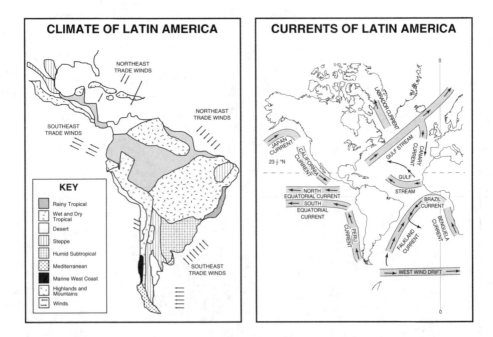

266

Mountains, Plateaus, and Highlands

The mountain ranges and high plateaus have influenced the economic, social, and political life in much of Latin America. Paralleling the Pacific Ocean, there are a number of large mountain chains in the Americas. In Mexico, the Sierra Madres (Occidental and Oriental) run north and south. Between these two mountain ranges is a vast central plateau, where more than half the nation's population lives. The Sierra Madre del Sur run through Central America. In South America the Andes Mountains run along much of the continent's western coast. The Andes rank second only to the Himalayas as the world's highest mountain range. They have served to isolate cultures and delayed cultural diffusion.

The Atacama Desert, the strip of land on the Pacific Coast in Peru and Chile, results because the Andes act as a barrier to block rainfall. To the east of the Andes lies the high plateau region (altiplano).

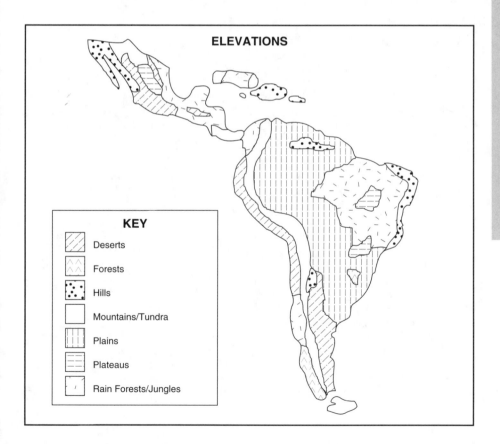

ELEVATIONS

KEY

Deserts

Forests

Hills

Mountains/Tundra

Plains

Plateaus

Rain Forests/Jungles

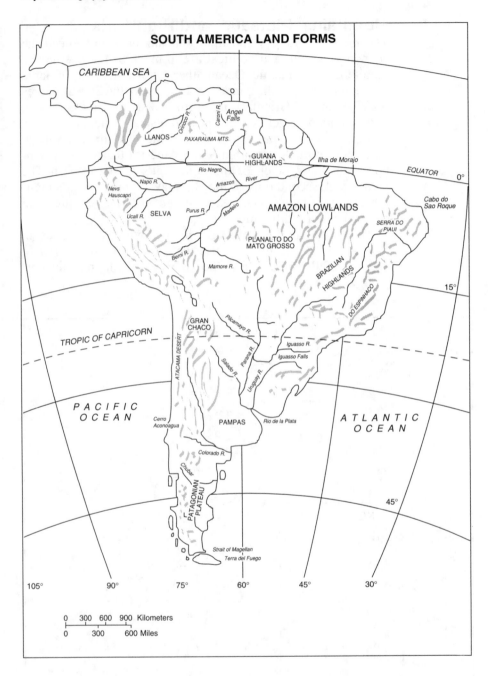

SOUTH AMERICA LAND FORMS

CARIBBEAN SEA

Orinoco R.

Caroni R.

Angel Falls

LLANOS

PAXARAUMA MTS.

GUIANA HIGHLANDS

Ilha de Morajo

EQUATOR 0°

Rio Negro

Napo R.

Amazon River

Nevs Hauscapri

SELVA

Purus R.

Madeiro

AMAZON LOWLANDS

Cabo do Sao Roque

Ucall R.

SERRA DO PIAUI

PLANALTO DO MATO GROSSO

Berni R.

BRAZILIAN

Mamore R.

HIGHLANDS

15°

GRAN CHACO

Pilcamayo R.

DO ESPINHACO

TROPIC OF CAPRICORN

ATACAMA DESERT

Iguasso R.

Salsedo R.

Parana R.

Iguasso Falls

Uruguay R.

PACIFIC OCEAN

Cerro Aconoagua

PAMPAS

Rio de la Plata

ATLANTIC OCEAN

Colorado R.

45°

Chubar

PATAGONIAN PLATEAU

Strait of Magellan

Terra del Fuego

105°   90°   75°   60°   45°   30°

0   300   600   900   Kilometers

0   300   600   Miles

The Guiana Highlands and Brazilian Highlands are the two other regions in South America that in otherwise tropical areas have helped offset the difficult climatic conditions of the surrounding lowland area.

Water Bodies

In South America a number of rivers have significantly influenced the development of the regions through which they flow.

The Amazon River, the world's second longest river, and its tributaries, which reach into Colombia, Venezuela, Ecuador, Peru, and Bolivia, has until recently been the only transportation network in the Amazon Basin. The Río de la Plata, which is a large estuary fed by the Uruguay and Paraná rivers, forms a water transportation network that serves Argentina, Bolivia, southern Brazil, Uruguay, and Paraguay.

In Venezuela, the Orinoco River runs for about 1,500 miles until it empties into the Atlantic Ocean. The Orinoco basin's agriculture production and ranching industry rely on this river system.

Latin America has very few large lakes. Lake Maracaibo in northwest Venezuela is within the petroleum-producing region. Lake Titicaca, one of the world's highest lakes, borders on Bolivia and Peru and serves primarily as a source of fish for the largely Native American population. In Mexico, Lake Chapala is a large lake that still serves as a source of fresh water fish. Lake Texcoco, once a major lake, has all but disappeared due to drainage to facilitate the growth of Mexico City.

GLOBAL
CONCEPTS

Environment

CONCEPTS
GLOBAL

Review Questions

Multiple Choice. Select the letter of the answer that correctly completes each statement.

1. The major religion in most of Latin America is
   A. Roman Catholicism
   B. Protestantism
   C. Islam
   D. Buddhism

2. Most nations of Latin America have a colonial heritage that is
   A. Spanish
   B. Portuguese
   C. French
   D. British

3. The nation with the largest land area in Latin America is
   A. Brazil
   B. Argentina
   C. Mexico
   D. Peru

4. Most of Latin America lies within the climatic zone known as the
   A. tropics
   B. tundra
   C. Arctic circle
   D. humid continental

5. The term "Latin America" refers to the three geopolitical regions: South America, Meso (Middle) America, and the
   A. Caribbean Sea islands
   B. Sahel region
   C. Indian subcontinent
   D. East Indies islands

6. All the following are examples of cultural diffusion *except*
   A. Japanese immigrants in Brazil speaking Portuguese
   B. Native Americans listening to rock music
   C. French missionaries in Haiti learning Creole
   D. Mexican citizens in Spain speaking Spanish

Matching. Match the geographical items in Column 2 with the correct countries or regions in Column 1.

Column 1

_____ 1. Brazil

_____ 2. Mexico

_____ 3. Argentina

_____ 4. Chile

_____ 5. Central America

Column 2

A. Río de la Plata

B. Atacama Desert

C. Sierra Madre del Sur

D. Amazon River

E. Lake Chapala

ESSAYS

1. Why can Latin America be described as an area of cultural diffusion and diversity?

2. How does the physical geography of Latin America determine its climate, rainfall, and vegetation?

II. ECONOMIC GEOGRAPHY OF LATIN AMERICA

Economic Development in Latin America

WORLD ISSUES

World
Trade and
Finance

Latin America has had a history of economic dependence dating from the colonial period. During the colonial period, because of the mercantilist policies of Spain and Portugal, the future Latin American nations were primarily exporters of raw materials and importers of manufactured goods. The Dutch, French, and most notably the British dominated trade with Latin America in the 1800s.

The economies of the newly independent Latin American nations continued to have a colonial character. Latin America was heavily dependent on imported consumer goods, food, and machinery and on the export of raw materials as payment for these imports. The dependence on one or two commodities made many smaller Latin American countries vulnerable to economic pressure. Even large countries like Brazil (coffee and sugar) and Argentina (cowhides, wheat) were dependent on the prices that their major exports earned.

In the second half of the 19th century, first Germany and then the United States began to trade with and invest in Latin America. This was a challenge to Britain's economic dominance of the region. The Latin American countries continued to export agricultural products and raw materials. Coffee, tobacco, sugar, copper, and nitrates paid for the increased imports of luxury goods, machinery, and other manufactured products.

Before World War I, the European nations accounted for 60 percent of the foreign investment in Latin America. U.S. trade and investment grew substantially between the wars. North American capital investment concentrated on mines and railroads, which stimulated the import of American machinery. Although German and British trade and investment resumed after World War I, the United States' dominance, particularly in the Caribbean, Mexico, and northern South America, continued. During these years, the Latin American nations faced increased competition to sell their raw materials in Europe because of new sources of these raw materials in Asia and elsewhere.

WORLD ISSUES

Economic
Growth and
Development

Since World War II, Latin American trade has undergone rapid changes in volume and direction. By the end of the 1960s, the region's economic giants—Brazil, Mexico, Argentina, and oil-rich Venezuela—accounted for 56 percent of the total value of Latin American trade. These nations began to produce more manufactured goods. By the late 1980s, Brazil had become the world's eighth largest economy. Mexico, Venezuela, Peru, Argentina, and other nations to a lesser extent became more industrialized because of foreign investment and loans. Foreign capital was also used by the Latin American nations to develop their infrastructures and establish credit to buy needed technology. However, in the 1970s the foreign debt of the Latin American nations increased enormously, and in the late 1980s it began to have a negative impact on their economies.

GLOBAL
CONCEPTS
Choice
CONCEPTS
GLOBAL

In the 1990s the United States, Mexico, and Canada approved the North American Free Trade Agreement (NAFTA). These nations are already trading partners, and with NAFTA they will increase their economic interdependence by abolishing tariffs on most goods traded among them. Chile is slated as the next possible NAFTA member.

Freer world trade is also now possible as a result of the Uruguay round of trade talks, which led to the General Agreement on Tariffs and Trade (GATT). Latin America could benefit from this agreement if NAFTA and European Union (EU) nations do not violate its intent to promote trade.

Industry

Industrial development started in the late 19th century. In Argentina, Brazil, and Mexico, the first manufacturing involved small workshops and factories that produced textiles and food products. There was also some production of machine tools

WORLD ISSUES

Economic
Growth and
Development

and spare parts for the operation of sugar-refining mills, railroads, and other service needs. Before World War I industrial growth took place in the larger Latin American nations.The types of industries that developed were import-substitutive because they sought to replace imports for an already existing market. Factories producing textiles, food products, and other light consumer goods expanded their output. In the 1930s there were also attempts to develop heavy industry. For example, in Brazil, steel production began.

World War II encouraged the growth of industry because it became difficult to import manufactured goods. Existing factories were used to capacity, and new plants were added. After World War II, Latin American governments promoted industrialization, which was financed largely by American capital. Various methods used to promote industrialization were protective tariffs, preferential exchange rates for fuels and industrial raw materials, government construction of infrastructure projects (transportation and power facilities), and government investment in some heavy industries such as steel and petroleum.

In Argentina, Chile, and Venezuela, consumer-goods industries were first encouraged. Heavy industry for such products as steel and chemicals came later. In Mexico and Brazil, the governments sought to promote consumer and capital goods at the same time. By the late 1960s, in Argentina, Brazil, and Mexico, industry produced about 30 percent of the gross national product (GNP). Steel output increased enormously, and automobile production in these nations rose to a combined total of over 1 million cars.

By the 1980s Brazil was in the top ten nations in terms of industrial production, producing airplanes, computers, automobiles, and military goods that competed in global markets. Mexico City was a great center of industrial production, while Venezuela developed an important petroleum industry.

The stress on industrialization has had mixed results. On the positive side, many new jobs for the increasing population have been created; national pride increased because of reduced dependence on foreign imports; manufacturing centers developed and spurred the growth of cities; and an industrial class of manufacturers and factory workers grew. Moreover, new wealth has been created, which has stimulated overall economic growth, and national financial institutions have grown. However, there have also been negative aspects to industrialization. The stress on manufacturing has led to a neglect of agricultural exports, which traditionally accounted for much of the foreign exchange earned. Industry has not been able to employ all the rural workers who have left agriculture. Moreover, some industries are not competitive, are too costly to run profitably, and have been a drain on the national budget. Pollution, urban squalor, and crime have often been byproducts of industrial growth.

WORLD ISSUES

World
Trade and
Finance

The money borrowed to finance this industrialization has created crises in Brazil, Mexico, Venezuela, Argentina, Peru, and smaller economies that cannot repay their growing foreign public and private debt. This debt crisis has seriously affected growth rates, destroyed national currencies due to spiraling inflation, and led to political instability.

In the 1990s Latin American nations are hoping for increased economic growth. Their hopes rest on each nation's ability to combat inflation and ease the debt crisis. Foreign banks and governments want to be repaid the billions owed to them. The International Monetary Fund (IMF) also has set conditions for future lending. For example, the IMF wants an end to price-support systems and subsidies to lower food costs. Unless the demands of investors are met, Latin American nations will not receive the necessary funding to support their economic plans.

Agriculture

GLOBAL
CONCEPTS

Interdependence

CONCEPTS
GLOBAL

WORLD ISSUES

Environmental
Concerns

Since the pre-Columbian period, agriculture has been the most important part of the economy in the Latin American nations. More than half the population is employed in agriculture in almost all Latin American countries. However, in proportion to the population employed, agriculture produces a small percentage of the gross national product. The region produces large crops of coffee, bananas, cacao, sugar, and cotton, but their export value often does not justify the amount of labor and investment. Agriculture supplies both food and raw materials for the region, and most Latin American countries depend heavily on the export of agricultural products to earn foreign currency. Latin America suffers from cultural and physical obstacles that hold back the development of more modern agriculture.

Since the pre-Columbian period the slash-and-burn method of bringing new lands under cultivation has been used. For example, even today in the Amazon region huge areas of virgin forest are being destroyed by burning to create land for cattle ranching and farming. Often, lands have been overused until the effects of erosion, mineral depletion, and single-crop usage soon make the land increasingly incapable of production. Climate and topography have played important roles in reducing the fertility of arable lands. For example, in pre-Columbian times, Native Americans in the Andes region used a terrace farming system to lessen the effects of erosion, but during the colonial period this system was abandoned.

The arrival of the Europeans changed the landholding system. Large landed estates, latifundia, were created, which were inefficiently operated. Absentee landlords still control huge tracts of land. In contrast, millions of Latin American families are subsistence farmers, growing a handful of food staple crops such as corn, beans, potatoes, plantains, manioc, and rice. The growing demand for land reform has been strongly resisted by the traditional landed elite.

Commercial agriculture, however, is increasing throughout Latin America. Crops for export began to be grown in the colonial period, especially in Brazil and the Caribbean, where sugar and cacao became important. In the 1800s coffee, wheat, wool, and beef made the agricultural exports of Brazil, Argentina, and Uruguay increasingly important. In the 20th century the development of refrigerated transportation made bananas and other fruits valuable exports. However, the heavy reliance on one-crop economies in Central American nations such as Honduras has had a negative effect on commercial agriculture. By contrast, in Brazil, where agriculture diversification is possible, export crops such as soya have earned needed foreign currency.

Latin America needs to increase its agricultural production to meet its high rate of population growth. In the Andean region and elsewhere, farmers have turned to the growing of coca leaves, marijuana, and poppy plants to escape the endless cycle of poverty. Without land reform, agricultural productivity will continue to be held back by culture and physical problems. Many of these subsistence farmers are the ones who are fleeing the rural areas for the cities.

AGRICULTURAL PRODUCTS OF LATIN AMERICA

KEY

Bananas
Beef Cattle
Cacao
Cassava
Coffee
Corn
Cotton
Fish
Potatoes
Soybeans
Sugarcane
Timber
Wheat
Corn zone
Rice zone
Wheat zone

Mineral and Energy Sources

During the conquest of Latin America, the Europeans searched for precious metals, especially gold and silver. Much of the mineral wealth, primarily gold and silver objects taken from the more advanced pre-Columbian peoples, was shipped to Europe. From the 1500s to the 1700s, new deposits of gold, silver, and diamonds were found in Mexico, Peru, Bolivia, and Brazil. Although other mineral deposits—for example, iron ore, lead, tin, copper, and zinc—were discovered, they were not used to any great extent.

In the late 19th century, mining activities were extended to new areas. Increased foreign investment from Western Europe

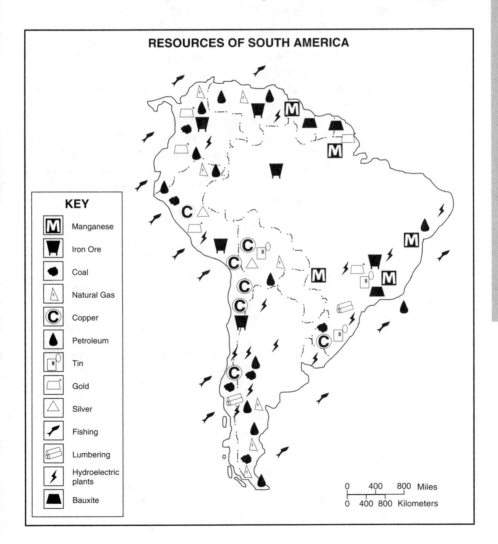

RESOURCES OF SOUTH AMERICA

KEY

M	Manganese
▼	Iron Ore
●	Coal
△	Natural Gas
C	Copper
▲	Petroleum
▯	Tin
▱	Gold
△	Silver
✈	Fishing
▱	Lumbering
⚡	Hydroelectric plants
◼	Bauxite

0   400   800 Miles

0   400 800 Kilometers

and the United States provided capital, technology, and management. In the 20th century, in Peru, Chile, Bolivia, Mexico, Brazil, and elsewhere, mining production increased and contributed significantly to the GNPs of these nations. Certain nations became increasingly dependent on their mineral wealth. For example, Bolivia (tin), Chile (copper), Peru (bismuth), and Brazil (manganese and iron ore) became major centers of the world production of these metals. Today, prospects for mining should continue to increase in many Latin American countries.

WORLD ISSUES

Energy:
Resources and
Allocations

Energy resources are less abundant in Latin America. Mexico is the leading producer of oil; Petroleos Mexicanos (Pemex) controls the distribution from Mexico's oil fields. Newly discovered fields in the Gulf of Mexico have increased Mexico's known reserves.

In South America, Venezuela is the leading producer of petroleum. In 1970 Venezuela produced approximately 70 percent of Latin America's petroleum. Argentina, Brazil, Colombia, Peru, Ecuador, and Chile are all petroleum-producing nations, but most of the oil produced by these nations is used to meet their own energy needs. Recent finds by Peru and Ecuador in their Amazon lands have raised hopes of exporting oil; however, in comparison with other regions, particularly the Middle East, the proven reserves are very limited. The lack of large oil reserves could handicap the long-term development of Latin America's industrial base.

MINERALS IN LATIN AMERICA

Mineral	Produced in
Silver	Mexico (number one in the world), Argentina, Colombia, Peru, Bolivia, Costa Rica, Ecuador
Tin	Bolivia
Copper	Chile (Atacama Desert), Argentina, Bolivia, Colombia, Cuba
Nitrates (fertilizer)	Chile (Atacama Desert) (world's leading producer)
Oil	Venezuela, Mexico, Colombia, Argentina, Trinidad, Peru
Iron ore	Venezuela, Peru, Chile, Brazil, Argentina, Guatemala
Aluminum (bauxite)	Surinam (first in the world), Guyana (second), Jamaica
Iodine	Chile
Manganese	Brazil, Cuba
Antimony	Bolivia, Mexico, Peru
Platinum	Colombia (third in the world)
Diamonds	Brazil (second in the world)
Uranium	Brazil

The Quest for Development in Latin America

Few areas of Latin America have the proper combination of industrial capacity, capital for investment, raw materials, energy resources and technology needed for developing their economies. Brazil comes the closest to having all the necessary factors. However, even Brazil, which has increased its industrial capacity, encountered enormous problems in the 1980s. The desire to satisfy the demand for consumer goods while providing manufactured goods and agricultural products for export led to a substantial increase of foreign investment capital. Today Brazil's foreign debt, the highest in Latin America, is over $100 billion. Despite a favorable balance of trade, Brazil can hardly meet its debt interest payments. Hyperinflation (extremely rapid rise in prices for goods and services), urban problems, such as poor housing and increasing crime, and a declining standard of living have affected the nation's political stability.

WORLD ISSUES

Hunger
and
Poverty

In other less well endowed nations, modernization and industrialization have resulted in many new and difficult problems. Mexico, Argentina, Peru, Colombia, and Venezuela face enormous economic uncertainties. Economic problems have led to increasing migration from rural to urban areas, and the search for economic opportunity has led people to migrate to other nations.

Multinational corporations have been established in Latin America that seek to profit from the cheap labor, available raw materials, and the need for investment capital for industrialization. Often they have a competitive advantage over national industries. Multinational corporations show the growing interdependence of the more industrialized and less-developed regions of the world. In Latin America multinationals take as profit the capital that is much needed instead of reinvesting it. This is a serious problem.

GLOBAL
CONCEPTS

Interdependence

CONCEPTS
GLOBAL

Some Latin American nations have sought to work together in regional projects in order to better develop their economies. Brazil and Paraguay are jointly building the Itaipu Dam to harness the energy of the Paraná River system for electrical power. There have been several attempts at regional economic cooperation by Andean nations, some Caribbean countries, and by Brazil and Argentina. In the Caribbean region, nations of the Caribbean Community and Common Market (CARICOM) are working on policies to liberalize trade among the organization's members. A more open trading system would stimulate economic growth and development. This is particularly important since economic trading blocs such as NAFTA and the EU, will favor trade among their member nations.

WORLD ISSUES

World
Trade and
Finance

Many countries that lack natural resources have turned to tourism. This is particularly true of the Caribbean island nations of the Dominican Republic and Jamaica. Even the more diversified economies of Mexico and Brazil have come to depend on tourism as a source of needed foreign currency. Tourism can be a mixed blessing in some situations, but it is one path to development in Latin America that is increasingly being tried.

Latin America in the Global Context

Today Latin American nations have ever more global trading relationships. For example, Japan's economic investment in and trade with Latin America have recently expanded. The more industrialized nations such as Brazil export such manufactured products as automobiles, military equipment, and commercial aircraft as well as agricultural products to Africa and the Middle East. The petroleum industries of Latin America, most notably that of Venezuela, are increasingly a part of the global oil network. U.S. economic relations with Latin America remain strong. However, global interdependence has led to more diversified economic relationships.

REVIEW QUESTIONS

Multiple Choice. Select the letter of the answer that correctly completes each statement.

1. The nation that dominated trade in Latin America during the 1800s was
   A. Great Britian
   B. France
   C. Germany
   D. the United States

2. By the 1980s the Latin American nation that was among the top ten nations in terms of industrial production was
   A. Brazil
   B. Mexico
   C. Argentina
   D. Peru

3. Large landed estates in Latin America are called
   A. latifundia
   B. terraced farms
   C. subsistence farms
   D. minifundia

4. Increased foreign investment from Western Europe, the United States, and Japan has provided Latin American nations with all the following *except*
   A. capital
   B. technology
   C. management
   D. raw materials

5. Brazil's foreign debt problem has caused all the following *except*
   A. hyperinflation
   B. high debt interest payments
   C. a rising standard of living
   D. a favorable balance of trade

6. The NAFTA nations are
   A. United States, Mexico, and Chile
   B. United States, Mexico, and Canada
   C. Mexico, Canada, and Chile
   D. Mexico, Canada, and Brazil

Matching. Match the correct minerals, agricultural problems and energy resources in Column 2 with the correct countries or regions in Column 1.

Column 1	Column 2
_____ 1. Argentina, Uruguay	A. Bananas
_____ 2. Central America	B. Beef cattle
_____ 3. Brazil, Cuba	C. Fish
_____ 4. Peru	D. Sugar cane
_____ 5. Bolivia	E. Tin

ESSAYS

1. Why do many areas of Latin America suffer from cultural and physical obstacles that hold back the development of more modern agriculture?

2. Why has foreign capital investment become a problem for many Latin American nations?

3. How will Latin American nations be affected by the NAFTA and GATT agreements?

III. HUMAN AND CULTURAL GEOGRAPHY OF LATIN AMERICA

Demographic Characteristics of Latin America: The People Today

A Latin American may be a person with a mixed racial, ethnic, and cultural composition. Native American, European, African, and Asian peoples have blended together in many Latin American countries to form heterogeneous populations. This is particularly true in the nations of Brazil, Mexico, and Venezuela, where rapid urbanization has led to a blurring of racial lines. However, in some Latin American countries major groups of homogeneous ethnic and racial populations exist. For example, in Argentina, Uruguay, and Costa Rica, a large percentage of the population has a primarily European heritage, whereas in parts of the Andean region and in Guatemala, many Bolivians, Peruvians, Ecuadorians, and Guatemalans would be classified demographically as Native American.

GLOBAL
CONCEPTS
Diversity
CONCEPTS
GLOBAL

The high population growth rate of Latin America has led to expanding populations, particularly in nations with large urban centers. In Brazil, Mexico, Peru, and elsewhere, the growth of urban areas has not only led to demographic changes but also has changed traditional patterns of economic activity. In addition, the pressures of urbanization have altered environmental conditions. For example, in the cities of São Paulo, Brazil, and Mexico City, the enormous increase in population and concentration of industry and automobiles have caused severe pollution and large areas of urban squalor. In the Amazon region, there has been an enormous deforestation due to the burning of rain forests, logging, and mining. This is in part a direct result of demographic changes.

WORLD ISSUES

Population

Latin America does not have as large a population as Asia, Africa, and Europe. Nevertheless, the trend toward urbanization, accompanied by increased mining, ranching, and other uses of previously unused land, has led to major environmental damage that has serious long-term global consequences.

WORLD ISSUES

Environmental
Concerns

Demographic Pressures

In the 1970s the annual population increases in Mexico, Costa Rica, the Dominican Republic, Colombia, Venezuela, and Paraguay were over 3 percent. This profound demographic growth in Latin America is a result of a number of factors. One is a persistent tradition that values high birth rates. Another is the stand of the Roman Catholic church against abortion and contraception. In addition, improvements in public health services have led to a higher survival rate after birth. Furthermore, the decline in the death rate, especially the infant mortality rate, has been a factor in increasing populations.

The massive migrations of people from rural areas to the cities has led to the rapid growth of urban centers. This migration is the result of depressed rural conditions and the belief that work and a better life can be found in the cities.

WORLD ISSUES

Population

By 1970 approximately 54 percent of the population of Latin America was classified as urban. The urban population has been increasing at a rate of 3 to 4 percent every five years, and this growth is expected to continue to the end of the century.

The largest cities of Latin America have experienced the greatest population increase. In a number of cities, the annual population increase has been 7 percent, which means that the city's population will double in about a decade. This rapid growth has led to the growth of squatter settlements, called barridas or favelas. They are inhabited by people who do not have access to enough productive work and many goods and services.

The rapid urban growth has placed severe strains on urban infrastructures and led to mounting problems. Shortages, congestion, pollution, overcrowding, and a growing crime rate are common in São Paulo, Rio de Janeiro, Mexico City, Lima, Bogotá, and elsewhere. In some Latin American cities, large numbers of poor urban youths are unemployed. The consequence is that too many young people have been marginalized. They are poor and lack health and social services, education, and adequate employment opportunities. Latin American youth need increased education and job possibilities.

In some Latin American nations, increased immigration from Europe, the Middle East, and Asia has led to other demographic changes. In Argentina and Brazil, massive immigration from Italy, Germany, Spain, Portugal, and elsewhere in Europe has resulted in a Europeanization of the urban populations. Immigration has had an effect not only on the industrial and agricultural sectors of the economies of Brazil, Argentina, Venezuela, Paraguay, and Uruguay but also on their cultures and their ethnic diversity. For example, in Brazil, a large community of Japanese immigrants has contributed to the development of an agricultural sector in São Paulo.

GLOBAL
CONCEPTS
Diversity
CONCEPTS
GLOBAL

Social Factors

In Latin America, the family has traditionally represented stability and security. Political and economic uncertainties have contributed to the importance of family ties and connections.

There has also been a tradition of male dominance in Latin American societies that has shaped male-female and family relationships into the 20th century.

In recent years, demographic growth, urbanization, and increased participation of women in the labor force have led to some changes in the traditional roles of men and women. There are increasing numbers of women who head families in large urban areas in Latin America. Most countries have granted suffrage to women. Nevertheless, obstacles to full equality still remain deeply ingrained in male-dominated societies, where machismo is the accepted social behavior.

The differences between urban and rural lifestyles have led to a breakdown of some family traditions. In the large Latin American cities, families face the same problems as in other societies. When both parents work or there is only one parent, it is difficult to raise children in traditional ways. Abandoned children are a problem in some Latin American countries, such as Brazil, Peru, and Colombia. There is also a rise in urban crime committed by young people.

Urban centers have been favored over rural areas in terms of development. As a result, the economic and social problems of rural areas have been largely ignored. This neglect is a major cause of the migration of rural people to the cities. However, the cities are not able to provide adequate housing and social services for the new city dwellers.

The migration of poor rural laborers has also had an effect on the remaining Native American populations. Certain tribes were able to preserve their culture because until recently they were isolated. In Brazil, for example, the building of highways in the Amazon basin, burning vegetation to claim land for cattle raising, and increased mining using technology that is destructive to the land and water have destroyed some Native American tribes. The invasion of lands set aside for tribal reservations by poor rural farmers and miners has led to increased violations of the Native Americans' human rights.

The continuing inequalities and differences between urban and rural areas reflect the power of the city over the countryside. The uneven distribution of economic development has led to increasing differences between social classes. The gap between rich and poor has increased in the Latin American nations. Urban areas have increasingly become the centers of wealth and power. Industrial production and financial affairs are concentrated in the cities.

The growth of industry has led to the rise of a group of urban elites, the factory owners, financial leaders, bankers, and merchants who have gained much political influence because of their economic power. The unwillingness of the urban elites to distribute more evenly their profits has often placed them on the side of the landed elite, the military, and the Roman Catholic church and against change.

Latin American Contributions to a Global Culture

The people of Latin America have made important contributions to world culture in the fields of arts, music, dance, and literature. The cultural achievements of the Native Americans prior to the arrival of European and African influences have not been very well preserved. The accomplishments of these pre-Columbian societies are mostly known through monuments, such as temples and other buildings. However, pottery, jewelry, statues, dance, music, and certain handicrafts that have survived clearly show the creativity and skill of these peoples. Unfortunately, the Spaniards destroyed much that existed of these peoples' writings.

GLOBAL
CONCEPTS

Culture

CONCEPTS
GLOBAL

The Europeans brought their own styles of art and music to the Americas during the colonial period. However, along with the dominant imported European culture, other cultures existed that had connections with Africa and the pre-Columbian heritage. Modern Latin American culture is a blend of Native American, African, and European cultures. Latin Americans have blended these together to form a rich, vibrant, changeable, but uniquely Latin American culture that varies from country to country.

GLOBAL
CONCEPTS

Diversity

CONCEPTS
GLOBAL

REVIEW QUESTIONS

Multiple Choice. Select the letter of the answer that correctly completes each statement.

1. Demographic growth in Latin America is the result of all of the following factors *except*
   A. Roman Catholic church's stand against abortion
   B. improvements in public health services
   C. a persistent tradition that values high birth rates
   D. the trend toward urbanization in many countries

2. A group of Latin American nations whose population is of primarily European heritage is
   A. Argentina, Costa Rica, Uruguay
   B. Guatemala, Nicaragua, Ecuador
   C. Mexico, Cuba, Bolivia
   D. Colombia, Venezuela, Peru

3. Rapid urban growth in Latin America has resulted in
   A. a decline in the crime rate in large cities
   B. a low percentage of unemployed urban youth
   C. the elimination of marginal populations
   D. the growth of squatter settlements

4. Full equality for women in Latin America has been difficult to obtain because
   A. urbanization has led to a decrease in women's rights
   B. women in Latin America are interested only in suffrage
   C. machismo is the accepted social behavior
   D. in most families both parents usually work

5. The invasion of lands set aside for tribal reservations by poor rural farmers and miners is a violation of Native Americans'
   A. human rights
   B. ethnic diversity
   C. demographic growth
   D. urbanization patterns

Matching. Match the correct definition in Column 2 with the correct vocabulary word in Column 1.

Column 1
_____ 1. elite
_____ 2. marginal population
_____ 3. technology
_____ 4. composition
_____ 5. urbanization

Column 2
A. the movement to cities
B. the different parts of a whole
C. practical application of knowledge
D. people without access to goods and services
E. leading member of society

ESSAYS

1. Describe the problems that rapid urbanization has caused in many Latin American nations?

2. How have the people of Latin America contributed to the development of a global culture?

3. How has the role of women changed in Latin America?

IV. HISTORY AND POLITICAL GEOGRAPHY OF LATIN AMERICA

Early History

Most probably, the first people came to North and South America thousands of years ago during the Ice Age, over a land bridge across the Bering Strait. These nomadic hunters from Asia moved into North America and over thousands of years spread throughout the Americas.

In Latin America, a number of Native American civilizations flourished independent of and isolated from developments in Africa, Asia, and Europe until Columbus's voyage in 1492. These pre-Columbian civilizations were as brilliant as the ancient civilizations of other continents. Yet, despite certain similarities in art, political systems, and religion, there were differences that hindered further development. The horse, mule, camel, and other work animals were not found in the Americas when these civilizations prospered. Also, the wheel and iron tools and weapons were not in use.

Olmec Culture

GLOBAL
CONCEPTS

Environment

CONCEPTS
GLOBAL

Olmec culture developed in Mexico along the Gulf of Mexico from about 1500 B.C. to 600 B.C. The Olmecs were an agricultural society capable of developing raised land platforms to plant in swamp areas. They were accomplished artists and traders who built what are believed to be some of the first ceremonial centers in Meso America. The Olmecs were probably the forerunners to other civilizations that later developed. The mystery of exactly who the Olmec were and why they disappeared has not been completely explained.

The Mayan Civilization

The Mayan civilization developed in what is today the Yucatán Peninsula of Mexico and Central America. By the 2nd century B.C., groups of Mayan clans were living in cultural communities. By the time of the classic period of their history (300–900 A.D.), a large number of rival city-states existed. They were ruled by nobles and a priestly class. Warriors, farmers, merchants, and slaves made up the vast majority of the highly rigid, stratified Mayan social structure.

The Mayans made great accomplishments in science, especially in astronomy and mathematics. The Mayan calendar was very accurate, and Mayan buildings rival those of other ancient peoples. Religion dominated Mayan life.

During the classic period, the Mayan city-states engaged in ruinous wars, which led to the destruction and abandonment of the centers that had developed in the heavily forested areas of the Peten jungle in present-day northern Guatemala and Chiapas, Mexico. These bloody wars among competing dynasties devastated Mayan life.

By 900 A.D. the Mayans had moved north to the Yucatan Peninsula and south to the Guatamalan highlands. Although new settlements were established after 1000 A.D., they did not reach the level of the earlier cities.

The Aztec Empire

GLOBAL
CONCEPTS

Political Systems

CONCEPTS
GLOBAL

The Aztecs were a warrior people with a rigid social structure who rose to the leadership of an alliance of city-states in the 1400s. The Aztec capital was Tenochtitlán, an island city in Lake Texcoco, the site of present-day Mexico City. The Aztec empire was ruled by a warrior king, who was supported by a warrior class and a priestly class who controlled the Aztec religious ceremonies. The Aztecs had, as did other Meso-American peoples, a polytheistic religion. Of particular importance was their god of war, Huitzilopochtli, who could only be worshiped properly through human sacrifice and the offering of blood. The Aztecs believed that their gods had great powers and required human sacrifice in ceremonies designed to win their favor in battle.

War was the policy of the Aztec empire towards all peoples who did not accept a tributary status, which included the supplying of slaves for sacrifice. Although the Aztec empire was expanding in the early 1500s, the Aztecs could not conquer all their enemies in central Mexico. The Aztec empire was the center of Meso-American civilization prior to the arrival of the Spaniards.

The Aztec Calendar

GLOBAL
CONCEPTS

Culture

CONCEPTS
GLOBAL

Cortés relied heavily on the military support of the Aztecs' enemies, particularly the Tlaxcalans, in his conquest of the empire in the 1520s. Trade played an important role in the Aztec empire. Farming was also of great importance. Corn, beans, squash, and peppers were the main staples. Landownership was controlled by the government. Land was given to families headed by male warriors and could be handed down.

The Aztecs were a literate people who spoke a language called Na'nhautl. The Aztecs were adept at making parchment paper and in gold and silver metallurgy. To measure time, they adopted the Mayan calendar. They were skilled engineers and architects.

The Incas

The Incas ruled a highly regimented empire that included much of the Andean region of South America, stretching from southern Colombia through Ecuador, Bolivia, Peru, into northern Chile and northwestern Argentina. Beginning in the 13th century, the Incas began to expand and conquer other peoples, including other advanced civilizations such as the Tihuanaco and the Chimu. The acceptance of Incan rule meant that a conquered people could retain its own rulers.

Religion played a crucial role in Inca life. The term "Inca" refers to the ruler of the empire and his extended family, which numbered in the thousands. The Inca was believed to be a descendent of the sun god, Inti, and was worshiped like a living god. The Incas sought through their worship to influence their gods to help them, and a large group of priests regulated the ceremonial life of the empire. Offerings of food, animals, and at times human sacrifice were made to the gods.

Land was not privately owned. It was given by the Inca to the tribe and distributed. The land was subdivided into four parts: one section was given to the farmers; a second was set aside for the sun and the crops given to the priests of the temples; a third went to the emperor, who used the crops for the government officials, the military, and his personal household use; and the last section was farmed for those who could not provide for themselves. Potatoes, cotton, maize, beans, squash, cotton, and tomatoes were the principal crops.

GLOBAL
CONCEPTS

Choice

CONCEPTS
GLOBAL

The Incas excelled in engineering and architecture. Remnants of the Inca road system, bridges, and building construction can still be found throughout the Andean region. Cuzco, located in the highlands of Peru, was their major capital. The official language of the Inca empire was Quechua, but the Incas allowed subject peoples to use their own languages. They had

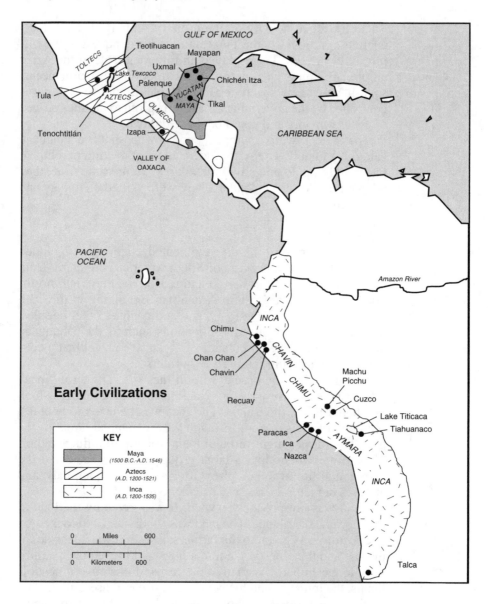

Early Civilizations

KEY

Maya
(1500 B.C.-A.D. 1546)

Aztecs
(A.D. 1200-1521)

Inca
(A.D. 1200-1535)

no written language and therefore kept no written records or books. Instead they used a quipu, which was a main string with small colored strings attached and tied into knots to record knowledge. The Incas were skillful artisans who excelled in metal work, pottery, and textiles. Cotton and the wool from the llama, alpaca, vicunya, and guanaco were used for clothing. The Incas were particularly adept in the use of gold and silver for fine jewelry and other ornaments. In the 1530s the Spanish conquistadores, led by Pizzarro, ended the reign of the Incas and destroyed their civilization.

The Spanish Colonial Empire

The Spanish and Portuguese were the first to make vast claims in the Americas and carve out colonial empires. In 1494, in the Treaty of Tordesillas, Spain obtained all of the Americas except for what is today Brazil, which went to Portugal.

As the Spanish empire in the New World was established, the Native American civilizations were for the most part destroyed by superior military forces and diseases. Forced labor on plantations and in the mines, the encomienda and mita systems, were other factors in the destruction of the Native American cultures and people.

The Spaniards brought the characteristics of their society to their New World empire. Spain imposed a political, religious, and linguistic unity on its colonial empire. The Spanish colonial organization penetrated wherever wealth could be found and Roman Catholicism could be preached.

The growing scarcity of Native American labor led to the importation of African slaves in the Americas for use on plantations, in the mines, and for other purposes. Efforts by the Roman Catholic church to protect the Native Americans from abuses of their human rights were largely ignored in a colonial economy, which operated on the principles of the mercantilist system. Bishop Bartolomé de Las Casas sought to enlist the Spanish crown in the protection of the Native Americans, but his efforts failed. The latifundio and hacienda (large, self-sufficient plantations) forms of landownership predominated. They were characterized by unproductive holdings, dependent labor, a low level of technology, and little capital investment.

GLOBAL
CONCEPTS
Human Rights
CONCEPTS
GLOBAL

The Spanish colonial organization was based on a hierarchical structure, which placed the Spanish at the top of colonial society. This privileged class of Spanish elite, peninsulars (Spanish-born nobles), and creoles (their American-born children) dominated the colonial economy and owned vast areas of land. Next were the mestizos (Caucasian and Native American ancestry), followed by mulattos (Caucasian and African ancestry), African slaves, and Native Americans.

GLOBAL
CONCEPTS
Diversity
CONCEPTS
GLOBAL

The Spanish Roman Catholic church helped in the subjugation and control of the Native American population and the ordering of colonial society. The hierarchical Roman Catholic church was a large landholder throughout the Spanish colonies in the Americas. Both the regular hierarchy and the religious

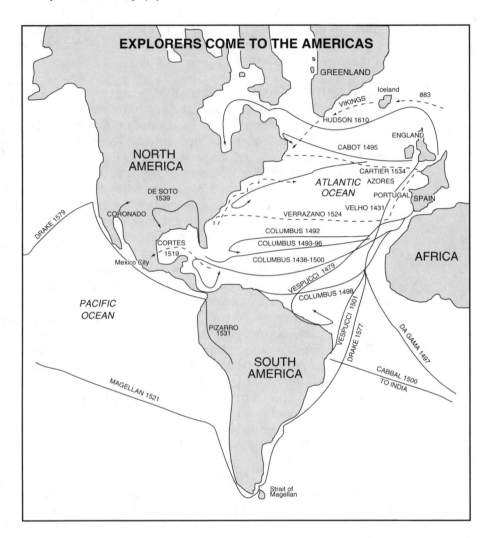

EXPLORERS COME TO THE AMERICAS

GREENLAND

Iceland

883

VIKINGS

HUDSON 1610

ENGLAND

CABOT 1495

NORTH AMERICA

CARTIER 1534

ATLANTIC OCEAN   AZORES

DE SOTO 1539

PORTUGAL SPAIN

VELHO 1431

CORONADO

VERRAZANO 1524

DRAKE 1579

COLUMBUS 1492

CORTES 1519

COLUMBUS 1493-96

Mexico City

COLUMBUS 1438-1500

AFRICA

VESPUCCI 1479

COLUMBUS 1498

PACIFIC OCEAN

VESPUCCI 1501

PIZARRO 1531

DRAKE 1577

DA GAMA 1497

SOUTH AMERICA

MAGELLAN 1521

CABBAL 1500 TO INDIA

Strait of Magellan

orders (the Jesuits, Franciscans, and Dominicans) took responsibility for the education of the Native American populations. The Jesuit order played a particularly important mission role in protecting the Native American populations. Jesuit interference with the Spanish colonists' exploitation of the Native American population led to their expulsion from Portuguese America (1759) and Spanish America (1767).

The Spanish empire was controlled by the crown through the royal Council of the Indies. Spanish territory in the New World was divided into viceroyalties headed by appointed governors, called viceroys. The governor was assisted by an administrative and judicial tribunal called the audiencia. Numerous other officials were appointed by the crown. The viceroyalties of New Spain, Peru, New Granada and La Plata were the four major territorial units of the Spanish colonial empire by 1800.

The Portuguese Empire in America

The Portuguese empire began to take shape in the 1400s due to the voyages of exploration sponsored by Prince Henry the Navigator. Credit for the discovery of Brazil is given to Pedro Cabral, who claimed the territory for the king of Portugal in 1500. Portugal's primary colonial interests were in Africa and Asia. This situation changed in the 1600s due to Portugal's loss of most of its colonies in Asia, the growing value of Brazil's sugar-cane production, and the discovery of gold and diamonds. Portugal had less of a dominating presence in Brazil than the Spanish had in their Latin American empire. The Portuguese did not settle in large numbers in Brazil, and since men greatly outnumbered women, the population increase resulted primarily from intermarriage. Class lines were more economic than racial in Brazil because of this intermixture of Portuguese, Native Americans, and Africans.

The Tupi-Guarani, an Amerindian grouping of tribes who spoke dialects of the Tupian language, inhabited the Brazilian coastline when the Portuguese arrived to trade and settle in the 1500s. The Tupian peoples survived on subsistence hunting and fishing and the cultivation of manioc, sweet potatoes, and beans. They were fierce and warlike, but contact with the Europeans eventually proved fatal due to disease, warfare, and attempted enslavement for labor.

The growing need for a reliable source of labor on the sugar-cane plantations led to the importation of large numbers of Africans as slaves starting in the mid-1500s. Since the Roman Catholic church did not play as wide a role in Brazil as in Spanish territory, the African slaves were able to retain some of their religious and cultural beliefs. These blended with Christian and Native American concepts and emerged as Candomble, an Africanized ritualistic and formalized cult that existed beneath the façade of the Roman Catholic church.

The Portuguese penetrated deeply into the interior of the South American continent. Bandeiras, quasi-Euro-Amerindian military expeditions in search of Indian slaves and precious mineral wealth, pushed Portuguese claims to the Andes Mountains.

The Dutch, French, and English in Latin America

In the second half of the 16th century, the Dutch, French, and English sought to establish colonies in the Americas. They took possession of territory primarily in the Caribbean region and along the northeastern coast of South America.

Starting in the 1580s the Dutch attempted to gain control of northeastern Brazil. The profitable sugar-cane industry was a target of growing Dutch sea power, financial strength, and technical and business expertise. The Dutch presence in the

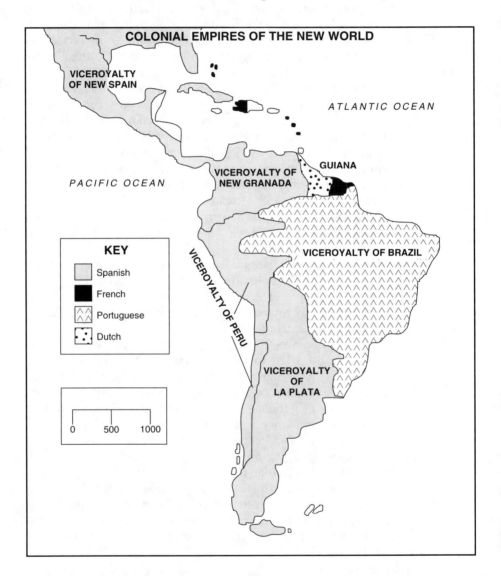

COLONIAL EMPIRES OF THE NEW WORLD

VICEROYALTY OF NEW SPAIN

ATLANTIC OCEAN

PACIFIC OCEAN

GUIANA

VICEROYALTY OF NEW GRANADA

VICEROYALTY OF PERU

VICEROYALTY OF BRAZIL

VICEROYALTY OF LA PLATA

KEY

Spanish
French
Portuguese
Dutch

0   500   1000

sugar-producing areas south of the Amazon River lasted until the 1640s, when Portugal reestablished its independence from Spain, which enabled the Portuguese to drive out the Dutch. The Dutch were able to hold onto Dutch Guiana, present-day Surinam, and they retained the Netherlands Antilles: the islands of Curaçao, Aruba, Bonaire, St. Eustatius, Saba, and part of St. Martin.

During the 1500s, besides laying claims to parts of North America, the French sought to establish a presence in the Caribbean and South America. Attempts to gain a foothold in Brazil were defeated by the Portuguese in the mid-1500s. Settlements in Cayenne in French Guiana began in 1604. Control of this territory shifted back and forth among the French, Dutch, Portuguese, and British. Martinique and Guadaloupe in the French West Indies were settled and colonized beginning in 1635 and became valuable sugar producers. Haiti was ceded by Spain to France in 1697. The western region of the island of Hispaniola became France's most prosperous colony in the Americas. The establishment of a plantation economy, based on slave labor and restrictive mercantilist trade policies, was promoted by the French crown.

WORLD ISSUES

Economic
Growth and
Development

Besides the settlements along the eastern coast of North America, the British were also able to establish themselves throughout the Caribbean. Jamaica, Barbados, and Trinidad-Tobago were their principal possessions in what became the British West Indies in the late 1600s. As elsewhere in the Caribbean, large numbers of African slaves were brought in to provide labor for the sugar-cane plantations in the British West Indies. The first English settlements of South America, in present-day Guyana, began in the 1600s.

The English, French, and Dutch colonies in the Caribbean basin all developed a highly profitable sugar-plantation economy, utilizing imported African slave labor. The colonies were controlled by trading policies that favored the "mother" country. The European colonial powers exploited the resources of the Caribbean islands to further their own economic development.

Establishment of Political Independence in Latin America

GLOBAL
CONCEPTS

Change

CONCEPTS
GLOBAL

The 1700s were a period of great political, social, and economic change for the European powers. Britain's thirteen colonies in North America won their independence as a result of the American Revolution. In the late 1700s the French Revolution shook the stability of Europe. The writings of the Enlightenment, expressed in the works of Locke, Rousseau, Voltaire, Montesquieu, and others, led to the spread of revolutionary ideas in Europe and the Americas. In the 1700s Spain sought to reform its American empire. New viceroyalties were created, and an intendancy system was introduced to increase revenues and improve the colonial administration. A Spanish officer appointed by the crown, an intendente, had complete control in matters of justice, war, fiscal problems and general public administration over a given area. Despite these reforms, the foreign policy of Spain's Bourbon monarchy, which allied the nation with France, led to a series of military engagements that greatly weakened the Spanish empire. Spain's economic situation and military power continued to decline into the 1790s.

The Napoleonic era that followed the French Revolution caused dislocations that eventually led to a period of Latin American revolutions from 1808 to 1826. Despite the distance and isolation of Spain's colonies from Europe, the political ideas of the Enlightenment and the American and French revolutions affected the people in the Spanish colonies. The English, Dutch, French, and Americans increasingly traded with Spain's American empire, thereby decreasing the loyalty and dependence of the colonies on Spain. Moreover, some of the creole elite in the Spanish colonies, such as the Venezuelan Francisco Miranda, promoted the independence of Spanish America.

WORLD ISSUES

War
and
Peace

Napoleon's armies invaded Spain and Portugal in 1806 to 1807. The capture and exile of the Spanish royal family to France and the placement of Joseph Bonaparte on the Spanish throne broke the bond that tied Spanish America to Spain. A movement that began as a rejection of French control ended as a series for wars of independence against Spain.

The liberators, Simón Bolívar and José San Martín, and their supporters, raised armies to drive the Spanish out of South America. In Mexico the leadership of Fathers Hidalgo and Morelos and other revolutionaries led to the eventual success of Agustín de Iturbide, who established Mexican independence in 1821. Creole nationalism was too strong to overcome, and with the help of the mestizo population, the Spanish were driven out.

Case Study in Independence: Haiti

WORLD ISSUES

Determination
of Political
and Economic
Systems

The movement towards Haitian independence was sparked by the French Revolution. Throughout the 1790s, the former slaves, first led by Toussaint l'Ouverture, increasingly sought to drive out the white slaveowners. Despite a major attempt to restore French authority by Napoleon in 1802, independence was inevitable. In 1804 Jean-Jacques Dessalines, an ex-slave, was able to drive out the French, and Haiti became the second nation in the Western Hemisphere to win complete independence.

Case Study in Independence: Mexico

In 1810, Miguel Hidalgo, a priest, joined with other creole plotters, most notably Ignacio de Allende, and issued the famous Grito de Dolores. This symbol raised the cry of rebellion against the Spanish government in New Spain. The first phase of the struggle for independence ended with the royalists' defeating the insurgents and executing many of the leaders of the rebellion. Despite this setback, one of Hidalgo's lieutenants, Jose Morelos, called together a congress, which wrote a constitution and declared independence. Morelos was captured and executed in 1815. However, independence was finally secured in 1821 when Agustín de Iturbide, a creole military officer who had helped defeat the earlier rebellions, negotiated with Vincente Guerrero, by then the principal insurgent leader, to form the Plan of Iguala, which called for independence under a monarchy. Iturbide forced the Spanish out and briefly ruled Mexico as emperor.

LATIN AMERICAN INDEPENDENCE MOVEMENTS TO 1828

Country	Year of Independence	Independence Movement Leaders
Haiti	1803–1804	Toussaint l'Ouverture
Mexico	1821	Father Miguel Hidalgo
		José Morelos
		Agustín de Iturbide
Colombia	1819	Simón Bolívar
Venezuela	1821	Francisco de Miranda
		Simon Bolívar
Ecuador	1822	José de Sucre
		Simón Bolívar
Argentina	1816	José de San Martín
Chile	1818	José de San Martín
		Bernardo O'Higgins
Peru	1824	José de Sucre
		Simón Bolívar
Bolivia	1825	Simón Bolívar
Uruguay	1814, 1828	José Artigas
Brazil	1822	José Benifacio
		Emperor Dom Pedro
Paraguay	1811	Fulgencio Yegros
Central American Republics	1812–1825	José Delgado
		José del Valle

Case Studies: Argentina, Chile, and the Role of José de San Martín

In 1810 a revolutionary regime in Buenos Aires declared independence. José de San Martín, the real architect of independence, had liberated the future Argentina by 1816. He crossed the Andes Mountains with an army in 1817 and helped Bernardo O'Higgins drive the Spanish army out of Chile the following year. San Martín was also involved in the liberation of Peru, but he left the final military struggle in that country after an historic meeting with Simón Bolívar, the Liberator.

Case Study: The Andean Region and the Role of Simón Bolívar, "the Liberator"

Simón Bolívar, by birth a member of the creole landowning elite, supported the growing independence movement. Between 1810 and 1821 the Liberator was involved in wars to free the future nations of Venezuela, Colombia, Ecuador, Bolivia, and Peru. He was made the first constitutional president of Gran Colombia in 1821. With the help of Francisco Santander and Antonio José de Sucre, Bolívar defeated the Spanish royalist forces by 1826, and they withdrew from Peru.

Case Study: Brazil

GLOBAL CONCEPTS

Change

CONCEPTS GLOBAL

Napoleon's invasion of Portugal resulted in the royal family's leaving for Brazil. Joao VI became king of Portugal, Brazil, and the Algarve in 1816. Joao helped the British commercial interests by opening the Brazilian ports to trade with friendly nations. This measure also resulted in promoting Brazil's economic autonomy. However, in 1821 political events in Portugal caused Joao to return there. He left behind his son, Pedro I, as regent of Brazil. In 1822, Pedro issued his famous "I am staying" statement after the Portuguese parliament ordered him to return to Portugal. Later that year, independence was declared. In contrast to Spanish America, Brazilian independence was achieved peacefully. Pedro I was declared emperor of Brazil in 1822.

Case Study: The Caribbean

The one area where Spain retained its colonies was in the Caribbean. Cuba and Puerto Rico remained possessions of Spain until the Spanish-American War in 1898. The economies of these two Greater Antilles islands were dominated by the sugar-plantation owners, and slavery was the main source of labor, particularly in Cuba. The cooperation of Spanish and creole landowners, merchants, and government officials prevented an independence movement from developing on these islands.

In the British, French, and Dutch Caribbean colonies, with the exception of Haiti, independence has been attained more recently, if at all. Many of the British-held islands did not achieve independence until the post-World War II period. Some islands have remained attached to Great Britain. The French-speaking islands were made overseas departments, which gave them the privilege of representation in the nation's politics and the right of French citizenship. However, the real political power remained in France.

Early Attempts at Unification Fail

The initial attempts at unification of the newly independent states did not last, mainly because nationalistic feelings in the Latin American countries led to political fragmentation. The political union of present-day Colombia, Venezuela, Ecuador, and Panama in Gran Colombia was established in 1819 through the efforts of Simón Bolívar, Francisco Santander, and others. At the Congress of Cucuta in 1821, a constitution was adopted. Bolívar and Santander were elected the first president and vice-president for all of Colombia. Santander remained to direct the government after Bolivar went off to liberate Peru. The central government promoted a program of liberal reform. However, attempts by the landed elites to safeguard their local authority and autonomy in Venezuela and Ecuador led in 1826 to an open revolt that broke out in Venezuela. The return of Bolivar temporarily brought unity and peace. However, a brief war soon began between Peru and Gran Colombia in 1828, and this caused the local landed elites to renew their struggle for a political entity that would be more easily influenced and run in their interests. In 1830 first Venezuela and then Ecuador formally seceded. The remaining part of Gran Colombia became the Republic of New Granada.

The Federation of Central America was created when the five provinces—Guatamala, El Salvador, Honduras, Nicaragua, and Costa Rica—declared independence in 1821 and joined the Mexican empire under Iturbide. They drafted a constitution and adopted a republican form of government. The new government immediately had political difficulties, and in 1823 the five provinces left the federation and became independent states. By the 1840s the federation had ceased to exist.

Sources of Stability and Power: The Landed Elite, the Military, and the Roman Catholic Church

The failure of unification in South America and in Central America was a result of the concentration of power in the hands of the creole landed elite in the independent nations of Latin America. The large landowners gained enormous power in their local areas and were unwilling to surrender it to a strong central government. The creole aristocracy, who owned large estates called latifundio, replaced the Spanish officials and peninsulars. They were unwilling to share political power, and the large landowners became a conservative force that sought to maintain stability and their traditional local powers. Instead of unity, Latin America fell victim to frequent disputes concerning landownership within each nation and along border areas. These problems have continued to our present day.

WORLD ISSUES

Determination of Political and Economic Systems

The role of the military also proved to be a continuing problem in Latin America. In the early years, military leaders were called on to maintain law and order and act as a stabilizing influence. The military shared a common goal with the landed elite, which was to preserve the status quo. In some countries, the military was the only organized force that could prevent chaos after the wars of national independence.

The rebellions that frequently broke out in the Spanish-speaking republics in the 1800s led the armed forces of many nations to control their countries for long periods. The rise of the military dictator, the caudillo, became a tradition in many countries. José Antonio Paez of Venezuela and Andres Santa Cruz of Bolivia are early examples of caudillos in their nations. Venezuela suffered 50 revolutions, and Bolivia 60 revolutions by 1900.

GLOBAL CONCEPTS

Political Systems

CONCEPTS GLOBAL

Military figures continued to gain and hold onto power in the 20th century. The military continues to see itself as the preserver of stability and tradition. Today, a military coup d'état is justified to prevent the possibility of a Communist takeover and social disintegration. This was the case in Chile when General Augusto Pinochet seized power in 1973.

After the wars of independence, the Roman Catholic church remained a key institution throughout Latin America. Until recently, the church often supported the landed elite and military in their efforts to preserve tradition and social order and showed little concern for social problems. However, in recent years the role of the church in some Latin American nations has changed, as the clergy has taken a more active role in causes concerning human rights. Some members of the clergy have supported the ideas of the liberation theology, a church of the people and even rebellions against the government in power. The struggle within the church between conservatives, who believe that the clergy should continue its traditional historic role, and radicals, who want the clergy to play a more social and political role, continues. In addition, the Roman Catholic church is also under pressure due to inroads made by Protestant denominations, particularly the evangelical movements that stress the importance of reconciliation and personal experience with God.

Political Evolution Since Independence

GLOBAL CONCEPTS

Citizenship

CONCEPTS GLOBAL

In Latin America, a concept of citizenship was slow to develop after independence. There also were difficulties in attempting to institute a republican form of government. Political participation was open primarily to the wealthy members of society. The landed elite consolidated their hold on the executive and legislative branches of government. In theory, some democratic traditions were established in many Latin American countries in the 19th century. For example, constitutions were written, elected legislative bodies were provided for, and judicial systems were created. However, in practice, the caudillo acted as a dictator and often ignored the democratic features of government.

Case Study: Argentina (1820s to Today)

The landed elite, primarily cattle ranchers, were the real source of power in Argentina. Argentinian nationalism developed during the rule of the caudillo tyrant Juan Manuel de Rosas. Rosas ignored the constitution and often used his military power to persecute and terrorize his enemies. Although the provinces of Argentina remained loosely associated under Rosa's federalist control, by the time of his overthrow in 1852, he had, to a large measure, forged national unity. However, the establishment of democratic traditions did not come until later in the 1800s.

In the 1940s a military officer, Juan D. Perón, rose to power. Perón was a populist caudillo who used the democratic process to promote a program that favored the middle and labor sectors of society. Perón was elected president twice. Juan Perón and his first wife, Eva Perón, relied on the support of the workers. His program, Justicialismo, sought a balance between society's opposing forces. Perón was overthrown in 1955 by the military, with the support of the traditional elite who found his programs threatening. However, Perónism continued to be a political force. In 1972 Perón was reelected but died shortly thereafter. His new wife, Isabel, succeeded him but soon was overthrown by a military coup d'état. A period of harsh military rule followed.

In 1976, as terrorist attacks worsened, the military started a brutal campaign known as the dirty war. As many as 25,000 people, mainly students and workers, were killed or "disappeared" during this time. In 1982 the military launched a campaign to gain control of the Malvinas Islands, also called the Falkland Islands, about 300 miles off the coast of Argentina. These islands had been ruled by the British since the 1830s. The British refused to recognize the Argentine claim and soundly defeated the Argentine military. With this defeat, the military lost all credibility and popular support.

WORLD ISSUES

Terrorism

In 1983 democratic elections were allowed. The Radical and Perónist parties once again vied for political power. Raul Alfonsin, a Radical, was elected president and worked to restore democracy to Argentina. Alfonsin brought some of the military leaders responsible for the dirty war and the defeat in the Malvinas to justice. In 1989 voters elected a new president, Carlos Menem. President Menem, a Perónist, instituted drastic reforms, which resulted in curbing inflation and restoring economic growth. Argentina's constitution was amended in 1993 to allow President Menem to run for a second term.

WORLD ISSUES

Economic
Growth and
Development

Case Study: Mexico

In the late 1820s a military caudillo, Antonio Santa Anna, rose to power. He dominated Mexican politics to the mid-1850s and supported a conservative and centralist concept of government. Unfortunately, Santa Anna resorted to dictatorial rule and corrupt policies that had disastrous consequences. Mexico, under Santa Anna's leadership, fell victim to U.S. expansionism. The successful rebellion led by Americans in Texas in the 1830s and the Mexican War in the 1840s led to a loss of over 40 percent of Mexico's territory.

GLOBAL
CONCEPTS

Change

CONCEPTS
GLOBAL

After Santa Anna's exile in 1855, Benito Juárez tried to rule Mexico under more democratic ideals. In the mid-1870s, Porfirio Díaz, a soldier and protegé of Juárez, was elected president and held political power until the revolution of 1911. During Díaz's rule, Mexico was transformed into a politically stable and economically progressive nation, but at the expense of political freedom and democratic government. Foreign investment was encouraged in railroads, oil, and mining. Díaz's political power was based on the use of a repressive police force, the rurales, to control his opponents. The peasants continued to live under terrible conditions, and the urban labor movement was suppressed. Díaz was supported by the elite hacienda owners, the Roman Catholic church, and the military.

Political Revolutions

In the 20th century, several revolutions have led to important changes in some nations of Latin America. Their long-term effects are not yet clear. However, traditional institutions are faced with increasing social and economic problems brought on by demographic change.

Case Study: Mexico Since 1911

The Mexican Revolution of 1911 led to important changes in that nation. After the fall of Díaz, military leaders succeeded one another as president and created a constitutional government based on a one-party political system. The Roman Catholic church lost much of its influence and power. The Mexican labor movement was allowed to develop and became an important force. The labor unions competed with the new developing industrial oligarchy to influence the government.

Mexico became more nationalistic, and the nationalization of the petroleum industry in the 1930s by Lazaro Cardinas symbolized the nation's change of direction. In the years after 1940, the leaders of the ruling political party, the PRI, sought to create political stability by allowing a middle class to develop and by encouraging economic change. However, the PRI has continued to hold power despite growing political opposition.

In 1988 Carlos Salinas de Gotari was chosen by the PRI as its official candidate and took office after a disputed presidential election. President Salinas made a number of painful budgetary reductions. There were cuts in spending on education, health care, and other social services. Thousands of government workers were laid off and state-owned industries were sold to private investors. President Salinas also moved toward freer trade, and the Mexican government ratified NAFTA.

In 1994 President Salinas handpicked Ernest Zedillo as PRI's presidential candidate after the original candidate Luis Donaldo Colosio was assassinated. President Zedillo was elected in August 1994 for a six-year term. Salinas promised that the PRI, in power for more than six decades, would not resort to fraud or irregularities to win the scheduled August 1994 elections. In early 1994 a rebellion took place in Chiapas, a poor state in southern Mexico where descendants of the Maya live mostly in poverty. This rebellion is further indication that political, economic, and social reforms are needed.

The question remains whether the political system in Mexico is open to change.

Case Study: The Cuban Revolution (1959–)

Cuba remained a Spanish colony until 1898 when independence was established as part of the treaty that settled the Spanish-American War. The U.S. influence in Cuba continued after its military occupation ended in 1902. Between 1933 and 1959 Fulgencio Batista dominated, and although he provided political stability, economic problems led to increased suffering. A rebellion supported by young professionals, students, urban workers, and some farmers was led by Fidel Castro. By 1959 Castro's military forces had defeated Batista's army and seized power.

GLOBAL
CONCEPTS
Political Systems
CONCEPTS
GLOBAL

Castro brought about great political, social, and economic changes. He turned to the Communist nations, especially the former Soviet Union, for economic support and protection from the United States. By 1965 Castro's socialist state was officially ruled by the Cuban Communist party and guided by the principles of Marxism-Leninism.

Castro sought to export the Cuban Revolution by supporting guerrilla movements in Bolivia, Colombia, Nicaragua, El Salvador, and elsewhere. This forced the United States to pay greater attention to the social and economic problems in Latin America. Starting in the 1960s, the United States began to work to politically and economically isolate Cuba.

The United States has continued its trade embargo against Cuba despite opposition from some Latin American countries. The collapse of Communism ended the massive support of the former Soviet Union and Eastern European nations for Cuba. In the early 1990s Cuba has suffered increased economic and social problems. The United States insists that Cuba make political reforms if the trade embargo is to be lifted. Fidel Castro is increasingly faced with difficult choices as the Cuban economy continues to deteriorate. There is growing doubt as to whether Castro can continue the Cuban Revolution and retain his power. In 1994, Cuba and the United States reached an agreement concerning increased Cuban immigration after another wave of Cubans left the island nation for the U.S. to escape the harsh economic conditions.

Case Study: The Sandinista Revolution in Nicaragua

U.S. interest in Nicaragua dates from the late 1840s when the American government contested British supremacy in Central America. The United States began a military occupation of the nation in 1912, which lasted until 1933. In the mid-1930s, the national guard, trained by U.S. military officers, took responsibility for maintaining order. The national guard was the instrument for the rise of the Somoza dictatorship, which ruled Nicaragua from 1936 through most of the 1970s. Although there was economic progress under Somoza in agricultural production and then in the industrial sector, there was little real distribution of income.

The assassination of Pedro Chamorro, the publisher of an opposition newspaper in 1978, sparked an uprising that toppled the Somozoa dictatorship and brought the Sandinista Front to power in 1979. The Sandinistas sought to create a socialist-type state in Nicaragua, and Daniel Ortega became the nation's leader. The Sandinistas soon faced opposition from the United States. Moreover, the Sandinista government faced serious economic problems brought on by alienating important segments of the agricultural and industrial sectors.

Hostility toward the Sandinista government because of its ties to Castro's Cuba, the former Soviet Union, and the insurgency in El Salvador led the United States to support the contra military forces, which were seeking to overthrow the Sandinistas. The costly civil war in Nicaragua led to large numbers of casualties, increased emigration, and a further deterioration of the Nicaraguan economy.

GLOBAL
CONCEPTS

Change

CONCEPTS
GLOBAL

In 1990 a democratically elected government headed by Violeta Chamorro, the wife of Pedro Chamorro, took power. The Sandinistas peacefully gave up power but continue part of the government. In Nicaragua, problems remain, but there is hope that they can be peacefully solved.

Case Study: Brazil (1930s to Today)

Getulio Vargas came to power as a result of the Revolution of 1930. Vargas ruled Brazil from 1930 to 1945 and set up programs to promote industrial growth. In the 1950s, Juscelino Kubitschek was elected president. Kubitschek created the new capitol city, Brasilia, in the interior of the country. He also began programs to develop Brazil's highways, universities, airports, factories, and hydroelectric plants.

WORLD ISSUES

Economic
Growth and
Development

In 1964, the military overthrew President Joao Goulart after the economy faltered and as a result of political disagreements. The military governments that ruled Brazil to the end of the 1980s banned political parties and encouraged economic growth. The generals encouraged foreign investment, and in the 1970s, an economic boom called the Brazilian miracle took place. The upper and middle classes obtained most of the benefits during this time of greater prosperity.

By the late 1980s, Brazil's staggering debt of $110 billion and widespread economic and social problems forced the military to give up power slowly to the politicians. In 1990, Fernando Collor de Mello was elected president. President Collor began a series of drastic economic reforms to control Brazil's spiraling inflation.

In 1993 President Collor was removed from office because of corruption. The vice president, Itamar Franco, took over the presidency. In 1990s Brazil's leaders must find solutions to the problems of high inflation, widespread poverty, malnutrition, lack of adequate health care, and crime in the Western Hemisphere's second largest nation in terms of territory, population, and economy. Brazil is placing its hope in Fernando Henrique Cardosa, the newly elected president in 1994 to resolve its many problems.

Political Integration

In 1823, when Spain threatened to try to regain its colonial empire in Latin America, the United States responded with the Monroe Doctrine. President James Monroe in a statement issued to Congress declared that the American continents were henceforth not to be considered as subjects for future colonization by European nations. The statement also said that any attempt by European powers to extend their system to this hemisphere would be considered dangerous to the peace and safety of the United States. In addition, the United States declared that it would not interfere in European affairs.

The Monroe Doctrine was favorably received by the Latin American nations. Although the United States did not possess the military force to back up this bold statement, it knew that the British navy would protect Latin America because of Britain's commercial interests in the region.

Prior to the 1860s, the United States had done little to protect Latin America from European intrusions. However, in the late 1800s the United States began to play a greater role in the affairs of Latin America. In 1898 the United States defeated Spain in the Spanish-American War and gained control of Puerto Rico and Cuba. Cuba soon gained its independence, but the era of U.S. domination of much of Latin America, especially Central America and the Caribbean, had begun.

President Theodore Roosevelt changed the role of the United States in Latin America from protector to that of an international police power. In 1904 the Roosevelt Corollary to the Monroe Doctrine stated that if the Latin American nations failed to properly maintain their political and financial affairs, the United States would intervene to restore order. This corollary led to interventions in the Dominican Republic, Nicaragua, Haiti, and elsewhere. In addition, the U.S. desire to build a canal to connect the Atlantic and Pacific oceans led it to defend Panama's secession from Colombia in 1903. The Hay-Bunau-Varilla Treaty negotiated with the newly independent nation to build the Panama Canal was very favorable to U.S. interests.

This policy of interference in Latin American affairs caused a growing resentment in the region toward the "colossus of the north" as other presidents continued Theodore Roosevelt's aggressive policy. President Taft supported dollar diplomacy, which encouraged American bankers to make loans to Central America and the Caribbean nations. This led to intervention to protect American creditors.

During the 1930s President Franklin D. Roosevelt sought to modify U.S. policy toward Latin America in his Good Neighbor policy. Under Roosevelt, the United States succeeded in its economic and security objectives, but the Good Neighbor policy did little to resolve Latin America's fundamental political, social, and economic problems or reduce the region's distrust of the United States.

After World War II, a new inter-American system, known as the Organization of American States (OAS), was established. At first, it included 20 Latin American nations and the United States, but it has since admitted Canada, Trinidad and Tobago, Barbados, and Jamaica. The charter of the OAS provides a legal framework for a permanent inter-American organization. In 1967 a series of changes amended the charter. A general assembly of member nations that meets annually was established, and a secretary general elected to a five-year term was approved. The amended charter stresses economic development, social justice, and regional integration.

The OAS record of preserving hemispheric peace has been mixed. The United States has sought to involve the OAS in its attempts to regulate Latin American political affairs. The American-sponsored Bay of Pigs invasion of Cuba in 1961 and the United States' military occupation of the Dominican Republic in 1965 were seen as violations of the OAS charter by many Latin American nations. However, Latin America did support the United States by voting to exclude Cuba from the OAS in the early 1960s.

In the 1980s the United States invaded Grenada and Panama to overthrow dictatorships. The Latin American nations resent these interventions and favor a legal channel for solving

GLOBAL
CONCEPTS

Power

CONCEPTS
GLOBAL

international disputes. The Latin American nations also opposed U.S. intervention in Nicaragua. The Contadora peace plan drafted by a group of Latin American nations, most notably Costa Rica, was an attempt to stop armed conflict and to establish regional peace in Central America. The Nicaraguan election in February 1990, won by Violeta Chamorro over the Sandinistas, is a hopeful sign that electoral politics will replace armed conflict in Central America.

The Case of Puerto Rico

U.S. rule over Puerto Rico has changed since the Spanish-American War. This evolutionary process transformed the original military government in 1898 into a civilian government under the Foraker Act of 1900. The Jones Act of 1917 allowed the popular election of both houses of the bicameral legislature and a voice in appointing the governor's cabinet.

The Muñoz Rivera and Muñoz Marín political dynasty that dominated Puerto Rican politics from 1900 to the mid-1960s was supported by the United States. The idea of independence did not have much political support in this period. Under Public Law 600 in 1952, Puerto Rico became an associated free state with full autonomy in internal matters and its own constitution. As citizens of the United States, Puerto Ricans share a common currency and the right to defense by U.S. government. In 1967, a plebiscite (vote) resulted in a large majority favoring commonwealth status rather than statehood. Less than one percent of the people voted for independence. In recent years, although some favor independence the vast majority of the Puerto Rican people favor either statehood or commonwealth status.

WORLD ISSUES

Determination
of Political
and Economic
Systems

In the 1950s reforms initiated by Muñoz Marín led to the development of industry and the growth of tourism on the island. Operation Bootstrap, a U.S.-sponsored program, offered companies tax savings to build plants in Puerto Rico. Despite economic progress, unemployment in Puerto Rico remains high. Puerto Rico's status for the next number of years was settled after a vote in 1993, which resulted in a victory for the supporters of commonwealth status.

REVIEW QUESTIONS

Multiple Choice. Select the letter of the answer that correctly completes each statement.

1. All the following are examples of advanced pre-Columbian civilizations *except* the
   A. Mayan
   B. Aztecs
   C. Incas
   D. Tupi-Guarani

2. The Portuguese empire in America differed from the Spanish empire in that the Portuguese
   A. did not practice the Roman Catholic religion
   B. were only interested in agricultural production
   C. did not settle in large numbers in Brazil
   D. treated the Native Americans better than the Spaniards

3. The European nations that colonized Latin America supported trade policies that were
   A. mercantilist
   B. laissez faire
   C. unrestrictive
   D. pro free trade

4. Early attempts at unification failed in Latin America after independence because
   A. there were no strong nationalist sentiments
   B. the great leaders of the independence movements did not support unification.
   C. the new nations had no common heritage
   D. the landed elites wanted to preserve their local power

5. All of the following are sources of stability and power in Latin America *except* the
   A. landed elite
   B. military
   C. Roman Catholic church
   D. liberation theology movement

6. The earliest of these pre-Columbian civilizations was
   A. Aztec
   B. Mayan
   C. Olmec
   D. Inca

Matching. Match the correct hero of the independence of Latin America with
the nation liberated in Column 1.

Column 1	Column 2
_____ 1. Mexico	A. José San Martín
_____ 2. Argentina	B. Pedro I
_____ 3. Chile	C. Simón Bolívar
_____ 4. Brazil	D. Miguel Hidalgo
_____ 5. Colombia	E. Bernardo O'Higgins

Essays

1. Why do the nations of Latin America fear United States interference in Latin American affairs?

2. Why has the military in many Latin American countries seized power so often?

3. Why did Mayan civilization decline in the late classic period?

4. Why is the Roman Catholic church experiencing problems in Latin America?

5. How has the PRI dominated politics in Mexico since 1940?

6. What problems does Brazil face today?

UNIT SIX

Western Europe

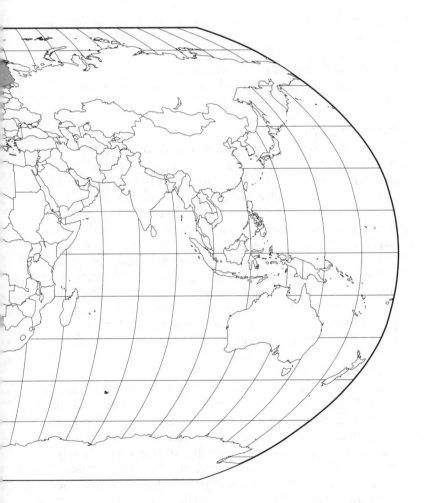

I. PHYSICAL GEOGRAPHY OF WESTERN EUROPE

Overview

The region known as Western Europe consists of 20 nations that lie in the western part of the European continent. These nations may be grouped in the following ways:

1. Northwestern Europe, which consists of Ireland, the United Kingdom (England, Scotland, Wales, and Northern Ireland), France, and the Benelux countries (Belgium, the Netherlands, and Luxembourg).

2. Southern Europe, consisting of Portugal, Spain, Italy, and Greece.

3. Middle (Central) Europe, which consists of Germany, Switzerland, Austria, and Liechtenstein.

4. Scandinavia, made up of Iceland, Norway, Sweden, Finland, Denmark, and Greenland.

Topography

Western Europe has many different kinds of landforms, which have affected political, economic, and cultural ways of life. The major mountains are the Alps, Apennines, and Pyrenees. The Pyrenees have restricted movement between France and Spain, thereby separating the Iberian Peninsula (Spain and Portugal) from the rest of the region. The mountainous terrain in Greece was responsible for the growth of separate city-states in ancient Greece. The lowlands in the Netherlands made that country concerned about frequent flooding from the North Sea, and many dams and canals have been built for protection. The low plains in the other Benelux nations as well as in northeastern France have been the sites of invasions and battlegrounds throughout European history.

GLOBAL
CONCEPTS
Environment
CONCEPTS
GLOBAL

Water Bodies

The major water bodies surrounding Western Europe are the Baltic Sea and the North Sea in the north, the Atlantic Ocean in the west, and the Mediterranean Sea in the south. The Atlantic Ocean has been a highway of commerce and a migration path for peoples between Europe and the Americas, particularly for those nations touching the Atlantic, such as Britain, France, Ireland, and Spain. The nearness to large bodies of water led to the build-up of fishing fleets and eventually to great naval power for several nations. At different times in history, these nations—

GLOBAL
CONCEPTS
Change
CONCEPTS
GLOBAL

WESTERN EUROPE

ICELAND

✪ Reykjavik

ATLANTIC OCEAN

NORWAY

SWEDEN

FINLAND

Oslo ✪

✪ Helsinki

✪ Stockholm

NORTH SEA

SCOTLAND

BALTIC SEA

DENMARK

✪ Edinburgh

NORTHERN IRELAND

✪ Copenhagen

✪ Belfast

GREAT BRITAIN

NETHERLANDS

IRELAND

Amsterdam ✪

✪ Dublin

WALES

ENGLAND

GERMANY

✪ London

✪ Bonn

BELGIUM

LUXEMBOURG

✪ Vienna

ENGLISH CHANNEL

Paris ✪

SWITZERLAND

AUSTRIA

Bern ✪

✪ **LIECHTENSTEIN**

FRANCE

ITALY

SPAIN

✪ Rome

PORTUGAL

GREECE

✪ Madrid

✪ Lisbon

✪ Athens

MEDITERRANEAN SEA

KEY

- Central Europe
- Scandinavia
- Mediterranean Europe
- United Kingdom and Ireland
- ✪ Capital City

Britain, France, Holland, Portugal, and Spain—established overseas colonial empires. Historically, the Mediterranean Sea has made cultural diffusion possible between Europe, Africa, and the Middle East, especially by way of the Italian Peninsula. In the 20th century, the North Sea has been developed as an important source of oil. The many warm-water ports on these major bodies of water have helped in the movement of goods and people. The Dutch port of Rotterdam, for example, is the largest in Europe and handles more cargo than New York City.

Several navigable rivers are found in the region, providing for easy access between cities and nations. Among these are the Rhine, Po, Seine, Danube, and Thames.

GLOBAL
CONCEPTS

Change

CONCEPTS
GLOBAL

The English Channel separates Britain from the European mainland and, consequently, has provided protection for the British Isles most of British history. However, times change; a tunnel has been built underneath the English Channel that will provide for the passage of trains and cars. Called the Chunnel, it opened in May 1994.

The North Atlantic Drift brings moderate temperature patterns to the Atlantic coast nations. The Mediterranean Sea affects the climate in the nations of southern Europe, causing hot, dry summers.

REVIEW QUESTIONS

Multiple Choice. Select the letter of the answer that correctly completes each statement.

1. Which of the following is in Northwestern Europe?
   A. Portugal
   B. France
   C. Italy
   D. Austria

2. Norway and Sweden are in a region known as
   A. Central Europe
   B. the Iberian Peninsula
   C. the lowlands
   D. Scandinavia

3. In recent years, the area that has been developed as a source of oil is the
   A. North Sea
   B. Baltic Sea
   C. Mediterranean Sea
   D. Atlantic Ocean

ESSAY

Geography has affected the lives of people in Western Europe. Explain two ways in which each of the following has affected life in Western Europe.

   1. Water bodies
   2. Mountains

II. ECONOMIC GEOGRAPHY OF WESTERN EUROPE

Agriculture

Europe's farmers, although declining in number in this century, produce large amounts of food. Careful use of land, along with pesticides and modern technology, have contributed to food surpluses in many areas. The major agricultural products are wheat, potatoes, meat, wine, and dairy products.

Industrial Production

Western Europe has long been one of the world's leading areas in manufacturing and industrial development. The large deposits of coal in Britain and Germany and scientific technology (beginning with the 19th-century Industrial Revolution) have been primary factors in this development. Major industrial products are automobiles, chemicals, electronics, steel, and machinery.

Advances in agricultural and industrial production have resulted in a high standard of living for Western Europe's people. Germany has the highest GNP (gross national product) on the European continent.

The Marshall Plan

WORLD ISSUES

Economic

Growth and

Development

The Marshall Plan is named after George C. Marshall, U.S. secretary of state, who proposed a way in which the United States could help build up Europe's economy after World War II. His plan, passed by Congress in 1947, was officially known as the European Recovery Act. It made about $12.5 billion in aid available to countries that suffered damage and devastation from the war and called upon the European countries to draw up their own plans for recovery. Most non-Communist European nations accepted the aid offered by the Marshall Plan and as a result achieved much economic progress.

Although the plan included all the European nations, the aid was refused by the Communist nations. Instead, they accepted aid from the Council of Mutual Economic Assistance, a Soviet version of the Marshall Plan.

Economic Systems and Decision Making

Today, different types of economic systems exist in the Western European nations. An economic system is a way of making decisions about such basic economic questions as: What should be produced? Who should produce it? How should it be produced? What should the price be? Who should own the land and the means of production? How is the product to be distributed? To whom should it be distributed?

In a capitalist system, most of these economic questions are decided privately and freely by individual citizens. Under capitalism, a society's government has very little to do with making economic decisions. This kind of system permits a free market economy to exist. Societies that have a market economy and economic freedom also allow other kinds of freedom, such as freedom of religion, speech, the press, etc. In *The Wealth of Nations,* written in 1776, Adam Smith provided a good description of a capitalist system.

In a socialist system, most of the basic economic issues are decided by the government. A socialist government is freely elected by the people, and its main goal is to improve the conditions of workers. Democratic freedoms are allowed, as are many political parties.

In a Communist system, the government makes all the economic decisions. Communist governments come to power as a result of violence and revolution. Only one party, the Communist party, is allowed to exist. *The Communist Manifesto,* written by Karl Marx and Friedrich Engels in 1848, explained certain aspects of Communist theory. (See also Part IV dealing with the Industrial Revolution.)

GLOBAL
CONCEPTS

Diversity

CONCEPTS
GLOBAL

The countries in Western Europe today are said to have a mixed economy; that is, they have elements of both capitalism and socialism. Each nation has a different degree of government ownership (nationalization) of industries. In the field of health and other social services, some nations, such as England, Denmark, and Sweden, have extensive social welfare programs. For example, the British National Health Service provides free dental and medical benefits. The costs of these programs are paid for by taxes on employers and workers.

Although Communist parties have existed in almost every Western European nation, the Communists have been weak and have never won control of a government. In the late 1970s, a movement called Eurocommunism arose. These Communist parties claimed to have somewhat different views from the Soviet and East European Communists, thereby hoping to gain more support. However, this movement was not successful.

Attempts at Economic Cooperation

World War II brought economic ruin to Western Europe and also signaled an end to almost 500 years of European economic dominance in the world. During these many centuries, eco-

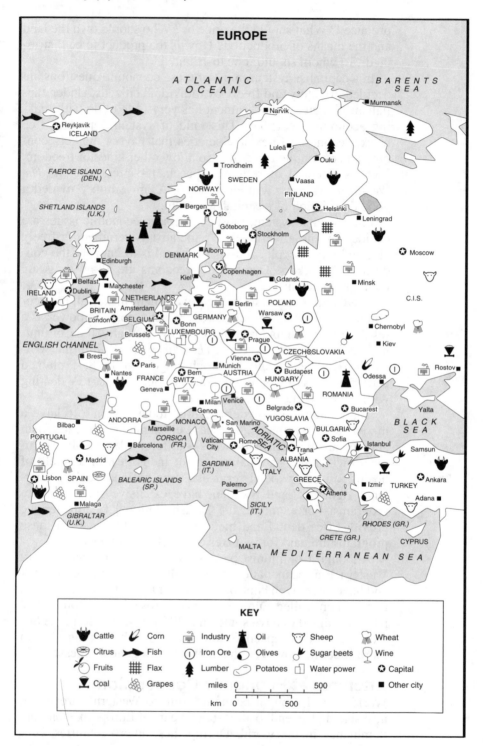

EUROPE

KEY

Cattle	Corn	Industry	Oil	Sheep	Wheat
Citrus	Fish	Iron Ore	Olives	Sugar beets	Wine
Fruits	Flax	Lumber	Potatoes	Water power	Capital
Coal	Grapes				Other city

miles 0 500

km 0 500

nomic rivalry and competition grew among European nations. Since World War II, however, there has been a movement to promote economic unity and cooperation.

The European Union. Once known as the Common Market, this organization was originally created in 1951 as the ECSC (European Coal and Steel Community). Its aim, as stated by French Foreign Minister Robert Schuman in his Schuman Plan, was to bring together the coal and steel industries of six nations—Belgium, France, Italy, Luxembourg, the Netherlands, and West Germany. This group was also known as the Inner Six.

1. In 1957 the Inner Six agreed to bring together their economies and reduce economic barriers such as tariffs. As a result, there was more free trade among these nations, and they changed their name from the ECSC to the EEC (European Economic Community). They also created Euratom to tie together the six nations' research in nuclear power.

2. The EEC came to be known as the European Community (EC) and was very successful in increasing economic activity among its members. By 1985, six other nations were accepted for membership—Denmark, Ireland, England, Greece, Portugal, and Spain.

GLOBAL
CONCEPTS

Change

CONCEPTS
GLOBAL

3. In 1987 the 12 nations of the EC agreed to bring their economies even closer together by 1992 and to create a frontier-free Europe. This plan called for one large common market in which nations could sell their goods more easily to other members; it would allow citizens of a member nation to work in any member nation of the EC; and it would subject goods coming into the EC from outside to a high tax (tariff). The EC's 12 nations would thus make up a single economic unit, with 330 million citizens that could compete with the world's two current economic giants—the United States and Japan. Eventually, the 12 nations might join together politically, creating a United States of Europe. Discussions about this took place in Dublin and Rome in 1990.

GLOBAL
CONCEPTS

Interdependence

CONCEPTS
GLOBAL

The hopes described above, for greater econmic unity by 1992, received a boost with the signing in that year of the Maastricht Treaty. Although the treaty sparked debate in many countries, notably Denmark, England, France, and Germany, it was approved by all members by 1993. These nations were concerned about their voting rights under the treaty as well as the extent to which regulations would affect their sovereignty and the lives of their citizens. The treaty became effective in November 1993. The EC is now know as the European Union. In March 1994 the foreign ministers of the 12 member nations

WORLD ISSUES

Determination
of Political
and Economic
Systems

voted to admit four more nations—Austria, Finland, Norway, and Sweden. It is expected that, subject to working out further details on the admission, these four nations will become members as of January 1, 1995.

The European Free Trade Association (EFTRA). Also known as the Outer Seven, this organization, which came into existence in 1960, contains seven member nations—Austria, Finland, Iceland, Liechtenstein, Norway, Sweden, and Switzerland. EFTRA has not established as strong links as the EU, but it has similar economic goals. EFTRA will probably cease to exist, once four of its members gain entry into the EU.

Economic Issues

The term post-industrial society refers to a society in which more people work in service industries (accounting, health) than in production industries (steel, textiles). This situation is becoming more and more common in Western Europe, as it is in the United States.

Inflation refers to rising prices, which have caused a decrease in the value of the European currencies. The increase in oil prices charged by the Middle Eastern nations during the 1970s was one reason for inflation in Western Europe. Another reason was the attempt by the United States to cut down the flow of European imports into the United States and to increase the flow of American exports. Most Western European nations are dependent on outside areas for raw materials, such as oil from the Middle East.

Of increasing importance to Western Europe in the 1990s will be its economic relations with Japan and the United States, as well as with the former Soviet Union and Eastern European nations, and the former European colonies in Africa and Asia.

REVIEW QUESTIONS

Multiple Choice. Select the letter of the answer that correctly completes each statement.

1. Which nation has the highest GNP (gross national product) in Western Europe?
   A. France
   B. England
   C. Holland
   D. Germany

2. The Marshall Plan provided aid that was
   A. cultural
   B. military
   C. financial
   D. agricultural

3. The person most responsible for the growth of the European Common Market was
   A. Karl Marx
   B. Robert Schuman
   C. Friedrich Engels
   D. George Marshall

ESSAY

Show how each of the following has affected or will affect economic activity in Western Europe:

1. the European Union
2. social welfare programs
3. Euratom
4. capitalism

III. HUMAN AND CULTURAL GEOGRAPHY OF WESTERN EUROPE

Overview

Western Europe, with over 300 million people, has a variety of religious, ethnic, and linguistic groups. The largest nations are Germany (80 million), Italy (57 million), and France (56 million). Overpopulation and overcrowding (high population density) are not problems in Western Europe. In fact, population growth rates are among the lowest in the world. One reason for the absence of demographic (population) problems is that Western Europe is very industrialized and has high standards of living and modern health care. Compared with people in less industrialized areas, such as South Asia and sub-Saharan Africa, Western Europeans tend to live longer, marry later, and have smaller families. In addition, more women are in the work force. Urbanization—the movement of people from rural to city areas—is also characteristic of Western Europe.

Religion

GLOBAL
CONCEPTS

Culture

CONCEPTS
GLOBAL

Christianity is the predominant religion in Western Europe. The majority of people are Catholic, with the largest concentrations in the south, in Spain and Italy. Members of Protestant denominations are found mainly in the north, in nations such as England and Sweden. (For reasons explaining the connection between geography and religion, see the section on the Reformation in Part IV of this unit.)

Jews have been a minority in the Western European nations for centuries. They share some basic beliefs with Christians, such as the belief in one God and in the Ten Commandments. The combined basic beliefs and ideals of Jews and Christians make up the Judeo-Christian tradition. This tradition has influenced life in Western Europe for the last 2,000 years. It has also influenced life in areas that had the greatest amount of overseas European settlement, such as North and South America. Jews accept the part of the Bible popularly known as the Old Testament (known to Jews as the Tanach); Christians accept both the Old and New Testaments. (For a comparison of Judaism, Christianity, and Islam, see the unit on the Middle East.)

A growing number of Muslims and Hindus today live in some Western European nations, mostly those nations that once had colonies in Africa and Asia. France's Islamic community comes mainly from Algeria and Morocco. Most Hindus and Muslims in England come from the Indian subcontinent (India,

Pakistan, and Bangladesh). The Muslims in Germany are mainly Turks who have immigrated for economic reasons.

Ethnic Minority Groups

From Outside Europe. Besides the groups listed above, people from other areas of the world are found throughout Western Europe. They include people from the Caribbean, Africa, the Middle East, and East Asia. With the British colony of Hong Kong scheduled to come under rule of the People's Republic of China in 1997, many Hong Kong Chinese are interested in imigrating to England. However, the British have mixed feelings about whether to admit great numbers of Chinese and other non-British people to their nation. Some of this concern in England (as well as in other European nations) results from prejudice against foreigners. This prejudice is rooted in the issues of race as well as competition for employment, and at times it has even led to riots.

From Inside Europe. The more industrialized nations, such as Germany and France, have guest workers from other parts of Europe. These workers often take jobs for short periods of time and send money back to their families. Such workers are from Turkey, Greece, the former country of Yugoslavia, Italy, and Portugal. Although there have been attempts by the host countries to assimilate these workers and provide education, instances of ill feeling and prejudice have also been evident.

GLOBAL
CONCEPTS

Empathy

CONCEPTS
GLOBAL

Languages

While a variety of languages exists in the Western European nations, many have striking similarities. All languages in Western Europe are written using the Roman alphabet. There are also similarities in the ways some words are put together and are spoken. As a result, people in one nation are frequently able to understand the language of another nation. Because of the similarities between the languages, many Europeans are multilingual. Other reasons for the large numbers of Europeans who are multilingual are the nearness of nations to one another and the frequent travel and economic exchanges between them.

GLOBAL
CONCEPTS

Diversity

CONCEPTS
GLOBAL

French, Spanish, Portuguese, and Italian are Romance languages and have words constructed in a similar pattern. English is a Germanic language. German and Dutch have much in common, while the Scandinavian languages, except for Finnish, are similar. Some nations are officially bilingual because large segments of their populations speak distinct languages. For example, in Switzerland, French and German are spoken, while in Belgium, Flemish and French are used.

Cultural Achievements

Western European achievements in such fields as art, literature, architecture, sculpture, and music have been very extensive. They are treated in the next section, dealing with history and political geography.

REVIEW QUESTIONS

Multiple Choice. Select the letter of the answer that correctly completes each statement.

1. Which nation has the largest population in Western Europe?
   A. France
   B. Ireland
   C. Germany
   D. Italy

2. In which pair of nations is Catholicism the predominant religion?
   A. England and Italy
   B. France and Denmark
   C. Spain and Portugal
   D. Sweden and Holland

3. Which pair of nations have Romance languages?
   A. Italy and Spain
   B. England and Germany
   C. France and Holland
   D. Norway and Austria

4. A nation that is officially bilingual is
   A. Finland
   B. Belgium
   C. Sweden
   D. Austria

ESSAY

Overpopulation and high population growth rates are *not* considered to be major problems in Western Europe. Discuss two reasons for this situation.

IV. HISTORY AND POLITICAL GEOGRAPHY OF WESTERN EUROPE

Overview

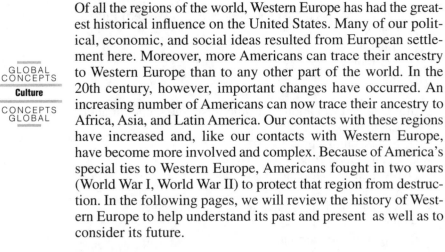

Of all the regions of the world, Western Europe has had the greatest historical influence on the United States. Many of our political, economic, and social ideas resulted from European settlement here. Moreover, more Americans can trace their ancestry to Western Europe than to any other part of the world. In the 20th century, however, important changes have occurred. An increasing number of Americans can now trace their ancestry to Africa, Asia, and Latin America. Our contacts with these regions have increased and, like our contacts with Western Europe, have become more involved and complex. Because of America's special ties to Western Europe, Americans fought in two wars (World War I, World War II) to protect that region from destruction. In the following pages, we will review the history of Western Europe to help understand its past and present as well as to consider its future.

GLOBAL
CONCEPTS

Culture

CONCEPTS
GLOBAL

Ancient Mediterranean Civilizations: Greece and Rome

The time period when the civilizations of Greece and Rome were at their height is called both the classical period and the Age of Antiquity. For ancient Greece this period was from 750 B.C. to 150 B.C. For Rome it was from 500 B.C. to 200 A.D., even though the Roman Empire lasted until 476 A.D.

Greece. The Greeks were the first people of Western Europe to develop an advanced culture. This was accomplished even though Greece's geography made unity very difficult. Because of the many mountains in the Greek Peninsula, the Greek people were isolated from one another and formed individual city-states, small governmental units organized around urban centers. Of the hundreds of these city-states dotting the Greek mainland and islands, the most famous were Athens and Sparta. There were major political, economic, and cultural differences between these two city-states.

GLOBAL
CONCEPTS

Environment

CONCEPTS
GLOBAL

Sparta developed as a militaristic city-state. It emphasized military strength and rule by just a few people—the landowners and nobility. The majority of Spartans, including the slaves, or helots, had no voice in the government. Sparta could also be called an aristocracy because it was ruled by a small number of people. Sparta did not promote individual freedom or progress

GLOBAL
CONCEPTS

Political Systems

CONCEPTS
GLOBAL

in the arts and sciences, and thus it had little impact on Western European history.

Athens eventually developed into a democratic city-state and had a lasting influence on the history of both Western Europe and the United States. By 450 B.C. Athens had developed the world's first democracy, that is, a system in which citizens take part and have a voice in their government. Because Athenian citizens voted directly for or against the laws, this system is called a direct democracy. However, there were limitations in Athenian democracy. Women, for example, could not vote for office-holders. Athenian democratic ideals were expressed in the famous Funeral Oration of Pericles. During the years of Pericles's leadership in the 5th century B.C. (461–429 B.C.) Athens made great progress in democracy as well as in the arts and sciences. Consequently, this period, called the Age of Pericles, also became known as the Golden Age of Athens. Some examples of Greek cultural progress in the Hellenic period (750–336 B.C.) are:

GLOBAL
CONCEPTS

Citizenship

CONCEPTS
GLOBAL

1. *Philosophy.* The ancient Greeks believed in the ideal of the well-rounded person, that is, one who was intelligent, thoughtful, asked questions, and had a "sound mind in a sound body." According to the famous Greek philosopher Socrates, one should "know thyself." He also said, "The unexamined life is not worth living." Plato, his most famous student, wrote *The Dialogues.* One of these dialogues, called *The Republic,* contains Plato's ideas about government. Plato's most famous student was Aristotle, whose thoughts on reason, logic, science, ethics, and government are found in his extensive writings, such as the *Nicomachean Ethics* and *Politics.*

2. *Literature.* Drama was the most outstanding Greek contribution in literature. The Greeks invented tragedy and comedy. Some famous Greek writers were Homer *(The Iliad* and *The Odyssey),* Sophocles *(Oedipus Rex),* and Aristophanes *(Lysistrata).* Also notable were the poet Pindar and the historians Herodotus and Thucydides.

3. *Mathematics and science.* Noteworthy achievements were made by Pythagoras (geometry), Hippocrates (medicine), and Democritus (matter composed of atoms).

4. *Architecture and sculpture.* The Parthenon was a temple built on a hill called the Acropolis. As with other Greek buildings, the Parthenon combined balance and symmetry and the use of tall, graceful columns. Many buildings throughout the Western world have imitated Greek architecture. The three basic styles of Greek columns or pillars are called Doric, Ionic, and Corinthian. Greek sculpture displayed dignity, realism, and simplicity, and it idealized the human form.

The famous Parthenon in Athens

5. *The Olympic Games.* These major athletic events were held in honor of the god Zeus, and they are the basis of the modern-day Olympics.

Military conflicts. Although the Greek city-states often quarreled among themselves, they were able to unite against the Persians. In the Persian Wars (500–479 B.C.) the Greeks were able to stop the westward expansion of the Persian Empire. Important Greek victories were at the battles of Marathon and Thermopylae.

The Peloponnesian War (431–404 B.C.) was a conflict between Athens and Sparta. Sparta was victorious and brought Athens under its control but was unable to unite all the Greek city-states.

Eventually, most of the Greek city-states were united by the conquests of King Philip of Macedon (a region to the north) in 338 B.C. When he died, his title, power, and lands were passed on to his son Alexander.

Alexander's Empire. Alexander the Great built an empire that extended as far south as Egypt and as far east as India. His conquests were made between 336 and 323 B.C. and resulted in the largest world empire up to that time. Alexander, who had been taught by Aristotle, was an admirer of the culture of Greece, and he spread Greek culture wherever he went. The mixture of Greek culture with the cultures of conquered areas—of Egypt, the Middle East, and South Asia—became known as Hellenism. This period of cultural mixing and cultural diffusion lasted beyond Alexander's death in 323 B.C. and is referred to as the Hellenistic period. When Alexander died, his empire was divided into three parts, each part ruled by one of his generals. In less than 200 years, these three parts were once again united under the rule of the Roman Empire. Important cultural achievements during the Hellenistic period (336–150 B.C.) included:

GLOBAL
CONCEPTS

Diversity

CONCEPTS
GLOBAL

1. *Philosophy.* During this period, philosophers developed new and different ideas about life. Diogenes founded the philosophical school of Cynics. The idea of Cynicism included criticism of materialism and social conventions and a distrust of human virtue. Zeno founded Stoicism, advocating freedom from passions and desires and detachment from the outside world. Epicurus founded Epicureanism, advocating the search for pleasure and happiness while maintaining a sense of moderation.

2. *Mathematics and science.* The leading figures were Aristarchus (astronomy), Euclid (geometry), Archimedes (physics), and Eratosthenes (geography).

GLOBAL
CONCEPTS

Political Systems

CONCEPTS
GLOBAL

Rome. By 500 B.C. the Latin peoples of central Italy, also known as Romans, had created a republic. In a republic, citizens participate in government by electing the rulers who represent them. The early Roman Republic was controlled by a few nobles, the patricians, and was thus actually an aristocracy. Over the next 200 years, however, important political gains were made by the plebians, the farmers and workers, who won the right to become members of the government assembly and to vote for tribunes. The tribunes could take action against the patrician-controlled consuls and the Senate. Plebian gains also included the codification (writing down) of Roman law into the Twelve Tables, which enabled all to know what the laws were.

GLOBAL
CONCEPTS

Justice

CONCEPTS
GLOBAL

Roman law established forms of justice and protection of human rights and property that have influenced legal systems throughout the Western world. In its period as a republic, Rome made progress as a democracy.

The Roman Republic Becomes an Empire (340–27 B.C.).

WORLD ISSUES

War
and
Peace

After conquering and uniting the Italian Peninsula, Rome took control of the lands bordering the western Mediterranean Sea. These lands came under Rome's control after its success in the Punic Wars (264–146 B.C.) against Carthage, a rival city located in North Africa. Roman forces next turned their attention to the eastern Mediterranean area and conquered the Greek lands that had once been part of Alexander's empire (Greece, Egypt, the Middle East). The Mediterranean had become a

Roman soldiers prior to a battle.

Roman lake. The Romans admired the Hellenistic culture of the Greeks, and it is said that even though Roman force conquered Greece, Greek culture conquered Rome.

Under Julius Caesar, Roman legions conquered most of central and western Europe. Rome now held land on three continents, and by 50 B.C. it had become the largest empire known to the world. However, during this period of conquest, many changes took place in Rome. The Roman army changed from a civilian force to a selectively trained group of professional soldiers. As a result, soldiers were more loyal to their individual generals than to the republican government elected in Rome. As the military commanders gained more power, they fought among themselves in civil wars for control of Rome, and the republic was changed into a dictatorship. In 46 B.C. Julius Caesar became a dictator. He was succeeded by three generals after his death. Among these was Octavian, who became the first emperor of Rome when he took the title Caesar Augustus and established the Roman Empire. He ruled from 27 B.C. to 14 A.D.

GLOBAL
CONCEPTS

Power

CONCEPTS
GLOBAL

The so-called Augustan Age, which began with Octavian, was the start of 200 years of stability, peace, and progress in the Roman Empire, a period known as the *Pax Romana,* or Roman Peace (27 B.C.–180 A.D.).

The Roman Empire Declines and Falls (180–476). During these years, the Roman Empire slowly declined for several reasons:

1. *Division of the empire.* The emperor Constantine moved from Rome and made Constantinople (now Istanbul) his capital in the 4th century. This move split the empire into two parts— the western part, with its capital remaining at Rome, and the eastern part, or the Byzantine Empire, headed by Constantine.

2. *Political weaknesses.* The government in Rome became corrupt and because of the size of the empire was unable to keep control over all the territory under its rule.

3. *Economic problems.* The rulers wasted money, and heavy taxation led to anger among the people. A trade imbalance caused by importing many goods lowered the value of Rome's money.

4. *Social factors.* A decline in morality and patriotism was widespread. A rigid class system developed. Many slaves and non-Romans who lived in the major cities were badly treated.

5. *Invasions.* Beginning in the 3rd century, Germanic tribes invaded Roman lands and eventually were able to defeat Roman armies. In 476, Rome itself was conquered. (The Eastern Roman Empire, however, survived beyond 476. See the unit on the Middle East.)

6. *Impact of Christianity.* The teachings of Christianity conflicted with the dictatorial policies of the emperors.

Achievements of the Ancient Romans. The Romans made many achievements in the arts and sciences and had a lasting impact on the Western world.

1. *Law.* Roman law was codified in the Twelve Tables. Over the years, many new statutes were added, and Roman law became the basis of the legal systems of Western Europe and South America.

2. *Language.* Latin was the basis for Romance languages, such as Spanish, French, and Italian. Many English words also come from Latin.

3. *Literature.* The speeches of Cicero and the works of Vergil *(The Aeneid)* and Horace are well known. The historians Livy, Plutarch, and Tacitus are still studied today.

4. *Architecture.* Roman-built roads, aqueducts, and buildings were found all over the empire and helped unite the terri-

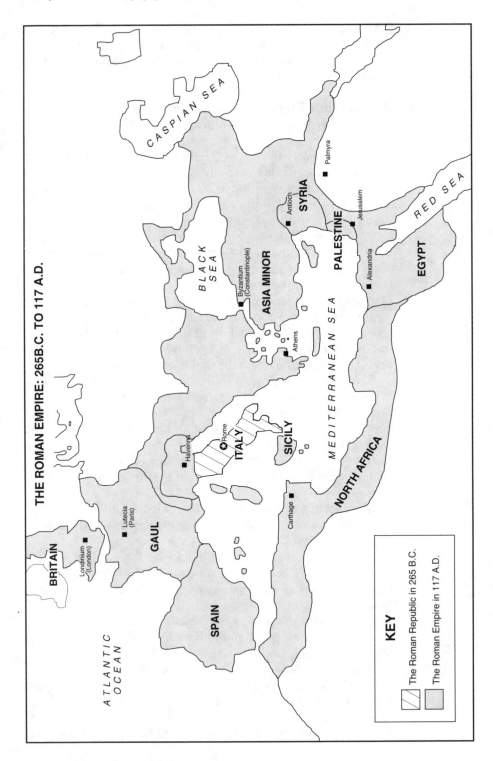

THE ROMAN EMPIRE: 265 B.C. TO 117 A.D.

CASPIAN SEA

Palmyra

RED SEA

Antioch
SYRIA

Jerusalem

PALESTINE

Alexandria

EGYPT

BLACK
SEA

ASIA MINOR

Byzantium
(Constantinople)

Athens

MEDITERRANEAN SEA

Ravenna

Rome
ITALY

SICILY

NORTH AFRICA

Carthage

Lutecia
(Paris)

GAUL

BRITAIN

Londinium
(London)

ATLANTIC
OCEAN

SPAIN

KEY

The Roman Republic in 265 B.C.

The Roman Empire in 117 A.D.

tories. Some structures, such as the Colosseum in Rome, still stand. The Romans used the arch and were the first to use concrete as a building material.

5. *Government administration.* A good civil service of government officials helped to run the far-flung empire. Under the Pax Romana and a strong central government, unity and peace were brought to many areas of Europe. However, when the empire collapsed, disunity and disorder were common in the former Roman lands.

The Roman Colosseum

The Middle Ages (500–1500)

The time between the fall of the Roman Empire and the start of the modern era is known as the Middle Ages, or the medieval period. The first 500 years of this period is sometimes called the Dark Ages, due to the disruptive economic and social conditions as well as the absence of a strong and stable central government. During this time, Europe experienced many invasions. The first group of invaders were the Germanic tribes, some of whom eventually settled down and formed kingdoms. Later invaders included the Norse, the Magyars, and the Muslims. These invasions ended about the year 1000. Political power was decentralized, that is, it was held by several small, weak groups throughout Europe. Among these were the Franks (in Gaul, or France), the Ostrogoths (in Italy), the Visigoths (in Spain), and the Angles and Saxons (in England). People felt more loyalty to a local ruler in a small territory than to a larger political unit. The protection given by a local ruler, or lord, to people who performed services for him in return was the basis of feudalism, which developed in the 800s. This was the form of government prevalent in Europe until the 1400s.

Charlemagne and the Holy Roman Empire. One group of Germans, the Franks, were able to create a strong kingdom by the 5th century. The kingdom of the Franks grew in power during the early Middle Ages. Under Charles Martel, the Franks stopped the advance of Muslim forces in 732 at the Battle of Tours in France. Martel's grandson was Charlemagne (768–814), who became the most important ruler in medieval Europe.

Charlemagne conquered and united lands in central and western Europe, some of which had been part of the Roman Empire. These included parts of present-day Italy, Spain, France, Germany, Czechoslovakia, Austria, Belgium, and Holland. For these efforts and for spreading Christianity, Charlemagne was crowned as the first Holy Roman Emperor by Pope Leo III in 800. Charlemagne's empire became known as the Holy Roman Empire.

Charlemagne built schools and was able to run his empire's provinces with the help of the *missi dominici*, appointed officials who traveled in the provinces and kept Charlemagne informed about various nobles. Consequently, under Charlemagne's rule, a rare example of a stable, centralized government existed in the Middle Ages. After his death, however, the empire was divided, and his successors were not able to maintain order and stability.

GLOBAL CONCEPTS
Political Systems
CONCEPTS GLOBAL

Feudalism. Feudalism developed in Europe in response to the breakdown in central authority in the Frankish empire following Charlemagne's death and also because of the instability and chaos caused by the numerous invasions in the 9th and 10th centuries, especially those of the dreaded Vikings or Norse. Feudalism began in France in the late 9th century and spread throughout much of Europe. It was a way of life that involved agreements, promises, and exchanges between different groups of people to help them live together. It involved social, economic, and political relationships.

GLOBAL CONCEPTS
Change
CONCEPTS GLOBAL

1. *Social.* A strict class system existed, based on land and military power. Each class had specific rights as well as responsibilities and obligations to the other classes. The classes were serfs, knights, and landowning nobles and lords. A code of chivalry set rules of behavior that everyone followed, especially the knights and lords.

2. *Economic*. Serfs worked the land on a manor (a large estate held by a lord) and supplied food to the landowner, who promised protection and shelter in return. The landowner in turn also promised to fight for a higher noble, such as an over-lord or a king, who gave him a piece of land in return. In this relationship, the landowner owed loyalty, or fealty, to the king and became a vassal of the king. In this manorial system, each manor supported itself economically and was self-sufficient. The three-field system was used for growing food.

GLOBAL
CONCEPTS

Human Rights

CONCEPTS
GLOBAL

3. *Political*. The serfs were bound to the land and had no say in political matters. The king's power rested on his relationship with his vassals. By receiving a fief (a grant of land) from the king (as suzerain), in a ceremony called investiture, the vassals came under the king's protection and in return owed homage, promising allegiance and military service. Although a vassal, the landowning noble exercised great political power in his area because he passed laws, levied taxes, and acted as a judge.

GLOBAL
CONCEPTS

Culture

CONCEPTS
GLOBAL

The Role of the Roman Catholic Church. The Christian or Roman Catholic church was the most powerful and influential institution in Europe in the Middle Ages. It was the only insti-tution able to provide some order amid the chaos in Europe. The Roman Catholic church was a major force in the lives of people, providing education, the means to salvation, and many services usually provided by governments.

Although early Christians were persecuted in the Roman Em-pire for almost 300 years after the crucifixion of Jesus, Christian-ity continued to gain converts and to grow in power. Christianity was spread through the efforts of St. Paul and other followers of Jesus. In 313 the Edict of Milan, under the Emperor Constantine, permitted religious freedom for Christians. In 392 the Emperor Theodosius made Christianity the official state religion of the empire. By this time the Roman Empire had split into an eastern part centered in Constantinople and a western part centered in Rome. Different views on religious authority and teachings de-veloped between the church in Rome (headed by the Pope) and the church in Constantinople (headed by the Patriarch). Eventu-ally, these differences led to an official division of the Christian church in 1054 into the Roman Catholic church in Rome and the Greek Orthodox church in Constantinople. While the Greek Or-thodox church divided into several Eastern Orthodox churches in Eastern Europe, it was the Roman Catholic church that was to exert a strong influence in Western Europe.

GLOBAL
CONCEPTS

Change

CONCEPTS
GLOBAL

1. *Political*. Besides having the power to crown Charlemagne as Holy Roman Emperor in 800, the church could use excom-

EUROPE IN THE 14TH CENTURY

■ Important trading cities

NORWAY
SWEDEN
Stockholm
SCOTLAND
Edinburgh
DENMARK
IRELAND
Copenhagen
ENGLAND
WALES
London
HOLLAND
Amsterdam
POMERANIA
BRANDENBURG
FLANDERS
Ghent
SILESIA
HOLY ROMAN
BRITTANY
Frankfurt
Paris
EMPIRE
MORAVIA
FRANCE
Augsberg
BURGUNDY
AUSTRIA
BAVARIA
Lyons
SAVOY
GASCONY
Avignon
DAUPHINE
NAVARRE
REPUBLIC OF VENICE
Lisbon
PORTUGAL
CASTILE
ARAGON
PROVENCE
Florence
Barcelona
PAPAL
STATES
Granada
Rome
KINGDOM
OF NAPLES
Naples
Athens
DUCHY OF
ATHENS
KINGDOM
OF SICILY
MOORISH STATES

GLOBAL
CONCEPTS

Power

CONCEPTS
GLOBAL

munication as a weapon against any ruler or person who did not follow the church's teachings. A person who was excommunicated was no longer considered a member of the Christian faith and was thus denied salvation. In an era of faith, this was a very strong threat. In the 13th century, the church created a special court, called the Holy Inquisition, to investigate anyone who disobeyed or disagreed with its teachings. If a person was found guilty as a heretic, that individual could be tortured or put to death.

2. *Economic*. The church grew wealthy from its many lands and from taxes such as the tithe. With this wealth, convents, monasteries, and great cathedrals were built. Many were built in the Gothic style. The church's role in the economy of Western Europe was so great that it was able to forbid usury, the practice of lending money with interest. However, the prohibi-

340

tion on interest was only for Christians; Jews were permitted to become moneylenders and to charge interest. As a result, many Jews created banking houses. Some became wealthy but suffered prejudice because of their financial activities.

3. *Social and cultural.* The church's teachings were the rules by which most people led their lives. Bishops, priests, and other religious figures were looked to for guidance, especially since they could explain the Bible and were usually the only people who could read and write. Members of the clergy were educated and preserved the classical culture of ancient Greece and Rome. Many members of the clergy encouraged writers, painters, and sculptors to produce works with religious themes. The church was a stabilizing and unifying influence at a time when Western Europe was going through a period of disorder and confusion.

Since the Jews of Western Europe did not follow church teachings, they were often the target of prejudice, persecution, and expulsion. Moreover, laws that restricted where Jews could worship and live (ghettos were the result) were frequent (as were forced conversions). These anti-Jewish actions are examples of anti-Semitism.

The Crusades. These were attempts by the Christians of Western Europe to regain control of Jerusalem and other parts of the Holy Land from the Muslims. These holy wars lasted for approximately 200 years. There were eight Crusades. The first Crusade came in response to a request from Pope Urban II in

GLOBAL
CONCEPTS

Culture

CONCEPTS
GLOBAL

WORLD ISSUES

Human
Rights

Crusaders leave to fight in the Middle East.

1095 and was successful. Other Crusades and fighting between Christians and Muslims continued until 1291, with the Muslims finally emerging victorious. Muslims kept control of the Holy Land until World War I. (For the history of the Holy Land prior to the Crusades, see Unit One on the Middle East.)

Besides hoping to regain the Holy Land in the Crusades, the church had other goals. It wanted to increase its power and wealth and unite the Western (Roman) and Eastern (Byzantine) branches of Christianity. Although the Crusades failed to achieve these goals, they had important results for European history.

1. *Political.* European kings gained more power, especially since many feudal lords were killed while fighting in the Crusades. Other lords sold their lands to get money to go on the Crusades. As kings increased their power, they eventually were able to create nation-states, which they ruled.

2. *Economic.* Trade and commerce increased, especially in towns and port cities used by the Crusaders. Goods from the Middle East, such as spices, pepper, and carpets, began to appear throughout Europe. Feudalism was weakened, as many serfs joined armies or left their manors to settle in the cities that began to grow because of increased trade.

3. *Social and cultural.* Europeans learned much from the more advanced culture of the Muslim world at the time of the Crusades. Developments from the Golden Age of Islam made their way into Europe. These developments were in such fields as mathematics, science, art, and literature. The Europeans also discovered many Greek and Roman writings that had been lost to them but preserved by Muslim scholars. Classical civilization was reintroduced. The new ideas and new goods brought to Europe because of the Crusades were factors that slowly helped to bring an end to the Middle Ages and led to the period we call modern history. Other factors that brought on this change from medieval to modern times included: the growth of towns and a merchant middle class (the bourgeoisie); increased use of gunpowder and more effective weapons; renewed interest in learning, both about humans and about the world they lived in; increased contact with people outside of Europe; and the rise of nation-states.

The Renaissance (1400–1700)

The Renaissance refers to the period between 1400 and 1700 when there was a great rebirth of cultural and scholarly activity in Western Europe. This activity began with a revival of interest in the cultures of ancient Greece and Rome. These classical cultures had stressed human endeavor and human conduct, and the Renaissance was marked by a return to the concerns of individual humans and their lives. The Renaissance had other characteristics.

1. An emphasis on the individual as a reasoning, thinking, and questioning person. Human beings were seen as the center of all things, as was life here on earth. These were secular, or worldly, concerns. (This was in direct contrast to the Middle Ages, when there was concern with matters of religion, authority, and tradition. Salvation and the hereafter were emphasized.)

2. Humanism was an important influence in the arts and sciences. This meant that paintings of people were more realistic and "human" than in the Middle Ages. Writers wrote about simple, everyday events. Much writing was done in the vernacular languages—that is, in everyday speech in national languages, such as Italian, that were commonly spoken—rather than in Latin, the language used chiefly by church officials and educated people. Scientists questioned traditional ideas about humans and the universe. They used reason and experimentation to try to understand those things that had previously been accepted on faith or because of religious beliefs.

3. The Renaissance began in Italy and was supported by wealthy families who were patrons of the arts. The Medicis in Florence were one such family.

4. The Renaissance gradually spread to other parts of Europe, northward to Holland, Germany, France, and England, and to Spain.

The characteristics described above can be seen in the achievements of several famous people in the fields of art, literature, and science presented in the table below.

RENAISSANCE ACHIEVEMENTS

Field	Name	Nationality	Achievement
Art	da Vinci	Italian	*The Last Supper; Mona Lisa*
	Michelangelo	Italian	Sistine Chapel; *Piéta; David*
	Titian	Spanish	*Assumption of the Virgin*
	El Greco	Spanish	*Views of Toledo*
	Rembrandt	Dutch	*The Night Watch; The Anatomy Lesson*
Literature	Dante	Italian	*The Divine Comedy*
	Chaucer	English	*Canterbury Tales*
	Erasmus	Dutch	*In Praise of Folly*
	Shakespeare	English	*Macbeth; Julius Caesar; Hamlet*

continued on next page

RENAISSANCE ACHIEVEMENTS

Field	Name	Nationality	Achievement
Literature (cont.)	Rabelais	French	*Gargantua and Pantagruel*
	Machiavelli	liItalian	*The Prince*
	Cervantes	Spanish	*Don Quixote*
Science	Copernicus	Polish	"The sun is the center of the universe."
	Galileo	Italian	Telescope; law of falling bodies
	Gutenberg	German	Printing press
	Harvey	English	Circulation of blood in the body
	Leeuwenhoek	Dutch	The microscope
	Newton	English	Laws of motion and gravity

The Reformation and Counter-Reformation

The Reformation, which is also called the Protestant Reformation, was a movement to reform or change certain ideas and practices of the Roman Catholic church. It began in 1517 when Martin Luther, a German priest, placed his Ninety-Five Theses, or statements, on a church door in Wittenburg, Germany. In this document Luther protested against certain church practices and also stated his own religious beliefs, which differed from those of the Roman Catholic church.

1. Luther protested certain church practices, such as the sale of indulgences (paying money for church pardons), simony (selling of church offices), and nepotism (giving church positions to relatives). He also protested against the worldly and materialistic life led by some church officials and against the power of the Pope to do certain things. Luther saw these practices as church abuses.

2. Luther believed that the Bible and not the Pope was the final authority on religious matters. He wanted the Bible to be translated into German so that each person could read it and interpret it for himself or herself. Luther believed that salvation was achieved through faith alone, not through both faith and good works as the church claimed. Faith was a free gift given to humans through God's grace, and it was God's mercy that permitted humans to be saved.

Factors That Led to the Reformation. Luther's protests against church practices and beliefs about salvation were

GLOBAL
CONCEPTS

Change

CONCEPTS
GLOBAL

shared by many people, especially in northern Europe. Other factors that caused the Reformation were:

1. *Economic.* Some rulers were upset about the economic power and wealth of the church. This power and wealth came from taxes imposed by the church as well as from the vast amounts of land that it owned. These rulers hoped to obtain this wealth for themselves and their subjects.

2. *Political.* Many felt that the Pope had too much power over political and other secular, or nonreligious, matters. Many rulers challenged the Pope's claim to being supreme in secular as well as religious affairs. They resisted the church's claim to having power over them and other civil officials and to its interference in political matters concerning their nation.

3. *Renaissance thought.* The Renaissance emphasized the ability of humans to think and reason for themselves. Along with this came the questioning of traditional authority. In this atmosphere, many people during the Renaissance began to disagree with certain church practices and ideas.

4. *Previous church problems and reform attempts.* Even before Luther, there had been problems within the church, such as the Babylonian Captivity of 1309–1377, when the Popes lived in France and were under the control of the king of France, and the Great Schism of 1378–1417, when two Popes competed for control of the church. Other reformers had attacked some of the same practices that Luther protested against. These included John Wycliffe (England), John Hus (Bohemia), and Desiderius Erasmus (Holland).

GLOBAL
CONCEPTS

Choice

CONCEPTS
GLOBAL

Immediate Impact of Luther's Actions. Luther established the Lutheran church in Germany. Lutheranism was the first of the new Protestant religions. It was accepted as a new religion in northern Germany as well as in most of Scandinavia (Norway and Sweden). Other Protestant religions also began as the result of activities of additional reformers who challenged the Catholic church, such as Ulrich Zwingli in Switzerland, John Knox in Scotland, and John Calvin, whose ideas, especially that of predestination, won acceptance in Switzerland, Scotland, Holland, England, and parts of France. (According to predestination, God chose certain people, called the elect, to be saved, while those who had not been chosen could never achieve salvation, no matter what they did on earth.)

GLOBAL
CONCEPTS

Power

CONCEPTS
GLOBAL

The Protestant Reformation also spread to England, where King Henry VIII broke with the church because of marriage problems. He defied the authority of the Pope and divorced Catherine of Aragon. During his rule, Parliament passed the

Act of Supremacy in 1534, which made the Anglican church of England independent from the Pope, with the king as its head. Afterwards, Henry took over some church lands.

Luther's ideas as well as those of other reformers throughout Europe were spread more easily due to the printing press, which was invented in Germany in 1450.

The Reaction of the Catholic Church. While the Protestant Reformation was underway, the Roman Catholic church acted to maintain its power and to reform itself. This movement to revise the spiritual mission of the Catholic church and to stop the spread of Protestantism was called the Counter-Reformation. Among the actions it carried out were:

1. Luther was excommunicated.

2. At the Council of Trent (1545–1563), the church upheld its traditional beliefs and practices, including the supreme power of the Pope over the church and the necessity of both faith and good works for salvation. It also corrected some abuses, banning the sale of indulgences and forbidding simony. It also drew up the Index. This was a list of books that Catholics were not allowed to read because they contained heretical ideas.

3. The Inquisition, or the church courts established during the Middle Ages, took measures against heretics. The Inquisition was very effective in southern Europe, especially in Italy and Spain.

4. The Jesuit order was founded in 1534 by Ignatius Loyola and known officially as the Society of Jesus. The Jesuits helped to defend and preserve Catholic teachings.

Results of the Reformation. The Reformation shattered the religious unity of Western Europe and led to the development of Protestant religions. By 1600 almost all of Western Europe was divided into Protestants and Catholics, with each group hostile to the other. In the 1600s these feelings erupted into wars. Several religious wars were fought, the most serious of which was the Thirty Years War (1618–1648).

The monarchs of the European nations and local civil officials, especially in central and northern Europe, gained in power and wealth as the strength of the Catholic church declined. They were able to take over church lands and taxes.

Progress was made in education and literacy, especially because of the greater interest in reading the Bible.

At first, because of the growing competition between Protestants and Catholics, religious intolerance grew. Some religious

WORLD ISSUES

Human

Rights

WORLD ISSUES

War

and

Peace

GLOBAL
CONCEPTS

Change

CONCEPTS
GLOBAL

WORLD ISSUES

Human
Rights

conflicts even turned into civil wars, as in France in the 16th century. However, in time, some small steps were taken toward religious freedom and tolerance. In the Edict of Nantes (1598), France, a Catholic nation, permitted Protestants to practice their faith. In England, the Toleration Act of 1689 granted some religious freedom to various Protestant groups.

The Age of Exploration

From the late 1400s to about 1750, the economic life of Western Europe changed greatly. This transformation was caused by an explosion of trade. In time, the search for trade and for alternate routes to Asian markets caused explorers to sail across the oceans, and the Europeans discovered lands which previously had been unknown to them. Spain and Portugal opened up the Age of Exploration and colonization, as they ventured overseas to find new trade routes and markets. The first voyages explored the coast of Africa, and eventually Vasco da Gama of Portugal sailed around the Cape of Good Hope to India. Christopher Columbus, explorer for Spain, was the first to sail westward, reaching the Americas in 1492. These overseas explorations continued for a period of about 250 years, ending European isolation and eventually leading to European global domination.

WORLD ISSUES

World
Trade and
Finance

Reasons for the Age of Exploration. There were many reasons why the nations of Western Europe undertook these voyages. These included:

1. The Renaissance spirit of inquiry and curiosity, which aroused interest in other parts of the world.

2. Scientific advances in navigational instruments and improved sailing vessels that made such voyages possible.

GLOBAL
CONCEPTS

Technology

CONCEPTS
GLOBAL

3. Interest in finding new routes to South and East Asia, stirred by the Crusades and the stories of Marco Polo. The Europeans wanted the products of the Asians, such as spices, but they had to pay high prices for them because the Arabs and Italian city-states controlled the routes to the East.

4. The desire for land and resources by the new nation-states of Europe.

5. Many adventurers were stirred by the desires of gold, God, and the glory. Many Europeans who ventured overseas went in search of riches and fame, while others wanted to spread their religion.

The major explorers and their achievements are presented in the table on the next page.

EXPLORERS AND THEIR ACHIEVEMENTS

Name	Nation	Achievement/Area of Exploration
Columbus	Spain	Americas; the "New World"
da Gama	Portugal	East and west coasts of Africa; India
Magellan	Spain	Philippines; one of his ships circumnavigated the globe, proving that the earth was round.
Cortés	Spain	Conquered Mexico
Pizarro	Spain	Conquered Peru
Cartier	France	St. Lawrence River
Verrazano	France	East coast of North America
Champlain	France	Canada
Cabot	England	Northeast coast of North America; Labrador
Drake	England	Circumnavigation of the world
Hudson	Holland	New York

Results of the Age of Exploration. The European voyages of discovery had many far-reaching effects. One was the establishment of colonial empires. Spain colonized Central and South America, while England colonized part of North America. Other Western European nations also established colonies. Eventually the rivalry among European nations for control of colonies and for sea routes led to wars. These included the French and Indian War in North America (1756–1763) and the defeat of the Spanish Armada by England in 1588. As the Europeans colonized overseas areas, they came to dominate native peoples. Also, colonies enabled the nations of Western Europe to acquire sources of raw materials, which they turned into manufactured goods. This made them rich. Finally, the Age of Exploration was made possible by the start of a commercial revolution that was further expanded by the voyages of discovery.

GLOBAL CONCEPTS

Interdependence

CONCEPTS GLOBAL

The Commercial Revolution

WORLD ISSUES

Economic

Growth and

Development

The term "commercial revolution" refers to the changes in trade and business practices that began in the 1400s and continued throughout the Age of Exploration. They were to transform the economies of Europe. This was not a revolution in the way goods were manufactured but in the way goods were bought and sold. It took place over three centuries. The changes included:

1. The growth of trade within Western Europe. Also, trade became more worldwide, and goods were traded between Europe and Asia and the Americas.

2. The growth of capitalism as an economic system. Under this system, property is privately owned and capital (money) is used to make a profit. A new type of business called a joint stock company was formed to undertake risky ventures that

required large amounts of capital, such as traveling overseas and establishing colonies. Joint stock companies, such as the Dutch East India Company, were privately owned and sold stock to investors who were willing to risk their money in the hope of making a profit. Capitalism also came to be known as the free-enterprise system. To meet the needs of this system, a banking system arose. These developments eventually led to the concept of a market economy.

GLOBAL CONCEPTS

Change

CONCEPTS GLOBAL

3. The Atlantic Ocean replaced the Mediterranean Sea as the center of economic activity. Also, the nations located on the Atlantic Ocean became wealthier and more powerful than the other nations of Europe.

4. The development of mercantilism, or the economic theory that claimed it was important for a nation to acquire overseas colonies because they could provide gold, silver, and raw materials that would make that nation wealthy and more powerful. The raw materials obtained from the colonies were used to make manufactured goods, which could be sold at high prices in the colonies. Mercantilists also said that a nation should export more than it imports, thereby achieving a favorable balance of trade. This would result in a nation's becoming highly self-sufficient.

5. The increase in manufactured goods spurred an increased demand for these goods by consumers.

WORLD ISSUES

Economic
Growth and
Development

WORLD ISSUES

Population

Effects of the Commercial Revolution. Because of the commercial revolution, the power of several European nation-states and their absolute monarchs increased. (See the following section.) Trade and overseas empires made nations such as England, Spain, and France wealthy and powerful. Also, population shifts occurred. Many Africans were brought as slaves to work in the Americas. Many Europeans left their homelands to settle in the colonies. As a result, European culture was spread to areas around the world. Finally, a new production system, the domestic system, was developed in Europe. Under this system, goods were produced in the home rather than in a shop. Although the domestic system was used mainly to produce wool, other items such as buttons and gloves were also made this way. It enabled merchants to increase production. In time, it would be replaced by the factory system.

WORLD ISSUES

Human
Rights

WORLD ISSUES

Economic
Growth and
Development

The Rise of Nation-States; Royal Power and Absolutism

Besides the profound cultural (Renaissance), religious (Reformation), and economic (commercial revolution and exploration) changes that took place in Western Europe between the late

WORLD ISSUES

Determination
of Political
and Economic
Systems

1400s and early 1700s, there were also a series of great political changes. The changes involved the creation of nation-states with strong monarchs and centralized governments in England, France, and Spain. The term "nation-state" refers to a specific area of land with fixed boundaries, united under the rule of a central government. The people in a nation-state are usually united by many common factors, such as language, religion, race, and culture. The growth of nation-states in Western Europe began as feudalism declined. Two countries, England and France, had developed into nation-states by the end of the Middle Ages, in 1500. Their governments were under the rule of strong kings. In many nations of Western Europe, the king ruled as an absolute monarch, that is, the king had complete or absolute rule over his nation and subjects. Such monarchs are also called autocrats, and their governments are referred to as autocracies.

GLOBAL
CONCEPTS

Power

CONCEPTS
GLOBAL

England. William the Conqueror, the Duke of Normandy in France, crossed the English Channel with his Norman army and invaded England. After his victory in the Battle of Hastings in 1066, he was crowned king of England, and he ruled as a strong monarch. To determine the population and wealth of England, he carried out a survey. The result was a list of all the property in England called the Domesday Book. William introduced feudalism in England, but he made all the feudal lords and knights take the Salisbury Oath in which they promised allegiance to him. William's successors grew more powerful, uniting England under their control. The Hundred Years War and the period of Tudor rule increased the power of English monarchs.

The Hundred Years War (1337–1453) was fought between England and France. Although the British lost their territories in France, they increased their feelings of loyalty to their kings and their homeland. During the period of Tudor rule (1485–1603), two monarchs became very popular as they expanded royal power and the nation's prosperity. Henry VIII (1509–1547) defied the Pope and helped establish the Anglican church. His daughter, Queen Elizabeth I (1558–1603), defeated the Spanish Armada and encouraged the growth of the British navy and overseas exploration.

WORLD ISSUES

War
and
Peace

Although the Tudor monarchs were powerful, they could not be called absolute rulers. Limitations on their power had been set by the Magna Carta and the British Parliament. However, in the 17th century the Stuart rulers who succeeded the Tudors became absolute rulers and disregarded the traditional limitations on a monarch's powers. (See the section on the growth of democracy.)

France. After the Hundred Years War, royal power in France became more centralized. Louis XI (1461–1483) increased his power by decreasing the power of the feudal lords, taking their lands and thereby laying the foundation for a strong monarchy. The rulers of France in the 1500s continued to centralize authority in the crown. Henry IV (1589–1610), the first Bourbon ruler, ended the religious strife and civil wars between French Protestants and Catholics. A Protestant, he adopted Catholicism to avoid bloodshed and issued the Edict of Nantes in 1598, which granted a measure of religious freedom to French Protestants, who were called Huguenots. Henry and other members of the Bourbon family ruled France until the Revolution of 1789.

GLOBAL CONCEPTS
Human Rights
CONCEPTS GLOBAL

Louis XIII, Henry's son, made Cardinal Richelieu his adviser and chief minister. From 1624 to 1642, Richelieu laid the foundations for a strong French monarchy by weakening the nobles and increasing taxes, which added to royal wealth. Richelieu made the monarchy absolute within France, and his foreign policy made France the strongest power in Europe.

GLOBAL CONCEPTS
Power
CONCEPTS GLOBAL

By the mid-1600s King Louis XIV (1643–1715), who was known as the Sun King, ruled as an absolute monarch. Examples of his form of absolutism were:

1. He believed in the divine right theory of government, which held that a monarch's power came from God and that the monarch was accountable not to the people he ruled but only to God.

2. He used his wealth for his own benefit rather than for the people. The great palace at Versailles, near Paris, was built at his direction. The construction of the palace seemed to support his statement: "L'état, c'est moi" (I am the state).

3. He never summoned the Estates-General, a lawmaking body, to meet.

4. He led France into many wars, hoping to gain territory. Few of these were successful, and their major result was to increase the dissatisfaction of the French people because of many deaths and high taxes.

5. His control over the French economy was aided by the actions of his finance minister, Jean Colbert.

6. He promoted artistic and musical works to glorify his rule, and he made France the cultural center of Europe. These activities also increased the spirit of French nationalism.

7. He revoked the Edict of Nantes, which was a blow to religious freedom and forced many Huguenots to leave France.

The absolutism in England and France eventually sparked strong political reactions and resulted in important democratic developments.

The Growth of Democracy

A democracy is a system of government that has two basic features:

1. Popular sovereignty—the people have the freedom to choose those who govern. Generally, they elect representatives to carry out their wishes.

2. Equality and respect for the individual—each person has specific freedoms and rights that are protected by the government.

By the year 1800, democracy had made significant advances in England, France, and the United States.

England—Democratic Progress up to 1603. Many democratic reforms had been instituted before the 1600s. Generally, they placed limits on the powers of the monarchy and outlined the rights of the English people. These included:

1. *Jury system.* The idea of a trial by jury began under King Henry II (1154–1189).

2. *Limit on royal power.* The Magna Carta (Great Charter) was signed by King John in 1215. It placed limits on the king's powers to imprison people and to levy taxes. The king needed the consent of the Great Council, an advisory body composed of England's leading nobles and bishops, in order to levy taxes. The Magna Carta established that the king was not above the law; like his subjects, he had to obey the law.

3. *Legislative power.* The Great Council gained greater power under the rule of King Edward I. In 1295 he decided to include members of the middle class, the burgesses (representatives of the towns), and knights (small landholders). This council was the beginning of Parliament and became known as the Model Parliament. Afterwards, all Parliamentary meetings included representatives of the nobles and "commons." At first, they met together. However, Parliament was eventually divided into two parts, the House of Commons and the House of Lords. This was the first step toward representative government in England.

4. *Judicial power.* During the later Middle Ages (1000–1500), the verdicts of the judges were written down, collected, and became the basis for future legal decisions. These common practices and legal decisions, which were based on judges' decisions rather than on a code of laws, formed a body of law known as the English common law.

England—Stuart Absolutism and Its Downfall in the 17th Century

GLOBAL
CONCEPTS

Power

CONCEPTS
GLOBAL

GLOBAL
CONCEPTS

Human Rights

CONCEPTS
GLOBAL

Following Queen Elizabeth I were the rulers of the Stuart dynasty (1603–1649), James I and Charles I. They ruled as absolute monarchs, believing they should have no limits set on their power. The Stuart rulers did not respect previous democratic traditions and preferred to rule by divine right. They came into conflict with Parliament because they disregarded it in raising money, imprisoned people unfairly, and persecuted Puritans. However, the underlying conflict was the question of where power would be centered—in the monarchy or in the Parliament.

In 1628, in exchange for its granting more revenues, Parliament made Charles I agree to the Petition of Right (see chart on the development of democracy) which limited the power of the monarch. As soon as he received the money, Charles dissolved Parliament and ruled for eleven years (1629–1640) without Parliament. Ignoring the Petition of Right, Charles appointed special royal courts, such as the Court of Star Chamber, to try individuals who disagreed with him, particularly Puritans. These royal courts ignored the traditional common law.

In 1640, when Scotland invaded England, Charles was forced to call Parliament into session. Led by Puritans, this Parliament, which sat from 1640 to 1660, is known as the Long Parliament, and it changed English history by limiting the absolute powers of the monarchy. In 1641 Parliament denied Charles's request for money to raise an army to fight the Irish rebellion. In response, Charles led troops into the House of Commons to arrest some of its Puritan members. The attempt by Charles to arrest members of Parliament sparked the beginning of a civil war, as Parliament soon raised an army to fight the king.

WORLD ISSUES

War
and
Peace

The English Civil War (1642–1645). This conflict, which lasted from 1642 to 1645, was between the supporters of King Charles, called the Cavaliers, and the supporters of Parliament, called the Roundheads. The Parliamentary forces emerged victorious under the leadership of Oliver Cromwell, a Puritan.

The Puritan Revolution (1642–1660). This period included the Civil War and the rule by Oliver Cromwell, which began in 1649. Under Cromwell's leadership, the Parliament voted to abolish the monarchy, and Charles I was tried and beheaded in 1649. England was now a republic or, as it called itself, a commonwealth. However, in 1653, supported by his army, Cromwell

Unit Six **WESTERN EUROPE**

353

took the title of Lord Protector and ruled as a military dictator. His dictatorial policies, which included religious intolerance, strict moral codes, and violence against the Irish, caused resentment. Soon after his death, Parliament invited Charles II, the son of Charles I who was in exile, to take the throne.

The Stuart Restoration (1660–1688). Aware of English democratic traditions and the fate of his father, Charles II was careful not to anger Parliament. He acknowledged the rights of the people established by the Magna Carta and the Petition of Right. In 1679, he agreed to the Habeas Corpus Act. (See the chart on democracy). On his death in 1685, his brother James II became king. James angered Parliament because of his pro-Catholic actions and his claim to divine right rule. Parliament invited James's older daughter, Mary, and her husband, William of Orange, a Dutch prince who was Protestant, to take the throne.

GLOBAL
CONCEPTS

Change

CONCEPTS
GLOBAL

The Glorious Revolution (1688–1689). William and Mary accepted Parliament's offer and arrived in England with an army. They were proclaimed king and queen, as James II fled to France. As a result of this bloodless revolution, which is known as the Glorious Revolution, Parliament gained in power and prestige. To protect its newly won supremacy over the monarchy, Parliament passed a Bill of Rights that was signed by William and Mary in 1689. (See chart.) Thus, by the end of the 17th century, England had become a limited, or constitutional, monarchy, the first in Europe. All the major decisions were made by Parliament, and the ruler's actions were limited by Parliament. Key steps in this development as well as other democratic advances up to the year 1800 are in the chart on the next page.

WORLD ISSUES

Determination
of Political
and Economic
Systems

Impact of the Growth of Democracy in England. The growth of democracy in England was to have worldwide influence.

1. The democratic advances in England influenced political revolutions in the British colonies in North America (1776) and in France (1789). These ideas also influenced the emergence of some democratic nations from imperialism in the 20th century (India, 1947). A major factor in the American Revolution was the emphasis by colonists on their rights as English subjects. Indeed, many democratic ideas and practices developed in England were included in American documents, such as the original Constitution and the first ten amendments, called the Bill of Rights.

GLOBAL
CONCEPTS

Choice

CONCEPTS
GLOBAL

2. The writings of John Locke, a 17th-century English philosopher, were a source of democratic ideas. They influenced the

DEVELOPMENT OF DEMOCRACY IN ENGLAND

Democratic Achievements	Their Importance
Petition of Right, 1628	Parliament's consent needed for taxes; the king could not imprison someone without a trial or quarter soldiers in someone's home without permission.
Habeas Corpus Act, 1679	An arrested person has the right to know the charges against him, to be brought before a judge, and to be given a fair and impartial chance to defend himself.
Bill of Rights, 1689	Strictly limited the power of the monarch in such matters as levying taxes, maintaining an army, and interfering in the affairs of Parliament; basic civil liberties are guaranteed to to the people, such as a speedy trial, protection from cruel and unusual punishment and from excessive fines and bail.
Toleration Act, 1689	Freedom of worship permitted for all Protestant religions.
Political parties	Two political groups arose in Parliament, each having members with common backgrounds, interests, and goals. They competed peacefully with each other for control of Parliament and became known as political parties. They were the Tories (later called Conservatives) and Whigs (later called Liberals). Political parties are an example of freedom of expression and give voters a chance to choose between different candidates and policies.
Cabinet system	The Cabinet consisted of members of Parliament who became advisers, or ministers, to William and Mary. These ministers eventually came from the majority party, with the leader becoming the prime minister. Over the years, their power increased because they were chosen from the elected officials in Parliament. The monarch became just a figurehead—a symbol of the nation, with the power to reign but not to rule.

American colonists, and had a direct impact on the writing of our Declaration of Independence. Locke's ideas also influenced the leaders of the French Revolution. Locke believed that governments get their power from the consent of the governed (the people) and that the people have the right to change the government when the government abuses its power. For Locke, the chief purpose of any government was to protect the rights of the people. His idea of a social contract concerned an exchange of rights and responsibilities between a government and its citizens. Locke's chief work was *Two Treatises on Civil Government*.

The French Revolution

France: Conditions Prior to the Revolution of 1789. The underlying causes of the French Revolution were the conditions under the Old Régime. This term refers to life in France during the 17th and 18th centuries, while the nation was ruled by the Bourbon kings.

1. *Political causes.* The absolute rule of King Louis XIV (see France in the section "The Rise of Nation-States; Royal Power and Absolutism") was continued by King Louis XVI (1774–1792) and his wife, Marie Antoinette. Louis XVI did not permit any criticism of himself and imprisoned without a trial anyone who spoke out against his policies. Imprisonment was often carried out by *lettres de cachet*, letters with the royal seal. He was a poor leader and very unpopular. The population was divided into three classes. The First Estate was the clergy; the Second Estate was the nobles; and the Third Estate was made up of everyone else—city workers, peasants, and the bourgeoisie. (The bourgeoisie were mainly bankers, businesspeople, professional people, and others who made up the middle class.) The Third Estate, which included 90 percent of the population, had little say in the government. In the Estates-General, a lawmaking body, each estate had one vote. The Third Estate felt powerless because the other two estates always voted together.

Most of the French people were aware of the democratic revolutions in England (17th century) and America (18th century) and were impressed with the results of these events.

2. *Economic causes.* The Third Estate was more heavily taxed than the other two estates. Taxes imposed on the Third Estate included the *taille* (a land tax) and the *corvée* (labor on roads). They also paid a tithe to the church and feudal dues to certain lords. The bourgeoisie were upset with strict restrictions on their commercial activities.

3. *Social causes.* Although the first two estates consisted of less than 5 percent of the population, they had many more priv-

ileges than the Third Estate. They owned much of the land, were exempt from most taxes, and generally lived much better than members of the Third Estate.

4. *Influence of the Enlightenment.* The Enlightenment, also called the Age of Reason, was an intellectual movement in the 17th and 18th centuries. It was sparked by the scientific progress of the previous age (the Scientific Revolution). Educated Europeans had learned that natural laws governed the physical universe. They reasoned that similar laws must govern human society as well. If people were able to discover these laws, they might be used to construct a better government and more just societies. The thinkers, philosophers, and writers who examined the political and social problems of the time were known as philosophes. They believed that everything, even government and religion, should be open to reason and criticism. They were convinced that through the use of reason, logic, and experience, people could improve their society—its laws, economy, and so on. The philosophes claimed that humans had certain natural rights. Traditional royal and church authority, particularly in France, were in conflict with these rights and had to undergo change. The most important French writers of the Enlightenment are listed in the chart below.

GLOBAL
CONCEPTS

Change

CONCEPTS
GLOBAL

FRENCH WRITERS OF THE ENLIGHTENMENT

Name	Major Work and Ideas
Montesquieu (1689–1755)	*The Spirit of the Laws.* There should be a separation of powers in government as well as a system of checks and balances. These features would prevent tyranny and absolutism.
Voltaire (1694–1778)	*Letters Concerning the English.* Written in support of the concepts of England's limited monarchy and its ideas on freedom of speech and religion.
Rousseau (1712–1778)	*The Social Contract.* Inequality among people can be ended by citizens' coming together and agreeing to a general will. The general will is what the majority desires and should be carried out by the government.
Diderot (1713–1784)	*The Encyclopedia.* Absolutism and the injustices of the Old Regime were wrong.

There were also other important Enlightenment writers. Adam Smith of England *(The Wealth of Nations)* said that people should be free to conduct business without government interference. This was the laissez-faire philosophy of economics. The American Thomas Paine *(Common Sense)* claimed that it was right and natural for the American colonists to revolt against England, a tyrannical government that was thousands of miles across the Atlantic Ocean. John Locke was also a major Enlightenment writer. (See the section "Impact of the Growth of Democracy.")

The Enlightenment's concern with natural rights and the use of reason, logic, and experience was seen in the field of science as well as in politics and economics. During the 16th and 17th centuries, the way the people of Europe viewed themselves and the universe underwent a dramatic transformation in what was called the Scientific Revolution. The discoveries of a succession of astronomers, physicists, and mathematicians undermined many ideas that had been accepted for centuries. A new system of ideas and theories was created, based on the direct observation of nature and a belief in the power of reason. The scientific method, based on carefully planned experiments, observation of results, and the formulation of general laws, was the basis of the Scientific Revolution. Scientists such as Isaac Newton (1642–1727) of England used the scientific method to investigate nature. Newton, the leading figure in the Scientific Revolution, put forth important theories about gravity and the movement of planets. His famous book was the *Principia Mathematica*.

The French Revolution of 1789: Outbreak and Major Developments. In 1789 King Louis XVI called the Estates-General into session because he needed money to solve France's financial problems. This was the first time this body had been summoned since 1614 (175 years before). When the Estates-General met, the Third Estate refused to accept the traditional method of voting—each estate met separately and had one vote—because it would be outvoted by the other two estates. It demanded that all three estates meet together and that each deputy have a vote. When the king refused, the Third Estate, on June 17, 1789, declared itself to be the National Assembly and in the Tennis Court Oath pledged to write a constitution for the nation. This declaration was the beginning of the French Revolution. On July 14, 1789, the revolution spread as a mob stormed and destroyed the Bastille—a prison that was a symbol of the Old Regime. The next day the king recognized the National Assembly. The National Assembly, which was made up of moderates, took power and began to carry out reforms. They passed the Declaration of the Rights of Man on August 27, 1789. This document was similar to the American Declaration of Independence and the English Bill of Rights. It stated the following democratic ideals:

1. The class structure and privileges connected with the three estates were ended, abolishing the remains of feudalism.

GLOBAL CONCEPTS

Change

CONCEPTS GLOBAL

GLOBAL CONCEPTS

Justice

CONCEPTS GLOBAL

2. All people were equal before the law and had certain basic freedoms, including freedom of religion, speech, and the press.

3. The spirit of Liberty, Equality, and Fraternity was to guide the nation. In 1790 the National Assembly abolished the special taxes and privileges of the Catholic church in the Civil Constitution of the Clergy. It also granted freedom of worship, confiscated all church land, and placed the church under the government's control.

The French constitution was written in 1791, and it created a limited, or constitutional, monarchy and established separate executive, legislative, and judicial branches of government.

However, King Louis's unsuccessful attempt to flee the country and war with Austria and Prussia enabled radicals, such as Robespierre, Danton, and Marat, to take over the revolution. In 1792 delegates were elected by universal manhood suffrage to the National Convention, which took the place of the National Assembly and contained more radical members, such as the Jacobins. The first act of the National Convention was to declare France a republic. Louis XVI was brought to trial and executed in 1792.

GLOBAL
CONCEPTS
—
Human Rights
CONCEPTS
GLOBAL
—

The National Convention was soon taken over by extremist groups, who formed the Committee of Public Safety, which put the executive, legislative, and judicial powers of government in the hands of a small group of revolutionaries. The committee was given power to conduct the war with France's enemies and to enforce the ideals of the revolution by all means possible. The leading figures were Danton and Robespierre, who began a Reign of Terror (1793–1794) in which they executed at the guillotine all enemies of the revolution, who were to them the nobles or anybody who spoke out against them.

Eventually, more moderate groups, anti-Jacobins, took over the National Convention. Danton and Robespierre were themselves sentenced to die by the guillotine in 1795. The Convention wrote a new constitution in 1795 that made France a republic. It established a five-member Directory government that ruled France until 1799, when it was replaced by the military dictatorship of Napoleon Bonaparte. (See the next section.) This return of government to moderate control is called the Thermidorian Reaction.

Importance of the French Revolution. The French Revolution had many important and long-lasting results. It brought about a basic change in the relationship between the government and the governed. Along with the revolutions in England and the United States, the French Revolution advanced democracy by recognizing the value and worth of the individual.

Political power passed from an absolutist monarch who ruled by divine right and the nobles to the masses of people. A greater sense of nationalism and patriotism developed. Also, the remaining feudal features of French society were removed. The growing power of the bourgeoisie helped France to become a strong capitalist nation.

The Rise and Fall of Napoleon (1799–1815)

Napoleon Bonaparte was an ambitious, brilliant military officer who won many victories in wars against France's enemies. In 1799 in a coup d'etat (a sudden takeover of a government), he came to power in France in a new government called the Consulate. The Directory had lost support because of worsening economic problems and its inability to defeat Russia and Austria in the war. The Consulate was headed by three consuls, with Napoleon as First Consul. The new government, France's fourth in ten years, was called a republic, but it was a military dictatorship under the control of Napoleon. He took the title of Emperor Napoleon I in 1804. The French people accepted his ruthless methods because they believed he would bring peace and stability to the nation.

GLOBAL CONCEPTS

Political Systems

CONCEPTS GLOBAL

At first, Napoleon was brilliantly successful in his war against France's European enemies. Under Napoleon's leadership, French forces won victories and took large amounts of land in Europe. By 1808 Napoleon dominated Europe, and he reorganized many parts of Europe, making members of his family rulers in Italy, Spain, and other places.

The Napoleonic Empire soon became too large to control, however, and in time Napoleon suffered severe military setbacks. His attempt to conquer Russia in 1812 failed due to the harsh winter conditions and the scorched-earth fighting tactics of the Russians. At the Battle of Waterloo in 1815, fought near Brussels in Belgium, Napoleon's forces were defeated by the combined forces of European nations led by the Duke of Wellington of Britain.

WORLD ISSUES

War
and
Peace

Results of the Napoleonic Era. Napoleon made many significant contributions to governing France. Both within France and in the areas he conquered, Napoleon sought to carry out the ideals of the French Revolution as he interpreted them. Indeed, he called himself a son of the revolution and carried out the following reforms:

1. The Code Napoleon brought all the laws, regulations, and reforms of the revolution into a single system of law. Based on the belief that all people are equal before the law, the Napoleonic

Code became the fundamental law of France and the parts of Europe governed by France.

2. The Concordat of 1801 provided for a peaceful relationship between the French government and the Catholic church.

3. An efficient, centralized government was created in France, with specific power over the education and banking systems. Government officials were selected based on merit through an examination system, and a public school system was established.

4. Many European monarchs lost their thrones to Napoleon's armies. Peoples in these areas, such as Spain and Italy, learned of the ideals of the French Revolution. At first, some of these people welcomed Napoleon because they believed he had liberated them from foreign and unjust rule. Eventually, they turned against Napoleon's dictatorial rule and fought against him. However, as a result of Napoleon's conquests, the ideas of the French Revolution were spread throughout Europe. The ideals of social justice, liberty, and democracy became rallying cries for reformers. Combined with the rise of the spirit of nationalism, which was stirred by the struggle against Napoleon's armies, the dreams of liberty and equality made many national groups determined to gain self-government in the years after 1815.

The Metternich Age and the Growth of Nationalism (1815–1871)

After Napoleon's defeat, five major European powers—England, Russia, Prussia, France, and Austria—met at the Congress of Vienna in 1814 and 1815 to draw up peace plans and settle a number of important territorial questions by redrawing the map of Europe. Under the leadership of Austria's Count Metternich, the Congress of Vienna sought to restore political life in Europe, including former rulers and boundaries, to what it had been prior to Napoleon and to maintain peace and stability. Such a policy of restoring past ways and turning the clock back is called reactionary. Metternich wanted to wipe out the ideas spread by the Napoleonic era and return to the old days of absolutism and special privilege. The decisions reached at the Congress of Vienna were based on three principles—legitimacy, the balance of power, and compensation. Legitimacy meant restoring the ruling families that reigned before the French Revolution to their thrones. Balance of power meant that no one nation should be strong enough to threaten the security of the others. To do this, shifts of territory were necessary. This involved compensation, or providing one state with territory to pay for territory taken away from that state.

Metternich opposed the French Revolution ideas of freedom and equality. He sought to maintain what had been the status quo prior to the French Revolution. During the Metternich age (1815–1848), there were challenges to the status quo. However, most attempts by European peoples against these reactionary policies in order to achieve national unity were put down by force. These attempts, which led to revolutions in 1830 and in 1848, were inspired by a nationalistic spirit, whereby a group of people, such as the Italians, Poles, or Germans, sought to create their own nation and establish self-government. Although most of these revolutions failed, two successful attempts were made in Belgium and Greece in 1830. The Quadruple Alliance, representing the four powers that had defeated Napoleon, did not want these revolutionary movements to succeed. From this alliance emerged the Concert of Europe. This was a form of international government, arranged by concert, or agreement, among its members. It wanted to keep the balance of power that the Congress of Vienna had set up. Although the Congress could not suppress nationalism permanently, it was able to postpone its success for a half a century. The unification of Italy and of Germany in the later 1800s were the first breaks in the territorial settlements of 1815.

The spirit of nationalism influenced the political history of Europe from 1815 to 1914. Nationalism is the belief that a group of people who share a common culture, language, and historical tradition should have their own nation in a specific area of land. Once the people accomplish their nationalistic goals and form a nation-state, they can then make their own laws and are said to be sovereign and to have autonomy. Nationalism was the guiding force that led to the unification of both Italy and Germany in the late 19th century. The Italians, Poles, Hungarians, Turks, and others who were ruled by the large dynastic states that dominated Europe—the Austrian Empire, the Russian Empire, and the Ottoman Empire—all struggled to win freedom and form their own nation-states.

GLOBAL CONCEPTS
Change
CONCEPTS GLOBAL

Unification of Italy. In 1815 there was no nation called Italy; Italy was really a geographic expression. The Italian Peninsula was divided among large and small states, such as the Lombardy province and the kingdom of Sardinia-Piedmont. Austria, which controlled the states in the northern part of the Italian Peninsula, was against any kind of unity. But by 1861 all the Italian states had become unified into a nation. Those most responsible for bringing unification about were:

GLOBAL CONCEPTS
Identity
CONCEPTS GLOBAL

1. *Cavour.* Considered the brain of unification, he was a successful diplomat who got France to help him fight the Austrians. He also expanded the power of Sardinia-Piedmont by adding to it other Italian states.

2. *Mazzini*. The soul of unification, he wrote and spoke eloquently about his desires for Italian unity. He was the founder of the Young Italy movement.

3. *Garibaldi*. The sword of unification, he conquered southern Italy and joined it to the state that Cavour had unified under the control of Sardinia-Piedmont in the north.

4. *King Victor Emmanuel*. Formerly the king of Sardinia-Piedmont, he became the king of a united Italy in March 1861.

Unification of Germany. In 1815 there was no nation called Germany. Instead, there were more than 30 independent German states that had their own traditions, laws, and economic regulations. The largest of these states, Prussia, located in northern Germany, led the movement for unification. The chief obstacle to Prussia's leadership was Austria. It sought to dominate German affairs and did not want to see the German states unified. But by 1871, under the leadership of Prussia's chief minister, Otto von Bismarck, Austria's power was weakened and the German states achieved unification.

GLOBAL
CONCEPTS

Change

CONCEPTS
GLOBAL

Otto von Bismarck

Following a policy of blood and iron, Bismarck used military means to achieve his goal of German unity under Prussia's leadership. Under this policy, Prussia won victories in the Danish War (1864), the Austro-Prussian War (or Seven Weeks' War, 1866), and the Franco-Prussian War (1870–71). As a result of these wars, Prussia was able to gain land, such as Schleswig-Holstein from Denmark and Alsace-Lorraine from France, unite other German states with Prussia, and reduce the influence of Austria in German affairs. King William I of Prussia became the ruler of a united Germany in 1871 and was called emperor, or kaiser.

WORLD ISSUES

War
and
Peace

Conclusion. Nationalism can be positive (a force for good) or negative (a force for evil). The desire by Italians and Germans to form their own nations brought together people with common ties and histories. The wishes of a group of people to achieve sovereignty and self-determination are common themes throughout history and exist even in our own day. However, nationalistic desires can become so intense that hatred and unnecessary bloodshed can result. The reign of terror in France was one example; Bismarck's humiliation of France after the Franco-Prussian war was another. Intense nationalism can also be dangerous when it turns into chauvinism and excessive ethnocentrism. This occurs when a group of people claim to be superior to another group of people. Such claims have often led to prejudice and wars.

GLOBAL
CONCEPTS

Identity

CONCEPTS
GLOBAL

The Industrial Revolution

A major upheaval in the way people live, work, and think began about 200 years ago and in many ways is still going on today. This change is called the Industrial Revolution, and it accomplished on a massive scale the replacement of human power and animal power with the power of machines. The Industrial Revolution began in England in the 1750s and involved vast changes in the production of goods. These changes were as follows:

WORLD ISSUES

Economic
Growth and
Development

1. From handmade goods to machine-made goods.

2. From production at home to production in factories (from the domestic system to the factory system).

3. From producing small amounts to producing large amounts (mass production).

4. The increased use of science and new forms of energy (steam power, for example) to speed up production and meet human needs. The use of science in these ways is referred to as technology.

GLOBAL
CONCEPTS

Technology

CONCEPTS
GLOBAL

Causes and Preconditions in 18th-Century England. The Industrial Revolution began in England because of a combination of fortunate conditions that existed at the time.

1. *Natural resources.* Britain was fortunate to have large amounts of coal and iron ore.

2. *Geography.* England had many good harbors, and coastal and river trade was well developed. England also had relatively good roads and numerous canals for the cheap transport of raw materials and finished goods.

3. *Investment capital.* Entrepreneurs and other private individuals had money that they, as capitalists, were willing to invest and risk in business ventures.

4. *Labor supply.* There were large numbers of skilled workers in the population.

5. *Increased demand.* There was a great demand for British products, both in the domestic market (within the nation) and in foreign markets.

6. *Transportation and colonial empire.* Britain had a good navy and had built up a shipping industry. Its expanding colonial empire furnished raw materials and markets for goods.

7. *Agricultural changes.* An agricultural revolution that occurred in the 1700s brought changes in farming that made the Industrial Revolution possible. These changes resulted in the production of more food and required fewer farmers to produce it. Many people left the farms and went to the cities to find work in factories.

8. *Role of government.* Britain had a stable government that had established a good banking system, promoted scientific experimentation, and passed laws to protect business.

9. *Inventions.* The changes in production came first in the cotton textile industry. Several inventors devised inventions that sped up and improved the manufacture of textiles.

EUROPEAN INVENTORS OF THE INDUSTRIAL REVOLUTION

Inventor	Invention and Its Importance
John Kay	Flying shuttle—speeded up the weaving process
James Hargreaves	Spinning jenny—could spin many threads at one time
Richard Arkwright	Water frame—used water power to increase spinning; first machine to replace human hand power with another power source
Edmund Cartwright	Power loom—used water power to make weaving faster
James Watt	Steam engine—use of steam as a source of power
George Stephenson	Steam locomotive—improved ground transportation

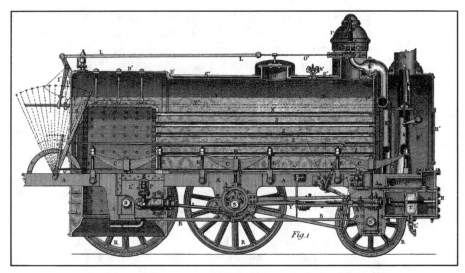

The locomotive was developed during the Industrial Revolution.

Responses to the Industrial Revolution. The Industrial Revolution fundamentally changed the way people lived. Families moved to industrial cities by the millions to work in the new factories. The first years of adjustment to the new industrial society were a period of severe difficulty for workers. Men, women, and children worked long hours under deplorable conditions in factories. People were crowded into towns and cities that had made little provision for housing or for sanitation. With more people working in factories and living in cities, occupational, health, and housing problems developed. Moreover, even though they were becoming more populated than rural areas, cities had not gained political power. These problems associated with industrialization developed in Britain as well as in other areas of Europe where industrialization took place. In response to workers' protests and reformers' appeals, various reform measures were adopted. These reforms indicated that Europeans had begun to understand the changes in the working and living conditions of those who labored under the factory system. Reform measures in Britain were as follows:

1. *Social and economic reforms.* Harmful working conditions such as child labor, low wages, faulty ventilation, and dangerous equipment were brought to public attention by the Sadler Report on factories and the Ashley Report on mines. In time, members of Parliament became concerned about children as young as five or six working long hours in factories and mines and about the dangerous, unhealthful conditions for all workers

in factories. Laws such as the Factory Act (1833) and the Mines Act (1842) were passed to improve conditions for workers. The need for workers to unite to protect and advance their interests led to the formation of labor unions.

2. *Political reforms.* The move to reduce property rights as the basis for suffrage (the right to vote) and to give cities more representation in Parliament led to the passage of the Reform Bill of 1832. This bill also did away with most "rotten boroughs" (areas that no longer had many people but had kept the same amount of representation in Parliament). The middle class, workers, and women were to benefit from the Reform Bill of 1832 and similar legislation passed in the 19th and early 20th centuries. By 1928, for example, Britain provided for universal suffrage. This meant that both women and men had the right to vote. The expansion of suffrage in Britain and other European countries was partially due to changes brought about by the Industrial Revolution.

GLOBAL CONCEPTS

Citizenship

CONCEPTS GLOBAL

The Development of Socialism. Political scientists and philosophers struggled with the problems presented by industrialization, seeking to discover how the political system should respond. One of these solutions was socialism, which was a criticism of capitalism and called for a basic change in the economic system in order to correct these problems. Socialists maintained that it was necessary to transfer ownership of the means of production (factories, mines, railroads, land) from private individuals to the state. According to socialist theory, the government, as elected by the people, should own all the means of production and should also make all the key economic decisions. These decisions included: What should be produced? Who should produce it? What should the price be? and How should the product be distributed? This kind of planned, or command, economy is in contrast to a free-enterprise or market economy. In a market economy, according to capitalist principles, the key economic decisions are basically made by private individuals acting on their own.

One group of socialists wanted to create an ideal society, or a utopia. Utopian socialists believed that a socialist society would emerge peacefully and that even capitalists would be willing to help create it. Among the utopian socialists of the 19th century were a wealthy British manufacturer, Robert Owen, and a French philosopher, Charles Fourier.

In contrast to utopian socialists were those people who believed in a radically different type of socialism called scientific socialism or communism. That was a type of socialism based on what they believed were scientific ideas about the way society operates. The leading scientific socialist thinkers were

Karl Marx

Karl Marx and Friedrich Engels of Germany. Their ideas were contained in two books: *The Communist Manifesto* (1848) and *Das Kapital* (1867). Their major ideas came to be known as Marxism and included:

1. *Economic interpretation of history*. All history is determined by economic conditions. Whichever group or class controls the means of production will control the government.

2. *Class struggle*. In all societies throughout history, there have been struggles for power between two economic groups—the haves and the have nots. In industrial societies the struggle has taken place between the capitalists, or bourgeoisie, and the workers, or proletariat.

3. *Surplus value theory*. Surplus value was the difference between the price of a good and the wage paid to a worker. According to Marx, this difference was kept by the capitalists as their profit. For Marx, this was wrong, especially as he felt that workers were paid far too little in wages. Such abuse, or exploitation of workers, was unjust.

4. *Inevitability of socialism*. Eventually all these conditions would lead to depressions and poverty and would result in a violent overthrow by the workers of the government, primarily because the capitalists would not peacefully give up their economic and political power. This Communist revolution would result in a dictatorship of the proletariat, a government that would be more just and would rule on behalf of the working class. The government would operate under the theory of socialism. Eventually, a classless society would emerge, and there would be no need for a government; the government would wither away.

The Impact of Communism. The history of Communism since Marx put forth his ideas shows a wide difference between what Marx said and what has actually happened.

1. His prediction that Communist revolutions would occur mostly in Western European industrialized societies was wrong. The first two Communist revolutions took place in agricultural societies—Russia (1917) and China (1949).

2. Communism never won control in industrialized societies in Western Europe or in North America. Marx failed to see the growth of unions and their ability to work toward their goals in a free, democratic system. He also did not realize that the living conditions of the workers would improve in the 19th century and that workers would become part of the middle class.

3. As the 1990s began, it was clear that Communist societies had failed to achieve their goals. Economic and political problems in Eastern Europe and the Soviet Union led to the collapse of Communism in those areas (1989–1991). In addition, throughout this century, there have been constant attempts by people in these Communist nations to leave, seeking a better life elsewhere, specifically in non-Communist countries.

Imperialism

Imperialism can be defined as the control by one nation over a weaker area or nation. This control has usually been both political and economic. Since the areas under control are called colonies, the practice of imperialism can be referred to as

WORLD ISSUES

World
Trade and
Finance

colonialism. There were two distinct periods of imperialism—the "old imperialism" (1500–1800) and the "new imperialism" (beginning in the 1880s). The old imperialism had the following characteristics: concerned with establishing trade routes and obtaining resources; carried on at first by private individuals and companies; took place mainly in the Western Hemisphere, the Americas. (See the unit on Latin America.) The new imperialism had these general characteristics: concerned with establishing trade and markets, obtaining resources, and making large financial investments; carried on by governments as official policy; took place mainly in the Eastern Hemisphere, Africa, and Asia. There were many reasons for the new imperialism.

1. *Economic.* The increased supply of manufactured goods produced by the Industrial Revolution encouraged European

GLOBAL
CONCEPTS

Interdependence

CONCEPTS
GLOBAL

nations to find new markets for these goods. Investors with surplus capital looked overseas to make investments that would bring them profits. The need for raw materials to produce more goods was another important consideration.

2. *Political.* Nations hoped to gain prestige and glory by expanding their power. These nationalistic desires sparked nations to achieve a balance of power with other nations that were also seeking to build colonial empires.

3. *Social.* European nations felt that they were superior to other global areas. They felt that they had both an obligation and a right to spread their culture and way of life into these areas. These feelings of ethnocentrism can be seen in Rudyard Kipling's poem *The White Man's Burden,* which concerns the obligation of carrying Western civilization to those considered less fortunate. These feelings were also the result of 19th-century notions of white racial superiority and the theory of social Darwinism. This was the belief that social progress depended on competition among human beings, resulting in the survival of the fittest.

Forms of Imperialist Control. Imperialism took many different forms in the 19th century.

1. *Sphere of influence.* A nation gained sole economic power in a region and had exclusive economic rights to trade, to invest, and to develop mines, railroads, or factories. It could not be interfered with by other nations. This form of imperialism was used in China, where each foreign nation—for example, Germany—had economic control in a specific area.

2. *Concession.* In this form, a foreign nation obtained special privileges. An underdeveloped area gave permission to a technologically advanced nation to do something of economic value in the area. (For example, the Arabs let the British drill for oil and build a railroad in the Middle East.)

3. *Protectorate.* A colonial nation allowed the native ruler of an area to remain in office as a figurehead, while in reality the colonial power made all the major decisions (France in Tunisia). The former Eastern European satellite nations controlled by the former Soviet Union after World War II can be thought of as protectorates.

4. *Colony.* An imperialist nation takes total control over an area and makes it part of its empire. (France in Indochina, the Netherlands in Indonesia, Britain in India.)

Colonial Policies. The major imperialist nations followed different policies in ruling their empires. These policies influenced the patterns of independence that took place after 1945.

GLOBAL
CONCEPTS
Choice
CONCEPTS
GLOBAL

1. *England.* Its policy of indirect rule permitted local rulers to retain some power in an area. Nevertheless, because the British felt that their democratic values were superior and should be spread, they sought to educate selected Africans and

Asians in English schools. It was hoped that these natives would plant British political and social ideals in their native lands. People who received such an education, such as Gandhi and Nehru in India, eventually led their people to independence in nonviolent ways, based on democratic ideas. Britain was never involved in harsh colonial wars for independence as were some of the other European nations.

2. *France.* Its policy of direct rule viewed colonies as if they were actually parts of France. Decisions for the colonies were made directly in Paris. Since the French language and culture were assumed to be preferable, all people were to learn them in colonized areas. These attitudes were the basis for France's claim to carry out a civilizing mission and to accomplish assimilation of native peoples. Since France viewed areas such as Algeria and Indochina as much a part of French territory as Paris, the French were unwilling to give into demands for independence that grew after the end of World War II. Consequently, France fought bitter, unsuccessful colonial wars in these areas. (See the units on the Middle East and South-east Asia.)

3. *Portugal.* Its policy of paternalism viewed colonies as though they were children, and Portugal did little to prepare its colonies for independence. As with France, it looked on its colonies as parts of Portugal. Consequently, it too was unwilling to grant independence to its colonies in Angola and Mozambique without military struggle.

4. *Belgium.* It followed policies of paternalism and exploitation in the Congo. Belgium did little to pave the way for independence and left the area amid much bloodshed in 1960. Consequently, this former colony had severe political problems in creating a stable government when it became independent. (See the units on Africa, Asia, and the Middle East for additional information on areas once under European imperialist control.)

Independence and Decolonization. During the period after World War II, independence came to almost all areas that had come under European imperialist control. This period of decolonization saw the emergence of over 50 new nations. The end of imperialism after 1945 was a result of many factors: nationalist movements in the colonies grew powerful, gaining support from native people as well as from some people in the imperialist nations; the Western European nations were weary after fighting World War II; the creation of the United Nations was linked to global concern for human rights and recognition of the need for people to achieve self-determination.

GLOBAL
CONCEPTS

Change

CONCEPTS
GLOBAL

Although decolonization was achieved in both peaceful and violent ways, many former colonies retain ties today to their former foreign rulers. Many of Britain's colonies, after independence, voluntarily chose membership in the British Commonwealth of Nations. The organization meets to discuss matters of mutual interest and provides certain economic privileges for members. Although it no longer exists, the French Community was an organization similar to the British Commonwealth. It included France and several of its former colonies. France's interest in its former colonies can be seen in its giving economic aid and in providing military support when requested. For example, in recent years, French forces were sent to the African nations of Chad and Gabon to put down armed opposition to the governments there.

WORLD ISSUES

Human
Rights

Evaluation of Imperialism. European imperialism had both positive and negative consequences, as summarized in the table below.

EUROPEAN IMPERIALISM

Consequence	Positive	Negative
Political	Brought stability and unification; training for independence; promoted the nation-state idea	Colonial wars; discrimination; drew boundaries without consulting native peoples
Economic	Introduced modernization; improved means of transportation and communication; created industries; taught new skills; improved the standard of living; provided employment	Took wealth away from colony; treated workers badly; did not provide for advancement or mangement by colonized people; destroyed traditional industries and patterns of trade
Social	Introduced Christianity and other aspects of Western culture; built schools and hospitals; modern medicine	Looked down on native cultures; promoted racism and cultural inferiority; introduced Western vices and diseases

World War I (1914–1918)

The Congress of Vienna laid the foundation for a century of peace in Europe, broken only by a few brief and local wars (Franco-Prussian, Russo-Turkish, and Crimean). Beginning about 1870, a series of forces combined to move Europe toward war. These forces included a growing spirit of nationalism, increasingly dangerous colonial conflicts, a complex system of entangling alliances, and a rising tide of militarism.

WORLD ISSUES

War
and
Peace

Between 1914 and 1918 war swept across Europe. This war was far more destructive of lives and property than any other previous conflict and was considered the first total war. Civilian populations became targets along with soldiers. Terrifying new weapons were used for the first time.

Basic (Fundamental, Underlying) Causes of World War I.

Many factors contributed to the start of World War I. All the major European powers shared some blame, although historians disagree on whether one nation was more to blame than the others.

1. *Imperialism.* The desire to control other areas led to sharp competition and rivalry among nations of Western Europe. Examples include: Britain and Germany in Africa and the Middle East; France and Germany in Morocco; and Austria-Hungary and Russia in the Balkans. As European nations struggled to claim more territories in Africa and Asia, they approached the brink of war several times.

2. *Nationalism.* Strong ties to one's nation and/or ethnic group stirred strong emotions. Many groups of people wanted to be free of the control of other nations. For example, Bosnia-Hercegovina wanted to be free from Austria-Hungary so they could be united with Serbia. Other nationalities in the Balkans also wished to be free of control by Austria or the Ottoman Empire and to create their own nations. The Balkans were called the tinderbox of Europe. Nationalism was also a factor in France's wanting *revanche* (revenge) against Germany for Germany's taking Alsace-Lorraine after the Franco-Prussian War.

GLOBAL
CONCEPTS

Identity

CONCEPTS
GLOBAL

3. *Alliances and the Lack of World Peacekeeping Machinery.* Two alliances, the Triple Entente (France, Russia, and Britain) and the Triple Alliance (Germany, Austria-Hungary, and Italy) were formed for defensive purposes, but they soon became two armed camps. At this time no organization existed, such as the United Nations, to foster world peace or to help settle disputes among the major powers.

4. *Militarism.* As the alliance system divided Europe into two opposing camps, each nation began to increase its military strength. The growth of armies and navies, as well as the development of weaponry, added to the mood of belligerence (warlike attitude) and a tendency to settle disputes by fighting. Manufacturers of arms increased production, as governments sought to build up their military strength. Economic rivalry between Germany and Britain poisoned relations between the two nations. Germany's growing navy was seen by Britain as a threat to its security.

Immediate Cause of the War. The spark that set off World War I was the assassination of the Austrian Archduke Francis Ferdinand in June 1914 in the town of Sarajevo. The assassin was a Serbian nationalist, Gavrilo Princip, who wanted to free Bosnia-Hercegovina from the Austro-Hungarian Empire and unite them with Serbia.

Developments in the War. Austria, backed up by Germany and glad to receive Germany's blank check, threatened Serbia. This angered Russia, causing it to get its armed forces ready for war. Because of the alliance system, country after country was

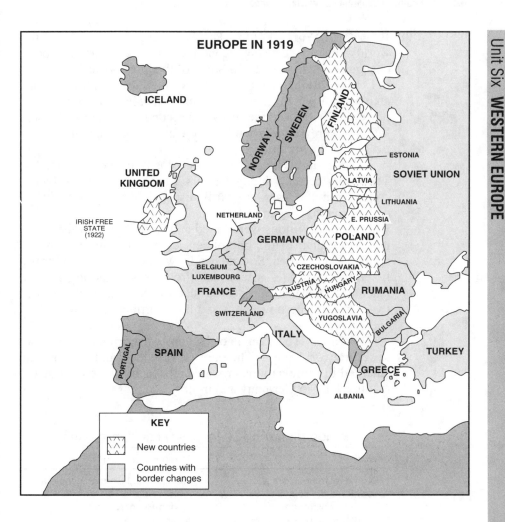

EUROPE IN 1919

ICELAND

NORWAY

SWEDEN

FINLAND

ESTONIA

SOVIET UNION

LATVIA

LITHUANIA

UNITED KINGDOM

IRISH FREE STATE (1922)

NETHERLAND

E. PRUSSIA

GERMANY   POLAND

BELGIUM
LUXEMBOURG

CZECHOSLOVAKIA

FRANCE

AUSTRIA   HUNGARY   RUMANIA

SWITZERLAND

YUGOSLAVIA   BULGARIA

ITALY

PORTUGAL

SPAIN

TURKEY

GREECE

ALBANIA

KEY

New countries

Countries with
border changes

drawn into the conflict and all the major powers were soon
fighting each other. A local, regional crisis thus became the
spark of a major war. The war, known as the Great War at first,
turned into the most violent European conflict since the
Napoleonic Wars, almost 100 years before. With neither side
able to win, the armies faced one another from trenches. The
war was a stalemate until 1917, when the United States entered
the war on the side of the Triple Entente nations, or the Allies
(Britain, France, and Russia). This helped to bring victory
against the Central Powers (Germany, Austria-Hungary, Italy,
and Turkey—a late entrant into the war). The war ended in November 1918, having lasted over four years.

Results of World War I. The war changed the course of the world's history, causing economic chaos and radical social changes in many countries. Some of the most powerful nations in Europe lost their influence and began to decline. Many monarchs lost their thrones. A Communist government came to power in Russia, and the seeds of a second great conflict (World War II) were sown when World War I ended and the peace treaty was drawn up.

1. *Economic.* The war was very costly to the participants. The losers became debtor nations. Many economic problems arising from the war were partly responsible for the worldwide depression that began in 1929.

2. *Social.* Millions were killed and wounded from the fighting. More than 8 million soldiers died, and almost as many civilians were killed. Several deadly weapons were used for the first time in warfare—gas, tanks, airplanes, submarines, and the machine gun. Most Europeans failed to understand the destructive power of these weapons and how horrible modern warfare had become.

3. *Political.* The League of Nations was formed in an effort to secure world peace. The political problems and hatreds that emerged in some nations provided a basis for the rise of dictatorships later in Germany and in Italy.

MAJOR TERRITORIAL CHANGES AFTER WORLD WAR I

Changes	Taken From
1. Poland recreated, with a corridor to the sea	Germany and German-conquered area of Russia
2. Romania enlarged	Austria-Hungary
3. Yugoslavia and Czechoslovakia created as new nations	Austria-Hungary
4. Austria and Hungary become separate nations	Austria-Hungary
5. Finland, Estonia, Latvia, and Lithuania created	Russia
6. Alsace-Lorraine to France	Germany
7. Syria, Lebanon, and Palestine became mandates (see Middle East unit)	Turkey

The Versailles Treaty (1919). The Versailles Treaty officially ended World War I. It was drawn up at the Paris Peace Conference by David Lloyd George (Britain), Georges Clemenceau (France), Vittorio Orlando (Italy), and Woodrow Wilson (United States). It forced Germany to accept "war guilt" and stripped

Germany and Austria-Hungary of much territory (see chart on previous page). Germany was also forced to pay huge amounts of money to the victors as reparations. It was prohibited from uniting with Austria and required to limit its armed forces (demilitarization). This *diktat* (dictated peace), as it was called by Germany, caused much resentment in that country and was later used by Hitler as propaganda in his rise to power in the 1930s. The treaty also created the League of Nations. The League was one of the Fourteen Points that America's Wilson had asked for in an attempt to prevent future wars. The United States Senate refused to ratify (approve) the Versailles Treaty. Therefore, the United States did not become a member of the League. For this reason, as well as the fact that it had no enforcement powers, the League was seen as a weak organization.

The Rise of the Modern Totalitarian State

Totalitarianism is a political philosophy that emerged in the 20th century. Totalitarianism describes governments in which one political party monopolizes all power and exercises complete authority over the people and their activities. It involves total control of all aspects of an individual's life by the government, with both civil and political rights being curtailed. Although various forms of totalitarianism exist in parts of the world today, its earliest examples were in three European nations during the 20-year period following World War I. These

nations were the Soviet Union (under Communism; see Unit Seven), Italy (under Fascism), and Germany (under Nazism). Totalitarian societies look down on individual human rights and civil liberties. The values of democracy are not found in such societies. Totalitarian states emphasize: (1) glorification of the whole community (that is, the state); (2) authoritarian rule by a dictator or by selected members of the one political party allowed to exist; (3) control of the individual citizen's life; (4) belief in the idea that the individual should benefit the state and exists solely to serve the state's interests. In Western Europe, these features of totalitarianism were most characteristic of Germany under the control of Adolf Hitler and the Nazi party, from 1933 to 1945. This government, known as the Third Reich, arose after the period of the Weimar Republic.

Germany Under the Weimar Republic (1919–1933). The Weimar Republic was the name of the German government that came to power after World War I. It was a democratic government, with a constitution that was drawn up in the city of Weimar. However, this experiment with democracy in Germany faced many problems, including economic chaos and street violence. It was not successful for a number of reasons.

1. In the early 1920s the Weimar government printed paper money with little to back it, resulting in severe inflation. This devastated the German economy and resulted in severe unemployment and street violence.

2. When Germany was unable to meet its reparations payments in 1923, France sent troops to occupy the Ruhr Valley, Germany's chief industrial area.

WORLD ISSUES

Hunger

and

Poverty

3. There was terrible unemployment in Germany in the early 1920s and again in the 1930s.

4. The German economy was restored after 1923 and conditions improved. However, in 1929 a worldwide depression that threatened the stability of democratic governments everywhere brought much suffering to Germany. Unemployment rose to 6 million in 1932, and Germans lost faith in their political leaders. This further fueled the bad feelings that had been caused by the Versailles Treaty.

5. The government was unstable because no single party was able to achieve a majority in the Reichstag, the more powerful of the two legislative houses created by the Weimar constitution. As a result, German political leaders seemed helpless to deal with the severe economic problems.

These problems led many Germans to conclude that democracy was ill suited to their nation and that autocracy was preferable, especially since it had brought Germany political unification, economic growth, and respect as an international power. A strong democratic tradition did not exist in German history.

The Role of Adolf Hitler. Hitler was born in Austria and served in the German army during World War I. He joined the Nazi party (National Socialist German Workers party). He spoke out against the Weimar government and was arrested for his role in the Munich Putsch of 1923, an unsuccessful attempt to overthrow the government. While imprisoned, he wrote the book *Mein Kampf* (My Struggle) that contained his ideas for a stronger and more powerful German nation. It also revealed his racist beliefs concerning the alleged superiority of Aryans as a "master race" and the need to eliminate all groups he considered inferior, such as Jews, Slavs, Gypsies, and blacks. Hitler was a stirring and charismatic speaker when addressing large crowds, thereby attracting many people to the Nazi party.

Rise of the Nazis to Power. In addition to the problems of the Weimar government and the powerful role played by Hitler, a number of other factors led to the rise of the Nazis in Germany:

1. *Economic problems.* The Nazis offered simple explanations for both the causes of Germany's economic problems and its cures. These problems, as described above, affected millions of Germans. The reparations demanded by the Versailles Treaty were condemned as unjust and blamed for causing the economic crisis.

2. *Patriotic appeals.* The Nazi program stirred German nationalism. It called for:

- a large increase in the armed forces;
- the expansion of the German fatherland to include territory in Europe where people of German descent lived (Austria, parts of Poland, and Czechoslovakia);
- control over educational and cultural institutions to teach Nazi principles of racism and physical fitness for the glory of the state;
- ignoring the Versailles Treaty and refusing to accept the war-guilt clause;
- regaining land that Germany had held in Europe and its overseas colonies prior to World War I;
- the use of violence as a legitimate means to achieve domestic and international goals;
- the importance of looking back to and glorifying the mythical German race (the so-called *Volk*) as the source of all strength and power.

The Nazis also claimed that Nordic Germans were destined to rule the world and to eliminate undesirable peoples. They blamed the Weimar government for accepting the Versailles Treaty and said it had been forced to do so by Jews, Communists, and others. Finally, the Nazis claimed that German forces had not been defeated in World War I but had been stabbed in the back.

WORLD ISSUES

Terrorism

3. *Anti-Semitism.* Prejudice toward Jews had existed in Germany for hundreds of years, resulting in exile, loss of life and property, and hatred. However, Hitler's prejudice against Jews was fanatical; he used Jews as scapegoats and blamed them for his own personal failures and also for Germany's problems. These false notions became persuasive parts of Nazi propaganda, especially when they were blended with Hitler's master race theories. Hitler claimed that the Aryans (Germans) were a

WORLD ISSUES

Human
Rights

master race who were naturally entitled to control and rule peoples of less "pure" blood, such as Slavs and Jews. (The Holocaust, in which 6 million Jews were systematically murdered after Hitler came to power, was the tragic consequence of these misguided notions.)

4. *Fear of Communism and of Soviet Russia.* The Nazis played upon these fears with much success and portrayed themselves as the only ones capable of protecting Germany from foreign beliefs and potential aggressors. In this way, they were able to win the support of large segments of the German population, such as bankers and industrialists.

5. *Use of private, illegal armed groups.* Many of Hitler's followers were organized into private armies. One such group was the Storm Troopers (S.A.), or Brown Shirts, who used scare tactics and violence to terrorize Jews and opponents of the Nazis.

6. *Lack of meaningful opposition.* Few strong voices inside Germany spoke out against the Nazis. Many Germans came to gradually support Hitler, while others were apathetic. Others feared speaking against him, and many who did were intimidated. Internationally, there was little awareness of or concern about the Nazi movement.

The Nazis Come to Power. The formal takeover of Germany by the Nazis took place in January 1933 when the president of the Weimar Republic, Paul von Hindenburg, appointed Hitler as chancellor. By this time, the Nazis had become the largest political party in Germany, and they formed the single largest block in the Reichstag, the German parliament. Yet they had never won a clear majority in any national election. (In 1932, for example, they won slightly less than 40 percent of the seats in the Reichstag.) Although Hitler promised to preserve the Weimar constitution, he soon carried out policies that destroyed the democracy that had existed under the Weimar Republic. The result was a totalitarian dictatorship that eventually brought about World War II and brought devastation to Germany and to most of Europe. Hitler's distorted ideas, along

with his antidemocratic beliefs and tactics, unfortunately found a receptive audience in post-World War I Germany. He was called der Führer, or leader.

Italy Under a Fascist Government (1922–1943). Italy experienced totalitarian rule under a Fascist government headed by Benito Mussolini. The word "fascist" comes from the word

"fasces," an axe-like weapon that was a symbol of the ancient Roman Empire. Mussolini wanted Italians to feel a strong sense of nationalism and to remember the glory of the Roman Empire. Mussolini and his Black Shirt followers came to power for some of the same reasons that led to the rise of the Nazis in Germany.

1. *Economic.* The costs of World War I had been staggering. After the war, there was high unemployment, strikes, and severe inflation.

2. *Political.* The weak and divided government of King Victor Emmanuel III was unable to provide leadership or to inspire confidence in its ability to solve the postwar crisis. Also, there was no strong democratic tradition in Italy. Moreover, the fear of Communism and a Communist-led revolution was seized upon by Mussolini, who promised to defend Italy and thereby won followers.

3. *Social.* Italy was suffering from low morale, and was saddened by the many deaths in World War I. Mussolini promised the Italian people security, order, and economic progress in exchange for their liberties and freedom.

Mussolini in Power. As a result of his famous March on Rome in 1922 supposedly to save Italy from a Communist revolution, Mussolini came to power. Neither the king nor the army opposed him. He soon established a police state, destroying civil liberties and demanding that people recognize him as Il Duce, the leader. Mussolini reorganized the economy of Italy, establishing Fascist-controlled associations in all industries, and Italy was run as a corporate state.

GLOBAL
CONCEPTS

Power

CONCEPTS
GLOBAL

World War II (1939–1945)

Although the war started in Europe, it soon became a global conflict that dwarfed all previous wars in geographical extent and in human and material losses suffered. Fighting took place on three continents—Europe, Africa, and Asia—and on the seas, lands, and oceans around the globe. More nations (over 50) were belligerents (fighters in the war) than in any war in history. The chief antagonists on the Allied side were Great Britain, France, the United States, the Soviet Union, and China. On the opposing side were Germany, Italy, and Japan, the so-called Axis powers.

WORLD ISSUES

War
and
Peace

Causes. Many of the causes of World War II were similar to those that brought on the first world war. After World War I, many nations hoped to prevent another war by establishing what could be called a house of peace. The foundations of this house included: the Versailles Treaty, the League of Nations, disarmament conferences (held in Washington, D.C., and in London), and the Kellogg-Briand Pact, which attempted to outlaw war. Unfortunately, the house of peace crumbled for a number of reasons, most of them due to the actions of the Axis powers (Germany, Italy, and Japan). The basic causes of the war were:

1. *Militarism.* Large amounts of money were spent on weapons. Military strength was seen as a source of national pride. The leaders of the Axis nations were always seen in military dress.

2. *Nationalism and racism.* The Axis nations saw themselves as superior to others and with the right therefore to extend their culture and their borders (the German "master race" theory, the Italian wish to revive the ancient Roman Empire, the Japanese pride based on Shinto teachings and the necessity to establish a new order in Asia).

3. *Imperialism.* The Axis nations sought to take over other lands for political, racist, and economic reasons. Japan moved into China (1931, 1937); Italy conquered Ethiopia (1938); and Germany annexed Austria (the Anschluss, or union) and Czechoslovakia (1938, 1939).

4. *Failure of collective security.* The democratic nations of Europe and the United States did little to curb the aggressive policies of Germany, Italy, and Japan. The League of Nations condemned some of these aggressive moves but was unable to take any other action.

5. *Appeasement.* To give in to a potential aggressor, hoping that the aggressor will be content and not commit any further harmful acts is called appeasement. It later came to mean the policy of accepting territorial aggression against small nations in the hope of avoiding a general war. This policy was followed by the British prime minister, Neville Chamberlain, at the Munich Conference in 1938. Here, he agreed to accept German annexation of the Sudetenland portion of Czechoslovakia in return for Hitler's guarantee of independence for the rest of Czechoslovakia. The policy proved to be a failure when Hitler later sent the German army to occupy all of Czechoslovakia in violation of the Munich Agreement.

The Start of the War. The German attack on Poland in September 1939 was the actual start of the war. Britain and France finally realized that they would have to use military force to stop Hitler's aggression and threat to conquer all of Europe. Just prior to its attack on Poland, Germany signed a nonaggression pact with the Soviet Union. Under this agreement, Russia would take over eastern Poland and the Baltic states of Estonia, Latvia, and Lithuania and would not contest Hitler's attempt to take over western Poland. Also, Russia and Germany promised not to fight each other.

GLOBAL
CONCEPTS

Power

CONCEPTS
GLOBAL

Developments in the War. Using blitzkreig warfare ("lightning war"), Germany overran most of Europe, except for England, by 1941. In June of that year, Germany broke its promise not to attack Russia and invaded that nation. The Russians suffered great losses and were driven back to the outskirts of Moscow, Leningrad, and the Volga River, where they held and gradually began to turn the tide. Also, in 1941 the United States entered the war after its navy was attacked by Japan at Pearl Harbor, Hawaii. The nations now fighting the Axis powers were known as the Allies (United States, Britain, France, Soviet Union). With the invasion of Normandy in western France on June 6, 1944 ("D-Day"), Allied forces began to retake German-held lands and pushed the Germans eastward. Russian forces entered the German-held Eastern European nations and pushed the Germans westward. On May 8, 1945 ("V-E Day"), Germany surrendered. In Asia, by 1941 Japan had conquered large areas of East and Southeast Asia. These Pacific areas were slowly retaken by U.S. forces between 1942 and 1945. In August 1945 the United States dropped two atomic bombs on the Japanese cities of Hiroshima and Nagasaki. On September 2, 1945 ("V-J Day"), Japan surrendered.

The Holocaust. This word refers to the intentional persecution and systematic murder of European Jews by the Germans from 1933 to 1945. Six million Jews were exterminated, mostly in concentration camps such as Auschwitz, Dachau, and Treblinka. The planned extermination of a group of people because of their religion, race, or ethnicity is called genocide. The genocidal tactics of the Nazis were a horrible extension of Hitler's anti-Semitic attitudes. The world stood by and did nothing while these tactics such as gas chambers, ovens, and firing squads were being used. There were scattered instances of Jewish armed resistance, such as in the Warsaw Ghetto Uprising in 1943. After the war, at the Nuremberg War Crimes Trials, several Nazis were found guilty of genocide and of crimes against humanity.

In addition to Jews, other groups of people labeled "inferior" by the Nazis were also sent to the concentration camps. These included homosexuals, Jehovah's Witnesses, Gypsies, Slavs, and mentally retarded people.

Results of World War II. The world of 1945 bore little resemblance to the world of the 1930s. Europe was shattered and lay in ruins, its people facing an uncertain future.

1. *Political.* The United States and the Soviet Union became the two leading superpowers and eventually clashed on many issues in what became known as the cold war. Germany was divided into four zones of occupation—American, British,

French, and Soviet. Poland's boundaries with the Soviet Union were changed, adding some to its own land. The Soviets established a sphere of influence, as an imperialist power, in many Eastern European nations. Some Soviet activities were in violation of the Yalta agreements of 1945. Britain and France lost some of their status as world powers; nationalistic movements in their colonies were to lead to a loss of their empires. The Allies helped to create the United Nations.

2. *Economic.* The war proved to be the most costly ever fought. The loss of life and property in World War II far surpassed that of any previous conflict. The economies of many European nations were destroyed. Communism spread into the nations of Eastern Europe.

3. *Social.* More people, soldiers and civilians, were killed than in any other war. Much of this was due to new highly destructive weapons, as well as to the racist policies of the Axis powers. At war's end, millions of people had become refugees and displaced persons.

GLOBAL
CONCEPTS
Technology
CONCEPTS
GLOBAL

4. *Scientific.* The Atomic Age had begun with the dropping of atomic bombs on Hiroshima and Nagasaki.

The United Nations

The United Nations was created in 1945. Its founders included the United States and the other World War II Allies. They hoped to make the UN a more effective international peacekeeping organization than the League of Nations had been. The UN Charter listed the organization's goals: to maintain peace and prevent war; to fight against hunger, disease, and ignorance; to improve social and economic conditions; and to build friendship and cooperation among nations. To accomplish these goals, the UN is structured as follows:

WORLD ISSUES

War

and

Peace

The General Assembly. The General Assembly has 184 member nations. Each nation has one vote. This figure contrasts with the 50 member nations that signed the UN Charter in 1945. The General Assembly meets to consider international problems. It has the power to admit and expel members and to make recommendations to members and to other UN bodies. A decision on important questions requires a two-thirds majority.

The Security Council. The Security Council has 15 members. Five are permanent members, while ten are nonpermanent members. The five permanent members are the United States, Britain, France, Russia, and China. The other members are elected by the General Assembly for a two-year term. The

TERRITORIAL CHANGES IN EUROPE 1945–1948

NORWAY

0   300 miles
0   300 km

NORTH SEA

SWEDEN

DENMARK

BALTIC SEA

ESTONIA

LATVIA

LITHUANIA

Leningrad ■

NETH.

BELG.

LUX.

FRANCE

SWITZ.

U.S.

BR. ZONE

GERMANY

Stettin ■

Berlin ■

SOV. ZONE

Nuremberg

ODER-NEISSE LINE

(TO POLAND)

E. PRUSSIA

Warsaw ■

POLAND

U.S.S.R.

(TO U.S.S.R.)

■ Prague

CZECHOSLOVAKIA

(TO CZECH.)

U.S. ZONE

SOV. ZONE

FR. ZONE

AUSTRIA Vienna ■

FR. ZONE *U.S. ZONE*

BR. ZONE

■ Budapest

HUNGARY

ROMANIA

(TO FRANCE)

Trieste ■

(TO YUGOSLAVIA 1954)

Belgrade ■

Bucharest ■

YUGOSLAVIA

ITALY

ADRIATIC SEA

(TO BULGARIA)

BULGARIA

CORSICA

■ Rome

ALBANIA

SARDINIA

GREECE

DODECANESE ISLANDS
(TO GREECE)

MEDITERRANEAN SEA

KEY

Territorial changes after World War II

Soviet occupation zones

Occupation zones of Western powers

International boundaries after World War II

Unit Six WESTERN EUROPE

Security Council functions as the UN's executive body; it can investigate problems and take action to maintain international peace.

1. Resolutions for action in the Security Council require nine votes, including the votes of all the five permanent members. Therefore, each permanent member has veto power over Security Council proposals.

2. The most important UN official is the head of the Security Council—the Secretary-General. The individuals who have served in that post include Trygve Lie of Norway (1946–1953), Dag Hammarskjöld of Sweden (1953–1961), U Thant of Burma (1961–1971), Kurt Waldheim of Austria (1972–1981), Javier Perez de Cuellar of Peru (1981–1992), and Boutros Boutros-Ghali of Egypt (1992–present).

Specialized Agencies. These are bodies in the UN that carry out specific social and economic tasks. Some of these agencies are UNESCO (United Nations Educational, Scientific, and Cultural Organization), WHO (World Health Organization), and FAO (Food and Agriculture Organization).

Evaluation. The UN has been more successful in dealing with social and economic issues than with political issues. Examples of its success can be seen in eliminating smallpox, fighting famines, and drawing attention to women's rights. On political matters, the UN has had mixed results. Examples of effective political action include the following: peacekeeping forces in Cyprus, the Middle East, and South Asia; truce in the Korean War; overseeing the transition to independence for Namibia. UN resolutions have been disobeyed, however, in other disputes: Soviet troops in Hungary, apartheid in South Africa, India's seizure of Goa, Serbs fighting in Bosnia.

The Cold War and the Era of the Superpowers

WORLD ISSUES

Determination
of Political
and Economic
Systems

The period after World War II (the postwar period) was marked by the dominance of two superpowers—the United States and the former Soviet Union. Each nation had different philosophies about politics, economics, and human rights. Each thought it was superior to the other. The two nations engaged in a cold war, which was not a shooting war but a war of words and propaganda; it also involved competition in science, weapons, and seeking friends among the new emerging nations in Africa and Asia. Western European nations sided with the United States in what was called the free world. The Soviet Union occupied the

WORLD ISSUES

Determination

of Political

and Economic

Systems

Eastern European nations and, with them, formed the Communist bloc. As the 1990s began, however, the cold war came to an end, seen in the peaceful overthrow of Communist governments in Eastern European nations such as Poland and Czechoslovakia. But the most striking event marking the end of the cold war and the decline of Communism occurred on December 8, 1991, when the leaders of Russia and other Soviet republics announced that the Soviet Union no longer existed. Taking its place would be several independent nations, for example, Russia, Ukraine, and Belarus, that would be members of the Commonwealth of Independent States. (For more on these developments, see Unit Seven on the Commonwealth of Independent States and Eastern Europe.) The cold war era, from 1945 to 1991, was distinguished by certain key events in Western Europe.

NATO. NATO, the North Atlantic Treaty Organization, was formed in 1949. It was a defensive alliance consisting of the United States, Canada, and ten Western European nations. It now has 16 member nations. Its formation was part of the U.S. policy of containment, through which the United States and its European allies hoped to prevent the spread of Communism by the threat of military power. Two important parts of the containment policy in 1947 were the Marshall Plan (to provide economic aid) and the Truman Doctrine (to provide military aid to prevent a Communist takeover in Greece and Turkey). To counter NATO, the Soviet Union and its allies formed the seven-member Warsaw Pact in 1955.

However, in March 1991 the former Soviet Union and five Eastern European nations agreed to dissolve the Warsaw Pact. This dramatic event, along with others that marked the end of the cold war, caused NATO members to reconsider the role of the organization. They discussed the possibility of changing NATO from an alliance focused on collective defense against a specific threat to an alliance based on extending democracy and providing stability throughout Europe. Key episodes during 1994 illustrated how such changes could develop.

1. In April, the NATO alliance carried out its first bombing raid. NATO bombed Serbian positions in Bosnia-Hercegovina to protect UN officials under fire and to protect thousands of people in the town of Gorazde from being attacked.

2. In January, U.S. President Bill Clinton and other NATO leaders proposed a Partnership for Peace program, that was intended to bring about closer ties between NATO and its former Warsaw Pact enemies. It would allow these former Communist nations to join military exercises, peacekeeping operations, and

other activities without actually granting them NATO membership or security guarantees. As of June 1994, 18 Eastern European nations and former Soviet republics had signed the partnership agreement. Although it was not yet a signatory at that time, Russia indicated that, under certain conditions, it would be willing to join the program.

Germany. In the years immediately after World War II, the question of what to do about Germany caused much tension between the superpowers. At the end of the war, most of Germany was divided into four occupation zones—American, British, French, and Soviet. The city of Berlin was also divided into four such zones. Some territories in East Germany were put under Polish control. Since the four Allies were unable to agree on a plan for German reunification, the Western nations permitted their zones to come together in 1949 as the Federal Republic of Germany (West Germany), with its capital at Bonn. The Soviet zone became the German Democratic Republic (East Germany), with its capital in East Berlin. West Berlin, although surrounded by East Germany, became part of West Germany. The Soviets tried to cut off access to West Berlin in 1948 and 1949

GLOBAL
CONCEPTS

Change

CONCEPTS
GLOBAL

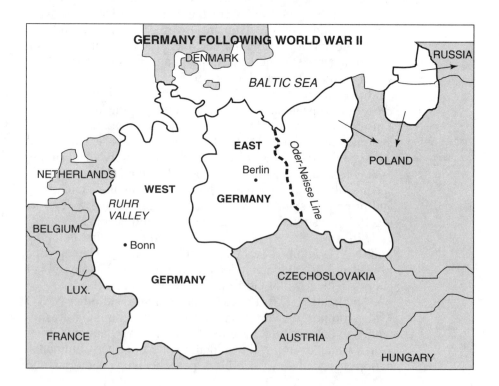

GERMANY FOLLOWING WORLD WAR II

by imposing the Berlin Blockade. However, the Western Allies sent in food and supplies by plane (the Berlin Airlift). The Soviet Union subsequently backed down and ended the blockade.

1. *The Berlin Wall.* The Soviets again made Berlin a tension spot in 1961 when they built a wall (the Berlin Wall) separating the Western section from the Eastern section. These areas had been used as escape routes for people who wanted to flee from Communist rule. The wall was another example of the Soviet policy of restricting the flow of ideas, goods, and people between the free world and the Communist world. This restrictive policy became known, in the words of former British Prime Minister Winston Churchill, as the iron curtain.

WORLD ISSUES

Political and Economic

Refugees

The many historic changes in the European Communist world that occurred in 1989 and 1990 can be thought of as cracks in the iron curtain. One crack was the destruction of the Berlin Wall by the Communist authorities, making Berlin a more open city. From November 1989 onward, when the wall was opened, it lost its significance as a political, economic, and social barrier.

2. *German reunification.* With the end of the Berlin Wall and the friendlier relationship (détente) between the superpowers, the chances of reunifying Germany became a very distinct possibility. In 1990 free elections were held in East Germany. West German political parties, such as the Christian Democrats and Social Democrats, ran candidates and won the support of some voters. In July 1990 an economic merger occurred when the West German mark became the unit of currency in East Germany. This meant that even though Germans were still living in two separate nations, they would use the same money. East Germans were allowed to move into West Germany; West German companies were allowed to set up capitalist-style businesses in East Germany. With these developments, it became likely that German reunification would occur by 1991. Indeed, discussions about a reunited Germany were held throughout 1990. The major discussants were the four victorious World War II Allies, as well as representatives from the two Germanies. These discussions were thus known as the four-plus-two negotiations. Poland wanted to be included in the talks, because it had suffered more from German occupation in World War II than any other European nation. It wanted assurance that a reunited Germany would respect Polish sovereignty and would not seek to retake any land given to Poland after the war. Specifically, Poland wanted to be sure that the Oder-Neisse boundary line between East Germany and Poland would remain intact. A promise to maintain this boundary was made by

West German Chancellor Helmut Kohl in the spring of 1990, on the assumption that he would become the first head of a re-united German nation.

A reunited Germany came into being on October 3, 1990. In December 1990 the first all-German elections were held. The winner was the Christian Democratic Union (C.D.U.) coalition party and its leader, Helmut Kohl. To finance the huge cost of reunification and to fight the economic depression that now affected the eastern part of the new nation, taxes had to be raised. The new government also decided to move the capital from Bonn to Berlin by the year 2000. Two events would occur in 1994, to mark the new Germany: (1) By August, all American, British, French, and Russian troops would leave Berlin; (2) In October, highlighting 1994 as the Super Election Year, the second all-German elections would be held.

Political Issues for the Decade of the Nineties

The consequences of German reunification is one of several political issues that will concern Western European nations in the 1990s. Some of the others are:

Ireland. The Irish question has been a source of controversy between Ireland and England for centuries. By 1600, Protestant England had gained control over Catholic Ireland. From that time until the 20th century, British imperialist treatment of the Irish was cruel and harsh. During the 17th century, when Oliver Cromwell ruled England, many Irish were killed by British forces; in addition, Protestants from England and Scotland took over large areas of land in Northern Ireland. Until the 1800s, Irish Catholics could not hold political office and were taxed to support the Anglican (Protestant) church.

In 1905 the Sinn Fein party was formed as a nationalist group to press Britain for Irish independence. Its leader was Eamon de Valera. Although the Easter Rebellion in 1916 against the British was unsuccessful, the Sinn Fein continued its campaign for independence. In 1922, the southern four-fifths of the island of Ireland became a free nation known as the Republic of Ireland. The remaining one-fifth, Northern Ireland, also known as Ulster, decided to remain as part of the United Kingdom (Great Britain). Catholics in Northern Ireland wanted the area to be united with the Irish Republic to the south, as did the new Republic of Ireland itself. These requests were turned down by Britain, particularly because the majority of Ulster citizens were Protestants and wanted to stay under the

British Crown. Extremist groups, both Catholic and Protestant, began to fight an undeclared civil war in Northern Ireland. The I.R.A. (Irish Republican Army) spoke for many Ulster Catholics and demanded a united Ireland. Militant Protestants, headed by the Reverend Ian Paisley, are against unification. British troops have been sent to Ulster since 1976 to help maintain peace and stop the killings and terrorist actions of both sides. These efforts have not been very successful. A 1985 agreement between Ireland and Britain, the Hillsborough Agreement, attempted to end what has been called the Troubles. It provided for greater cooperation against extremist groups, stopping discrimination toward the Catholic minority in the north, and giving the Republic of Ireland some involvement in the governing of Northern Ireland. The agreement has had mixed results and has been criticized by both Catholics and Protestants.

In December 1993, Prime Ministers John Major of Britain and Albert Reynolds of Ireland signed a declaration of principles in London to encourage talks for a peace plan. The agreement's highlights were: (1) all groups that promise to renounce violence, such as the I.R.A. and Protestant guerrilla organizations, would be invited to join negotiations on the future of Northern Ireland; (2) Northern Ireland would remain a province of Britain for as long as most of its people want it to; (3) the Irish government agreed to amend its constitutional claim to the territory of Northern Ireland. Although little progress toward peace was made in the early months of 1994, there was a reduction in the bloodshed that had claimed over 3,100 lives in the preceding 25 years.

Political Union and a "United States of Europe." The political unification of European nations is an idea that has been under consideration since the end of World War II. There already exists a European Parliament, a European Court of Justice, and a European Commission. These organizations have limited powers but stand for some attempt at international cooperation. The twelve nation European Union (EU) (formerly known as the European Community), has made great strides toward economic cooperation. (See Section II, Economic Geography, in this unit). At its June 1990 meeting in Dublin, the EU agreed to consider proposals for political union. These have been discussed further in conferences at Rome and elsewhere. French President Francois Mitterand and West German Chancellor Helmut Kohl have spoken of a single European currency as well as possible political unification.

One factor that helped to set the stage for consideration of political and economic cooperation was the Helsinki Pact of 1975. This was a treaty signed by the United States, Canada, and 33 European nations, at what was called the Conference on Security and Cooperation in Europe. The signing nations agreed to accept the post-World War II boundaries in Europe. They also agreed to recognize the importance of promoting human rights throughout Europe and to investigate any governmental actions that violated such rights. A Helsinki Watch Committee was established to conduct such investigations.

REVIEW QUESTIONS

Multiple Choice. Select the letter of the answer that correctly completes each statement.

1. The political system of the ancient Roman Empire was characterized by
   A. a strong central government
   B. rule by a coalition of emperors and religious leaders
   C. universal suffrage in national elections
   D. a strict adherence to constitutional ideas

2. Which was a major characteristic of democracy in ancient Athens?
   A. All adult male citizens were eligible to vote.
   B. All residents were given voting rights.
   C. Women were allowed to vote in major elections.
   D. Slaves were permitted to vote in major elections.

3. Which ancient civilization established the basis of Western political thought?
   A. Phoenician
   B. Egyptian
   C. Babylonian
   D. Greek

4. Which statement best describes the role of the Roman Catholic church in Europe during the Middle Ages?
   A. It encouraged individuals to question authority.
   B. Church leaders were involved solely in spiritual activities.
   C. It gained influence as the world became more secular.
   D. It provided a sense of stability, unity, and order.

5. Which is the most valid generalization about the Crusades?
   A. The Crusades strengthened the power of the serfs in Europe.
   B. The Crusades increased trade between Europe and Asia.
   C. The Crusades brought European influence to Africa.
   D. The Crusades supported the idea of religious tolerance.

6. Which was a result of the Commercial Revolution?
   A. decline in population growth in Europe
   B. shift of power from Western Europe to Eastern Europe
   C. spread of feudalism throughout Western Europe
   D. expansion of European influence overseas

393

7. Which is a valid conclusion based on a study of European art during the Renaissance in Europe?
   A. Emphasis on artistic creativity can discourage a society from pursuing reforms.
   B. The development of guilds prevented artistic creativity.
   C. The presence of a wealthy leisure class contributes to artistic achievement.
   D. An economy based on subsistence agriculture encourages artistic development.

8. The humanists of the Renaissance differed from the traditional medieval philosophers in their
   A. interest in the spiritual life of the people
   B. lack of interest in ancient Greek and Roman culture
   C. rejection of Christian ideas
   D. emphasis on the importance of the individual

9. An immediate result of the Protestant Reformation was the
   A. breaking of the religious unity of Europe
   B. strengthening of the political power of the Pope
   C. increase in the influence of the Roman Catholic church
   D. restoration of political unity to Western Europe

10. Martin Luther's Ninety-five Theses were a call for
    A. religious revolt against the German princes
    B. reforms within the Roman Catholic church
    C. greater papal authority
    D. crusades to spread Christianity

11. The theory of laissez-faire capitalism advocates
    A. government control of the economy
    B. noninvolvement of the government in the economy
    C. government regulation of big business
    D. government sponsorship of labor unions

12. One important result of the French Revolution was that
    A. France enjoyed a lengthy period of peace and prosperity
    B. the Roman Catholic church was restored to its former role and power in the French government
    C. political power shifted to the bourgeoisie
    D. France lost its spirit of nationalism

13. In Europe, which group benefited most from the industrialization of the 19th century?
    A. rural farmers
    B. middle class
    C. factory workers
    D. clergy

14. A main idea of Karl Marx and Friedrich Engels's *Communist Manifesto* is that the proletariat
    A. would need foreign help to achieve its revolutionary ends
    B. had to cooperate with the capitalists to gain economic rewards
    C. should allow the capitalists to control the means of production
    D. must unite to overthrow the capitalist class

15. Which statement best reflects the theories of Karl Marx and Friedrich Engels?
    A. Workers can expect that working conditions will improve as a result of government legislation.
    B. Owners of businesses will eventually realize that conditions for workers must be improved.
    C. Workers will experience an improved standard of living as capitalism matures.
    D. Workers will change working conditions by revolutionary means.

16. The Magna Carta, the Reform Bill of 1832, and the Parliament Act of 1911 were all steps by which Great Britain
    A. evolved toward democratic principles
    B. extended British imperialism
    C. created a classless society
    D. promoted socialist policies

17. Which was a major effect of European rule in Africa?
    A. decreased dependence of African nations on imports
    B. development of subsistence agriculture
    C. improved transportation and communication systems
    D. increased use of barter

18. Which group suffered from anti-Semitism during the Hitler era?
    A. Czechs
    B. Jews
    C. Muslims
    D. Aryans

19. Which was a major result of World War II?
  A. Military alliances were abolished.
  B. Efforts to develop new weapons decreased.
  C. European colonialism began to decline.
  D. Democracy spread in Eastern Europe.

20. The Berlin Wall was built
  A. with the help of the United Nations
  B. to prevent people from escaping to West Berlin from East Berlin
  C. to stop West German forces from reaching the Soviet Union
  D. with the cooperation of the two Germanys

21. The cold war era was characterized by
  A. cooperation between the superpowers
  B. increased tension between Communist nations and Western democracies
  C. United Nations control of nuclear weapons
  D. worldwide acceptance of Marxist ideas

22. The League of Nations and the United Nations were both created for the purpose of
  A. stopping the spread of Communism
  B. eliminating military dictatorships
  C. maintaining international peace
  D. building a single world culture

23. The Helsinki Conference sought to establish secure boundaries and protect human rights several years after
  A. the Napoleonic Wars
  B. the Franco-Prussian War
  C. World War I
  D. World War II

Essays

1. Throughout Europe's history, several individuals have acted in ways that have had a major impact on one or more nations.

  Alexander the Great
  Caesar Augustus
  Martin Luther
  Elizabeth I
  Robespierre
  Metternich

Select any five of the above. For each one chosen:
  A. State the nation or homeland of the person.
  B. Describe one title the person had.
  C. Describe something this person did that had a major historical impact.
  D. Explain one reason why the person acted this way and one result of that action.

2. Nationalism has been a major force in shaping world events.

   Nationalistic Struggles
   French Revolution (1789–1815)
   Unification of Germany (1860–1871)
   World War I (1914–1918)
   Unification of Italy (1850–1861)
   The Irish Question (1650–present)

Choose three of the nationalistic struggles listed. For each one chosen:
  A. Identify one nationalistic leader or group involved in the struggle
  B. Describe one nationalistic goal of the leader or group
  C. Describe one action taken by the leader or group to achieve the goal

3. During the twentieth century, major events or situations have affected nations as well as regions of the world.

Twentieth-Century Event/Situation	*Nation/Region*
Creation of NATO	Western Europe
Helsinki Conference	Europe
Unification of East and West Germany	Germany

  A. Describe one reason for each event or situation.
  B. State one effect of this event or situation on the nation or region with which it is paired.

UNIT SEVEN

The Commonwealth of Independent States and Eastern Europe

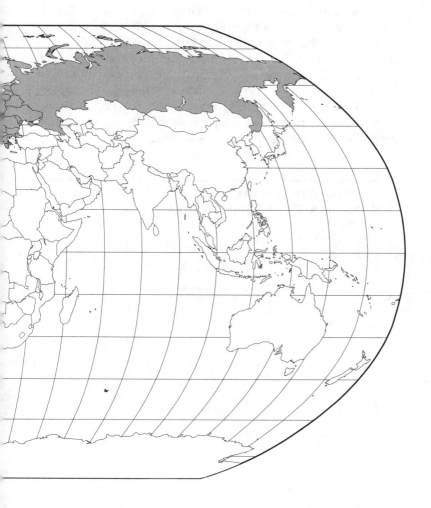

I. PHYSICAL GEOGRAPHY OF THE C.I.S.

Overview

The Commonwealth of Independent States (C.I.S.), formerly the Union of Soviet Socialist Republics or U.S.S.R., is an immense federation of countries that is more than two and one-half times the size of the United States. It is located in both Europe and Asia, occupying two-fifths of the continent or land mass referred to as Eurasia. Its geographic location in two continents, particularly that of Russia, was often reflected in the political and cultural developments of the region. Before 1917, the Soviet Union was called the Russian Empire. Today Russia is the largest country in the Commonwealth of Independent States. The Baltic nations and Georgia, formerly part of both the Russian Empire and the U.S.S.R., are not currently members of the C.I.S. Russia's great size (more than a quarter of the globe) has brought both problems and advantages to its inhabitants. With over 283 million people, the population of the C.I.S. is made up of more ethnic groups than any other area. Over a hundred languages are spoken there.

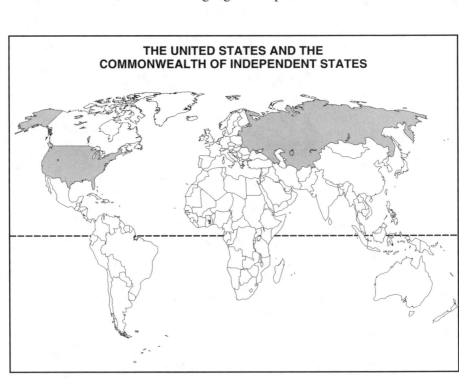

THE UNITED STATES AND THE COMMONWEALTH OF INDEPENDENT STATES

Topography

The topographical diversity of Russia has had an enormous impact on its political, economic, and cultural development. Originally, Russia was a much smaller country, landlocked (no access to the sea) and isolated by the Eurasian land mass. The desire to gain access to the sea for trading purposes led many Russian rulers to adopt a policy of expansion. This goal of gaining warm-water ports has always been central to Russian foreign policy. The numerous rivers that run throughout Russia long served as its only connections to the outside world. It was through these water trade routes that the Kievan princes made contact with the Byzantine or Eastern Roman Empire, which eventually gave Russia its religion and culture. Invasions from both Europe and Asia made it clear to later Russian rulers that if Russia did not gain access to the sea, it would be absorbed by other nations and cease to exist as a nation. As a result, the Russian kings, called czars, followed an expansionist policy. First they set out on a path of conquest to the North and White seas, then south to the Black Sea, and finally east through Siberia to the Pacific Ocean. Yet, despite the acquisition of several thousand miles of coastline by the early 20th century, Russia's access to the Mediterranean, which carried the great bulk of commerce, was limited. Russian ships must leave from a port on the Black Sea and travel through the Dardanelles and the Sea of Mamara to reach the Mediterranean. Moreover, the ports gained by the Soviet Union were cold-water ports locked in ice during the winter.

The plain of northern Eurasia consists of several thousand miles of flat land, often referred to as the Northern European Plain. This area stretches from the Atlantic Ocean, across Western Europe and Eastern Europe until it reaches Russia, where it becomes the Siberian Plain. Only some mountain ranges, such as the Urals (the traditional dividing line between Europe and Asia), interrupt the plain. The geographic feature made Russia open to invasion. For example, during the Middle Ages, Russia suffered attacks by the Teutonic (German) knights as well as by Swedish and Polish armies from the west, while Mongols and Tartars invaded from the east.

The Great Caucasus, the highest mountains in the European part of Russia, stretch between the Black and Caspian seas. This series of mountain ranges, which run eastward from the Great Caucasus along the borders of Iran, Afghanistan, Pakistan, and India and then north along Tibet and China, separates Russia from its southern neighbors. Although these mountains are an obstacle, they have not prevented Russian attempts at expansion.

GLOBAL
CONCEPTS

Environment

CONCEPTS
GLOBAL

Bodies of Water

As you have read, the rivers of Russia have played an important role in its history and development. In the European part of Russia, the Volga (the longest river in Europe), Dneiper, Dvina, and Don rivers were essential for internal trade and commerce. The Neva River still serves as an important link between Russia's industrial centers and the Baltic Sea. In the Asian part of Russia, the Ob, Yen, and Lena rivers have recently become valuable as sources for hydroelectric industrial power.

Russia's seas and lakes also have great importance. The Caspian Sea (the largest inland body of water in the world) provides food and a passageway for commerce. The Black Sea also provides an important trade route. Russia's fresh-water lakes, such as Lake Baikal (the deepest lake in the world) and Lake Ladoga (the largest inland body of water in Europe), also provide important links in a generally landlocked country.

Vegetation Belt

The vegetation belts of the region consist of three zones: the tundra, the taiga, and the steppes. The northern rim, including the islands of the Arctic Circle, is known as the tundra and covers about 10 percent of the country. It consists of a thick layer of permanently frozen ground, called permafrost. Its severe climate makes the tundra uninhabitable.

WORLD ISSUES

Population

The taiga, which covers nearly half of Russia, is a great forest that provides wood and limited crops. These conditions have kept the population there small.

The steppes is a very fertile region that has attracted both farmers and nomadic tribes. The southwestern region of the steppes, now the nation of Ukraine, is an important agricultural area that was known as the breadbasket of Russia. It has the most fertile land in the C.I.S. Because it has no natural barriers, the steppes has always served as an invasion route for armies from both the west and the east.

GLOBAL
CONCEPTS

Environment

CONCEPTS
GLOBAL

The territories between the steppes and frontier mountains of the southeast are mainly uninhabited desert. The majority of people in the Russian Empire lived in European Russia, particularly in the steppes. It was only during the Soviet period that large numbers of people moved north and east, largely to exploit the natural resources in these areas. Russia's vast size has always presented great obstacles for travel, communication, and trade. However, it has also helped to save the Russians from invaders. For example, the invasions of both Napoleon's and Hitler's armies were defeated by Russia's vast size and harsh climate. The relative isolation of much of the population

GLOBAL
CONCEPTS

Culture

CONCEPTS
GLOBAL

has resulted in the often stubborn and conservative nature of the Russian people.

Climate

The climate of Russia has played an important role in shaping the character of its people. The lack of warming ocean winds and the cool Arctic blasts make Russia's winters the coldest in the populated world. Even Russia's warmest areas have a climate similar to that of the Great Lakes or Canada. The harsh winters and short growing season have made the Russians both patient and able to endure great hardships.

REVIEW QUESTIONS

Multiple Choice. Select the letter of the answer that correctly completes the statement.

1. The C.I.S. is physically
   A. twice the size of the United States
   B. more than two and a half times the size of the United States
   C. half the size of the United States
   D. larger than Europe but smaller than the United States

2. Until the 18th century, Russia
   A. was landlocked and isolated by the Eurasian land mass
   B. only had ports on the Black Sea
   C. had Baltic ports with limited use
   D. had easy access to the Mediterranean via the Black Sea

3. The most fertile region of Russia that attracted both farmers and nomadic tribes is the
   A. taiga
   B. steppe
   C. tundra
   D. plain

4. Covered with permafrost and uninhabitable, Russia's northern rim is known as the
   A. taiga
   B. tundra
   C. steppe
   D. plain

5. Which of the following rivers has not been important in the development of Russia?
   A. Dnieper
   B. Neva
   C. Sava
   D. Volga

The geography of Russia has been extremely important to its development.

    A. To what extent did Russia's diverse topography (mountains, plains, vegetation belts) influence its development? Show two ways this occurred.

    B. Give two examples of how Russia's rivers have shaped its economic development.

    C. Discuss two ways Russia's diverse and often extreme climate have affected the development of the Russian people.

II. ECONOMIC GEOGRAPHY OF THE C.I.S.

Agriculture

Until the 20th century, Russia's economy was almost completely agricultural. Ukraine was the primary source of crops. Called the breadbasket of Russia, Ukraine was able to grow enough grain to supply the entire Russian Empire with enough surplus to make it a major food-exporting nation. Ukraine still produces wheat, rye, barley, cabbage, and potatoes. The Caucasus region supplies cotton, tea, and subtropical fruit such as oranges and grapes.

However, certain geographic conditions have been harmful to Russia's agricultural production. These include droughts that severely affect crop production and Russia's vast size, which makes the transportation of crops difficult.

In addition to these geographic factors, other conditions have affected agricultural production in the region. The policy of collectivization (a Soviet government policy that forced

farmers to work together on state land in accordance with Communist philosophy) under Stalin reduced agricultural output. State control of the Soviet economy (the government decided what was produced, who should produce it, and how much it should cost) interfered with the farmers' free choice and did not respond to the demands of the population. Also, in 1986 the nuclear power plant at Chernobyl near Kiev (the capital city of Ukraine) exploded. As a result, much of the soil in Ukraine was contaminated, and the produce was not safe for humans. For that reason, the Soviet Union was dependent on outside sources, especially the United States, for much of its wheat.

Industrial Production Resources

Major Resources. Southwest Russia and Ukraine are rich in coal, iron ore, manganese, natural gas, and other minerals, es-

pecially metallic ores and precious and semiprecious stones. It is also a major source of oil. Siberia supplies the C.I.S. with 90 percent of its coal and half its natural gas. Siberia also has a huge supply of oil and immense deposits of iron and other minerals. However, the severe climate conditions make these resources difficult to obtain. In addition, Siberia provides over 60 percent of the Commonwealth's hydroelectric power. The rich forests of the taiga provide the C.I.S. with timber and fur. The

Pacific Ocean in the Far East yields one-third of the Soviet fish supply, while the Baltic and Black seas provide the balance.

Major Industries. The C.I.S. is the world's largest producer of coal. The most important centers of this production are in Ukraine, the Urals, and eastern Siberia. Petroleum is also an important part of the Russian economy. The largest oil-producing area is the Volga-Ural region, which provides over 70 percent of the C.I.S.'s oil, followed by Azerbaijan and western Siberia. Most natural gas is produced in the Volga-Ural region as well. The C.I.S. is also the world's largest producer of iron and manganese, with Ukraine serving as the major center of this industry. The production of chemicals, essential to Russian technology, is also centered in the Volga-Ural region.

Guns vs. Butter Controversy. The GNP, or gross national product (total value of goods and services produced in a country) of the nations of the C.I.S. was severely strained during the years of Soviet rule. In the former U.S.S.R., it was estimated that between 16 and 20 percent of the GNP was spent on national defense. This led to a guns vs. butter controversy, that is, a disagreement over whether more of the GNP should be spent on the military or on food production and consumer goods. For example, much of the iron produced in the C.I.S. nations was used to manufacture tanks rather than consumer goods. As a result, few consumer goods were available. This lowered the general standard of living for most Russian citizens.

WORLD ISSUES

Economic

Growth and

Development

GLOBAL
CONCEPTS

Choice

CONCEPTS
GLOBAL

Perestroika. In the 1980s the Soviet Union faced an enormous economic crisis. It had become evident that the Communist system had failed. In an effort to revive the Soviet economy, President Gorbachëv (who had taken power in 1985) began a series of economic reforms known as *Perestroika* (restructuring). Beginning with an attempt to improve the quality of products, Gorbachëv decentralized Soviet industrial and agricultural management (the Enterprise Law of 1987). Factory and farm managers were given greater control over determining both production and distribution of profits. Worker incentives, such as a pay increase for greater individual productivity, were adopted. The goal of this law was to make factories and farms independent, self-sufficient, and profitable so that they no longer needed government subsidies (money to make up losses). The Law of Cooperatives of 1987 allowed Soviet citizens to set up private businesses free of state control and keep the profits. The goal of this law was to encourage

WORLD ISSUES

Economic

Growth and

Development

more production and better products or services by beginning a system of individual enterprise. The Agricultural Reform Law of 1988 broke up the state and collective farms, replacing them with a private leasing system. Individual farmers could own and profit from their farms after paying off a long-term lease. The goal of this reform was to promote greater productivity through private ownership of land.

While the purpose of Perestroika was to "restructure" and thereby improve the Soviet economy, it faced many problems. These included:

1. The Soviet people had been used to a state-dependency system that provided security and undemanding work, not individual initiative and productivity.

2. Consumers expected immediate improvements (greater availability of goods and services), while Perestroika needed time in order to be effective.

3. Opposition by conservatives, especially government officials and party members who had benefited from the Communist system, made it difficult to carry out the reforms.

Economic Reforms in the Post-Soviet Period

With the collapse of the Soviet regime in 1991, the economic controversy started to resolve itself, as the newly independent nations began reforms to develop capitalist economies. However, the political instability and ethnic/religious conflicts in many regions of the C.I.S. threaten these changes as well as attempts to establish democratic governments. A further problem faced by the nations of the C.I.S. was to dismantle the huge Soviet nuclear and military arsenals and reduce the armed forces.

REVIEW QUESTIONS

Multiple Choice. Select the letter of the answer that correctly completes the statement.

1. Originally called the breadbasket of Russia, the greatest agricultural output has always come from
   A. Belarussia
   B. Georgia
   C. Siberia
   D. Ukraine

2. The Soviet government's policy of forcing farmers to work on state farms was known as
   A. collectivization
   B. cooperatives
   C. Russification
   D. Perestroika

3. The guns vs. butter controversy was a disagreement over
   A. the quality of arms and food production
   B. whether or not to nationalize heavy and light industries
   C. whether or not to decentralize industry
   D. the amount of the GNP spent on arms as opposed to consumer goods

4. In 1986 Mikhail Gorbachëv began a series of reforms designed to restructure the Soviet economy. It was known as
   A. Glastnost
   B. Perestroika
   C. N.E.P.
   D. collectivization

5. Both the Enterprise Law of 1987 and the Law of Cooperatives are examples of
   A. capitalist incentives
   B. Marxist economic principles
   C. a command economy
   D. economic nationalism

Essay

Why did Perestroika fail to solve the U.S.S.R.'s economic problems?

A. Describe two economic problems the Communists faced after taking power in 1917.

B. To what extent did Communist economic principles create obstacles in trying to solve these problems?

C. How did Gorbachëv's reforms attempt to resolve these problems? Why were they unsuccessful?

III. HUMAN AND CULTURAL GEOGRAPHY OF THE C.I.S.

Demography

The population of the C.I.S. is approximately 283 million, slightly more than that of the United States. However, when one considers that Russia is two and one-half times the size of the United States, it is really underpopulated. In fact, the Commonwealth's population density is only 33 people per square mile, compared with 68 people per square mile in the United States and over 288 people per square mile in China. Yet, most of the population is located in European Russia and Ukraine. The small populations in Siberia, the taiga, the Central Asian nations, and the countries of the Caucasus have grown only slightly in the present century. Most of this increase is due to industrialization of these areas.

Ethnic Groups, Languages, and Religion

There are many ethnic groups in the C.I.S. and its surrounding regions. (The Baltic nations and Georgia, which are not presently C.I.S. members, are included because of their historical importance as part of both the Russian Empire and the U.S.S.R.) The largest of these groups, the Great Russians, Ukrainians, and Belarussians (White Russians), share a common culture and religious heritage. They also have common

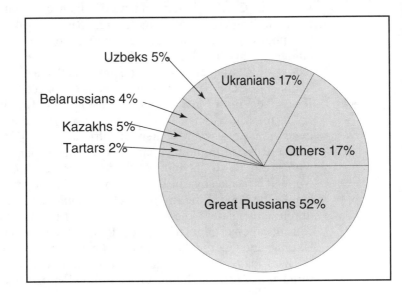

linguistic roots in Slavonic, the ancient language of the Slavic Eastern Orthodox churches. The Georgians, while distinct in their cultural and linguistic origins, also share the Orthodox Christian faith. The Armenians, who share a cultural and linguistic heritage with the Georgians, come from an eastern Anatolian nation that was forced into Russia by Turkish aggression between 1915 and 1923. The Armenians are also Eastern Orthodox Christians, but have their own church that differs slightly in ritual and practice. The Azerbaijanis, Turkmen, Uzbeks, and Kazahks are descended from the Turkish invaders of Russia in the Middle Ages. The Tartars are descendants of the Mongols, who ruled Russia from 1237 to 1450. Among the peoples of the Baltic region, the Latvians and Lithuanians share a common linguistic, cultural, and religious heritage, while the Estonians speak a language closely related to Finnish and Hungarian.

The Orthodox Church

GLOBAL
CONCEPTS

Culture

CONCEPTS
GLOBAL

Christianity came to Eastern Europe and Russia from the Byzantine Empire. It played an essential role in the development of the Russian language, culture, art, and architecture.

In 988 Prince Vladimir of Kiev adopted Eastern Orthodox Christianity and had the people of Ukraine, Russia, and Belarussia baptized along with him. The Russian Orthodox church dominated the culture of Russia until the 18th century. It continued to play a major role in the life of most Russians until the Communist Revolution in 1917. The Russian language is written in Cyrillic letters and was influenced greatly by the Slavonic language used by the church. Russian folk music and polyphony (using four-part harmony) were incorporated into church hymns. The building of churches became the chief objective of Russian architects, who developed a distinctive onion dome style. The painting of holy pictures, or icons, depicting Jesus, the Virgin Mary, and the saints, became Russia's major art form. Monasticism became very popular in Russia, and large monasteries were centers of spirituality and pilgrimages.

GLOBAL
CONCEPTS

Identity

CONCEPTS
GLOBAL

The Russian Orthodox church is an independent institution with strong ties to the other Orthodox churches throughout the world. It is headed by a bishop known as the Patriarch of Moscow. Unlike the Pope of the Roman Catholic church, who is supreme in religious matters, the patriarch is one of many bishops who consult together regularly to decide important church matters. Ukraine and Georgia have their own patriarchs as well.

Historically, the Russian Orthodox church was often pressured and controlled by the czars. Following the Russian Revolution of 1917, it was subjected to violent persecution by the Soviet government. In the Soviet regime's last years, the hostility of Communist authorities to the church lessened and a small measure of religious freedom was allowed. Despite years of great persecution, many Russians remained faithful. While precise figures are difficult to obtain, the majority of Russians, Ukrainians, Belarussians, and Georgians remained Orthodox Christians.

Other Religions in Russia

The Armenians, who are also Eastern Christians, have their own church that differs slightly in ritual and practice. The majority of Roman Catholics in Russia are Uniates, or Eastern Rite Catholics (Orthodox in ritual but officially under the authority of the Pope). Most Uniates are located in Ukraine. Otherwise, Lithuania has the only large Roman Catholic population. The other Baltic states, Estonia and Latvia, are primarily Lutheran (Protestant). The Azerbaijanis, Turkmen, Uzbeks, Kazakhs, Tartars, and other peoples of Turkish or Mongol origin are mainly Muslims. Finally, there is a sizable minority of Jews living in the C.I.S.

Cultural Achievements

Russia's culture had two great influences—Byzantium and Western Europe. From the 10th to the 17th centuries, the Byzantine Empire, and consequently the Orthodox church, were the main influences on Russian art, architecture, music, and literature. Religion played the key role in the early development of these forms. Most art was religious, usually in the form of icons, while Russian architects distinguished themselves building churches. (See "The Orthodox Church" on previous page.) Russian composers were usually monks who devoted themselves to writing church hymns, often based on traditional folk music. The ban on the use of musical instruments by the Orthodox church encouraged the development of a cappella (without instrumental accompaniment) choirs. Literature written in Slavonic, the language of the church, consisted for the most part of chronicles (narratives that combined history and legend) and hagiography (the lives of saints). As with music, literature was also written almost exclusively by monks.

At the beginning of the 18th century, Czar Peter the Great carried out a policy of Westernization that drastically changed the direction of Russian culture. Combining traditional Russian themes while imitating Western European styles, uniquely Russian schools of art, architecture, music, and literature developed.

Artists painted portraits and landscape series as well as icons, while architects created lavish palaces and churches that combined the best of Western European and Russian styles. It was, however, in music and literature that the Russians most distinguished themselves.

Russia's best-known composers in the Czarist period were Aleksandr Borodin (1833–1887), Modest Moussorgskii (1839–1881), Piotr Illich Tchaikovskii (1840–1893), and Nikolai Rimskii-Korsakov (1844–1908). These musical giants composed operas, choral works, symphonies, concertos, and chamber music that featured traditional Russian melodies. This tradition was continued in the Soviet period by composers such as Sergei Prokofiev (1891–1953), Dimitrii Shostakovich (1906–1975), and Aram Kachaturian (1903–1978). Certain composers, such as Sergei Rachmaninov (1873–1943) and Igor Stravinskii (1882–1971), forced into exile by the Russian Revolution in 1917, continued to create music and win acclaim for their work.

Russia's literary giants also brought a unique perspective to their work. These include: Aleksandr Pushkin (1799–1837), best known for his poetry and short stories; Nikolai Gogol

Count Lev Tolstoy

(1809–1852), noted for his short stories and the novel *Dead Souls* (which criticized serfdom); Ivan Turgenev (1818–1883), famous for his novels, particularly *Fathers and Sons*; Theodor Dostoievskii (1821–1881), whose psychological novels *Crime and Punishment* and *The Brothers Karamazov* won him worldwide acclaim; Count Lev Tolstoy (1828–1910), author of the masterpiece novels *Anna Karenina* and *War and Peace*; and Anton Chekhov (1860–1904), whose plays (*The Cherry Orchard*, *The Seagull*, *The Three Sisters*) have become world theater classics. In the Soviet period, most distinguished writers were dissidents, often punished for their work. One of the most famous, Boris Pasternak (1890–1960), was forced by the government to reject the Nobel Prize in Literature for his novel *Doctor Zhivago*. Another is Aleksandr Solzhenitsyn (1918–), whose stories ("One Day in the Life of Ivan Denisovich"), novels (*Cancer Ward*), and history of the Stalinist concentration camps (*The Gulag Archipelago*) brought him exile. However, as times and attitudes have changed, Solzhenitsyn was able to return to live in Russia in 1994.

REVIEW QUESTIONS

Multiple Choice. Select the letter of the answer that correctly completes the statement.

1. Most of the population in the C.I.S. lives in
   A. Central Asia
   B. European Russia and Ukraine
   C. Siberia
   D. the Far East

2. The largest ethnic group in the C.I.S. is the
   A. Kazakhs
   B. Georgians
   C. Slavs
   D. Armenians

3. In 988 Russia adopted
   A. Eastern Orthodox Christianity and medieval Latin culture
   B. Roman Catholicism and medieval Latin culture
   C. Eastern Orthodox Christianity and Byzantine culture
   D. Roman Catholicism and Byzantine culture

4. The spiritual leader of the Russian Orthodox church is the
   A. Patriarch of Constantinople
   B. Pope of Rome
   C. Patriarch of Kiev
   D. Patriarch of Moscow

5. Russia's most notable cultural achievements were in
   A. art and architecture
   B. literature and art
   C. music and art
   D. literature and music

6. Select the correct match of author and work.
   A. Nikolai Gogol—   *War and Peace*
   B. Count Lev Tolstoy—   *Dead Souls*
   C. Theodor Dostoievskii—   *The Brothers Karamazov*
   D. Aleksandr Solzhenitsyn—   *Father and Sons*

7. Russia's architecture is characterized by the
   A. baroque style
   B. basilica style
   C. onion dome style
   D. classical style

ESSAY

Religion played a major role in the development of Russia.

A. Discuss the role of religion in the creation of the Russian language, literature, art, and architecture. Give one example of each.
B. To what extent did religion hold various ethnic groups and nationalities together in the Russian Empire? Show two ways it unified and two ways it divided them.
C. In what ways did the church reinforce the social order through its teachings, institutions, and administrations?

IV. HISTORY AND POLITICAL GEOGRAPHY OF THE C.I.S.

Early Rus' (862–879)

The earliest settlers in Russia were Slavic tribes who migrated there between 600 and 700. These settlers depended on trade (furs, beeswax, and honey) rather than agriculture, and their settlements grew from towns into prosperous cities. These cities depended upon the Vikings (whom the Slavs called Varangians) to protect the trade routes. The Varangians soon became a ruling class, intermarrying with the Slavs, founding both a royal dynasty known as the House of Rurik and a new state called Rus'.

The Kievan State (879–1237)

By 879 the center of trade (and therefore power) in the state of Rus' had become the city of Kiev in Ukraine. Kiev's location in the most fertile region of Rus', with excellent river transportation to encourage trade, made it wealthy and powerful. The Kievan princes led a loose federation of Russian cities for mutual protection and the expansion of trade. Kiev's prosperity and prominence brought it into a close relationship with the Byzantine Empire. In 988 the Kievan Prince Vladimir was converted to Orthodox Christianity, bringing both Kiev and all Rus' with him. With the adoption of Byzantine religion came new political and social ideas. New artistic and cultural forms were also introduced. (See "The Orthodox Church" on page 412.) In addition, this brought Rus' into the political orbit of Byzantium and its Eastern European allies.

GLOBAL
CONCEPTS

Power

CONCEPTS
GLOBAL

The Mongol Period (1237–1450)

In 1237 Kievan Russia was invaded by Mongol armies under the leadership of Batu Khan, a grandson of Genghis Khan. (See Part IV of China in Unit Three.) Called Tartars by the Russians, these nomadic warriors on horseback conquered Russia and ruled it for more than 200 years. The Khanate of the Golden Horde, as the Mongol princes who ruled Russia were called, exercised control from their capital city of Sarai, located in the steppes. Mongol rule was indirect and usually consisted of collecting tribute from the local inhabitants. Frequently, local Russian princes served as representatives for the Mongol government and ruled their principalities with little or no interference. Only Novgorod, city of the legendary Rurik, was able to repulse the Mongols (as well as Swedes and Teuton Knights—

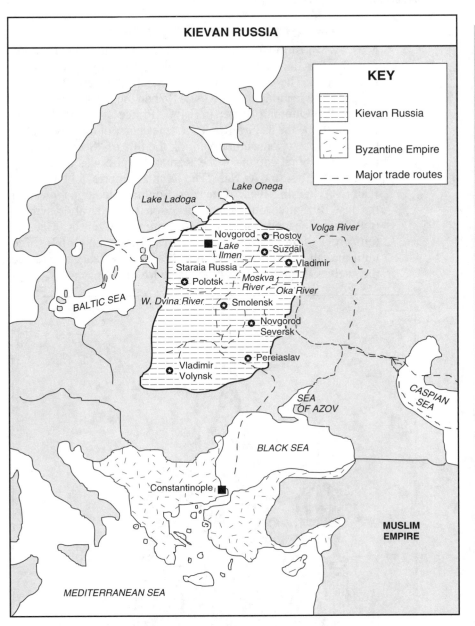

KIEVAN RUSSIA

KEY

Kievan Russia

Byzantine Empire

– – – Major trade routes

Lake Onega

Lake Ladoga

Volga River

Novgorod · Rostov
Lake Ilmen · Suzdal
Staraia Russia · Vladimir
Moskva River
Polotsk · Oka River
BALTIC SEA W. Dvina River · Smolensk

Novgorod Seversk

Pereiaslav

Vladimir Volynsk

SEA OF AZOV

CASPIAN SEA

BLACK SEA

Constantinople

MUSLIM EMPIRE

MEDITERRANEAN SEA

GLOBAL
CONCEPTS

Political Systems

CONCEPTS
GLOBAL

German crusaders—who attacked from 1240 to 1242) and remain free of Mongol rule. Mongol domination of Russia did
not last, as attacks by armies in Asia and the uprisings of Russian princes soon overextended Mongol military forces. By
1395 every major Mongol city, including Sarai, had been destroyed. Between 1450 and 1480 the last remains of Mongol
rule were wiped out by the princes of Moscow.

The Rise of Moscow (1450–1685)

Moscow's position as the headquarters of the Russian Orthodox church after the fall of Kiev contributed greatly to its rise to prominence. The support of the patriarch enhanced Moscow's image as the leading city of Russia. When the Byzantine Empire fell to the Ottoman Turks in 1453, Prince Ivan III declared Moscow to be the "Third Rome," or the center of the Eastern Orthodox church (Constantinople took the title of "Second Rome" after the original capital of the Roman Empire was overrun by Germanic tribes in 476. See "The Roman Empire" in Part IV of Unit Six). In 1462 Ivan III married Sophia Paleologos, niece of the last Byzantine emperor, and adopted her family's symbol (the double-headed eagle), declaring himself Czar, or "Caesar" (emperor), of all the Russias. From Ivan III's reign (1462–1505) until the fall of the monarchy in 1917, Russia's czars considered themselves the defenders of the Orthodox church.

Church in the Kremlin

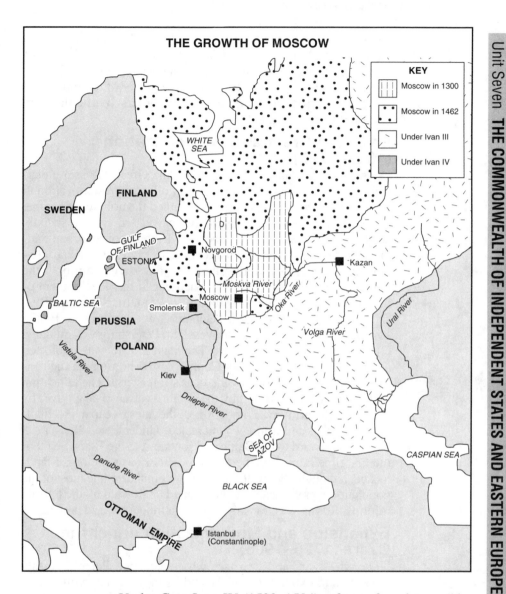

THE GROWTH OF MOSCOW

KEY

- |||| Moscow in 1300
- ·.·. Moscow in 1462
- Under Ivan III
- Under Ivan IV

WHITE SEA

FINLAND

SWEDEN

GULF OF FINLAND

ESTONIA

BALTIC SEA

PRUSSIA

POLAND

Vistula River

Novgorod

Moskva River

Moscow

Smolensk

Oka River

Kazan

Ural River

Volga River

Kiev

Dnieper River

SEA OF AZOV

CASPIAN SEA

Danube River

BLACK SEA

OTTOMAN EMPIRE

Istanbul (Constantinople)

GLOBAL
CONCEPTS

Power

CONCEPTS
GLOBAL

Under Czar Ivan IV (1533–1584), often referred to as "the Terrible," Russia's government became centralized. Often using brutal and ruthless force, Ivan ended the independent authority of local princes and boyars (nobles), making the aristocracy subservient to an autocratic central monarchy. He also created a new "service nobility" that was loyal only to the czar. By the year of his death, Ivan had extended Moscow's control over most of Russian land formerly controlled by the Mongols.

Ivan's weak successor, Theodor, died without an heir in 1598, ending the House of Rurik and beginning a period of anarchy known as the "Time of Troubles." This ended in 1613 with the selection by the Zemskii Sobor (Council of Nobles) of a new czar, Mikhail Romanov, and the establishment of a new dynasty. Under the early Romanovs the power of the monarchy grew even stronger, while Russia's borders (particularly in Ukraine) were expanded.

Peter the Great and Westernization (1685–1725)

Under Peter I, usually referred to as "the Great," Russia underwent important changes. Following a policy of Westernization in order to modernize his nation, Peter forced the nobility and upper classes to imitate their counterparts in Western Europe socially and culturally. A Western European-style bourgeoisie (urban middle class) was also created. An enormous civil service and government bureaucracy were established that drew from both the upper and middle classes. Peter encouraged the development of new industries and the importation of Westerners to train Russians. A new capital city, St. Petersburg, was built on the Baltic. Known as the "Window to the West," St. Petersburg was modeled after Western European cities. The Patriarchate was abolished and replaced with the Synod (Council) of Bishops under the control of a Procurator (one of the czar's ministers). The education system, once administered by the church, was also taken over by the state. The army was modernized, the latest weapons technology imported, and a navy was created. Under Peter, Russia expanded westward to the Baltic and southeast to the Black Sea. For the first time in history, the nation of Russia was no longer landlocked, although both water routes were limited. While most of the population were peasants and remained unaffected by the Petrine reforms, Russia was transformed into a modern world power.

GLOBAL CONCEPTS

Change

CONCEPTS GLOBAL

Expansion and Modernization under the Czars (1725–1905)

Under the czars and czaritsas who succeeded Peter I, Russia continued to expand its empire and its involvement with Western Europe. During the reign of Catherine II (1762–1796), usually referred to as "the Great," Russia regained the parts of Ukraine and Belarussia lost under the last Rurik czars, as well as Lithuania. In the southeast, the last of the Tartar tribes were defeated, thus gaining the entire Crimea and much of the northern coast of the Black Sea at the expense of the Ottoman Turks. This began a traditional policy that was pursued by the Soviet government as well as the later czars—to gain Constantinople (modern-day Istanbul) and the straits that connect the Black Sea with the Aegean and the Mediterranean (the Dardanelles)

GLOBAL CONCEPTS

Empathy

CONCEPTS GLOBAL

in order to have access to major trade routes. In addition, much of Siberia was explored and settled by Russians.

Czar Alexander I (1801–1825) was credited as the monarch who defeated Napoleon. This victory was due to the scorched earth policy (retreating and burning anything that could not be taken rather than leaving it for the enemy) that the Russians adopted in response to Napoleon's invasion. A lack of supplies and the severely cold winter devastated the French army. Thousands died during the chaotic retreat. (See "The Rise and Fall of Napoleon" in Part IV of Unit Six.) At the Congress of Vienna, Russia acquired most of Poland. (See the "Metternich Age and the Growth of Nationalism" in Part IV of Unit Six.) Alexander also gained Finland from Sweden in 1809.

Under the strong autocratic rule of Nikolai or Nicholas I (1825–1855), Russia was unsuccessful in further expansion. Greatly shaken by the Decembrist Revolt of 1825 (in which officers favoring democratic reforms tried to overthrow Nicholas), the czar fought any movement for change. Fearing that reform would undermine his authority, Nicholas followed repressive policies at home and abroad (he earned the title policeman of Europe). Yet, Russia's defeat in the Crimean War (1854–1856) revealed the need for both reform and modernization.

WORLD ISSUES

War
and
Peace

Czar Nicholas I

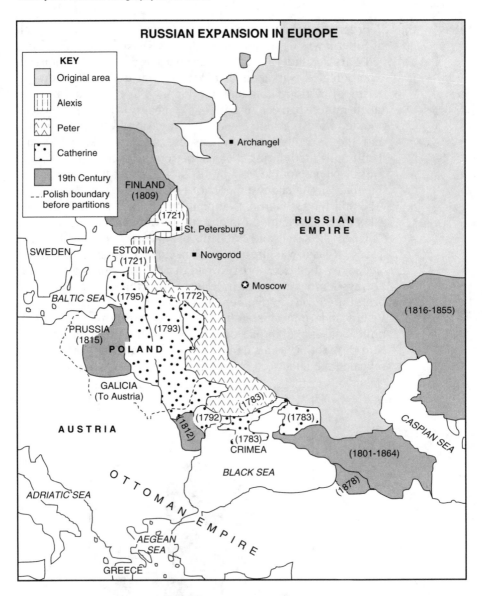

RUSSIAN EXPANSION IN EUROPE

KEY

- Original area
- Alexis
- Peter
- Catherine
- 19th Century
- - - Polish boundary before partitions

Archangel

FINLAND (1809)

(1721)

St. Petersburg

RUSSIAN EMPIRE

SWEDEN

ESTONIA (1721)

Novgorod

BALTIC SEA (1795)

(1772)

Moscow

(1816-1855)

PRUSSIA (1815)

(1793)

POLAND

GALICIA (To Austria)

(1783)

AUSTRIA

(1812)

(1792)

(1783)

CASPIAN SEA

(1783) CRIMEA

(1801-1864)

BLACK SEA

(1878)

ADRIATIC SEA

OTTOMAN EMPIRE

AEGEAN SEA

GREECE

GLOBAL CONCEPTS

Human Rights

CONCEPTS GLOBAL

Alexander II (1855–1881), the son of Nicholas I, made many of the necessary changes that his father would not. Known as the Czar Liberator, Alexander ended the institution of serfdom (peasants were bound to the land they farmed and were therefore controlled by the landowner), which held back the expansion of Russian agriculture and promoted many abuses and social evils. Industrialization was also started in order to make Russia competitive with other European nations. Finally, Alexander instituted reforms in government, education, and the military that ended many abuses and cruelties and modernized the Russian system. Despite the many changes made by Alexander II, new problems were created by the reforms themselves.

1. The liberation of the serfs created many small farmers who could not pay off their debts. This resulted in mass foreclosures and enormous migrations of unskilled workers to the cities.

2. The abundance of unskilled labor gave factory owners the opportunity to exploit (take advantage of) the workers, or proletariat.

3. Widespread exploitation of workers resulted in poverty, slums, and unsafe working conditions in Russian cities and industrial centers.

4. The exploited workers became strong supporters of revolutionary ideas and parties, particularly the Socialists, Communists, and Anarchists. The assassination of Alexander II in 1881 resulted in the end of reform and a renewal of repression.

Czar Alexander II

Alexander III (1881–1894) reacted to his father's murder by enforcing strict control over his subjects. Reinstituting a policy of Russification (forcing Russian language, culture, and religion on all peoples in the Russian Empire), Alexander created resentment and revolutionary feelings.

GLOBAL
CONCEPTS
Choice
CONCEPTS
GLOBAL

GLOBAL
CONCEPTS
Justice
CONCEPTS
GLOBAL

The Russian Revolution (1905–1917)

During the reign of Nicholas II (1894–1917), Russia made its greatest strides toward reform, modernization, and, ironically, revolution. From 1894 to 1905, Nicholas followed his father's (Alexander III) policies in opposing reform. Despite great gains made in the industrialization program under the direction of Finance Minister Sergei Witte, the conditions in urban slums and factories were still terrible. After the embarrassing defeat in the Russo-Japanese War (1904–1905) and the massacre of peaceful demonstraters in St. Petersburg in January of 1905, known as *Bloody Sunday*, uprisings broke out in every major Russian city and industrial center. Known as the 1905 Revolution, this series of revolts frightened the government into mak-

Czar Nicholas II

ing reforms, most notably the creation of the *Duma*, or parliament. While Russia technically became a constitutional democracy, the Duma was little more than an advisory body that could be dissolved by the czar at will.

In 1906 the monarchy instituted its own reforms in order to restore public confidence. Under the guidance of Prime Minister Peter Stolypin, a program of industrial expansion, foreign investment, and land reform (which made millions of peasants private landowners) was instituted. The Stolypin Reforms helped to overcome revolutionary feelings and restored a strong base of support for the monarchy, especially in the countryside.

In 1914 Russia entered World War I (1914–1918), a conflict that it was neither militarily nor economically ready to fight. For three years the Russians suffered defeats by the technologically superior German forces. (See "World War I" in Part IV of Unit Six.) Enormous casualties and government inefficiency led to widespread dissatisfaction with the conduct of the war. Scandal within the royal family also hurt the prestige of the monarchy. Czaritsa Aleksandra had fallen under the influence of a fraudulent "holy man," Grigory Efimovich Rasputin, who was able to control the Czarevitch (Prince) Alexis' hemophilia (probably through hypnosis).

While the czar was away at the front running the war, Rasputin exercised a destructive domination over the German-born czaritsa, who was already suspected by many of being a spy. His interference produced corruption and even greater inefficiency. By February 1917, food shortages and an outbreak of strikes and riots led to the collapse of the czar's authority in St. Petersburg and other cities. Nicholas II was forced to abdicate, and a provisional (temporary) democratic government was formed by the Duma, headed first by Prince Georgii L'vov and later by Aleksandr Kerenskii.

GLOBAL
CONCEPTS

Change

CONCEPTS
GLOBAL

The Provisional Government attempted to make Russia a democracy by instituting political reforms. By October of 1917, however, the Provisional Government had been overthrown by force and the Bolshevik (Communist) party had taken power. There were a number of reasons for this:

1. Kerenskii's decision to continue fighting the war was very unpopular.

2. Russia did not have a democratic tradition. Most of the Provisional Government's goals were not understood and were irrelevant to the majority of the population.

3. The war continued to create shortages and strain the economy. Conditions in the cities did not improve, and unrest began again.

4. The Bolsheviks capitalized on the unpopularity of the war. They undermined support for the Provisional Government through antiwar propaganda.

5. The monarchy had held the Russian Empire together. With the traditional symbol of unity (the czar) gone, the Provisional Government could provide no equivalent institution.

6. Kerenskii was experimenting with democracy in a nation with no democratic heritage during a war, a time when most democracies temporarily suspend civil liberties.

7. The war wasted the best troops the Provisional Government had. The regiments that remained to protect the Provisional Government were poorly trained and unreliable.

8. The Bolshevik leader Lenin promised "bread, peace, and land" as well as a "workers' state," promises that were better understood than the democratic principles put forth by the Provisional Government.

9. The Bolsheviks influenced the soviets, or local committees, that represented workers, soldiers, and farmers. Closely linked throughout Russia, they became influential, especially in the cities.

Lenin (1917–1924)

Born Vladimir Illich Ulianov, Lenin founded the Bolshevik, or "Majority," party at a 1903 Socialist Party Conference in London. While the Bolsheviks were never a majority, they were "professional revolutionaries" who ruthlessly pursued power, using any means necessary in order to succeed. The other Russian Socialists, the Mensheviks, or "Minority," favored gradual, peaceful change, without the violence and terror advocated by the Bolsheviks.

When the Bolsheviks seized power in 1917, Lenin immediately made peace with Germany and took Russia out of the war. Giving away sizable parts of Russia in a peace agreement (Treaty of Brest-Litovsk) and having no widespread support, the Bolsheviks soon faced strong opposition throughout Russia. A civil war followed (1918–1921) in which the Bolsheviks, or Reds, fought the combined forces of anti-Bolshevik groups, or Whites. The dependence of the White army on foreign nations for military supplies as well as the disunity among its leadership eventually led to a Bolshevik victory.

Once the Bolsheviks were firmly in power, Lenin realized that Russia was not ready to become a Communist state. In the new political order, the Communist party ran Soviet Russia until such time as society could be transformed into a pure Communist state. The central government planned and controlled all aspects of political, social, and economic life through a series of party organs. (See chart on the Soviet government.)

WORLD ISSUES

Determination of Political and Economic Systems

Facing great opposition, especially from the peasants, Lenin tried to ease the population into Communism by instituting the N.E.P. (New Economic Program) in 1921. This policy combined features of both capitalism and socialism by allowing private enterprise on a small scale while the state retained control of large industries. Under the N.E.P. (1921– 1928), the Soviet economy experienced only limited growth.

When Lenin died in 1924, a struggle for power developed between Leon Trotskii, Lenin's chosen successor, and Joseph

Dzhugashvili, known as Stalin ("man of steel"), who was Communist Party Secretary. By 1925 Stalin had gained control and removed Trotskii from all official positions. In 1929 Trotskii was deported as Stalin began to remove all possible opposition and rivals (Trotskii was assassinated by Stalin's agents in Mexico in 1937).

Stalin (1925–1953)

Stalin's rule proved to be one of the most brutal and ruthless dictatorships in modern history. From his consolidation of

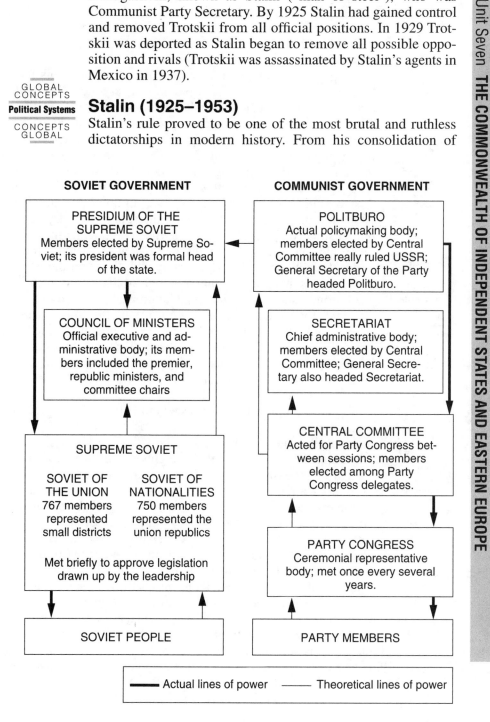

SOVIET GOVERNMENT

COMMUNIST GOVERNMENT

PRESIDIUM OF THE SUPREME SOVIET
Members elected by Supreme Soviet; its president was formal head of the state.

POLITBURO
Actual policymaking body; members elected by Central Committee really ruled USSR; General Secretary of the Party headed Politburo.

COUNCIL OF MINISTERS
Official executive and administrative body; its members included the premier, republic ministers, and committee chairs

SECRETARIAT
Chief administrative body; members elected by Central Committee; General Secretary also headed Secretariat.

CENTRAL COMMITTEE
Acted for Party Congress between sessions; members elected among Party Congress delegates.

SUPREME SOVIET

SOVIET OF THE UNION
767 members represented small districts

SOVIET OF NATIONALITIES
750 members represented the union republics

Met briefly to approve legislation drawn up by the leadership

PARTY CONGRESS
Ceremonial representative body; met once every several years.

SOVIET PEOPLE

PARTY MEMBERS

—— Actual lines of power —— Theoretical lines of power

complete power in 1929 until his death in 1953, he was responsible for millions of deaths, starting with the elimination of all possible rivals. Stalin created his own secret police, which spied on, arrested, tortured, and executed party members, government officials, artists, writers, clergy, workers, and peasants he suspected of not supporting his policies. In time, his fears became paranoia (fear and suspicion of everyone, often without cause), and even close friends and relatives were killed. From 1935 to 1936 Stalin conducted a series of show trials (hearings where the verdicts were decided in advance) known as the purges, in which hundreds of leading Communists were arrested, forced to confess to crimes they had never committed, and executed.

In 1928, dissatisfied with the slow growth rate of Soviet industry, Stalin abandoned Lenin's N.E.P. in favor of centralized economic planning. Goals for agriculture and industry (often unrealistically high), as well as the means for achieving them, were laid out in a series of Five-Year Plans. These were designed to make the U.S.S.R. catch up with the other industrialized nations by emphasizing the industrial development of steel, iron, coal, and oil. The population was expected to sacrifice and do without consumer goods until the Soviet Union could reach the level of industrial development attained by capitalist nations. Opposition to these plans was quickly and brutally put down. In order to pay for the importation of the technology needed to institute the Five-Year Plans, farms were collectivized. (See Part I of this section.)

To end the opposition of peasants to collectivization, Stalin began a series of genocides (mass killings) from 1932 to 1937, claiming that he was eliminating the *kulaks* (wealthy peasants who supposedly exploited their neighbors). In fact, few of the 14.5 million peasants who died by execution, perished in Siberian labor camps, or starved in Stalin's man-made famine in Ukraine (1932–1933) were kulaks. While outright opposition was finally crushed by these genocides, the peasants did not fully cooperate, and the collectivization program failed to achieve its goal. When World War II interrupted the Third Five-Year Plan in 1941, only heavy industry had made any progress. The loss of life and human suffering that this modest gain had cost was enormous. It is no wonder that many, especially Ukrainians, first saw the invading German armies as liberators.

When Nazi Germany invaded the U.S.S.R. in 1941, the population was forced once again to resort to the scorched earth policy used so effectively against Napoleon. By 1944 overextension of supply lines, the harsh Russian climate, and stiff military resistance by the Russians, despite heavy losses, had

GLOBAL CONCEPTS
Human Rights
CONCEPTS GLOBAL

GLOBAL CONCEPTS
Justice
CONCEPTS GLOBAL

WORLD ISSUES

Economic
Growth and
Development

WORLD ISSUES

Hunger
and
Poverty

WORLD ISSUES

War
and
Peace

worn down the German forces. By 1945 the Soviet army had pushed the Nazis out of Russia and Eastern Europe into Germany and occupied the eastern portion of that nation. Despite an agreement made with the Allies earlier that year (the Yalta Conference) that the U.S.S.R. would only occupy Eastern Europe temporarily, Soviet forces remained. Instead of holding free elections for self-determination in each Eastern European nation, Stalin placed puppet Communist governments throughout Eastern Europe. These countries became satellites, controlled

SOVIET TERRITORIAL GAINS, 1939–1945

KEY

U.S.S.R., 1939

Annexed 1939–1945

by the Soviet government. By Stalin's death in 1953, Eastern and Western Europe were divided by ideological differences and mutual fear. This last legacy of Stalin became known as the Iron Curtain.

The Cold War (1953–1990)

As a result of the division of Europe, a cold war (political, economic, and diplomatic conflict without open military conflict) developed. In 1949 the countries of Western Europe and the United States formed a military alliance, NATO (North Atlantic

THE DIVISION OF EUROPE

KEY

NATO Countries

Other NATO members include: Canada, Iceland, and the United States

Warsaw Pact Countries

Neutral Countries

0   200   400

Treaty Organization), in response to Stalin's takeover of Eastern Europe and his unsuccessful attempts to install Communist governments in Greece, Turkey, and Iran. This policy, called containment (to limit the spread of Communism to areas where it already existed), was answered by the U.S.S.R. with the creation of the Warsaw Pact, an alliance of the Soviet Union and the Eastern Bloc or Communist satellite countries. The military buildup that resulted from the cold war put an even greater strain on the Soviet economy, which was still suffering from the devastation of World War II. The U.S.S.R.'s new superpower status was expensive to maintain, and Soviet consumers bore the burden.

With the death of Stalin, there was a period of readjustment from the fear and suffering the Soviet dictator's rule had brought. This Great Thaw from Stalinism (1953–1958) allowed some freedom of political and cultural expression (mostly denouncing Stalin). However, this was short-lived. When Nikita Khrushchëv (1958–1964) took power as first secretary and premier, these freedoms ended. Khrushchëv attempted to increase industrial and agricultural production through a series of plans, particularly productivity incentives and an expansion of agricultural development into thinly populated areas (virgin lands program). Khrushchëv's policies failed due to the inefficiency of the bureaucratic Soviet system, the lack of incentives to produce in the factories, and the severe forces of nature in Russia. Many conservatives from the Stalinist period resented Khrushchëv. They used his setback in the Cuban missile crisis and the failures of his economic reforms to oust him from power in 1964.

Khrushchëv was succeeded by Leonid Brezhnev (1964–1982), who, unlike Stalin or Khrushchëv, did not have complete power and was answerable to top Communist party officials. Despite the great need for change that had prompted Khrushchëv's programs, Brezhnev feared that reform would undermine the authority of the Communist party. The policy of concentrating on heavy industry was therefore continued, except for one unsuccessful experiment to expand consumer goods production in the Ninth Five-Year Plan (1971–1975). By 1972 the antagonism between the Soviet Union and Communist China and the fear produced by improved relations between China and the United States forced Brezhnev to adopt a policy of Détente (understanding) with the United States and Western Europe. This first thaw in the cold war also resulted in the first of two SALT (Strategic Arms Limitation Talks) agreements, in which both NATO and the Warsaw Pact nations agreed to restrict the development of antiballistic missile systems. These were followed by START (Strategic Arms Reduction Talks) in the

WORLD ISSUES

Economic

Growth and

Development

GLOBAL
CONCEPTS

Choice

CONCEPTS
GLOBAL

Gorbachëv era. Despite Détente, Brezhnev continued to suppress dissent and oppose any domestic reform.

Gorbachëv (1985–1991)

After the brief period of rule by Yurii Andropov (1982–1984) and Konstantin Chernenko (1984–1985), Mikhail Gorbachëv became general secretary of the Communist party. He quickly consolidated his power by removing the older, more conservative members of the U.S.S.R.'s ruling Politboro (chief political committee of the Communist party) and replacing them with younger reformers like himself. The stagnation of the Soviet economy had reached a crisis, and Gorbachëv proposed sweeping economic reforms. (See "Perestroika" in the Economic Geography section of this unit.) Gorbachëv also adopted a policy of glasnost (openness), which was aimed at destroying the secrecy and suspicion of Soviet life. Public criticism and suggestions about national problems were encouraged as well as the expression of opposing ideas, which had previously been censored. Literature, films, music, and art that had been banned were now reinstated as cultural life was given new freedoms. As the Russian Orthodox church celebrated its millennium (1,000-year anniversary), Gorbachëv lifted many of the restrictions on Orthodox Christianity and the practice of religion in general.

GLOBAL CONCEPTS

Change

CONCEPTS GLOBAL

From 1988 to 1989, Gorbachëv reorganized the entire Soviet political system. Communist party control over the government was reduced, a popularly elected assembly (the Congress of People's Deputies) was established, which was a structure for a multiparty system, and a presidency with control over domestic and foreign affairs was created. In March 1989 the U.S.S.R. held its first elections in which many non-Communist party candidates were elected. Yet the majority of representatives were Communists who ran unopposed. When the Congress first met in June, it elected a smaller body (the Supreme Soviet) to deal with daily legislation. It also elected Mikhail Gorbachëv as the U.S.S.R.'s first (and only) president.

GLOBAL CONCEPTS

Political Systems

CONCEPTS GLOBAL

Gorbachëv also greatly improved relations between the U.S.S.R. and the West. In 1987 the U.S.S.R. and the United States agreed to the I.N.F. (Intermediate-Range Nuclear Forces) Treaty, in which both sides would destroy two classes of nuclear weapons. He also implemented the Gorbachëv Doctrine, a policy of noninterference in Eastern Europe. By the autumn of 1988, he began to reduce the number of Soviet troops in some of the satellite nations, which helped to bring about the collapse of the Communist regimes in those countries a year later (see Part IV of the Eastern Europe section of this unit).

The Decline and Collapse of the Soviet Regime (1989–1991)

By 1989 Gorbachëv began to retreat from his reforms. The election to the Congress of People's Deputies of dissidents, such as the prominent scientist Andrei Sakharov, and officials who were openly critical of the regime, such as the President of the Russian Republic Boris Yeltsin, was seen by Gorbachëv as a threat to the survival of the Soviet system. Yeltsin had risen to power by promoting Russian nationalism and downplaying the Soviet Union. This gave the population a new pride in their nation and directed their anger at the Soviet government. Gorbachëv, who never understood this, continued to support dominance by the Communist party. In so doing, he became as unpopular as the system he defended. By 1991 he had backed down from his reforms and appointed conservative Communists to important government positions.

With Gorbachëv's new policies, many of the U.S.S.R.'s republics, beginning with the Baltic nations, demanded independence. Gorbachëv was totally overwhelmed by the rise in nationalism and agreed to sign a union treaty with the leaders of most of the republics that would have given these nations greater autonomy. This frightened the conservative Communists into attempting a military coup d'état (an unexpected seizure of power) in August 1991. Gorbachëv, who was on vacation in the Crimea, was put under house arrest. The coup lacked any public support or the support of the bulk of the military, and it collapsed after three days. Yeltsin, who had defied the takeover, became a national hero. Gorbachëv returned, and the leaders of the coup were arrested or committed suicide. This series of events became known as the Russian Revolution of 1991.

The coup had made Gorbachëv seem weak and incompetent. Rumors circulated that he had actually planned and ordered the coup as a way of undoing his reforms before the Communist party leadership had completely lost power. The failed overthrow discredited both the Communist party and the KGB (secret police). Disregarding the unsigned agreement, Yeltsin declared Russia to be an independent state. One by one, the other republics also claimed independence. Unable to stop the swift breakup of the Soviet Union, Gorbachëv resigned on

GLOBAL CONCEPTS

Change

CONCEPTS GLOBAL

WORLD ISSUES

Determination of Political and Economic Systems

December 25, 1991, from the presidency of an empire that no longer existed. Communism in both Russia and the U.S.S.R. had ended.

The Commonwealth of Independent States (1991–   )

When the U.S.S.R. disbanded, each republic held its own elections and established its own independent government. Russia, as the largest and most populous of these states, took a leadership position in creating a new federation of autonomous nations, the Commonwealth of Independent States (C.I.S.). The United Nations recognized each new nation, giving them their own representatives in the world body.

Some republics did not make a smooth transition. Civil war flared up in Georgia between the newly elected government and rebels. Fighting between the Christians of Armenia and the Muslims of Azerbaijan, which had started in the last years of the Soviet Union, also continued. From 1992 to 1993, Russia and Ukraine negotiated a compromise over the Black Sea fleet in the Crimea (an area in southern Ukraine that had been a very important naval base for the Russians). The two nations finally agreed that it would belong to Ukraine, but the Russian fleet would be allowed to use it.

In the fall of 1993, President Yeltsin dismissed the Congress of People's Deptuies. Composed mainly of Communists from the Gorbachëv period, the former Soviet parliament had blocked all efforts to turn the Russian economy into a capitalist free market. Yeltsin demanded that new elections be held since most of the parliament's deputies had never been elected, but had run unopposed as Communist party candidates in 1989. Realizing it would probably not be returned to office, the Congress refused to stop meeting and the members barricaded themselves in the parliament building. Yeltsin brought in troops to storm it and arrest rebellious deputies. These decisive actions added to Yeltsin's popularity. He also took steps toward creating a new constitution that would give greater powers to the presidency. While some accused Yeltsin of trying to establish a dictatorship, most Russians still had confidence in him as a strong leader. Yet, the enormous suffering that the economic transformation has brought has created new problems that may threaten the development of democracy in Russia. This became evident in the national elections of December 1993, when ultra-nationalist Vladimir Zhirinovskii and his party won an impressive number of seats in the new Russian parliament.

As 1994 began, a spirit of cooperation existed between most of the nations of the C.I.S. All were still struggling, however, to solve their economic problems and make a smooth transition to capitalism and a free market. The success of their economic reforms may very well decide the extent to which these countries will become and remain democracies.

REVIEW QUESTIONS

Multiple Choice. Select the letter of the answer that correctly completes the statement.

1. The first ruling group in Russia was the
   A. Varangians
   B. Georgians
   C. Mongols
   D. Kazakhs

2. The period of Mongol domination
   A. resulted in the mass conversion of the Russians to Islam
   B. divided the nation into Christian and Muslim parts
   C. gave local princes greater autonomy
   D. restored the powers of the Kievan princes

3. The Petrine reforms
   A. gave Russia its first democratic government
   B. restored the power of the autocracy
   C. transformed Russia into a modern world power
   D. began a period of Russian isolation from the rest of the world

4. A traditional problem both the Russian Empire and the U.S.S.R. have faced in the expansion of trade is
   A. limited ports and lack of access to the Mediterranean
   B. aggressive attacks from Poland
   C. Chinese imperialism in the East
   D. lack of navigable rivers

5. The liberation of the serfs
   A. created a new middle class
   B. marked the beginning of democracy in Russia
   C. resulted in the mass migrations of impoverished farmers to the cities
   D. increased the number of productive farms in Russia

6. Which event did *not* lead to the Russian Revolution of 1917?
   A. Bloody Sunday massacre
   B. Russo-Japanese War
   C. Participation in World War I
   D. Creation of the Duma

7. One reason for the overthrow of the Provisional Government was that it
   A. did not appeal to the peasants
   B. had no army
   C. continued an unpopular war
   D. did not guarantee civil rights

8. Lenin's New Economic Program (N.E.P.) attempted to revive the
   Russian economy by
   A. combining features of capitalism with communism
   B. recreating a capitalist system in Russia
   C. transforming Russia's economy into a free-market system
   D. strictly applying Marxist economic principles

9. Starting with Brezhnev, the U.S.S.R. followed a policy of détente, or
   A. understanding with the West
   B. openness with the West
   C. standing firm to the West
   D. suspicion of the West

10. Gorbachëv's policy of glasnost was aimed at creating greater
    A. job opportunities and work incentives
    B. efficiency, especially in industry
    C. openness, with an end to the secrecy and suspicion in Soviet society
    D. patriotism and faith in communism

ESSAY

Throughout Russian history, determined individual rulers have significantly changed their nation's course.

   A. Choose three Russian rulers:
      1. Prince Vladimir of Kiev
      2. Czar Ivan IV ("the Terrible")
      3. Czar Peter I ("the Great")
      4. Czar Alexander II ("the Czar Liberator")
      5. Vladimir Illich Ulianov (Lenin)
      6. Joseph Dzhugashvili (Stalin)
      7. Mikhail Gorbachëv
      8. Boris Yeltsin
   B. Describe each ruler's most important policies and/or goals. Evaluate
      the success of each.
   C. Discuss two ways each individual significantly altered the course of
      Russian history.

I. PHYSICAL GEOGRAPHY OF EASTERN EUROPE

Overview

Eastern Europe consists of nations located between Western Europe and the C.I.S. Common religious, ethnic, and/or cultural ties distinguish the Eastern European countries. Despite a diverse mixture of peoples and influences, the Eastern European nations of Albania, Bulgaria, the Czech Republic, Hungary, Poland, Romania, Slovakia, and the countries that formerly constituted Yugoslavia (Bosnia-Hercegovina, Croatia, Montenegro, Serbia, Slovenia, and Yugoslavian Macedonia, or Skopje) have similar historical roots and have had similar experiences. Containing approximately 126 million people, with a wide range of languages and religions, these countries seem to have been brought together many times over the centuries by historical events.

Topography

Its topography and location have made Eastern Europe an invasion route throughout history. This has resulted in the mixing of many peoples, languages, and cultures. Mountains have played the most influential role in the development of Eastern Europe's nations. They have acted as barriers and trade routes, both protecting and/or unifying peoples in this region. Eastern Europe's mountains are low and relatively accessible when compared with other ranges in the world. The Carpathians are the longest mountain range (stretching through Romania, Hungary, the Czech Republic, Slovakia, and Poland), followed by the Balkans (which run from northern Bulgaria to eastern Serbia). Other important ranges are the Rhodopes (in southern Bulgaria), the Bohemian and Sudetens (in the Czech Republic), and the Julian and Dinaric Alps (running through Slovenia, Croatia, and Bosnia-Hercegovina, and the Transylvanian Alps in Romania).

Plains have also had a profound effect on the history of Eastern Europe. The Northern Plain stretches from the Atlantic Ocean across Western Europe through the north of Germany into Poland and continues across Eastern Europe into Russia (see Physical Geography in Part I of the C.I.S. section). This has served as a major invasion route for armies from both the east and west for centuries. The Great Hungarian Plain, located in the center of Eastern Europe, is both an agricultural and horse-breeding region and has also attracted invaders.

GLOBAL
CONCEPTS

Environment

CONCEPTS
GLOBAL

Bodies of Water

Rivers have played an important role in the development of Eastern Europe. They have served as major trade routes, linking the nations of Eastern Europe with the rest of Europe, particularly with Byzantium. The Danube is the most important of these waterways, connecting Hungary, Slovenia, Croatia, Serbia, Bulgaria, and Romania. In addition to trade, it has always been a source of fish, irrigation, and, in modern times, hydroelectric power. Other important rivers are the Morava (linking the Czech Republic, Slovakia, Hungary, Croatia, and Serbia), the Drava (flowing from Hungary to Croatia), the Drina (flowing from Serbia through Bosnia-Hercegovina to Montenegro), the Vandar (connecting Yugoslavian Macedonia with Greece), the Prut (which links Romania to Moldova and Ukraine), and the Bug (running from Poland through Belarussia into Ukraine). There are also several rivers that have been essential to trade and communication within countries: the Tisza (Hungary), the Vitava (the Czech Republic and Slovakia), the Vit (Bulgaria), the Sava (Yugoslavia), and the Vistula (Poland).

There are many scenic lakes throughout Eastern Europe, the most important of which is Lake Balton in Hungary. Slovenia, Croatia, Bosnia-Hercegovina, Monetenegro, and Albania are located on the coast of the Adriatic Sea, a rich source of fishing and tourism for all these nations except Albania. Bulgaria and Romania, which have access to the Black Sea, have experienced the same problems as the Russians—their only access to the Mediterranean is the Turkish-controlled Dardanelles. Poland's access to the Baltic has been limited since the 18th century, due to Russian expansion.

Vegetation Belts

As a whole, the region of Eastern Europe is mountainous. Yet, there are areas of abundant vegetation: the Pannonian Plain (located in Serbia and Montenegro); in Hungary, parts of the Great Hungarian Plain (particularly near Debrecen on the Romanian border); in the Danube Valley (the Czech provinces of Moravia, Bohemia, and eastern Slovakia); in Bulgaria, the Maritsa Valley, known as Bulgaria's California (located between the Balkan and Rhodope mountains), and the Balkan Plateau (in the north bordering Romania); in Romania, western Transylvania as well as the river valleys of the Danube and Prut; and in Poland, the Silesian region (southern plain).

There are also extensive forests in the uplands of Bosnia and Croatia-Hercegovina (along the coast of the Adriatic) and the northern plain of Poland. The exception is Albania, whose poor soil and lack of resources have only compounded other problems, making it an extremely poor nation.

Climate

The harshest climates of Eastern Europe are in the Czech Republic, Slovakia, and Poland, where very cold winters and cool summers have traditionally shortened growing seasons and lengthened people's endurance. There are less severe winters and warmer summers in Hungary, Bulgaria, and Romania. With hot, dry summers and milder winters (especially by the Adriatic coast), the former nations of Yugoslavia have benefited from the climate by expanding agriculture. Albania's internal problems make its climate of little use.

II. ECONOMIC GEOGRAPHY OF EASTERN EUROPE

Agriculture

Eastern Europe's economy was almost completely agricultural until the 20th century. Due to larger growing areas and richer soil, Serbia and Montenegro, followed by Bulgaria and Romania, provide the greatest agricultural output. Serbia and Montenegro also produce grains, fruits, tobacco, and wood; Bulgaria provides grains, fruit, rose oil, and tobacco; and Romania grows corn, wheat, and timber. Poland produces limited grain and timber, while Hungary provides grain and wine. The Czech Republic, unlike Slovakia, was almost completely industrial until recently. Albania's rigid Communist system, combined with its other problems, made its agricultural output barely self-sufficient.

Industrial Production/Resources

WORLD ISSUES

Economic
Growth and
Development

The Czech Republic is Eastern Europe's most industrialized nation. Rich in coal and ores used in the production of atomic energy, it also produces beer, glass, china, machinery, and light aircraft. Poland, with its wealthy deposits of iron ore, coal, zinc, and sulphur, provides iron, automobiles, textiles, and chemicals. Romania, rich in oil (for which it became a target in World War II), produces textiles, machinery, and metals in addition to oil, its greatest resource. Hungary provides steel, iron, aluminum, machinery, and railway equipment. Among the nations of the former Yugoslavia, Slovenia and Croatia were the most industrialized, producing steel, copper, lead, zinc, chrome, and wood products. Bulgaria's production is limited to machinery and chemicals. Albania's industrial production was limited to domestic consumption under Communist domination but is now in the process of changing.

"Guns vs. Butter" Controversy

As in the Soviet Union, the guns versus butter controversy (see Part II of the Soviet Union section of this unit) also raged in Eastern Europe. The question of whether to produce consumer goods or weapons for the military and defense had become very important, especially when most Eastern European nations started to reject Communist economic doctrines and develop democratic governments.

REVIEW QUESTIONS

Multiple Choice. Select the letter of the answer that correctly completes the statement.

1. Eastern Europe's topography and location have made it
   A. well protected from invaders
   B. an invasion route throughout history
   C. isolated and culturally homogeneous
   D. dominant in the affairs of Western Europe

2. All of the following are important Eastern European rivers *except* the
   A. Danube
   B. Don
   C. Vistula
   D. Bug

3. The nations of Eastern Europe that provide the largest agricultural output are
   A. Serbia, Montenegro, Bulgaria, and Romania
   B. Poland, Romania, Serbia, and Montenegro
   C. Bulgaria, Hungary, the Czech Republic, and Slovakia
   D. Albania, Bulgaria, Croatia, and Slovenia

4. The most industrialized Eastern European nation is
   A. the Czech Republic
   B. Hungary
   C. Poland
   D. Romania

5. Which is *not* true of Eastern Europe?
   A. It consists of nations located between Western Europe and the C.I.S.
   B. There is a diverse mixture of peoples
   C. It contains approximately 126 million people
   D. There is a unity of religious belief

ESSAY

The topography of Eastern Europe has been important to its development.

A. Show two ways in which Eastern Europe's diverse topography (mountains, valleys, plains) influence its development.
B. Give two examples of how Eastern Europe's rivers play in its economic development.
C. List two ways in which Eastern Europe's geography made its nations interdependent.

III. HUMAN AND CULTURAL GEOGRAPHY OF EASTERN EUROPE

Demography

The population of Eastern Europe is approximately 126 million people. A comparison of the population and area of each individual nation illustrates the breakdown: the Czech Republic and Slovakia, about the size of New York State, have a population of about 16 million; Albania, slightly larger than Maryland, has roughly 3 million; Bulgaria, as large as Ohio, has a population of about 10 million; Romania, twice the size of Pennsylvania, has a little over 23 million; and Poland, roughly the size of New Mexico, has a population of about 39 million. Due to the present disputes about borders and the conflict over territory in the former Yugoslavia, a breakdown for the nations of Bosnia-Hercegovina, Croatia, Montenegro, Serbia, Slovenia, and Yugoslavian Macedonia is not possible. The former nation of Yugoslavia was about the size of Wyoming and had approximately 24 million people.

Ethnic Groups and Languages

While many ethnic and linguistic groups make up the population of Eastern Europe, the largest and most dominant ethnic group are the Slavs (approximately 85 million), which include Great Russians, Belarussians, Ukrainians, Poles, Serbians, Croatians, Bulgarians, Slovenes, Slovaks, and Czechs. The larger non-Slavic groups of Eastern Europe are the Magyars (proper name for Hungarians), Romanians, Albanians, Greeks, Germans, Turks, and Gypsies. Each nation is divided ethnically and linguistically as follows:

Country	Ethnic Groups	Languages
Albania	Albanian 96% Greek 4%	Albanian, Greek
Bulgaria	Bulgarian 85% Turkish 8% Greek 7%	Bulgarian, Turkish, Greek
Czech Republic and Slovakia	Czech 64% Slovak 31% Magyar, German, Ukrainian, and Polish 5%	Czech, Slovak, Magyar, German, Ukrainian, Polish
Hungary	Magyar 94% German 3% Gypsy 3%	Magyar, German, Serbian, Croatian, Slovak, Romanian

Poland	Polish 98% Ukrainian and Belarussian 2%	Polish, Ukrainian, Byelo- Russian
Romania	Romanian 90% Magyar 8% German 2%	Romanian, Magyar, German
Former Nation of Yugoslavia	Serbian 40% Croat 20% Bosnian Muslim 9% Slovene 8% Macedonian Slav 6% Albanian 6% Others 11%	Serbian, Croatian, Slovenian, Albanian

Religion in Eastern Europe

The majority of Eastern Europeans are Eastern Orthodox Christians. The peoples of Albania, Bulgaria, the Czech Republic, Montenegro, Romania, and Yugoslavian Macedonia were Christianized by the Eastern Orthodox church and came under the influence of the Byzantine Empire. (The majority of Czechs became Roman Catholic while under Austrian rule and the majority of Albanians became Muslim under Turkish domination.) Croatia, Hungary, Poland, Slovakia, and Slovenia were converted to Christianity by Roman Catholic missionaries. Large groups of Uniates (Orthodox in practice while nominally under the Pope), Protestants, Muslims, and Jews also exist in Eastern Europe. Each nation is divided along religious lines as follows:

GLOBAL
CONCEPTS

Culture

CONCEPTS
GLOBAL

Country	Religion
Albania	Muslim 60% Eastern Orthodox 30% Roman Catholic 10%
Bulgaria	Eastern Orthodox 90% Muslim 10%
Czech Republic and Slovakia	Roman Catholic 65% Eastern Orthodox and Uniate 35%
Hungary	Roman Catholic 70% Protestant 25%
Poland	Roman Catholic 94% Eastern Orthodox 6%
Romania	Eastern Orthodox 85% Roman Catholic 10% Muslim 5%
Former Nation of Yugoslavia	Eastern Orthodox 60% (Serbians, Montenegrans, Yugoslavian Macedonians), Roman Catholic 30% (Croatians, Slovenes), Muslim 10% (Bosnians, Albanians)

REVIEW QUESTIONS

Multiple Choice. Select the letter of the answer that correctly completes the statement.

1. The largest and most dominant ethnic group in Eastern Europe are
   A. Romanians
   B. Slavs
   C. Magyars
   D. Albanians

2. Which Eastern European nation composed of many smaller nations is now involved in a civil war?
   A. Romania
   B. Hungary
   C. Yugoslavia
   D. Czechoslovakia

3. Uniates are
   A. Roman Catholics who support the union of all Christian churches
   B. Eastern Catholics who are Orthodox in practice but nominally under the Pope
   C. Christians married to Muslims
   D. Protestants who want union with Roman Catholics

ESSAY

Religion has played a major role in the development of Eastern Europe.

   A. Select three Eastern European nations.
   B. Give two examples of how religion influenced the creation of each nation's language, literature, and culture.
   C. Show two ways in which religion has acted as a disunifying factor for these nations.

IV. HISTORY AND POLITICAL GEOGRAPHY OF EASTERN EUROPE

Early Migrations

The earliest settlers in Eastern Europe were ancestors of the modern-day Romanians and Albanians, who were first brought under the influence of the ancient Romans. They were followed by waves of Slavic tribes migrating to present-day Russia, Belarussia, Ukraine, and eastern Poland. A second group of Slavs later settled in western Poland, the Czech Republic, and Slovakia. A third wave migrated to present-day Yugoslavia, Bulgaria, and Albania. Nomadic tribes from Central Asia followed the Slavs, settling throughout Eastern Europe, most notably the Magyars in Hungary and the Bulgars in Bulgaria (where they mixed and were absorbed by the Slavs living there).

Conversion to Christianity and the Byzantine Commonwealth (863–1453)

The conversion of the peoples of Eastern Europe to Orthodox Christianity and the adoption of elements of Byzantine culture created a sense of religious and cultural unity throughout the entire region. These factors gave the people of Eastern Europe a new identity. The work of two Byzantine missionaries, Cyril (826–869) and Methodius (815–885), was instrumental in the conversion of the Slavs. Preaching and conducting worship in the vernacular (the common spoken language), the brothers Cyril and Methodius were very successful in converting tribes of Slavs in Moravia (present-day Czech Republic). Cyril created an alphabet (Cyrillic), based on Greek and Coptic letters (language of Christian Egypt letters and grammar for the spoken Slavic language). This evolved into Church Slavonic, the liturgical language that unified early Slavic literature and culture. While the mission of Cyril and Methodius was confined to Moravia, their followers soon converted both Slavic and non-Slavic nations throughout Eastern Europe: Bulgaria, in 865; Serbia, in 874; Romania, in 900; Rus'/Ukraine, in 988. Poland and Hungary were converted by German missionaries and came under the influence of the Roman Catholic church.

By the year 1000, the Byzantine Empire and its Orthodox satellites (including Hungary) formed the Byzantine Commonwealth, an alliance to promote trade and economic expansion in Eastern Europe as well as to provide a common defense against the Arabs, Turks, and Germans. It was also a political

GLOBAL CONCEPTS

Choice

CONCEPTS GLOBAL

WORLD ISSUES

Determination of Political and Economic Systems

triumph for the Greek East over the Latin West in developing Eastern Europe as a sphere of influence. Poland joined forces with the Baltic peoples, particularly the Lithuanians, and became a Roman Catholic rival to the nations of the Byzantine Commonwealth, especially the Russians.

Turkish Domination (1453–1821)

Despite the establishment of the Byzantine Commonwealth, by 1450 the Ottoman Turks had captured much of the Byzantine Empire and Eastern Europe. The behavior of the Latin West, especially the Crusaders, created suspicion and hatred of both the papacy and Western Europe among Greeks and Slavs.

In 1453, when Constantinople was conquered by the Ottoman Turks, the czars of Russia claimed leadership of the Orthodox church. (See "The Rise of Moscow" on page 420 of this unit.) During the 19th century, a rivalry developed between the Russian czars (Romanovs) and the Austrian emperors (Habsburgs) to lead the Slavs out of Turkish rule. Each claimed to be the rightful heir to the Byzantine Empire (they both used the double-headed eagle in their coat-of-arms). Not surprisingly, the Orthodox nations favored the Russians, while the Catholic nations favored Austria.

Independence and Pan-Slavism (1821–1914)

The Greek struggle for independence in 1821 touched off a movement throughout Eastern Europe to end Turkish domination in that region. As revolutions broke out in each country, the rivalry between Russia and Austria intensified. The other major European powers became involved, trying to maintain the balance of power. In 1683 the Habsburgs defeated the Turks and captured Hungary. In 1815 Russia and Austria divided Poland at the Congress of Vienna after the Napoleonic Wars. By 1900, Austria had also gained Bohemia (modern day Czech Republic) and Croatia. Both Russia and Austria had great interest, therefore, in the shape of the new independent Eastern European states.

GLOBAL
CONCEPTS

Change

CONCEPTS
GLOBAL

Throughout the 19th century, Russia financed and supported wars for independence in Greece, Serbia, Bulgaria, and Romania. Developing the concept of Pan-Slavism (political, religious, and cultural unity of all Slavs and/or Orthodox Christians), Russian czars came into conflict with the British, Germans, and French, as well as the Austrians and Turks. The modern nation of Albania was created at the Congress of Berlin in 1878, as a compromise between Russia and the other Western powers concerning Serbian expansion. By 1914 tensions had grown so great in Eastern Europe, especially in the Balkans, that it was called the tinderbox of Europe. The incident that set off World War I, the assassination of the Austrian Archduke Franz Ferdinand by a Serbian nationalist, was one further example of how explosive the tension of Eastern Europe had become.

War and Communism (1914–1945)

With the exception of the Bulgarians, who fought against the Greeks, Serbians, and Romanians over territory from 1912 to 1913 (Second Balkan War), the Slavic/Orthodox nations joined Russia against Austria in World War I. When the war was over, the Russian Empire had collapsed and was involved in a bloody civil war (1918–1921). Ukraine (retaken by Soviet Russia in 1921) and Poland were independent, as were the Baltic states of Finland, Lithuania, Latvia, and Estonia. While Bulgaria and Romania remained as they were, three new nations were created by the Versailles Treaty: the independent states of Hungary and Czechoslovakia (Bohemia, Moravia, Slovakia, and the Sudentenland) from the Habsburg Empire, and Yugoslavia (Serbia, Croatia, Slovenia, Yugoslavian, Macedonia, Montenegro, and Bosnia-Hercegovina).

Eastern Europe developed constitutional monarchies and democratic governments between the wars. During World War II, fascist governments were set up in the nations of Eastern Europe under the Nazis. (See "The Rise of the Nazis to Power" in Part IV of Unit Six.) During the war, the Soviet army pushed the Nazis out of Eastern Europe. Puppet Communist governments (controlled by Stalin) were established by Stalin to replace the fascist governments, as the Soviets occupied Eastern Europe. (See Part IV in C.I.S. section in this unit.) The only exception was Yugoslavia, where Marshall Josip Broz (known as *Tito*) established an independent Communist government. Once again, the nations of Eastern Europe were satellites.

The Soviet Bloc (1945–1989)

Unlike the Byzantine Commonwealth or the Pan-Slavic alliances of the 19th century, the creation of the Communist Eastern, or Soviet Bloc was forced on the nations of Eastern Europe by Stalin. The bloc consisted of Hungary, Czechoslovakia, Bulgaria, Albania, Poland, Romania, and East Germany. From the start, Yugoslavia under Tito refused to take orders from Moscow. The formation of NATO in 1949 and the subsequent creation of the Warsaw Pact (see "NATO" in Part IV in Unit Six) in 1955 once again divided Europe into two camps, the East and the West.

WORLD ISSUES

War
and
Peace

GLOBAL CONCEPTS

Political Systems

CONCEPTS GLOBAL

Starting with riots after Stalin's death in 1953, the nations of the Eastern bloc began to oppose control by the U.S.S.R. In 1956 a revolution overthrew the puppet Communist government in Hungary, but Soviet troops were sent in to restore it. In 1961 Albania's extremist Communist government, under the leadership of the Stalinist dictator Enver Hoxha, left the sphere of Soviet domination and allied itself with Communist China. In Berlin, the Berlin Wall was built to stop the embarrassing flow of East Germans and Eastern Europeans from the East to the West. In 1968, after the Czechoslovakian government under Alexander Dubček tried to initiate democratic reforms (the Prague Spring), Soviet troops invaded that nation and installed a government more obedient to Moscow. From 1970 to 1980, food riots and worker unrest in Poland grew, as the trade union *Solidarity* was formed under the leadership of Lech Walesa. In 1981, the puppet Polish government began a series of unsuccessful moves (pressured by Moscow) to crush Solidarity. By 1989, Solidarity was legalized. In addition, domestic and international pressure forced the Polish government to hold free elections, in which the Communists were swept out of power. Solidarity formed a new government, with Solidarity leader Tadeusz Mazowiecki as prime minister. Encouraged by Mikhail Gorbachëv's reforms (see Part II and Part IV in C.I.S. section) and his policy not to interfere in Eastern Europe (Gorbachëv Doctrine), other countries began to break away from the Communist Bloc.

GLOBAL CONCEPTS

Change

CONCEPTS GLOBAL

The Collapse of Communism in Eastern Europe (1989–1992)

In the fall of 1989, Hungary allowed thousands of East Germans to escape through that nation. Faced with enormous protest and pressure, both internal and external, the East German government allowed free travel, and citizens began to dismantle the Berlin Wall. Realizing that their authority had gone when Gorbachëv refused to support them, the East German Communists resigned their monopoly of power. A non-Communist government was elected, and the reunification of Germany took place the following year.

In the manner of dominoes, Hungary followed by Czechoslovakia began reforms and free elections. By 1990 both nations had ousted their Communist governments and established democracies, electing former dissident writers Arpad Goncz (Hungary) and Vaclav Havel (Czechoslovakia) to lead the new governments. Tensions, however, soon developed between the Czech and Slovak leadership. In 1992 nationalist Slovak Prime Minister Vladimir Meciar succeeded in getting his country to

WORLD ISSUES

Determination of Political and Economic Systems

vote for independence. On January 1, 1993, Czechoslovakia separated into the nations of the Czech Republic and Slovakia.

In Romania, a major uprising in December 1989 overthrew the Communist dictator Nicolai Ceauşescu, who, along with his closest followers, was executed. The new Romanian government, the National Salvation Front, is led by a former associate of Ceauşescu, Ion Iliescu, and has come under much criticism as a disguised continuation of the previous dictatorship. Bulgaria's Communist government also started to make concessions to reform, following Gorbachëv's lead, but it seemed to stop short of making real changes. Bulgarian Communist party leader Todor Zhivkov tried to overcome criticism by launching a campaign to nationalize or oust the country's Turkish Muslim minority. However, Zhivkov was forced to resign in 1989 and parliamentary elections were held. In 1990 the Bulgarian Parliament ended the Communist party's domination of the government. Finally, the most xenophobic (fear of foreigners), isolated, and ruthless Communist regime, Albania, showed the first signs of change in 1990. Hoxha's successor, Ramiz Alia, was forced to begin political and economic reforms as he saw the rest of Eastern Europe abandoning the Communist system. He was forced to allow thousands of Albanians to leave the economically devastated country and held free elections for the first time. In the spring of 1992, the Communists were removed from power in Albania following national elections.

After Tito's death in 1980, the independent Communist government of Yugoslavia began to allow civil liberties unheard of in the Eastern bloc. Yet, despite these, a poor economy caused riots and strikes, forcing several of Tito's successors to resign. The forces of local nationalism also reappeared. This became evident in 1990 when the republics of Slovenia and Croatia declared independence from Yugoslavia. This led to conflict between those republics and the Yugoslavian government, which opposed the breakup of the federated nation. Slovenia was able to repulse the Yugoslav government's troops and force recognition of its independence. The Croatian government, however, became involved in a civil war against the sizable Serbian minority, which was assisted by the Serbian-dominated Yugoslav army. Acts of brutality were committed on both sides, with the term ethnic cleansing (killing with the intention of wiping out a race of people) used to describe the genocide. As a truce was finally reached between Croatia and its Serbians in 1991, hostilities broke out between the Serbians and Muslims of Bosnia-Hercegovina, after that republic declared its independence from the Yugoslav federation. The conflict soon became a three-way

---

WORLD ISSUES

Economic
Growth and
Development

WORLD ISSUES

War
and
Peace

WORLD ISSUES

Human
Rights

ethnic war between Bosnia's Serbs, Croats, and Muslims, with the Serbian and Croatian governments arming their Bosnian kin. The war was also encouraged by outside politicians, such as the Serbian President Slobodan Milošević and the Croatian President Franjo Tudtman. In late 1992, the nation of Yugoslavia officially disappeared as the remaining republics of Montenegro and Yugoslavian Macedonia declared independence. The killing in Bosnia-Hercegovina continued into 1994, despite the efforts of the United Nations and European Community to resolve the conflict.

The violence and disorder in Eastern Europe following the collapse of Communism presents new challenges to the world community. On July 6, 1990, NATO issued an official statement proclaiming the end of the cold war, but in its place old ethnic and religious hatreds have reappeared. While the Communist regimes were able to supress these conflicts, they did not resolve them. In addition, the nations of Eastern Europe must deal with the legacy of Communist "progress"—economic and environmental damage. In their new-found freedom, these countries face enormous obstacles that will require all their resources to surmount.

REVIEW QUESTIONS

Multiple Choice. Select the letter of the answer that correctly completes the statement.

1. The earliest settlers in Eastern Europe were the ancestors of modern-day
   A. Belarussians and Poles
   B. Albanians and Bulgarians
   C. Romanians and Albanians
   D. Bulgarians and Serbians

2. The mission of Cyril and Methodius was responsible for all of the following *except* the
   A. creation of a Slavic alphabet and grammar
   B. unity of Slavic literature and culture
   C. conversion of the Slavic peoples to Christianity
   D. introduction of Classical Greek and Roman learning

3. The Eastern European nations seeking independence in the 19th century were divided because of their support by
   A. Russia and France
   B. Austria and Germany
   C. Great Britain and France
   D. Austria and Russia

4. Before World War I, Eastern Europe was known as the tinderbox of Europe because
   A. tensions in that area had grown great and there was a danger of war
   B. it had many forests and provided Europe with lumber
   C. it was at odds with Western Europe and there was a danger of war
   D. it was very arid and susceptible to forest fires

5. After World War I, the nations of Eastern Europe developed
   A. constitutional monarchies and democratic governments
   B. autocratic monarchies
   C. fascist dictatorships
   D. Communist regimes

6. After World War II, Stalin occupied Eastern Europe establishing puppet Communist governments *except* in
   A. Bulgaria
   B. Yugoslavia
   C. Albania
   D. Romania

7. The formation of NATO in 1949 resulted in the creation of an Eastern European Communist military alliance under Soviet domination known as
   A. SEATO
   B. EEC
   C. the Eastern bloc
   D. the Warsaw Pact

8. The two Eastern European nations that unsuccessfully attempted to free themselves of Soviet domination in 1956 and 1968 were, respectively,
   A. East Germany and Czechoslovakia
   B. Hungary and Poland
   C. Hungary and Czechoslovakia
   D. Poland and Czechoslovakia

9. The Polish Communist party was forced out of power in 1989 largely due to
   A. the Polish Liberation Army
   B. the trade union Solidarity
   C. NATO
   D. Détente between the U.S.S.R. and the United States

10. Democratic reform and ethnic struggles began in Yugoslavia after the death of
   A. Josip Broz (Tito)
   B. Nicolae Ceausescu
   C. Joseph Stalin
   D. Alexander Dubček

ESSAY

The history of Eastern Europe is one of interdependence.

A. Select three Eastern European nations.
B. Discuss two ways each nation's history and politics were influenced by its neighbors.
C. Give two reasons why alliances between the nations of Eastern Europe keep recurring in their history.

UNIT EIGHT

The World Today

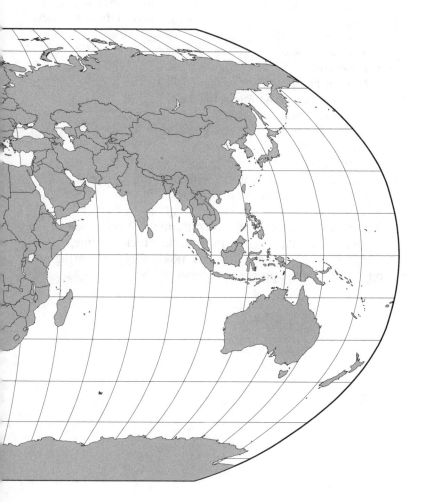

WORLD ISSUES

Today's world could be considered a global village, tied together by the ease of rapid travel and nearly instant communication. These ties create interdependence among culture regions and countries. Examples of this interdependence include: trade in agricultural and industrial products; the flow of knowledge and ideas from one region to another; and political alliances that provide mutual help and support.

Most importantly, however, our smaller world is united by the need to address common problems and concerns. All regions are challenged by several major world issues. These world issues are:

- War and peace
- Population
- Hunger and poverty
- Political and economic refugees
- Environmental concerns
- Economic growth and development
- Human rights
- World trade and finance
- Determination of political and economic systems
- Energy: resources and allocation
- Terrorism

These issues, which are shown throughout this book in the margins, show that we live in a world of global interdependence. Today, all regions share the possibility for sharing and cooperation and the progress that can result.

POPULATION ISSUES AND THEIR IMPACT

Population Growth in Developed and Developing Nations

WORLD ISSUES

Population

Population growth is the easiest issue to recognize but the most difficult with which to deal. In the year 1800 the world population was one billion. By 1900 the world population had doubled, reaching two billion, and by 1975 it had doubled again and there were four billion people. By the year 2000 the world population could reach six billion. Many believe that such a large number of people will strain the earth's "carrying capacity," that is, the ability of its resource base to support people at a reasonably safe and comfortable standard of living.

The changes brought about by the scientific and industrial revolutions have added to this population growth. Increased agricultural productivity has improved nutrition; modern medical knowledge has reduced the number of deaths caused by disease; and improvements in sanitation have bettered health conditions. As a result, more children survive through infancy and more people live longer and healthier lives in both the developed and developing nations.

GLOBAL
CONCEPTS

Technology

CONCEPTS
GLOBAL

In the developed nations where the production of material goods has increased and protective social and governmental services have been introduced, people have generally decided to have fewer children. Most of these nations have low population growth rates, and some have even reached zero percent population growth. Demographers (social scientists who study population patterns) and politicians agree that developing nations must make special efforts to control population growth.

Consequently, the governments of many developing nations have begun family planning or birth-control programs. They use many techniques, such as advertising and educational campaigns, economic incentives, and restrictive legislation to convince their citizens to have fewer children. China's one-child family law, India's transistor radios for vasectomies campaign, and Singapore's free education only for the first two children policy are examples of the different approaches that have been used.

Reducing the birth rate in many developing nations has proved to be difficult, however. Often cultural factors have worked against limiting population growth. In some cultures, economic and social conditions as well as religious beliefs lead to the desire, even the necessity, for large numbers of children.

Children may be needed to help with the family farm or business, to provide care for elders, or to contribute income from outside jobs. They may also be needed for religious ceremonies (especially funerals), to enhance a family's prestige, or to inherit the family occupation and property and carry the family name into the future.

ACTUAL AND PROJECTED POPULATION OF WORLD REGIONS

Region	1980	1990	2000 (est.)
Asia	2,583,477,000	3,112,695,000	3,712,542,000
Africa	477,231,000	642,111,000	866,585,000
Europe*	749,973,000	786,966,000	818,378,000
Latin America**	362,685,000	448,076,000	538,439,000
North America	251,909,000	275,866,000	294,712,000
Oceania	22,800,000	26,481,000	30,144,000
World	4,448,048,000	5,292,195,000	6,260,800,000

*Includes the former U.S.S.R.
**Includes Mexico, Central America, and the Caribbean

GLOBAL
CONCEPTS
Environment
CONCEPTS
GLOBAL

GLOBAL
CONCEPTS
Technology
CONCEPTS
GLOBAL

In some areas, other factors also make limiting population growth difficult. Geographic and historical circumstances have created an uneven distribution of population. Fertile river valleys and coastal plains are capable of producing vast amounts of food grain, and such production requires large labor forces. Consequently, dense populations are both possible and desirable. Eastern China, coastal Japan, and South Asia's Indo-Gangetic Plain are examples of this circumstance.

At the same time, modern agricultural technology has made areas that previously provided only small amounts of food extremely productive with small labor forces. The Great Plains of North America and the North European Plain are two such areas, and they help to provide Americans and Europeans with an abundant food supply and a high standard of living.

Urbanization stimulated by the Industrial Revolution has also contributed to uneven population distribution. Today, over 40 percent of the world's population lives in cities. Cities need workers for industries and services. Moreover, urban areas provide many economic and cultural opportunities for their inhabitants. As a result, people migrate from the rural agricultural areas to further crowd and congest urban areas, helping to create squalid, crime-ridden, and unhealthy slums. This trend of rural to urban migration is continuing today.

Population can also be unequally distributed by age. In the developed nations, more people live longer and couples have fewer children. As the population grows older, these societies need to provide services for retired people and care for many elderly. At the same time, there are fewer wage earners to provide tax revenues for such services.

Developing nations, with their growing populations, are faced with large numbers of school-age children. However, they do not have the money to fund education. This deprives young people of the skills and knowledge necessary to compete for jobs in modernized sectors of the economy and results in large numbers of young people being unemployed or underemployed.

SIZE, POPULATION, AND DENSITY OF THE WORLD'S LARGEST NATIONS AND REGIONS

Country	Size	Population (U.N. Estimate) 1968	1990	People Per Sq. Mi. 1968	1990
USSR*	8,600,000 Sq. Mi.	238,000,000	290,122,000	28	33.5
Canada	3,850,000 Sq. Mi.	21,000,000	26,620,000	5	7.5
China	3,700,000 Sq. Mi.	730,000,000	1,133,000,000	197	306.7
USA	3,600,000 Sq. Mi.	200,000,000	251,394,000	57	68.3
Brazil	3,300,000 Sq. Mi.	88,000,000	150,368,000	27	45.8
India	1,200,000 Sq. Mi.	534,000,000	853,373,000	437	698.0
Other Areas					
Japan	143,000 Sq. Mi.	101,000,000	123,692,000	706	848.0
Southeast Asia	1,692,000 Sq. Mi.	270,000,000	447,000,000	159	262.9
Middle East	3,784,000 Sq. Mi.	261,000,000	306,400,000	69	81.0
Africa— south of the Sahara	8,600,000 Sq. Mi.	254,000,000	500,000,000	30	62.2

(Note the great increase of population in the 22 years that separate the two sets of figures. Scientists estimate that the earth's present population will double in the next 50 years or sooner.)
*Note that "USSR" refers to all the former republics of the former Soviet Union.

World Hunger

Although population growth is an underlying cause of hunger and malnutrition in many parts of the world and the increasing numbers of people put a strain on food supplies, the issue is more complex. Many nations do not grow enough food crops. This is often because of policies carried out by former European colonial powers. In these areas, food production was frequently replaced by the production of cash crops for the European market. Also, in some areas, especially in Africa, borders were drawn without regard to natural and traditional agricultural ecosystems (the living community and nonliving environment working together in a cooperative economic system).

Since independence, the governments of some developing nations have ignored the development of agriculture. Instead,

WORLD ISSUES

Hunger
and
Poverty

WORLD ISSUES

Determination
of Political
and Economic
Systems

WORLD ISSUES

Environmental
Concerns

leaders have often emphasized industrialization and the growth of cities, hoping to build political support among city workers, the growing middle class, and the educated elite.

Climatic conditions and changes affect the food supply in some areas. Droughts (a long period of dryness, as in Africa's Sahel) often force people to overuse and damage the environment by digging deeper wells, which lower the water table, by allowing herds to strip sparse vegetation, or by cutting down trees and bushes for firewood. Floods and storms (as in Bangladesh) can wipe out harvests, ruin arable land, and destroy storage and transport facilities.

Although the developed nations produce a large enough food surplus to ease shortages in crisis areas, a number of obstacles prevent an equal distribution of these surpluses. Simply giving vast amounts of food to needy nations creates dependencies. It also interferes with agricultural prices in other areas. Political differences and policies may hamper the distribution of both food aid and local food supplies. Moreover, corruption, hoarding, and price fixing are often part of the political and economic systems of developing countries.

Finally, many developing nations do not have or cannot afford to develop the factories to produce the technological innovations (new ideas) that could bring about higher crop yields. They also are unable to purchase those items from more developed countries. New, improved seed varieties, chemical fertilizers, pesticides, and farm machinery are all expensive. Also, prices for fuels used in small engines that power farm machinery have increased.

Education—a Growing Gap

Development in Third World nations depends on information and technical skills. Education is necessary to make use of resources. However, as communication and information technology leap ahead in the industrialized nations, the developing nations are losing ground in gaining access to these essentials. This is due in part to the shortage of funds available for schools, colleges, and educational media. Also, social or economic limitations often take children out of the educational system. For example, they may be needed to contribute to family care or earnings, or tradition may exclude the participation of females. Also, governments sometimes ignore or attempt to eliminate long-standing methods or institutions, which makes it difficult for citizens to adapt to new ways.

Population pressure is not limited to particular culture regions, nor is the issue simply that of numbers of humans or even birth or population growth rates. It involves decisions about fairness and equity and how nations will deal with one another in the future. Developing nations react to criticisms of their high birth rates by criticizing how much of the world's natural resources are consumed by the industrialized countries. Indeed, one citizen of a developed nation may consume 20 to 30 times the amount of resources used by an individual in a developing nation.

Increased World Trade

WORLD ISSUES

World Trade and Finance

As it relates to the network of world trade, the population issue involves developing relationships that promote fairness in the prices paid for natural resources and agricultural products provided by developing nations. Increased prices for these products would help provide money for these nations to improve education, skill training, industrial capacity, transportation, and communication. These items make up a nation's infrastructure, a necessity for improving living standards and enabling societies to effectively deal with poverty, hunger, and population growth.

ECONOMIC DEVELOPMENT AND WORLD TRADE

Interdependence brought about by scientific, technological, and industrial progress has carried the message of economic development to every nation on earth. Every government strives to improve the standard of living of its citizens in a variety of ways. Improved health, sanitation, and nutrition; broader educational training and employment opportunities; better housing, clothing, and other basic necessities; affordable entertainment, reasonably priced consumer goods, and more leisure time—all of these are elements of economic development.

Accomplishing these things requires the investment of money and human effort, both of which may be strained by the great need. Political leaders must make decisions and set policies, although there may be differing opinions about how their nation can best develop economically.

Within a nation, even close political partners can disagree about how to achieve economic development. In Mahatma Gandhi's vision of independent India, he saw a nation of cottage industries with skilled craftspeople producing goods in their own homes or small shops. However, his follower and India's first prime minister, Jawaharlal Nehru, promoted industrial development and urban growth.

Global Power—the Gap Between Rich and Poor

Both developed and developing nations may suffer from an unfavorable balance of trade. Many developing nations earn foreign-exchange capital by selling natural resources at relatively low prices and then must pay high prices for manufactured and consumer goods. In addition, they must borrow capital to finance improvements in their infrastructure, which often leads to massive debts and huge interest costs.

Developed nations consume large quantities of material goods and provide many services for their citizens; also, their workers earn high wages. Consumers in these countries often find it cheaper to buy goods from other nations whose workers are paid less. Buying goods such as automobiles and TVs that are imported from other nations can lead to large trade deficits. Since the citizens of such countries expect high levels of public services, government borrowing and budget deficits may result. Nations with debts and deficits, whether developed or developing, may find the value of their money weak or declining

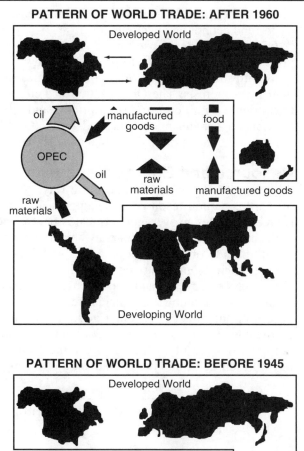

PATTERN OF WORLD TRADE: AFTER 1960

Developed World

oil

OPEC

oil

manufactured goods

food

raw materials

manufactured goods

raw materials

Developing World

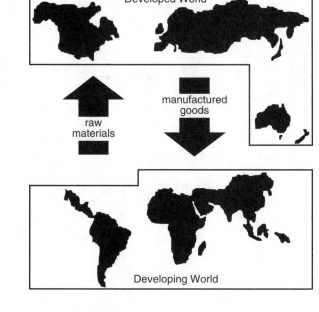

PATTERN OF WORLD TRADE: BEFORE 1945

Developed World

raw materials

manufactured goods

Developing World

from Nixon, Brian, *World Contrasts* Bell & Hyman: London 1986

in relation to that of other nations. This further limits their ability to fund economic development.

Often governments use tariffs (import taxes), which raise prices on imported goods, to protect their own industries. Nations with similar interests often form organizations to promote their own interests. The Organization of Petroleum Exporting Countries (OPEC) cooperates on pricing and other issues, and the General Agreement on Trade and Tariffs (GATT) is designed to benefit the industrial nations that have signed the agreement.

Resource and Energy Management

As science and technology find more ways to use up more of the earth's natural resources, managing scarce or declining resources becomes an ever more critical issue. Developing nations with abundant supplies of nonrenewable mineral resources need to sell them to obtain development capital. Developed nations who use such resources strive to keep the prices for them low and to find ways of recycling and using such resources more efficiently.

In industrial countries, financial resources may be spent on excessive amounts of consumer goods or lost to corruption or inefficiency (as in some former Communist nations). Developing countries are often forced to use much of their capital to pay off their debts and the interest on their loans. In developed

WORLD ISSUES

Energy:

Resources and

Allocations

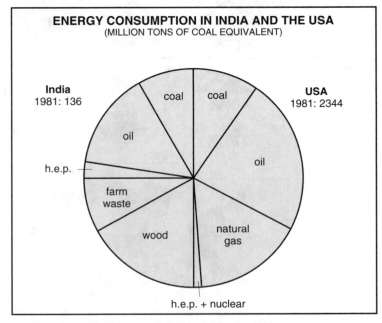

from Nixon, Brian, *World Contrasts* Bell & Hyman: London 1986

capitalist nations, dishonest investing techniques and conspicuous consumption may create waste and inequity.

Human resources are also crucial to development. Many African and Asian societies have suffered a so-called "brain drain," as many of their educated, skilled, or financially prosperous citizens have immigrated to developed nations for better opportunities. The lack of money for investment in education means that developing nations cannot fully develop the potential of the remainder of their population.

Tradition and Modernization: Finding a Balance

GLOBAL
CONCEPTS

Change

CONCEPTS
GLOBAL

As developing nations look for ways to improve living standards for their citizens, they often find that modern techniques disrupt or conflict with established cultural patterns. For example, family planning programs may violate religious beliefs (as with the Roman Catholic church in Latin America); migration from rural areas to urban areas upsets established social structures (for instance, India's caste system); changing roles for women threatens the traditional male-female relationships (as in some Islamic nations); and changing governmental structures may clash with centuries-old economic patterns (China's communes versus family farms).

CHANGING POLITICAL POWER STRUCTURES

The Superpowers

During much of the period after the end of World War II, world politics was dominated by the so-called superpower struggle, pitting the Communist ideology of the former Soviet Union against the capitalist ideas of the United States. This struggle, which involved military, political, and economic competition, has often been called the cold war, and each nation attempted to build and extend its power and influence. The cold war was an icy state of tension and hostility between the former Soviet Union and the United States without direct armed conflict.

Although competition between the superpowers was world-wide, it often focused on Europe, where their two opposing alliances faced one another across the "iron curtain." Here, the Soviet Union and its allies (the satellite states of Eastern Europe) in the Warsaw Pact confronted the United States and its Western European allies in NATO. The cold war led to an arms race in which both sides built more sophisticated and destructive weapons designed to maintain a balance of terror, or mutually assured destruction (MAD), preventing all-out warfare between the two sides.

During the cold war, there were periods of stability when both sides sought peaceful coexistence. These periods of détente (easing of hostility) alternated with times of heightened tensions, such as during the Cuban Missile Crisis of 1961 and the Soviet invasion of Afghanistan in 1979. From time to time, summit meetings were held between leaders of the two nations in order to improve communication and to seek conflict resolution.

Each of the superpowers attempted to extend its influence to other areas of the world. At times, the United States supported military or dictatorial governments opposed to Communism, often at the expense of real democracy in those countries. The Soviet Union supported national liberation movements in some nations, often condoning sabotage and terrorism.

Recently, however, dramatic political changes, especially in Eastern Europe, have disrupted this nearly 50-year-old pattern of relationships. The ideology of communism and its reliance on totalitarian control has been discredited and found ineffective in meeting people's economic and emotional needs. The desires for self-expression and self-determination of the people of Eastern Europe have been coupled with a need for higher material standards of living. The effect these political changes have on East-West relationships and political and economic structures will shape human history for the next few decades.

The Third World

Many African, Asian, and Latin American nations have held a different world view, that of a multipolar, or many-sided, pattern of power. The concept of nonalignment for nations that did not wish to be too closely allied with either the West or the Eastern bloc was formulated by Nehru of India. The first meeting of nonaligned nations was held by Sukarno in Indonesia in 1955.

from Morrish, Michael, *Development in the Third World* Oxford University Press 1983 Arms and the Third World. Is the cartoonist suggesting that Third World nations should continue or discontinue their spending on arms?

The superpowers often became involved in regional conflicts and disputes. At times, these involvements led to direct superpower confrontations, while at other times, the former Soviet Union and the United States were minimally involved, supplying only weapons or aid. The Korean War pitted Communist North Korea and China directly against the United States and its allies. American military involvement in Southeast Asia brought massive Russian support for North Vietnam. The Soviet invasion of Afghanistan brought American weapons and money to aid Afghan mujaheddin (freedom fighters) who were resisting Soviet control.

Soviet and American efforts to influence events in the Middle East were frustrated by the ongoing Arab-Israeli conflict. Arab nations used the superpower competition to gain weapons and aid from both sides.

WORLD ISSUES

War
and
Peace

Unit Eight **THE WORLD TODAY**

American President Jimmy Carter helped bring about an Egyptian-Israeli peace treaty (Camp David Accords—1979) and President Bill Clinton presided as Palestine Liberation Organization Chairman Yassir Arafat and Israeli Prime Minister Yitzhak Rabin took a major step toward a possible settlement in 1993.

WORLD ISSUES

Terrorism

American troops led a United Nations force in driving Iraq out of Kuwait in 1991 after an invasion by Iraq, but U.S. marines suffered losses to terrorists in trying to stabilize Lebanon in the midst of a civil conflict.

Elsewhere, many conflicts have been regional in nature and have not involved the United States or the Soviet Union. India and Pakistan have engaged in hostilities over Kashmir, and China and India have clashed along their disputed borders at several places in the Himalayas. Argentina and Great Britain fought a brief but bloody war over Los Islas Malvinas (the Falkland Islands) in the South Atlantic in 1982, and hostilities have broken out between Vietnam and China even though both are Communist nations.

Arms Control

The presence of nuclear weapons in the arsenals of the superpowers has led to a constant search for ways to reduce the massive sums of money spent on their development and deployment. Likewise, the potential for other nations to develop or acquire such weapons has led to efforts to control their spread.

GLOBAL
CONCEPTS

Identity

CONCEPTS
GLOBAL

During the 1960s, the Limited Test Ban Treaty (1963), the Nuclear Non-Proliferation Treaty (1968), and similar agreements were the focus of control efforts. Nations without nuclear capability, however, have claimed the right to it for both peaceful means (energy) and to protect themselves against enemies who already possess such weapons. India's 1974 nuclear test possibly spurred Pakistan's quest for an "Islamic bomb."

The United States and the former Soviet Union had many arms-control discussions, some of which have been successful. The 1970s saw limitations placed on certain types of missiles as a result of the first Strategic Arms Limitation Treaty (SALT), while SALT II set limits on the kinds of warheads, missile weights, and types of delivery vehicles. More recently, discussions focused on Strategic Arms Reduction Treaties (START), designed to "build down" (decrease) the numbers and types of weapons each nation possesses.

Terrorism as a Political Weapon

Today some groups frustrated by what they feel to be oppression by their own government or the policies of other governments often turn to terrorism. They use violence or the threat of it to publicize their grievances or to press their demands. Terrorism involves the use of violence against unarmed, innocent civilians. Its special horror lies in the fact that innocent men, women, and children are killed.

Terrorism can involve kidnapping or hijacking, assassination, random murder, or mass killing. It is usually carried out by small groups of highly dedicated, even fanatical individuals who believe they can obtain concessions, frustrate governments, or just gain revenge. Some believe in violence as the only way to fight conditions they view as evil, but most have specific goals.

Among those who have turned to terrorism to publicize their demands are the Palestinians, who have carried out global attacks against Israel and its supporters, especially the United States. Branches of the Irish Republican Army who are against Britain's role in Northern Ireland and groups like the Tuparmaros of Uruguay and the Shining Path (Sendoro Luminoso) in Peru have used terrorist tactics to defy the governments of those nations. State-supported terrorism has also become a problem. Countries such as Libya, Iran, and Syria have been accused of providing money and training for Palestinian and Islamic fundamentalist terrorist groups and have supported their activities.

ENVIRONMENTAL ISSUES

WORLD ISSUES

Environmental
Concerns

As humans increase their capacity to use the earth's resources through technology, they also become increasingly capable of destroying and polluting the very environment that sustains human and all other life. Human activities now affect the ecology and even the climate of the entire planet. As former President George Bush said, "Environmental problems respect no borders."

Chief among the environmental concerns are possible climate changes caused by the greenhouse effect. Carbon dioxide and other gases produced by modern industries trap more of the sun's heat and energy within the earth's atmosphere, causing global warming. While scientists disagree on the effects of global warming, many feel that even a slight increase in the earth's temperatures worldwide could melt the polar ice cap, raise sea levels, submerge coastal areas, and change growing seasons and agricultural production.

Associated with possible climate change is the issue of the destruction of forests, especially the tropical rain forests. Increasingly, the developing nations are clearing large areas of

GLOBAL
CONCEPTS

Environment

CONCEPTS
GLOBAL

tropical rain forests. They are exporting timber to obtain foreign capital, converting forests to farmland to grow cash crops such as rubber, and attempting to develop more land for settlement and to raise food crops. It is estimated that three thousand acres of tropical rain forest are destroyed every hour. At this rate, in a hundred years the rain forests could all be gone.

The destruction of the forests seems to add to the greenhouse effect because it decreases the number of trees and plants on the earth that change carbon dioxide to oxygen. In addition, thousands of plant and animal species may become extinct, reducing the earth's biological diversity and possibly its capacity to sustain other kinds of life. If the rain forests vanish, 40 percent of all living species will be destroyed. This means that millions of species, many of which have not yet even been discovered, will vanish. Finally, changing natural patterns can destroy the usefulness of the soil and the effectiveness of the water supply, thus defeating the original purpose of the attempted change in land use. The soil of the tropical rain forest is extremely poor in many nutrients and can sustain agriculture for only a short time. As a result, farmers move on and cut down more forest.

Also at issue is the need to protect endangered species and to conserve the wildlife of the earth. Animals such as leopards and alligators (for their skins), elephants and rhinos (for their tusks and horns), and ostriches (for their feathers) have been hunted almost to extinction to provide luxury consumer goods. The nets used by the tunafishing industry have endangered dolphins. Several nations have depleted the whale population for industrial purposes, and the spread of human settlement and recreation areas have reduced the land available for animals and plants.

Increased industrialization means increased pollution and an increased threat to human health. Pollution creates carcinogens that cause cancer. Respiratory diseases result from unhealthful substances in the air we breathe, and chemicals in the water supply and food chain create additional threats. Chlorofluorocarbons used in aerosol sprays and refrigeration units contribute to the depletion of the ozone layer, the part of the earth's atmosphere that filters out some of the most harmful of the sun's rays.

WORLD ISSUES

Environmental
Concerns

The waste byproducts of energy production are another threat. Acid rain is caused by the burning of fossil fuels and has the capacity to wipe out fish and aquatic plant life when it accumulates in bodies of water. Used-up radioactive fuel from nuclear power plants and other hazardous waste products must be disposed of and their transport across international borders regulated.

Safeguards must be developed to prevent industrial disasters such as those that occurred in Chernobyl in the former Soviet Union and Bhopal in India. Radiation from the accident at the Chernobyl nuclear power plant killed Soviet citizens and spread across northwestern Europe. A poisonous gas leak from an American chemical factory in Bhopal killed and injured thousands.

Governments around the world are beginning to cooperate in dealing with these environmental issues, though opinions differ about what to do in specific cases. For example, Brazilians see the clearing of the rain forest as essential to their nation's development. They consider American criticism unfair since the United States has been clearing forest lands for over two centuries. Agreements over the use of the resources of the oceans and areas such as Antarctica may establish patterns for dealing with global environmental issues in the future.

HUMAN RIGHTS

Along with the industrial and scientific revolutions of the past several centuries has come the democratic revolution. Fundamental to this has been the idea that all human beings possess certain political, social, and economic rights. In 1948 the United Nations adopted the *Universal Declaration of Human Rights*, which states the basic right to dignity for all people, as well as the right to freedom of speech, freedom of assembly, and an adequate standard of living.

In 1975, 33 nations of Europe along with the former Soviet Union and the United States signed the Helsinki Accords. This agreement included a statement of basic human rights. In spite of these documents, however, human-rights abuses continue around the world. Organizations such as Amnesty International monitor and publicize such abuses.

Recent Violations of Human Rights

Apartheid in South Africa. For over 40 years South Africa's government denied political rights to all citizens not of European background and attempted to establish homelands for blacks. This policy denied the nonwhite population the use of much of the land and resources of the nation. It severely limited economic opportunities for the majority of the population and preserved the white minority's control of the economy.

The South African system also severely limited the rights of those of Asian or mixed backgrounds and extended full political participation only to those of European ancestry. Efforts by the black majority to gain political rights, including the Freedom Charter of the 1950s as well as demonstrations, often led to violent repression. Several hundred blacks were killed by police at Sharpeville in 1965. Students protesting educational changes were gunned down in 1976, and protests and activism in the 1980s led to continued violence.

Individuals who criticized or campaigned against apartheid suffered banning, that is, restriction in their travel and contacts, or imprisonment. Some, such as Stephen Biko, who died in police custody, were murdered.

When change came, it occurred at a very rapid and surprising pace. Prime Minister F. W. deKlerk, elected in 1990, promised to "dismantle apartheid" and began by releasing revered South African leader Nelson Mandela after 30 years of imprisonment.

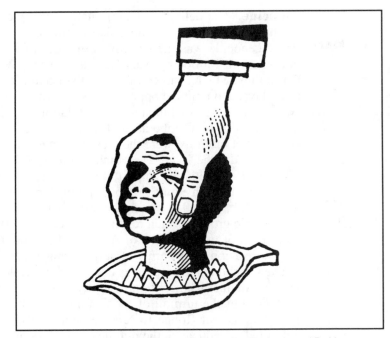

from MacLean, Kenneth, and Norman Thompson, *World Environmental Problems*
Bartholomew/Holmes McDougal: Edinburgh 1981.
Under apartheid the white minority in South Africa had much control over the lives of black South Africans.

The formerly outlawed African National Congress was legalized, many rules and laws were changed, and the first free universal elections were held in 1994. Nelson Mandela was inaugurated as the head of the nation.

GLOBAL
CONCEPTS
Political Systems
CONCEPTS
GLOBAL

Totalitarian Governments. Such governments are known for their violations of human rights. The former Soviet Union suppressed and imprisoned dissidents, those who criticized the Communist party or the government. Forced labor camps and psychiatric wards were used to punish those who spoke out or wrote critical articles or books.

In the spring of 1989, the democracy movement started by Chinese students and activists was violently repressed by the Chinese Communist government. It sent tanks and troops to clear the demonstrators out of Beijing's Tiananmen Square.

Military dictatorships in Latin American countries, such as Argentina and Chile in the 1980s, have imprisoned, tortured, and murdered those who opposed them. Central American death squads have used terrorist tactics to threaten and eliminate those who disagree with them.

WORLD ISSUES

Terrorism

GLOBAL
CONCEPTS

Human Rights

CONCEPTS
GLOBAL

Genocide. The deliberate extermination of a racial, cultural, or ethnic group is called genocide. The most devastating example of genocide was the systematic murder of Jewish people and others in Europe by Nazi Germany during World War II. This policy, which resulted in the death of 6 million Jews, gypsies, Slavs, and political opponents, is known as the Holocaust. Two recent cases of human-rights violations warrant special consideration. In Cambodia and Uganda, hundreds of thousands, if not millions, were the victims of genocide.

In Uganda, the issue was ethnic. Colonel Idi Amin seized power in 1971 with the support of an army largely made up of soldiers of his own ethnic group. After declaring himself president for life, he led a bloody campaign against members of other ethnic groups, which resulted in over 300,000 deaths, the emigration of most citizens of Asian background, and eventually an invasion by the army of neighboring Tanzania in 1979.

The Cambodian tragedy was even more horrible. The fanatical Communist Khmer Rouge, led by Pol Pot, gained control in 1977 after the turmoil of the Communist takeover in Vietnam. The Khmer Rouge forced the people to leave the cities and killed the educated, the middle class, Buddhist priests, and anyone else of power, authority, or uniqueness in the society. By the time Vietnam helped establish an opposition government in the capital of Phnom Penh in 1985, it is estimated that some four million Cambodians had died.

TECHNOLOGY

GLOBAL
CONCEPTS

Technology

CONCEPTS
GLOBAL

The post-Industrial Revolution refers to changes that have taken place in this century. These changes took place in such fields as the gathering of information technology, communications, and the manufacture of products. These changes have accelerated contact and diffusion among culture regions and promoted global interdependence. This has, in turn, widened the impact of machines and medical technology on the lifestyles, work patterns, and standard of living of people in all societies.

The Silicon Chip

Computers have been the key to the changes of the post-Industrial Revolution. The tiny low-cost silicon chip has brought the most important change in human communications since the printing press. A silicon chip makes it possible to perform millions of calculations in a second and to store vast amounts of information. Today's largest computers can perform as many as 800 million calculations a second and store 4 million words. These stored data can be retrieved instantly and transmitted to any location on earth or even into space. Computers today are used in many areas of human activity. These include: international financial and banking transactions and investments; automation of industrial production and product distribution; informational data, analysis, sharing, storage, and retrieval; news gathering and spreading via electronic telecommunication; and weapons development, monitoring, and control.

The Green Revolution

WORLD ISSUES

Economic

Growth and

Development

The developing nations need to increase their agricultural production to keep up with the population increases in their nations. The efforts of scientists and government leaders to find ways to do this have produced a Green Revolution, that is, an increase in the amount of agricultural production from land already under cultivation and expansion of farming onto previously nonproductive land.

The basis of these improvements has been the development by agronomists (agricultural scientists) of high-yielding plant varieties. These are seeds that can produce greater quantities of crops (especially food grains such as rice and wheat) from an area of land than traditional seeds can produce. However, the new grains are not always as hardy as the older ones, and they need chemical fertilizers, more water, and pesticides to protect them from diseases and insects. Different farming techniques are also necessary to use them effectively.

The Green Revolution needs government support to be carried out. Governments must provide education and information as well as loans to enable farmers to buy the new seeds and the necessary pesticides and fertilizers. They must also build irrigation and transportation systems and provide price supports to guarantee that farmers can sell their products at a profit. In addition, governments must carry out land reform, distributing land in a more equal fashion. Finally, the technology of the Green Revolution (appropriate farm machines and techniques) that are useful in small areas at low cost must be developed and made available.

FACT SHEET: THE GREEN REVOLUTION IN INDIA

Growth rate of agricultural production

1900–47	0.3%
1951–79	2.7%

Production of food grains (rice, wheat and other cereals) (million tons)

1950–1	55
1977–8	126.4
1978–9	131.4
1979–80	109.7

Average yields (kg per hectare)

	1950–1	1977–8
Wheat	655	1480
Rice	668	1308

Land growing high yield varieties of crops (million hectares)

1979–80	43
1985	56

Total irrigated area (million hectares)

1950–1	22
1978–9	58.5
1985	68

Use of chemical fertilizers (million tons)

1961	0.3
1979–80	5

---

from Graves, Norman, John Lidstone, and Michael Naish, *People and Environment: A World Perspective* Heinemann Educational Books, Ltd.: London 1987

Without such government support, the risk is too great for most farmers to try the new methods. One of the criticisms of the revolution in agriculture has been its failure to reach poorer farmers. Only those who already make a profit have the money to invest in new methods and techniques. Another criticism is that some of the changes create threats to the environment—irrigation may disrupt normal water systems; internal combustion engines in machinery as well as fertilizers and pesti-cides pollute the air and water; and overuse of the land can wear it out.

Medical Breakthroughs

The advances in medical technology over the past century have prolonged human life and increased its quality. Vaccinations have helped make humans immune to many deadly diseases, while new treatment techniques have increased survival rates for many others. Likewise, improved treatment of wounds and injuries, as well as organ transplants and artificial body parts, have enabled people to live full lives where in the past they might have been severely disabled.

Attitudes have also changed. People are now seen as "physically challenged" rather than handicapped and are encouraged to strive to reach their potential. Accessible public facilities and special activities and support groups have helped to enrich the lives of those with physical disabilities.

Preventing diseases has also become an important medical concern. Scientists have researched the effects of most human activities from smoking to jogging, from eating red meat to living near nuclear power plants. Although there is not always agreement on the implications of such studies, the information does provide people with knowledge and possible choices.

Biotechnology and genetic engineering hold both a promise and a threat for the future. The development of new organisms (biotechnology) may help control diseases or pollutants, but long-term effects may be hard to predict. And the capacity to alter human genes (genetic engineering) that control a person's individual makeup raises ethical as well as medical issues.

Underlying all this is the issue of cost. Medical treatment grows ever more expensive, even in developed nations. In the developing nations, it is one more factor that must be considered in making decisions regarding use of limited financial resources.

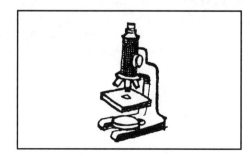

481

TRANSPORTATION AND COMMUNICATION

One aspect of our modern world is increased mobility—of resources, manufactured goods, ideas and techniques, and human beings themselves. The horizons of the average North American, Western European, or Japanese have been expanded by the automobile, the telephone, and satellite television, whereas in Asia and Africa, the bicycle or motorbike, the train or mini-bus, and the transistor radio have had a similar impact.

Improved transport systems move oil by supertanker from the Middle East to Japan's industries and move Korean technicians and engineers by jumbo jet to Saudi Arabian oil fields. Paved roads move fertilizer to the rural farms of India's Punjab and rural workers in search of jobs to the cities of Latin America.

China manufactures and uses more bicycles than any other nation. More people ride more trains over more miles in India than anywhere else. Job opportunities for rural Indonesians are increased by their ability to commute to a factory in a nearby town on small Japanese-built motorcycles and bus-vans.

Communication technology also improves people's standards of living. The American investor gathers data using cable TV and buys and sells using a computer. The Philippine farmer listens to the agricultural and weather reports; the Thai craftsperson watches traditional religious dramas on the government television station.

WORLD ISSUES

Environmental

Concerns

However, improved transportation and communications can also have negative effects. The massive oil spill from the ship *Exxon Valdez* in 1990 damaged Alaska's coastline and disrupted its economy. Tokyo commuters wear masks to keep airborne chemicals out of their lungs, and London cab drivers average only 9.2 miles per hour, hoping gridlock will not bring them to a complete standstill.

Terrorists hijack and destroy airliners. Computer hackers develop the potential to disrupt financial, informational, and perhaps even governmental communications systems. Smugglers make millions using boats and airplanes to transport illegal drugs. Each technological innovation also creates the possibility of dishonesty and abuse.

SPACE EXPLORATION

The space race began in 1957 when the former Soviet Union launched Sputnik, the first satellite. One of the highlights of the space race was the landing of American astronauts on the moon in 1969. Today the space program continues to be the focus of much attention and requires huge amounts of money and resources. Achievements in this area bring great prestige to the nations involved, but some think that the money could be used more effectively elsewhere.

Effects on Global Communication and International Relations

Electronic communication by satellite links has had important effects on both civilian and military aspects of human culture. News and entertainment can be shown live or almost immediately, and nations with "spy-in-the-sky" satellites can monitor the actions and movements of potential enemies.

International crises can develop more quickly but can often be dealt with more easily because of rapid communication. Moreover, when emergencies or disasters occur, aid and relief can be dispatched sooner and with greater effect.

Applications of Space and Space-based Technology

GLOBAL
CONCEPTS
Technology
CONCEPTS
GLOBAL

Both the United States and the former Soviet Union have applied rocket technology from their space programs to the development of intercontinental ballistic missiles (ICBMs) for use as carriers of atomic weapons. The American "star wars," or Strategic Defense Initiative (SDI), was an attempt to apply satellite techniques to the destruction of missiles in flight.

Astronomers have profited from the ability of satellites to look into the depths of space without the interference of the earth's atmosphere. Deep space probes to the farthest reaches of the solar system have extended scientific knowledge in a number of fields.

Meteorology and the analysis and prediction of weather patterns have been changed by satellite radar and photography. Such knowledge benefits travelers, businesspeople, farmers, and those threatened by storms or droughts. Other fields, such as medicine, may gain knowledge from the opportunity to conduct experiments in the weightless environment of an orbiting space vehicle. Geographers and geologists have new tools for mapping and analysis of land and water patterns and processes.

MUTUAL IMPACT AND INFLUENCE: EURO-AMERICAN AND AFRO-ASIAN

Much of the history of the past five hundred years has focused on the relationships between culture regions that experienced the direct effects of the Industrial Revolution and those that received those effects secondhand. The regions that directly experienced the Industrial Revolution, principally the nations of Europe and North America, are also areas whose cultures are based on the Judeo-Christian and Greco-Roman traditions.

The regions that did not directly experience the Industrial Revolution, such as the Native American cultures of the Americas, the ethnic groups (tribes) of Africa, the Islamic, Hindu, Buddhist, and Confucian societies of Asia, have been dominated by the West because of its technical and economic power for much of those five hundred years. During this period, there has not been much recognition of the contributions of African and Asian cultures to the development of Europe and North America.

GLOBAL CONCEPTS

Interdependence

CONCEPTS GLOBAL

Europe's reaction to the availability of trade and resources in Africa, Asia, and the Americas was colonialism and imperialism. The technology of the Industrial Revolution provided the weapons and tools and the development of capitalism provided the financial resources for Europe to colonize these areas of the world and to dominate them. This dominance profoundly affected European attitudes, resulting in feelings of cultural superiority, prejudice, discrimination, ethnocentrism, and racism.

GLOBAL CONCEPTS

Identity

CONCEPTS GLOBAL

In time, the cultures that came under European control reacted with an awakening of pride in their own cultures. As nationalism developed, Americans, Africans, and Asians often used European ideas of political revolution, democracy, and self-determination against the European colonial powers.

The political and economic policies carried out by the colonial powers often disrupted traditional patterns and weakened institutions in the colonies' cultures. Negative elements that already existed in colonized areas were also sometimes made worse—ethnic and social groups vied for power, corruption in government and the economy hurt development, and autocratic elites failed to use human and natural resources effectively.

Most of these difficulties that began in the colonial period have continued to hold back developing nations even after the achievement of independence from the colonial powers. Old dependencies have continued and are referred to as neocolonialism—that is, continued economic dependence on developed nations because of weaknesses in the economies of developing nations.

Stimulated by media images of the developed world, people in the developing nations have experienced a revolution of rising expectations. Consumer goods such as bicycles and radios, entertainment like rock music and movies, and fashionable clothing styles have prompted desires for a higher standard of living. So, too, has knowledge of the possibility of new technologies for increased production in agriculture and industry.

This interaction among culture regions has had a profound impact on both sides. The mutual impact has accelerated and broadened as a result of modern technology, global interdependence, and increased cultural diffusion. This stimulates changes in customs, beliefs, and institutions, often creating conflict between cultures and within cultures.

GLOBAL
CONCEPTS

Choice

CONCEPTS
GLOBAL

WORLD ISSUES

World

Trade and

Finance

Multiple Choice. Select the letter of the answer that correctly completes each statement.

1. People experiencing the revolution of rising expectations today are
   A. eager to accept democracy as the answer to political problems
   B. not interested in receiving assistance from developed nations
   C. dissatisfied with some aspects of their present way of life
   D. determined to follow all their traditional ways of living

2. Rapid population growth in a developing nation is due mainly to
   A. a high standard of living for most families
   B. the availability of medical and health care services
   C. a booming economy and many employment opportunities
   D. the number of marriages among younger teenagers

3. Nations have formed international organizations such as the European Community, the Organization of Petroleum Exporting Countries, and the Organization of African Unity in order to
   A. provide for increased military security and national defense
   B. insure that they receive a sufficient supply of natural resources
   C. carry out the decisions of the UN Security Council
   D. further their own national interests and improve their situation

4. Political leaders in both the United States and Great Britain have often spoken in favor of peaceful resolution of international conflicts. Yet during the 1980s the armed forces of both nations were involved in military encounters outside their own national boundaries. This observation best supports which of the following conclusions?
   A. Most armed conflicts are deliberately started by one side or the other.
   B. Industrialized nations tend to be more aggressive than developing ones.
   C. A popularly elected government must be warlike to satisfy its citizens.
   D. Nations often place greater value in their self-interest than in peace.

5. "Acid Rain Destroys North American Forests"
   "Chemical Leak in Bhopal, India, Kills Thousands"
   "Nuclear Accident at Soviet Power Plant in Chernobyl"
   These headlines best support which of the following conclusions?
   A. Communist nations produce more pollution than capitalist nations.
   B. Developing nations are responsible for most of the pollution in the world.
   C. Protecting the environment is an issue of worldwide importance.
   D. The United Nations is responsible for solving pollution problems.

6. A modern, well-organized infrastructure is necessary for the economic development of a nation. Which of the following factors would be included in a nation's infrastructure?
   A. network of transportation and communication
   B. written organizational plan for development
   C. technological system for using infrared rays
   D. strong system of family support and unity

COMPARISON OF INTERNATIONAL INEQUALITIES

| | Least-developed countries (total population 283 million) |
| | Developed countries (total population 1,131 million) |

Infant mortality (per 1,000 liveborn)	160
	19
Life expectancy (years)	45
	72
Adult literacy rate	28%
	96%
Per capita GNP	$170
	$6,230
Public expenditure on health per capita	$1.70
	$244

Note: The figures are weighted averages based on data for 1980 or latest available year.
Source: United Nations Children's Fund (UNICEF)

7. A valid conclusion that can be made from the chart above is that nations with a low per capita GNP have
   A. greater life expectancy
   B. greater public expenditure on health per capita
   C. a high infant mortality rate
   D. a high adult literacy rate

Base your answers to question 8 on the chart below.

What Americans Buy from Africans*

Crude petroleum	$9,900
Coffee beans	$599
Platinum	$352
Aluminum	$292
Diamonds (nonindustrial)	$286
Uranium	$200
Cocoa beans	$137
Iron alloys (for steel)	$119

*1982 U.S./sub-Saharan Africa trade ($ value in millions).

8. Most of the goods exported from Africa to the United States can be described as
   A. high-tech components
   B. consumer goods
   C. raw materials
   D. agricultural products

9. Global issues such as overcrowding and pollution are a direct result of
   A. high unemployment
   B. an agriculture-based economy
   C. population growth
   D. an imbalance in world trade

10. During the 1970s and 1980s, attempts were made by the United States and the former Soviet Union to
    A. share advances in military technology
    B. bring democracy to Eastern Europe
    C. form an alliance against Israel
    D. limit the build-up of nuclear weapons

11. In developing countries, the major reason that people move from rural areas to urban areas is to
    A. gain more political power
    B. escape dangerous chemical fertilizers
    C. find better job opportunities
    D. enjoy more varied entertainment

12. Terrorism in the 1980s was used by certain groups primarily to
    A. find a peaceful way of settling international conflicts
    B. draw the attention of the world to their causes
    C. increase humanitarian aid to their people
    D. put pressure on the superpowers to end the arms race

13. Which is most characteristic of a nation whose economy is dependent upon the production of one commodity?
    A. The economy is self-sufficient.
    B. The nation has a subsistence economy.
    C. Economic well-being is closely tied to world market prices.
    D. Industrialization makes it possible to export a variety of goods.

14. A policy of nonalignment may be attractive to a developing nation because it allows that nation to
    A. become a strong military power in its own right
    B. develop an overseas empire
    C. concentrate on domestic problems
    D. gain benefits from both sides in the superpower competition

15. Which has been an important result of improved means of communication and travel?
    A. Changes in one part of the world can greatly affect other areas.
    B. Countries have become more nationalistic.
    C. Barriers to international trade have been abolished.
    D. There is less need for international organizations.

ESSAYS

1. "Our world has become a 'global village.' What happens in one country not only affects the people in that nation, but also those in neighboring nations and possibly those on the other side of the planet."

   Choose one of the hypothetical issues listed below and explain
   A. its possible impact on the people of the nation in which it occurred;
   B. how it might affect neighboring nations;
   C. what impact it might have on distant nations.

   Issues
   The government of Brazil decides to clear 1 million acres of rain forest.
   Britain's Ministry of Industry issues strict rules limiting emissions from coal-burning power plants.
   The Indian Ministry of Family Planning is abolished.
   The government of South Africa grants equal rights to all residents.
   A cyclone kills thousands and destroys crops in Bangladesh.

2. The human rights of certain groups have been violated through official government policy and/or by traditional social patterns.

   Groups
   Blacks in South Africa
   Untouchables in India
   Inhabitants of Cambodia (Kampuchea)
   Jews in Europe
   Palestinian refugees in the Middle East
   Political dissidents in the Soviet Union

   Choose *three* of the groups from the list. For *each* group chosen:
   A. Describe a specific violation of human rights that the group suffered or is suffering.
   B. Describe the efforts that were made or are being made to overcome or compensate the group for the violations of its human rights.

490

3. In the 20th century, technological developments have had both positive and negative effects.

Technological Developments
Space technology
Nuclear energy
Computer revolution
Advanced medical techniques
Green Revolution
Internal combustion engine

Choose *three* technological developments from the list above. For *each* technological development chosen, discuss one positive effect and one negative effect it has had on 20th-century society. In your answer, include *one* specific example of *each* technological development.

ANSWER KEY FOR REVIEW QUESTIONS

INTRODUCTION

Pages xix–xx

Multiple Choice
1. C   2. C   3. C   4. C   5. D   6. A   7. D   8. C   9. A

UNIT ONE: THE MIDDLE EAST

Physical Geography, pages 9–10

Multiple Choice
1. C   2. C   3. B   4. B   5. C   6. D

Fact or Opinion
1. F   2. O   3. O

Economic Geography, pages 17–18

Multiple Choice
1. C   2. D   3. A   4. C   5. B   6. D   7. C   8. B

Human and Cultural Geography, page 24

Multiple Choice
1. C   2. C

History and Political Geography, pages 49–50

Matching
1. E   2. B   3. A   4. C   5. D

Timeline
1. 4   3. 4   5. 4   7. 5   9. 5   11. 5
2. 1   4. 2   6. 4   8. 5   10. 5   12. 5

Issues
1. B   3. A   5. A   7. C   9. B   11. D
2. C   4. B   6. D   8. B   10. D

UNIT TWO: SOUTH AND SOUTHEAST ASIA

SOUTH ASIA

Physical Geography, page 58

Fact or Opinion
1. F   2. O   3. F   4. F

Modified True-False
1. T   2. Himalayas   3. Pakistan   4. Arabian Sea   5. T

Economic Geography, page 64

1. B   2. C   3. C   4. C   5. D

Human and Cultural Geography, page 74–75

1. A   2. D   3. B   4. C   5. D   6. A   7. C

History and Political Geography, page 86

Matching
1. D   2. C   3. F   4. B   5. E   6. A

Multiple Choice
1. A   2. D   3. B

SOUTHEAST ASIA

Physical and Economic Geography, page 95

1. D   2. B   3. B   4. C   5. C   6. D

Human and Cultural Geography, page 99

1. B   2. B   3. A   4. B

History and Political Geography, page 106

1. A   2. B   3. C   4. C   5. B

UNIT THREE: EAST ASIA

CHINA

Physical Geography, pages 115–116

Multiple Choice
1. B   2. C   3. B   4. B   5. B   6. D   7. B   8. D   9. D   10. C

Economic Geography, pages 122–123

Multiple Choice
1. D   2. C   3. A   4. D   5. A   6. B   7. A   8. B   9. D   10. B

Human and Cultural Geography, pages 131–132

Multiple Choice
1. C   2. A   3. B   4. B   5. C   6. D   7. D   8. A   9. D   10. C

History and Political Geography, pages 151–154

Multiple Choice
1. B   3. A   5. A   7. A   9. C   11. B   13. D   15. C   17. B   19. D
2. B   4. B   6. B   8. B   10. B   12. C   14. A   16. A   18. A   20. D

JAPAN

Physical Geography, pages 159–160

Multiple Choice
1. C   2. B   3. B   4. A   5. D   6. C   7. D   8. C   9. C   10. C

Economic Geography, pages 166–167

Multiple Choice
1. C   2. B   3. A   4. A   5. C   6. A   7. A   8. B   9. C   10. D

Human and Cultural Geography, pages 176–178

Multiple Choice
1. A   3. D   5. C   7. C   9. C   11. B   13. B
2. A   4. C   6. B   8. A   10. D   12. D   14. B

History and Political Geography, pages 192–194

Multiple Choice
1. D   3. B   5. B   7. A   9. A   11. A   13. B   15. B
2. A   4. C   6. B   8. B   10. C   12. A   14. B

KOREA
page 201

Multiple Choice
1. C   2. A   3. C   4. B   5. C

UNIT FOUR: AFRICA

Physical Geography, pages 214–216

Multiple Choice

1. C	3. D	5. C	7. D	9. C	11. B	13. B
2. A	4. C	6. D	8. B	10. A	12. D	14. B

Economic Geography, pages 223–225

Multiple Choice

1. B	3. B	5. B	7. D	9. A	11. B	13. C	15. A	17. A
2. B	4. C	6. D	8. A	10. A	12. C	14. D	16. D

Human and Cultural Geography, pages 233–235

Multiple Choice

1. B	3. D	5. A	7. C	9. C	11. A	13. B
2. B	4. C	6. C	8. A	10. A	12. B	14. C

History and Political Geography, pages 257–261

Multiple Choice

1. C	4. C	7. A	10. B	13. A	16. C	19. B	22. B	25. C	28. A
2. C	5. B	8. D	11. D	14. D	17. A	20. D	23. B	26. B	29. C
3. C	6. C	9. D	12. C	15. D	18. C	21. D	24. A	27. C	30. D

UNIT FIVE: LATIN AMERICA

Physical Geography, pages 270–271

Multiple Choice

1. A	2. A	3. A	4. A	5. A	6. D

Matching

1. D	2. E	3. A	4. B	5. D

Economic Geography, pages 281–282

Multiple Choice

1. A	2. A	3. A	4. D	5. C	6. B

Matching

1. B	2. A	3. D	4. C	5. E

Human and Cultural Geography, pages 287–288

Multiple Choice
1. D   2. A   3. D   4. C   5. A

Matching
1. E   2. D   3. C   4. B   5. A

History and Political Geography, pages 311–312

Multiple Choice
1. D   2. C   3. A   4. D   5. D   6. C

Matching
1. D   2. A   3. E   4. B   5. C

UNIT SIX: WESTERN EUROPE

Physical Geography, page 319

Multiple Choice
1. B   2. D   3. A

Economic Geography, page 325

Multiple Choice
1. D   2. C   3. B

Human and Cultural Geography, page 329

Multiple Choice
1. C   2. C   3. A   4. B

History and Political Geography, pages 393–396

Multiple Choice
1. A   4. D   7. C   10. B   13. B   16. A   19. C   22. C
2. A   5. B   8. D   11. B   14. D   17. C   20. B   23. D
3. D   6. D   9. A   12. C   15. D   18. B   21. B

UNIT SEVEN: THE COMMONWEALTH OF EASTERN STATES AND EASTERN EUROPE

Physical Geography, page 404

Multiple Choice
1. B   2. A   3. B   4. C   5. C

Economic Geography, page 409

Multiple Choice
1. D   2. A   3. D   4. B   5. A

Human and Cultural Geography, page 416

Multiple Choice
1. B   2. C   3. C   4. D   5. D   6. C   7. C

History and Political Geography, pages 438–439

Multiple Choice
1. A   2. C   3. C   4. A   5. C   6. D   7. C   8. A   9. A   10. C

Physical and Economic Geography, page 444

Multiple Choice
1. B   2. B   3. A   4. A   5. D

Human and Cultural Geography, page 448

Multiple Choice
1. B   2. C   3. B   4. A   5. B

History and Political Geography, pages 455–456

Multiple Choice
1. C   2. D   3. D   4. A   5. A   6. B   7. D   8. C   9. B   10. A

UNIT EIGHT: THE WORLD TODAY

Pages 487–490

Multiple Choice
1. C   3. D   5. C   7. C   9. C   11. C   13. C   15. A
2. B   4. D   6. A   8. C   10. D   12. B   14. D

GLOSSARY

acupuncture an ancient Chinese practice of sticking needles into certain parts of the body to treat disease and to relieve pain

adaptation adjustment to the conditions of the environment or culture

agriculture using the land to produce crops and raise livestock; farming

agronomist a person who studies soil management and field crop production

ahimsa Indian idea of nonviolent action as suggested by Mohandas K. Gandhi

ainu among the earliest known people to live in Japan

Allah the one God of Islam

alliance joining together of groups by formal agreement

altitude height of the land above sea level

animism the worship of spirits that are part of the natural environment

annex to join or add to a larger or more important thing

anthropologist social scientist who studies people, their culture, and their different ways of living and behavior

anti-Semitism hostility and prejudice against Jews

apartheid a policy of segregation and political and economic discrimination against non-European groups in South Africa

arable fertile; suitable for growing crops

arbitrator a person chosen to settle a dispute between two groups

archaeologist scientist who studies the cultures of prehistoric and historic peoples through their artifacts, such as tools, pottery, building, and writing

archipelago a group of islands

artifacts objects made by either hand or machine representing a particular culture

artisan trained or skilled worker; craftsman

audiencia the highest court of Spanish colonial America

autonomous self-governing; independent

balance of payments a summary of international trade (exports and imports) of a country or region over a period of time

Bantu a large group of Africans who speak a common language

bedouins nomadic Arabic livestock-raisers and -herders

bicameral a two-house legislature

bilateral affecting two sides or parties in any negotiation

Boers South Africans of Dutch or Huguenot descent; from the Dutch word for farmers

boycott to refuse to buy and use certain goods

bride price payment made by a man to a woman's father to be allowed to marry her; bride wealth

Bunraku Japanese puppet play

Bushido Japanese Samurai Code of Behavior; similar to the feudal code of behavior of the European knights, called chivalry

cacao the seeds of a tree from which cocoa and chocolate are made

caliph a successor of Muhammad as spiritual and temporal head of Islam

calligraphy artistic writing, especially common in China and Japan

capital the things used to produce goods and services; money used to develop a country's economy

capitalism an economic system based on private rather than government ownership

cash crop crop that is raised for sale rather than for personal use

caste social system in which people are grouped according to occupation, wealth, inherited position, or religion

caudillo or **cacique** Powerful South American leader or dictator

civilization level of development of a group; includes food-producing ability, government, and methods of communication

clan people within an ethnic group who are descended from a common ancestor

class people grouped according to similar social and economic levels

climate the general existing weather conditions over an area for a long period of time

coalition voluntary union of interest groups, political parties, or nations

collectives a system in which a farming community shares ownership of land and farm machinery

colonialism a situation in which one group, often a nation, has control over and is depended upon by another area or people

colony a body of people living in a separate territory but retaining ties with the parent state

commonwealth a nation or state

commune often rural community characterized by collective ownership and use of property

communication the ability to send or receive information and ideas

communism economic system in which a single party controls the means of production with the aim of establishing a classless society

community a group living together, having the same laws, and sharing common interests

confederation alliance or league

conservation protection of natural resources; conserve, to save for the future

continent a large landmass; one of the seven great divisions of land on the globe

cooperative a community system operated by and benefiting all members who contribute to it

coup d'etat sudden and violent overthrow of a government by a small group

Creole (criollo) a white person descended from French or Spanish settlers of the U.S. Gulf states

crusades military campaigns and pilgrimages by European Christians to win the Holy Land from the Muslims (1096–1204)

cultivated prepared land for the raising of crops

cultural diffusion spread of cultural traits from one group to another

culture the customary beliefs, social forms, and material traits of an ethnic, religious, or social group

cuneiform writing in wedge-shaped characters

customs usual ways of acting in a particular situation

cyrillic the alphabet used for Russian and other Slavic languages

deficit lacking in amount or quantity

deforestation the action of clearing forests of their trees

deity a god or goddess

delta the land that is formed by mud and sand at the mouth of a river

democracy a political system in which the people participate in the making of their own laws or elect representatives to make the laws

desert a barren, extremely dry area

dharma the law in the Buddhist religion; correct behavior, virtue in Hinduism

dialects a regional or local variety of languages

dichotomy a division into two individual groups

dictator someone who has taken complete control of a country's government and the lives of the people

dissident one who disagrees with the general opinion or actions of a group

diversity not alike; variety

doctrine a position or principle taught and believed in by a church or government

drought a long period of dry weather over an area

dynasty a powerful group or family that rules for many years

economic relating to the production, distribution, and consumption of goods and services

ecosystem an ecological unit consisting of a community and its environment

elevation the height of land above sea level; altitude

embargo complete restriction or restraint of trade; refusal to buy a product

encomiendo a grant of land given by the King of Spain for loyal services

environment all of the natural, physical, and cultural conditions that surround and affect people

equator an imaginary line circling the earth and equally distant from the North Pole and the South Pole

ethnic group a group of people who have common physical traits, history, and culture

ethnocentrism belief that one's own group or culture is superior to others

exploit to make unfair or selfish use of something or someone

extended family a family that includes other members besides mother, father, sons, and daughters; for example, grandparents

extraterritoriality existing or taking place outside of the territory of a nation

extremists people who go to the greatest extent, including violence, to achieve their goals

faction clique; a party or a group

fallow plowed land that is not planted for one or more seasons

favela a part of a Brazilian town or city where the poor and landless live

federation a union of equal organizations that give power to a central group

fetish any real object worshipped by people for its supposed magical powers

feudalism the political and economic system in which the vassal pledges loyalty and service to a lord in return for land and protection

genocide the destruction of a particular group of people

gentry people belonging to the upper or ruling class of society

ghats low mountains on the east and west side of the Deccan in South India

"global village" describes the current state of our world, in which events or actions in one part of the world affect other parts of the world

greenhouse effect harmful warming of the earth's surface and lower layers of the atmosphere, caused by an increase in carbon dioxide in the atmosphere

gross domestic product (GDP) the total value of all goods and services provided in a country during a year

guerilla member of a group that carries on raids and fights an established government

habitat the natural environment in which people, animals, and plants live or grow

hacienda a large land estate or ranch in Spanish America, mainly in Mexico

haiku a Japanese form of poetry

haj the pilgrimage to Makkah that all Muslims should take as one of their five obligations

hegira Muhammed's journey from Makkah to Medina in 622 A.D.

heritage that which is passed from one generation to the next

hieroglyphics a writing system using mainly pictorial characters

Hindi the major language of India

Hinduism the major religion of India

hydroelectric relating to the production of electricity through the use of water power

imam leader of the Shi'ite Muslims; prayer leader of a mosque

imperialism a nation's policy of extending its power and dominion over other nations by using force or indirect economic and political control

inflation the great increase in the amount of paper money in relation to the available goods for sale; this situation leads to rising prices

infrastructure the basic transportation and communication system of a nation

interdependence people's dependence on one another

intervention the policy of interfering in the affairs of another nation

irrigation the watering of crops or other plants by pipes, canals, and ditches

Islam a major world religion that recognizes Allah as the only God and Muhammed as his Prophet

island a land mass completely surrounded by water

isolation separation from others

isthmus a narrow strip of land connecting two large land masses and separating two large bodies of water

jihad Islamic holy war

Judaism the oldest of the Middle East religions; the main idea of Judaism is the belief in one God (monotheism)

junta a board or ruling body

Kabbah a shrine located in the Great Mosque in Makkah and considered to be the holiest site for Muslims

Kabuki a form of Japanese drama with song and dance

kami good spirits of nature to the Japanese

Karma Hindu idea that every human action brings about certain reactions

kibbutz an Israeli community of farmers who work together and share all the property and income

Koran the holy book of Muslims

landlocked describes an area or region completely surrounded by land without access to a sea or ocean

language a systematic verbal method of communication among a group of people

latifundia large farms, ranches, or plantations in Spanish America

leaching the washing away of nutrients from the soil

leftist a person who favors change or reforms, usually in the name of greater freedom

lines of latitude imaginary parallel lines running east and west around the globe; these lines measure distance north and south of the equator

llanos plains in Colombia and Venezuela; from the Spanish word for "plains"

mandate an order or command; a commission set up to rule an area

marxist one who believes in socialism as a method of government

matriarchal a family group led by the mother

mercantile system a system in which a colony's only purpose is to provide raw materials for the mother country and act as a market in which products from the mother country can be sold; the colony exists solely for the support of the mother country

mestizo a person of mixed European and Native American ancestry

migration the movement of people from one area or country to another

militarism policy in which the armed forces are made powerful and military interests are most important

militia citizens who can be called to help defend a nation; this generally does not include the regular armed forces

minerals nonliving materials found on or near the earth's surface, such as gold, silver, and lead

missionary person who brings his religion to people who are not members of that religion

moderate not extreme

moksha the final resting place for all deserving Hindus

monarchy government headed by a king or queen

monotheism the belief in one god or supreme being

monsoon a wind in Asia that brings a wet season when it blows from the sea and a dry season when it blows from the land

mosque a building used for public worship by Muslims

most-favored nation a part of most trade agreements that gives each nation the same rights as all other trading partners

mouth the place where a river empties into a sea, lake, or ocean

mulatto a person having one European and one African parent, or a person of mixed European and African ancestry

Muslim someone who practices the religion of Islam

myth a traditional story of supposedly real events that explains a world view of a people or a practice, belief, or natural phenomenon

nationalism loyalty and devotion to one's own country, especially placing it above all others

nationality a group of people who feel they belong together because of common cultural characteristics like language, religion, history, and traditions

nationalization the government take-over of industry and property

natural resources industrial materials and capacities provided by nature

navigable deep enough and wide enough for ships to sail on

negotiate to confer or bargain in order to arrive at a settlement or solution to a problem

neutralism a policy of not taking sides in relation to the great world powers

nirvana the stopping of the wheel of rebirth (reincarnation); the goal of all Buddhists

Nō (Noh) a Japanese form of drama developed in the 14th century

nomad a member of a group that moves from place to place to secure its food supply

nonalignment a policy of not being allied with the great world powers

nuclear proliferation the possession of nuclear weapons by more and more countries

oasis a place in the desert where there is natural spring or surface water

ocean a great body of water that covers ¾ of the surface of the earth

opium an addictive narcotic drug

oral tradition the practice of passing down stories and information from generation to generation by word of mouth

origin thing from which anything comes; source; starting point

overpopulation a situation in which an area contains more people than available resources can support

pact an agreement between two or more nations

paddies rice fields in Asia

pagoda temple or sacred building with many stories (levels) found in India, Southeast Asia, and Japan

pampas the large grassy plains of southern Latin America, especially in Argentina

panchayat a local council in India

parliament a supreme legislative body

patois a local dialect

patriarchal a family group led by the father

patriotism love and devotion to one's own country

peasant a small landowner or laborer

peninsula land mass surrounded on three sides by water

peon in Latin America, a field worker who owns no land

per capita GDP the average value per person of the goods and services a country produces in a year

petrodollars money paid to oil-producing countries

petroleum an oily, inflammable liquid used in making gasoline and chemicals

pharaoh a ruler of ancient Egypt

pictograph an ancient or prehistoric drawing or painting on a rock wall

plain an extensive area of flat or rolling treeless country

plateau a broad land area with a usually level surface raised sharply above the land next to it on at least one side

population density the average number of persons per unit of area

possession an area under the control of another government

prehistoric refers to a period of time prior to written history

primitive very simple; of early times in a civilizaton

propaganda the spreading of ideas, information, or rumor for the purpose of furthering one's position or cause to injure another

provincial local; relating to a province or district

quarantine to blockade in order to prevent the transfer of goods

Quechua the language of the Incas, still spoken by the Indians of Peru, Bolivia, Ecuador, Chile, and Argentina

rabbi a Jewish religious leader

race a division of people having certain similar physical characteristics

radical one who favors extreme changes in government or society

rain forest a forest of hardwood evergreen trees that requires very heavy rainfall

rajah Indian ruler

realism a writing style which attempts to portray life as it really happens

rebellion armed resistance or fighting against one's government, political system, or culture

referendum a practice of submitting by popular vote a measure passed or proposed by a legislative body or by popular demands

region an area of land whose parts have one or more similar characteristics

regionalism loyalty to local economic and social affairs, customs, and traditions

reincarnation the act of returning to some form of life after death

republic a nation in which the leaders are elected by the people

revolution basic change in or complete overthrow of an existing government, political system, or culture

rift valley a split or separation in the earth's crust; the Great Rift Valley extends from southwest Asia (Jordan) to Mozambique in East Africa

rightist one who supports conservativism and resists change

romanticism a writing style that emphasizes human emotions rather than human reasoning

rural having to do with farming and the countryside

samuri the military class of feudal Japan

sanskrit an ancient Indian language; the classical language of Hinduism

savanna a grassland in subtropical areas with drought-resistant undergrowth and few trees

secede to withdraw from a group or organization

sect a group believing in a particular idea or leader

sectarian a member of a sect; or a narrow or bigoted person

self-sufficient able to meet one's own needs without help

sepoy a native of India employed as a soldier by the English

serf a member of a subservient feudal class bound to the soil and subject to the will of a lord; serfs had few rights or privileges

Shi'ite Muslims who believe Ali and the imams to be the only rightful successors of Muhammad

Shinto the original religion of Japan, having gods (Kami) of nature (sea, river, winds, forests, and sun)

shogun a military leader of Japan before 1867

silt a deposit of sand and mud along a river

slash-and-burn a method of clearing land so that it is temporarily usable for farming; used in tropical areas

social contract the idea that all people have a right to life, liberty, and property, and that, if a government tries to remove these rights, people also have the right to revolt

socialist economy a system in which the government owns the means for production and distribution of goods

source origin; place where something begins

sphere of influence an area or region within which the influence or the interest of one nation is more important than any other nation

stable steady; firm; not likely to fall

standard of living the level of comfort enjoyed by an individual or a group

steppe flat, treeless plain with short grass found in southeastern Europe or Asia

strait a narrow channel of water connecting two larger bodies of water

subcontinent a landmass of great size but smaller than a continent; for example, India

subsidy a grant or gift of money to assist an enterprise, business, or individual

subsistence farming the production of all or almost all the goods required by a farm family, usually without any significant surplus for sale

sultan ruler of a Muslim country

Sunni the Muslims of the part of Islam that follow the orthodox tradition

suttee the act or custom of a Hindu widow being cremated on the funeral pyre of her husband

Swahili a Bantu language of East Africa used for trade and government; has many Arabic, Persian, and Indian words

swaraj Indian term for self-rule

taiga a forested area in Russia and other places near the Arctic

Talmud books containing Jewish civil and religious law and tradition

tariff a tax on goods brought into a country from another country

terraced farmland flat shelves of land, arranged like wide steps on a mountainside

terrorism the idea of using violence and fear of violence to gain an objective

textiles fibers and yarns made into cloth and then into clothing

Third World refers to the developing nations of Asia, Africa, and Latin America

topography the surface features of a place or area

totalitarianism all parts of life— economic, social, political, religious, and educational—are controlled by the state

trade surplus exports of a nation are greater than the imports of that nation

tradition the handing down of information, beliefs, and customs from one generation to another

tribalism tribal relationships, feelings, and loyalties

tribe a group of people who share a common language and religion and are united under one leader

tributary the arms of a large river

tropical having to do with the hot areas near the equator

typhoon a tropical storm or cyclone found in the China Sea and Indian Ocean

underdeveloped an area with little industry that is in an early stage of economic development

unique one of a kind

untouchable a person belonging to the lowest caste of the Hindu social order

uprising revolt; rebellion; an act of popular violence in defiance of an established government

urban relating to a city

values attitudes or beliefs considered to be important by a group

vassal a person under the protection of a feudal lord to whom he has vowed his loyalty and service; a subordinate or follower

veld South African steppe or prairie

vernacular the style of language used in a certain area

viceroy the governor of a country or a province who rules as the king's representative

Yoruba an African tribe living in present-day Nigeria

zambo a person of mixed Native American and African parentage in Latin America

Zionism a theory for setting up a Jewish national community in the Middle East and supporting the modern state of Israel

Examination
June 1998
Global Studies

PART I [55 credits]

Answer all 48 questions in this part.

Directions (1–48): For each statement or question, write in the space provided, the *number* of the word or expression that, of those given, best completes the statement or answers the question.

1 One result of the Neolithic Revolution was

   1 an increase in the number of nomadic tribes
   2 a reliance on hunting and gathering for food
   3 the establishment of villages and the rise of governments
   4 a decrease in trade between cultural groups   1 _____

2 One reason the cultures of North Africa developed differently from the cultures of the rest of Africa was that these areas of Africa were separated by the

   1 Congo River Basin   3 Sahara Desert
   2 Great Rift Valley   4 Arabian Sea   2 _____

Base your answers to questions 3 and 4 on the poem below and on your knowledge of social studies.

> . . . , you, African, suffered like a beast
> Your ashes strewn to the wind that roams the desert,
> Your tyrants built the lustrous, magic temples
> To preserve your soul, preserve your suffering.
> Barbaric right of fist and the white right to whip,
> You had the right to die, you could also weep.
> — Patrice Lumumba, "Dawn in the Heart of Africa"

3 This African poem is discussing the evils of

  1 imperialism   3 nationalism

  2 communism   4 regionalism   3 _____

4 The tyrants referred to in the poem were

  1 communist revolutionaries who took over the newly independent African governments

  2 the European governments that had divided the continent of Africa into colonies

  3 tribal chieftains who fought each other to control African lands

  4 merchants who sought to expand the drug trade in colonial Africa   4 _____

5 Mansa Musa's journey to Mecca in the 1300's is evidence that

  1 the Crusades had a great influence on western Africa

  2 most African leaders were educated in the Middle East

  3 European culture was superior to the cultures of western Africa

  4 Islam had a major influence on the Mali Empire   5 _____

6 • Rebellion in the Congo during the 1960's
   • Civil war in Nigeria from 1967 to 1970
   • Fighting in the Sudan in the 1980's
   • Massacres in Rwanda in the 1990's

Which factor was the main reason for these conflicts?

1 poor food distribution systems
2 communist interference
3 demands for land reform
4 ethnic rivalries   6 _____

7 In which way has the end of apartheid had a positive economic effect on South Africa?

1 Black South African managers have increased industrial productivity throughout the nation.
2 The introduction of communism has led to a more equal distribution of income.
3 Many foreign companies have resumed trading and investing in South Africa.
4 All profits of South Africa's industries are now reinvested out of the country.   7 _____

8 In China, the development of ethnocentrism was most influenced by

1 its historic reliance on foreign nations
2 a long history of democratic government
3 a strong belief in Christianity
4 its geographic isolation   8 _____

Base your answer to question 9 on the cartoon below and on your knowledge of social studies.

9 What is the main idea of the cartoon?

1 Labor camps remain China's primary method of punishing political prisoners.
2 The Chinese consider the United States an imperialistic power.
3 Economic development in modern China has sometimes been achieved by ignoring human rights issues.
4 The Chinese believe that human rights abuses are also an issue in the United States.

9 _____

10 The Confucian view of government and the Chinese Communist view of government were similar in that both stressed

  1 loyalty to the government
  2 the need for filial piety
  3 a civil service system
  4 equality of men and women   10 _____

11 The results of the Opium War (1839–1842) indicate that China was

  1 still a major military power
  2 not strong enough to resist Western demands
  3 rapidly building a modern industrial economy
  4 accepting Western nations as equal trading partners   11 _____

12 The Tiananmen Square massacre in China was a reaction to

  1 Deng Xiaoping's plan to revive the Cultural Revolution
  2 student demands for greater individual rights and freedom of expression
  3 China's decision to seek Western investors
  4 Great Britain's decision to return Hong Kong to China   12 _____

13 Taoism and Shintoism are similar in that both religions stress

  1 adhering to the five Confucian relationships
  2 following the Eightfold Path
  3 developing harmony between humans and nature
  4 believing in one God   13 _____

14 In Japan between 1603 and 1868, the most notable action taken by the Tokugawa Shogunate was the

1 military conquest of China
2 development of extensive trade with the Americas
3 formation of cultural links with Europe
4 virtual isolation of the country from the outside world   14 _____

15 Between the Meiji Restoration and World War II, Japan tried to solve the problem of its scarcity of natural resources by

1 exporting agricultural products in exchange for new technology
2 establishing a policy of imperialism
3 building nuclear power plants
4 cooperating with the Soviet Union to gain needed resources   15 _____

16 In the past decade, Japanese automobile manufacturers have sought to improve Japanese-American trade relations by

1 drastically lowering the price of Japanese automobiles for American consumers
2 allowing an unlimited number of American automobiles to be sold in Japan
3 importing most spare parts from Mexico
4 building an increasing number of Japanese automobiles in the United States   16 _____

17 Which of these nations is located closest to the Philippines, Malaysia, and Indonesia?

1 Korea   3 Somalia
2 Vietnam   4 Pakistan   17 _____

18 In India, which aspect of society has been most heavily influenced by religious beliefs, tradition, and the division of labor?

  1 caste system
  2 policy of neutrality
  3 urbanization
  4 parliamentary government   18 _____

19 The "homespun movement" and the Salt March promoted by Mohandas Gandhi in India are examples of his policy of

  1 industrialization   3 nonalignment
  2 isolationism   4 nonviolent protest   19 _____

20 Which statement best explains why India was partitioned in 1947?

  1 The British feared a united India.
  2 One region wanted to remain under British control.
  3 Religious differences led to political division.
  4 Communist supporters wanted a separate state.   20 _____

21 From the perspective of the North Vietnamese, the war in Vietnam in the 1960's was a battle between

  1 fascism and liberalism
  2 nationalism and imperialism
  3 republicanism and totalitarianism
  4 theocracy and monarchy   21 _____

22 One similarity between the Five Pillars of Islam and the Ten Commandments is that both

  1 support a belief in reincarnation
  2 promote learning as a means to salvation
  3 encourage the use of statues to symbolize God
  4 provide a guide to proper ethical and moral behavior   22 _____

Base your answer to question 23 on the cartoon below and on your knowledge of social studies.

23 This 1994 cartoon suggests that peace in the Middle East will

1 never be achieved
2 put a stranglehold on the region's politics
3 occur only with the assistance of the United States
4 be accomplished only through negotiation and compromise

23 _____

Base your answer to question 24 on the map below and on your knowledge of social studies.

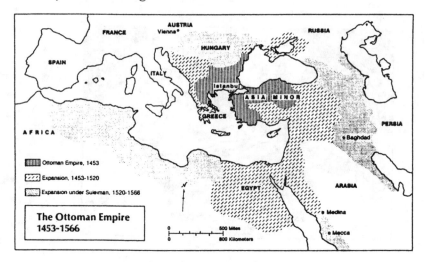

The Ottoman Empire
1453-1566

24 An observation about the Ottoman Empire in the 15th and 16th centuries is that the Empire

1 originated in Hungary
2 had a strategic location between Europe and Asia
3 was totally landlocked
4 had control over most of western Europe   24 _____

25 One major result of the Crusades was the

1 permanent occupation of the Holy Land by the Europeans
2 long-term decrease in European trade
3 conversion of most Muslims to Christianity
4 spread of Middle Eastern culture and technology to Europe   25 _____

26 One way in which the civilizations of the Sumerians, the Phoenicians, and the Mayas were similar is that each

1 developed extensive writing systems
2 emphasized equality in education
3 established monotheistic religions
4 encouraged democratic participation in government   26 _____

27 One reason the Spanish conquistadores were able to conquer the Aztec and Inca Empires rapidly is that

1 these empires had no standing armies
2 the Spanish had better weapons than the Aztecs and Incas did
3 the Spanish greatly outnumbered the Aztecs and Incas
4 the Aztecs and Incas joined together to fight the Spanish   27 _____

28 Which type of government has resulted from the changing political trends in much of Latin America during the 1990's?

1 monarchy   3 democracy
2 military junta   4 fascism   28 _____

Base your answer to question 29 on the cartoon below and on your knowledge of social studies.

29 What is the main idea of this cartoon?

1 Ancient ruins and artifacts are often destroyed by modern technology.
2 Trade agreements are sometimes used to reestablish direct colonial rule.
3 Trade agreements sometimes have negative consequences.
4 The civil rights of native peoples are usually recognized by industrialized nations.

29 _____

30 A major contribution of the Roman Empire to Western society was the development of

1 gunpowder
2 the principles of revolutionary socialism
3 monotheism
4 an effective legal system

30 _____

31 • Man is born free and everywhere he is in chains.
 • Everyone has the natural right to life, liberty, and property.
 • Slavery, torture, and religious persecution are wrong.

During which period in European history would the ideas in these statements have been expressed?

1 Pax Romana
2 Age of Exploration
3 Enlightenment
4 Age of Imperialism   31 _____

32 The growth of feudalism in Europe during the Middle Ages was primarily caused by the

1 rivalry between the colonial empires
2 suppression of internationalism
3 decline of the Roman Catholic Church
4 collapse of a strong central government   32 _____

33 Which idea about leadership would Niccolò Machiavelli most likely support?

1 Leaders should do whatever is necessary to achieve their goals.
2 Leaders should fight against discrimination and intolerance.
3 Leaders should listen to the desires of the people.
4 Elected leaders should be fair and good.   33 _____

34 European society during the Renaissance differed from European society during the Middle Ages in that during the Renaissance

1 the Church was no longer influential
2 the emphasis on individual worth increased
3 economic activity declined
4 art no longer contained religious themes   34 _____

35 A major result of the Industrial Revolution was the

    1 concentration of workers in urban areas
    2 increased desire of the wealthy class to share its power
    3 formation of powerful craft guilds
    4 control of agricultural production by governments   35 _____

36 According to the theories of Karl Marx, history can be viewed as a

    1 succession of famines that result in the destruction of civilizations
    2 repeating cycle of imperialism and colonialism
    3 listing of the accomplishments of the ruling classes
    4 continuous struggle between economic classes   36 _____

37 • Congress of Vienna redraws map of Europe.
    • Triple Entente is formed to combat the Triple Alliance.
    • Treaty of Versailles calls for the creation of the League of Nations.

These events are similar in that each reflects

    1 the aggressiveness of dictators
    2 an effort to establish a balance of power
    3 the rivalry between France, Germany, and Greece
    4 the concept of mercantilism   37 _____

38 After the breakup of the Austro-Hungarian Empire and the Soviet Union, new nations were formed. Which generalization accurately reflects the effect of the breakup on these new nations?

   1 New nations are generally too poor and weak to become active members of the United Nations.
   2 New nations rarely use their limited resources to wage war.
   3 National and ethnic differences often lead to instability and violence in new nations.
   4 Self-determination generally leads to democratic forms of government in new nations.

38 _____

39 Which series of events is arranged in the correct chronological order?

1	The Treaty of Versailles is signed. Adolf Hitler becomes Chancellor of Germany. German troops invade Poland.
2	German troops invade Poland. The Treaty of Versailles is signed. Adolf Hitler becomes Chancellor of Germany.
3	Adolf Hitler becomes Chancellor of Germany. The Treaty of Versailles is signed. German troops invade Poland.
4	The Treaty of Versailles is signed. German troops invade Poland. Adolf Hitler becomes Chancellor of Germany.

39 _____

Base your answer to question 40 on the cartoon below and on your knowledge of social studies.

Palma/Expresso/Lisbon

40 Which conclusion can be drawn from this cartoon?

   1 Many nations are interested in buying nuclear technology from the former Soviet Union.

   2 Developing countries are looking to the former Soviet Union for investment capital.

   3 Soviet nuclear scientists are looking for jobs in the Middle East.

   4 The nations of the Middle East are spending millions of dollars on nuclear disarmament.

40 _____

Base your answers to questions 41 and 42 on the map below and on your knowledge of social studies.

Eastern Europe in 1960

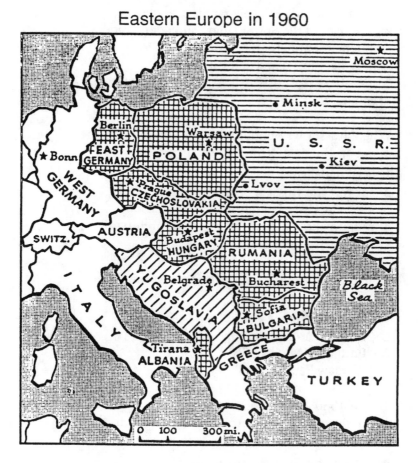

41 Which symbol is used on this map to identify nations that were considered satellites of the Soviet Union?

(1) ▤ (2) ☐ (3) ▦ (4) ▨ 41 ____

42 The reason that Ukraine, Lithuania, and Belarus are not included on this map is that they were

  1 located outside the geographic area shown
  2 republics of the Soviet Union and not considered independent nations
  3 provinces in Poland and Rumania
  4 members of the North Atlantic Treaty Organization (NATO)   42 _____

43 When Russia was under Mongol domination, the effect on Russia was to

  1 end feudalism
  2 convert the Russian people to Hinduism
  3 keep Russia isolated from western Europe
  4 reunite the Eastern Orthodox Church with the Roman Catholic Church   43 _____

44 Which headline concerning the Soviet Union refers to a Cold War event?

  1 **"Yeltsin Assumes Power"**
  2 **"Trotsky Forms Red Army"**
  3 **"Germany Invades USSR"**
  4 **"Warsaw Pact Formed"**   44 _____

45 In the 1980's, the governments of both Brazil and Malaysia supported the cutting of timber in their rain forests as a means of

  1 achieving economic prosperity
  2 increasing the national debt
  3 controlling rebellions of indigenous peoples
  4 preventing exploitation by imperialist nations   45 _____

46 **"Germany Will Make Reparations For WWI"**
"OPEC Supports Oil Embargo Against Western Nations"
"UN Imposes Sanctions on Iraq"

Which conclusion can be drawn from these headlines?

1 Economic measures are often designed to achieve political goals.
2 Communism as an economic system has failed.
3 Economic policies are often formulated to encourage investment.
4 Nationalism plays a small role in economic decision making.   46 _____

47 The code of bushido of the Japanese samurai is most similar to the

1 belief in reincarnation and karma of Hindus
2 practice of chivalry by European knights
3 teachings of Judaism
4 theory of natural rights of the Enlightenment writers   47 _____

48 One similarity between the leadership of the Meiji emperors of Japan, Peter the Great of Russia, and Shah Reza Pahlavi of Iran was that they all supported policies that

1 increased the power of the aristocracy
2 introduced new religious beliefs
3 kept their nations from industrial expansion
4 westernized their nations   48 _____

PART II

ANSWER THREE QUESTIONS FROM THIS PART. [45]

1 Geographic features have influenced the historical, economic, political, and social development of many nations and regions of the world. Several of these nations and regions and a geographic feature in that area are listed below.

> *Nations/Regions—Geographic Features*
> Egypt—Nile River
> Japan—Island location
> Poland—Northern European Plain
> Roman Empire—Mediterranean Sea
> Russia—Frozen rivers
> South Africa—Gold and diamond mines

Select *three* nations or regions and the geographic feature with which each is paired. For *each* one selected, discuss several specific ways that this feature has influenced the historical, economic, political, or social development of the nation or region.   [5,5,5]

2 Throughout history, the ideas of leaders have affected historical events within their own nation or region. The ideas of some leaders are reflected in the quotations below.

> I cannot and will not recant anything, for to go against conscience is neither right nor safe. . . . Here I stand. I cannot do otherwise.
>
> **Martin Luther**

> The position of the inhabitants of the American hemisphere has been for centuries purely passive. Politically they were nonexistent. We have been molested by a system which has not only deprived us of our rights but has kept us in a state of permanent childhood with regard to public affairs.
>
> **Simón Bolívar**

> Dear comrades, soldiers, sailors and workers, I am happy to greet in you the victorious Russian revolution, to greet you as the advance guard of the international proletarian army. . . .
>
> **V. I. Lenin**

> Extremes must be fought by extremes. Against the infection of [Marxism], against the Jewish pestilence, we must hold aloft a flaming ideal. And if others speak of the World and Humanity, we must say the Fatherland—and only the Fatherland!
>
> **Adolf Hitler**

> [British rule] has impoverished the dumb millions by a system of progressive exploitation. . . . It has reduced us politically to serfdom. It has sapped the foundations of our culture . . . and degraded us spiritually.
>
> **Mohandas Gandhi**

> A revolution is not a dinner party, or writing an essay, or painting a picture or doing embroidery; it cannot be so refined, so leisurely and gentle, so . . . kind, courteous, restrained, and generous. A revolution is an insurrection, an act of violence by which one class overthrows another.
>
> **Mao Zedong**

> . . . did the former regime not use the radio and television to render religious beliefs valueless and ignore national traditions and customs? In any case, . . . courage, patience, virtue, . . . avoiding dependence on the powers, and . . . sensing responsibility toward the masses, have revived the [leaders] and rendered them steadfast and popular.
>
> **Ayatollah Khomeini**

Select *three* of the quotations above and for *each* one selected:

- Explain the main idea of the quotation
- Describe the historical circumstances related to the quotation
- Explain the role or the action of the leader in the historical event   [5,5,5]

3 Turning points are events or key developments that change a nation's history.

Nations
Cuba
Egypt
France
Ireland
Kenya
Korea
Turkey

Select *three* nations from the list and for *each* one selected:

- Identify and describe a turning point in that nation's history
- Explain why that event or development was a turning point in that nation's history   [5,5,5]

4 Religion often has significant effects on different aspects of culture.

Aspects of Culture
Architecture
Dietary laws
Dress
Justice
Painting and sculpture
Social relationships

Select *three* of these aspects of culture and for *each* one selected:

- Identify a specific religion that has influenced that aspect of culture [You must use a different religion for each aspect of culture selected.]
- Discuss how the religion's teachings or beliefs have influenced that aspect of culture   [5,5,5]

5 Throughout history, technological developments have had a major impact on the global community and on specific nations. Several technological developments are listed below.

Technological Developments
Atomic energy
Chemical fertilizer
Computer
Genetic engineering
Gunpowder
Printing press
Steam engine

Select *three* of the technological developments and for *each* one selected:

- Discuss one specific positive or one specific negative impact of the technological development on the global community or on a specific nation [Do *not* use the United States in your answer.]
- Discuss why the technological development had a positive or a negative impact   [5,5,5]

6 Swedish inventor Alfred Nobel established a peace prize to be awarded annually ". . . to the person [or group] who shall have done the most or the best work for fraternity [brotherhood] between nations . . . and promotion of peace. . . ." In some years, the award has been shared by several individuals or groups who have worked toward a common goal.

Nobel Peace Prize Winners
Amnesty International (1977)
Mother Teresa (1979)
Lech Walesa (1983)
Elie Wiesel (1986)
Mikhail Gorbachev (1990)
Rigoberta Menchú (1992)
Nelson Mandela and F. W. de Klerk (1993)
Yasir Arafat, Yitzhak Rabin, and Shimon Peres (1994)

Select *three* winners (or group of winners) from the list and for *each* one selected:

• Identify and describe the issue for which the Nobel Peace Prize was given that year
• Discuss the specific contributions or actions of the winners in dealing with this issue   [5,5,5]

7 Every society must answer basic economic questions in order to survive.

Nations
France (1200–1500)
Belgian Congo (1890–1960)
Soviet Union (1917–1985)
Israel (1949–present)
Japan (1950–present)
Brazil (1950–present)

Select *three* nations from the list and for *each* one selected:

- Explain how these basic economic questions have been answered during the time period given:
  – What shall be produced?
  – How shall goods be produced?
  – Who will use the goods produced?
- Discuss the nation's economic system in that time period [In your discussion, identify who controls the resources and who makes the major economic decisions.] [5,5,5]

Examination January 1999

Global Studies

PART I [55 credits]

Answer all 48 questions in this part.

Directions (1–48): For each statement or question, write in the space provided, the *number* of the word or expression that, of those given, best completes the statement or answers the question.

1 Most traditional societies maintain social control and group cooperation through the use of

   1 subsistence farming
   2 regional elections
   3 democratic decision making
   4 the extended family   1 _____

2 Which statement is most closely associated with the economic policy of mercantilism?

   1 Colonies should exist for the benefit of the mother country.
   2 Local authority should determine the type of goods to be produced.
   3 Governments should not be involved in the economy.
   4 Business and industry should be owned by the state.   2 _____

3 India's earliest civilizations were located in

1 mountainous areas	3 coastal regions
2 river valleys	4 dry steppes

3 _____

4 The *Upanishads,* the *Ramayan,* and the *Bhagavad Gita* are considered to be significant pieces of Indian literature because they

1 provide guidelines for Hindu living and behavior
2 identify basic Buddhist principles
3 show the constant class struggle in Indian life
4 reflect the similarities between the Hindu and Muslim religions

4 _____

5 A newspaper published in India recently included these items.

- an article entitled "Toward Christian Unity in India"
- a picture of an Indian cricket team
- a review of an Elton John compact disc

Which is the most valid conclusion to be drawn from this information?

1 The Indian Government has abandoned its policy of nonalignment.
2 Cultural diffusion is a factor in Indian life.
3 The British still have control over Indian affairs.
4 The Indian people have abandoned their traditional religions.

5 _____

6 The Meiji Restoration in Japan was characterized by a movement toward

1 feudalism
2 modernization
3 isolationism
4 socialism

6 _____

Base your answer to question 7 on the cartoon below and on your knowledge of social studies.

7 In the 1930's, Japan decided that one way to solve its economic problems was by expanding its territory. Based on this cartoon, which statement reflects the result of this decision?

1 Japanese rule benefited many people in Asia.
2 Japan lost control of East Asia.
3 Imperialism can have unintended consequences.
4 Technological progress requires international cooperation.

7 _____

8 "Under the weight of winter snow
  The pine tree's branches bend
  But do not break."

—Emperor Hirohito

In this poem, what message was the Japanese Emperor trying to communicate to his people at the end of 1945?

1 As a victorious nation, Japan must treat those it conquered with kindness.
2 As a result of its defeat, Japan must adopt Confucian ideals.
3 Since Japan had been the strongest nation in Asia, the nation would try to defeat its enemies again.
4 Although Japan had been defeated in war, the economy and the nation would recover.   8 _____

9 The ethnocentric attitudes of various Chinese emperors can best be attributed to the

1 cultural isolation of China
2 failure of other nations to become interested in China
3 interest of Chinese scholars in other civilizations
4 great cultural diversity within China's borders   9 _____

10 In China, the terms "commune," "Great Leap Forward," and "Cultural Revolution" are associated with the

1 economic success of the Manchu dynasty
2 Mandate of Heaven
3 Confucian emphasis on the five human relationships
4 leadership of Mao Zedong   10 _____

Base your answer to question 11 on the quotation below and on your knowledge of social studies.

"It doesn't matter if the cat is black or white as long as it catches mice.

—Deng Xiaoping

11 In this quotation, Deng Xiaoping implies that to achieve success, China should

1 adhere to strict Marxian socialism
2 continue Mao Zedong's elimination of Western cultural influences in China
3 establish a policy of mercantilism
4 use whatever means necessary to improve its economy   11 _____

---

12 In the 17th and 18th centuries, the Dutch interest in the islands of Southeast Asia was mainly based on the

1 spice trade
2 large numbers of Christian converts
3 rich deposits of gold and silver
4 development of manufacturing sites   12 _____

13 Although many Southeast Asian nations have become independent, they have not been totally free of Western influence. One indication of this influence is that the governments in these nations have

1 joined the European Union
2 depended heavily on foreign capital for economic development
3 adopted Christianity as the official state religion
4 relied mainly on European nations for their food supply   13 _____

14 In the 19th century, opposition to the encomienda system in Latin America demonstrated the need for

1 landholding reforms
2 trade restrictions
3 female suffrage
4 a minimum-wage law   14 _____

15 In the 19th century, the independence movements in Latin America were greatly influenced by the

1 Glorious Revolution   3 Boer War
2 Hundred Years War   4 French Revolution   15 _____

16 "North Americans are always among us, even when they ignore us or turn their back on us. Their shadow covers the whole hemisphere. It is the shadow of a giant."

—Octavio Paz

Which attitude is being summarized by this Latin American writer?

1 admiration for United States technology and wealth
2 desire for American cultural values and traditions
3 resentment of United States economic and political influence
4 envy of American democratic institutions   16 _____

Base your answer to question 17 on the cartoon below and on your knowledge of social studies.

17 What is the main idea of this 1994 cartoon?

1 Haiti's lack of industrialization has led to economic stagnation.

2 Haiti's limited experience with democracy has made it difficult to establish this form of government.

3 The desire for democracy has led Haiti to neglect its development of modern technology.

4 The presence of American industry has failed to improve Haiti's economy.

17 _____

18 Archbishop Desmond Tutu and Nelson Mandela both won Nobel Peace Prizes for their opposition to

  1 the practice of apartheid in South Africa
  2 European imperialism in North Africa
  3 international sanctions against South Africa
  4 foreign religious influences in Africa   18 _____

19 Since the African National Congress came to power in South Africa in 1994, its primary aim has been to

  1 establish one-party rule in South Africa
  2 unite the people of South Africa in a democratic republic
  3 restore Dutch influence on South African culture
  4 create a homeland for white separatists   19 _____

Base your answer to question 20 on the map below and on your knowledge of social studies.

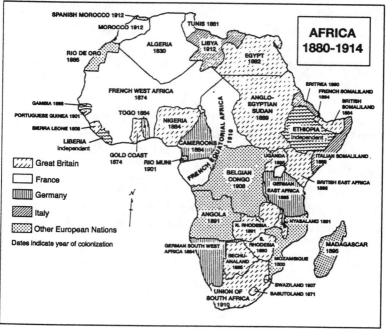

Source World History Patterns of Civilization

20 Which conclusion is valid, based on the information shown on this map of Africa in 1914?

    1 All of North Africa was controlled by France.

    2 Belgium was the last country to establish colonies in Africa.

    3 The Union of South Africa was settled by the Spanish in the early 20th century.

    4 Great Britain and France controlled most of Africa.   20 _____

---

21 The Code of Hammurabi of Sumeria, the Twelve Tables of Rome, and the Justinian Code of the Byzantine Empire were similar in that they

    1 provided a basis for behavior for medieval knights and Japanese samurai

    2 are legal systems developed to create order for the society

    3 are documents that maintained the position of the upper classes

    4 became examples of religious doctrine for other societies   21 _____

22 When Kemal Atatürk became the political leader of Turkey, his policies differed from those of the Ottoman Empire. One difference between these policies was that

    1 Western ideas and practices were adopted

    2 a limited monarchy was established

    3 Islamic fundamentalism became a major political force

    4 imperialism was used to gain territory in Europe   22 _____

23 Great Britain's primary motivation for acquiring control of the Suez Canal in the late 19th century was to

  1 protect British trade interests in Asia
  2 introduce democratic principles in this region
  3 make up for the loss of the Panama Canal
  4 prohibit the movement of ships from Russia   23 _____

24 In Iran under Ayatollah Khomeini and in Afghanistan throughout the 1990's, an effect of the Islamic fundamentalist government has been to

  1 produce an agrarian-based economy
  2 eliminate anti-Israeli terrorist groups
  3 create a strong military alliance with the United States
  4 limit rights for women   24 _____

25 Which European historical periods are in the proper chronological order?

  1 Middle Ages → Renaissance → Ancient Greece → Roman Empire
  2 Renaissance → Ancient Greece → Roman Empire → Middle Ages
  3 Ancient Greece → Roman Empire → Middle Ages → Renaissance
  4 Roman Empire → Middle Ages → Renaissance → Ancient Greece   25 _____

Base your answer to question 26 on the quotations below and on your knowledge of social studies.

"The pope is the only person whose feet are kissed by all princes. His title is unique in the world. He may depose [remove] emperors."

—Pope Gregory VII (11th century)

"An emperor is subject to no one but to God and justice."

—Frederick Barbarossa, Holy Roman Emperor (12th century)

26 The ideas expressed in these quotations show that during the Middle Ages in Europe

1 popes gave little attention to political matters
2 monarchs dominated the Church's leaders
3 popes and monarchs sometimes challenged the other's authority
4 monarchs and popes strengthened the role of the Church

26 _____

27 One similarity between the Renaissance and the Enlightenment is that both historic periods

1 produced major cultural changes
2 encouraged traditional values
3 limited technological advancements
4 ignored individual achievements

27 _____

28 A major effect of the Reformation in Europe was the

1 decline of religious unity
2 increased use of the divine right theory
3 emergence of mercantilism
4 increase in military dictatorships

28 _____

29 "I offer neither pay, nor quarters, nor provisions; I offer hunger, thirst, forced marches, battles, and death. Let him who loves his country in his heart, and not with his lips only, follow me."

—Giuseppe Garibaldi

Which concept is expressed by Garibaldi in this statement?

1 scarcity

2 nationalism

3 humanism

4 empathy

29 _____

Base your answers to questions 30 and 31 on the quotation below and on your knowledge of social studies.

"No observer of Manchester [England] in the 1830's and 1840's dwelt on its happy, well-fed people. 'Wretched, defrauded, oppressed, crushed human nature lying in bleeding fragments all over the face of society,' wrote an American in 1845. . . . Can we be surprised that the first generation of the labouring poor in . . . Britain looked at the results of capitalism and found them wanting?"

—E.J. Hobsbawm

30 This quotation describes some negative effects of the

1 Black Plague

2 Glorious Revolution

3 Napoleonic Wars

4 Industrial Revolution

30 _____

31 The conditions in England described in this quotation encouraged the growth of

1 socialism

2 Christianity

3 feudalism

4 Zionism

31 _____

Base your answer to question 32 on the map below and on your knowledge of social studies.

Mongol Empires, 1200–1350

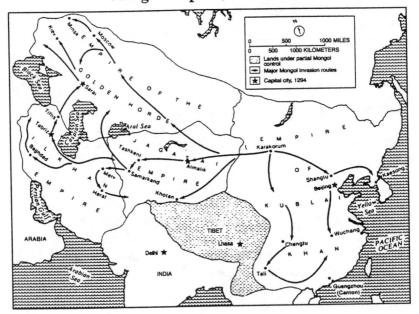

32 Which statement about the Mongol Empire is supported by information provided by the map?

1 Moscow became a capital city in 1294.
2 The Mongol Empire extended from the Pacific Ocean to the Atlantic Ocean.
3 Much of present-day Ukraine and Russia was under the rule of the Mongols.
4 The Mongol invasion routes passed through the city of Delhi.

32 _____

33 A study of the Byzantine civilization would show that this civilization

1 collapsed as a result of the Germanic invasions of the early Middle Ages
2 preserved Greek and Roman learning and passed it on to western and eastern Europe
3 based its economy on subsistence farming and slash-and-burn agriculture
4 reduced the influence of the Eastern Orthodox Church

33 _____

34 Which practice was similar under the rule of the Bolsheviks in Russia and of the Nazi Party in Germany?

1 establishing communism in their respective nations
2 permitting a series of multiparty elections
3 increasing the power of the middle class
4 limiting government opposition through intimidation and fear

34 _____

Base your answer to question 35 on the map below and on your knowledge of social studies.

35 Which event in the early 1990's resulted in the formation of the six new nations shown on the map?

1 unification of Eastern European ethnic groups
2 dismantling of the Berlin Wall
3 collapse of the Soviet Union
4 resolution of long-standing border disputes   35 _____

36 Under both the czarist regime of Russia and the Communist government of the Soviet Union, artistic expression was censored primarily because

1 the arts were considered unimportant
2 no markets existed for artistic or literary works
3 criticism of the government was sometimes reflected in the arts
4 support of the arts was considered a waste of money   36 _____

37 The strong showing by the Communist Party in the Russian Presidential election of 1996 suggests that large numbers of Russian people

1 favored a return to Stalin's policy of imprisoning dissidents
2 feared continuing economic instability and high inflation
3 wanted the Russian Orthodox Church to play a larger role in government
4 supported a return to isolationist policies   37 _____

38 One similarity between the feudal manors of Europe and the traditional villages of India is that

  1 peasants were seldom able to change their social status

  2 women dominated the political decisions of the local councils

  3 children could choose from a number of different occupations

  4 monarchs exerted absolute power over local governments

38 _____

39 • Aztec civilization

  • Roman Empire

  • Reign of the czars in Russia

During each of these historical periods, one similar development was the

  1 expansion of civil rights for the individual

  2 disruption of trade and commerce in that society

  3 centralization of legal and economic authority

  4 introduction of representative government

39 _____

40 One way in which the European Crusades, the Age of Exploration, and the Islamic Revolution in Iran were similar is that during each period

  1 religion played an important role in political events

  2 imperialism led to an increase in traditional values

  3 self-determination encouraged policies of home rule

  4 weak central governments led to a return to feudalism

40 _____

41 The creation of the United Nations, the expansion of the European Economic Community (European Union), and the signing of the North American Free Trade Agreement (NAFTA) resulted in an increase in

  1 political revolutions
  2 nonalignment policies
  3 military alliances
  4 international cooperation

41 _____

Base your answer to question 42 on the chart below and on your knowledge of social studies.

Nation	GDP (Per Capita)	Secondary School Enrollment (Women)	Fertility Rate
Germany	$16,200	93%	1.5
Greece	5,340	93	1.7
Peru	1,090	61	3.6
Morocco	900	30	4.2
Zimbabwe	640	42	5.3
Pakistan	370	11	5.9

42 Which generalization about the impact of the gross domestic product (GDP) on a nation can be drawn from this chart?

  1 The GDP has no relationship to the status of women.
  2 Women in nations with a low GDP tend to have fewer children.
  3 The percentage of women enrolled in secondary schools is higher in nations with a high GDP.
  4 Nations with a high GDP usually try to increase their population.

42 _____

43 Which action would best help developing nations improve their standard of living?

    1 borrowing from the World Bank to purchase food for their citizens

    2 relying on a few cash crops for export sale in the world market

    3 encouraging an increase in the trade deficit

    4 investing in the development of human resources   43 _____

44 The violence and destruction that occurred during World War II led to the

    1 expansion of colonial empires in Africa

    2 formation of the United Nations

    3 signing of the Versailles Treaty

    4 unification of Germany   44 _____

Base your answer to question 45 on the cartoon below and on your knowledge of social studies.

45 Which statement best reflects the viewpoint of the cartoonist?

1 Organizations such as the League of Nations and the United Nations will continue to maintain world peace.
2 Violence and bloodshed will continue to plague the world, despite efforts to end war.
3 The economy of the world will improve if wars are ended.
4 War will be eliminated by the 21st century since the world has learned from past conflicts.   45 _____

---

46 • Boxer Rebellion
• Solidarity Movement
• Intifada
• Shining Path Movement

One action that is common to the groups involved in these events is that each group

1 strengthened its ties with former imperialistic powers
2 established international terrorist organizations
3 used political demonstrations or revolts to bring about change
4 created religious unity in the group's nation   46 _____

47 In the late 1990's, international demands to conduct trials for war crimes similar to those conducted at Nuremberg after World War II are responses to war crimes taking place in

1 Bosnia   3 Poland
2 the Czech Republic   4 Russia   47 _____

48 Which nongovernmental organization has been
   most involved in the effort to achieve freedom for
   political prisoners throughout the world?

   1 Amnesty International
   2 Doctors Without Borders
   3 Greenpeace
   4 Red Cross   48 _____

Students Please Note:

In developing your answers to Part II, be sure to

(1) include specific factual information and evidence whenever possible
(2) keep to the questions asked; do not go off on tangents
(3) avoid overgeneralizations or sweeping statements without sufficient proof; do not overstate your case
(4) keep these general definitions in mind:
    (a) <u>discuss</u> means "to make observations about something using facts, reasoning, and argument; to present in some detail"
    (b) <u>describe</u> means "to illustrate something in words or tell about it"
    (c) <u>show</u> means "to point out; to set forth clearly a position or idea by stating it and giving data which support it"
    (d) <u>explain</u> means "to make plain or understandable; to give reasons for or causes of; to show the logical development or relationships of"
    (e) <u>evaluate</u> means "to examine and judge the significance, worth, or condition of; to determine the value of"

PART II

ANSWER THREE QUESTIONS FROM THIS PART. [45]

1 Geographic factors often have an important influence on the history, economy, and culture of regions and nations.

Geographic Factors

Amazon rain forest
Irregular coastlines
Island locations
Khyber Pass
Monsoons
Nile River valley
Sahara Desert

Select *three* geographic factors from the list and for *each* one selected:

- Identify *one* specific region or nation affected by the factor
- Discuss *two* effects of the factor on the history, economy, and/or culture of the specific region or nation [5,5,5]

2 Throughout history, men and women have attempted to change their societies through reform or revolution.

Reformers/Revolutionaries

Catherine the Great
Simón Bolívar
Sun Yat-sen
Mohandas Gandhi
Jomo Kenyatta
Anwar Sadat
Rigoberta Menchú

Select *three* of the reformers or revolutionaries from the list and for *each* one selected:

- Discuss the historical circumstances that led to the need to reform the nation or society
- Identify *one* specific action taken by the individual to bring about this reform
- Evaluate how successful the individual's action was in carrying out this reform [5,5,5]

3 Religions have influenced the development of various societies.

Religions

Animism
Buddhism
Christianity
Taoism (Daoism)
Hinduism
Islam
Judaism

Select *three* religions from the list and for *each* one selected:

- Identify *one* area of the world where that religion has had an influence on a particular society [Do *not* use the United States in your answer.]
- Discuss *one* major idea of the religion
- Explain *one* way that major idea influenced the society [5,5,5]

4 Historical concepts are often identified by descriptive titles. Several concepts with this type of title are listed below.

Concepts

Divine right of monarchs
Jihad
Liberation theology
Peristroika
Spheres of influence
The Four Modernizations
White Man's Burden

Select *three* historical concepts from the list and for *each* one selected:
- Identify a nation or region affected by this concept
- Explain the major idea expressed by the concept
- Discuss *one* social, economic, *or* political effect of the concept on the identified nation or region   [5,5,5]

5 Throughout history, a number of regions have experienced internal troubles, revolts, or wars.

Regions

Central Africa
Central America
Eastern Europe
Korean Peninsula
Middle East
Northern Ireland

Select *three* regions from the list and for *each* one selected:
- Discuss the historical background of the problem in that area [In your discussion, identify at least *two* of the major groups involved in the problem.]
- Discuss the extent to which the problem has been resolved [5,5,5]

6 The ideas contained in written works have often influenced societies.

Written Works

The Analects
Magna Carta
Mein Kampf
Ninety-five theses
Communist Manifesto
Two Treatises on Government
Vedas

Select *three* works from the list and for *each* one selected:
- Describe a major idea discussed in the work
- Identify a specific society or nation affected by the work [Do *not* use the United States in your answer.]
- Explain *one* way the society or nation changed as a result of this written work   [5.5,5]

7 Throughout history, inventions and technological changes have had both positive and negative impacts on nations and regions.

Inventions/Technological Changes

> Factory system
> Steam engine
> Computers
> Hydroelectric power
> Medical advances
> New types of fertilizers
> Nuclear power

a Select *three* inventions or technological changes from the list and for *each* one selected, discuss a positive *and* a negative impact of the invention or technological change on a specific nation or region. [Do *not* use the United States in your answer.] [4,4,4]

b For *one* of the inventions or technological changes you selected in part *a*, discuss whether the invention or technological change has had a greater positive *or* a greater negative impact on the nation or region.   [3]

Answers to the Regents Examinations

JUNE 1998

1.	3	11.	2	21.	2	31.	3	41.	3
2.	3	12.	2	22.	4	32.	4	42.	2
3.	1	13.	3	23.	4	33.	1	43.	3
4.	2	14.	4	24.	2	34.	2	44.	4
5.	4	15.	2	25.	4	35.	1	45.	1
6.	4	16.	4	26.	1	36.	4	46.	1
7.	3	17.	2	27.	2	37.	2	47.	2
8.	4	18.	1	28.	3	38.	3	48.	4
9.	3	19.	4	29.	3	39.	1		
10.	1	20.	3	30.	4	40.	1		

JANUARY 1999

1.	4	11.	4	21.	2	31.	1	41.	4
2.	1	12.	1	22.	1	32.	3	42.	3
3.	2	13.	2	23.	1	32.	3	43.	4
4.	1	14.	1	24.	4	34.	4	44.	2
5.	2	15.	4	25.	3	35.	3	45.	2
6.	2	16.	3	26.	3	36.	3	46.	3
7.	3	17.	2	27.	1	37.	2	47.	1
8.	4	18.	1	28.	1	38.	1	48.	1
9.	1	19.	2	29.	2	39.	3		
10.	4	20.	4	30.	4	40.	1		

INDEX

NOTES

NOTES

NOTES

NOTES

NOTES

NOTES

NOTES

NOTES